Nursing Leadership:
CONCEPTS
and
PRACTICE

Nursing Leadership:
CONCEPTS
and
PRACTICE

Ruth M. Tappen, R.N., Ed.D.
Associate Professor
University of Miami
Coral Gables, Florida

F. A. DAVIS COMPANY ✶ *Philadelphia*

Library of Congress Cataloging in Publication Data

Tappen, Ruth M.
  Nursing leadership.

  Includes bibliographical references and index.
  1. Nursing—Social aspects. 2. Leadership. I. Title. [DNLM:
1. Leadership—Nursing texts. 2. Nursing, texts.
3. Nursing, Supervisory.   WY 105 T175m]
RT86.5.T36   1983   362.1′73′068   82-22144
ISBN 0-8036-8334-0

Preface

When this book was first proposed, there was a limited choice of nursing leadership and management texts available. Since then, many more have appeared but some gaps in content continue to exist. For example, the stages of group development and group roles are not even touched upon in most texts. Teamwork has also been a neglected area and yet most nurses work as part of a team, often as parts of several different teams. The same is true for the more complex subjects of organizations and political action in the community.

An exclusive focus on the hospital setting ignores the variety of settings in which nurses at all levels are practicing today. Leadership has generally been treated as if it were a subject entirely separate from the rest of nursing practice although there are actually many concepts in common between the two. For example, good communication skills are helpful no matter with whom you are using them. Maslow's hierarchy of needs applies to both patient and coworker and sociocultural factors influence the behavior of both. In much the same way, effective leadership is needed equally (and probably more) when teaching a group of patients as when teaching a group of coworkers; therefore, this book contains examples of working with clients or patients as well as examples of working with colleagues.

The purpose of this book, then, is to provide a more comprehensive and readable text, one that contains all the leadership information needed by the practicing professional nurse and ample illustrations of the application of this information in practice. This book is written for the student or nurse who desires a strong basic foundation in leadership and management. Even the individual who is suddenly thrust into a supervisory or administrative role will find that, aside from learning the specific routines of the organization, these basic leadership concepts and skills are the most essential tools for effective functioning in these positions.

NURSING LEADERSHIP: Concepts and Practice can be used in a single course or in an integrated curriculum where leadership and management are taught in more than one course. One way to divide the chapters for use in separate courses would be to begin with Chapters 1 and 3 as an introduction to leadership, then proceed with Chapters 4 and 5 on communication and decision-making. Later courses would employ Chapter 2 on leadership and management theories, Chapters 6, 7, and 8 on groups, leading meetings, and teamwork, and Chapter 9 on implementing change would precede Chapters 10, 11, and 12 on working in organizations and in the community.

For me, the observation and study of people's behavior has always been a source of great fascination but the greatest rewards of studying leadership come from the opportunity to practice it. This is the real purpose of studying leadership and I hope that the reader will agree that it is a stimulating and constantly challenging experience.

Ruth M. Tappen

Acknowledgments

Cynthia Daubman, R.N., M.S., contributed the transcript of the conference included in Chapter 7 and assisted with the analysis of this conference and the writing of the section on Problem Discussion Meetings in the same chapter.

Phyllis George, R.N., M.A., contributed substantial information on formal evaluation methods and assisted with the writing of the section on Informal Evaluation in Chapter 8 and on Formal Evaluation Procedures in Chapter 11.

Contents

Introduction

Acquiring leadership knowledge and skills is an essential part of the health care professional's preparation for practice. In fact, experienced professional people often state that most of the major problems, conflicts, and challenges they face in their work are not technical problems but people problems, the kind of problems that leadership knowledge and skills can help you resolve.

The primary purpose for studying leadership is to learn how to work with people, individually or as members of groups, teams, organizations, and even whole communities. The acquisition and appropriate use of leadership concepts and skills can give you a feeling of greater understanding and control of events in a work situation. It can provide you with a sense of personal power and self-direction in situations that would otherwise be bewildering, frustrating, discouraging, or a combination of these.

The study of leadership encompasses many facets of human behavior. It includes the study of motivation, the effects of social roles and norms, leadership theories, group development, teamwork, organizational dynamics, and community structure. It also includes learning effective communication skills such as confrontation and negotiation, critical thinking, problem solving, leading teams, conducting meetings and conferences, providing evaluative feedback, collective bargaining, and implementing changes on both small and grand scales. All this is included because leaders need to know why the people with whom they work act the way they do and how to influence that behavior.

Leadership is often defined as the process of influencing others.[1] It is purposive behavior involving an exchange with other people. Although the emphasis in this book is on work situations, leadership behavior can also occur in social situations.

An act of leadership is an attempt to influence others, therefore, whenever you attempt to influence people, you are exercising leadership. The attempt defines the leadership action—it does not always have to be successful. It is also not necessary to be designated the leader. Any member of a group can act as its leader. You do not have to be called a team leader, manager, or supervisor to be a leader, although people in these positions do need to use leadership concepts and skills. The following example may help to clarify this point:

> A student is observing a hospital team attempting to resuscitate a patient. A nurse is ready to administer electroshock but others are still leaning against the patient's metal bed. The student calls out "Everybody off the bed!" and they quickly move back. Here, the student has exercised leadership in spite of junior status in the group.
> If the student had thought "Hmm, I don't think they ought to be leaning on the bed like that" but did not say anything, the student would not have shown any leadership although the student had the right idea.

In order to be a leader, you must implement your plans and ideas in some way. You must make a decision to act.

A leadership action always involves some kind of exchange with other people, an exchange in which there is some attempt to influence them, either directly or indirectly. The "other people" referred to may be a single coworker or client, the team to which you belong, the organization in which you are employed, or a whole community with which you are working to improve health care. The correct use of leadership concepts and skills can help you to improve your effectiveness in all these different exchanges and relationships.

Although the usual approach is to concentrate on leadership in institutional settings (especially hospitals), community situations are also included in order to better represent the whole spectrum of settings in which health care is given and leadership can be practiced. Much of what you will read in this book is also applicable to working with clients, again as individuals, small or large groups, or communities. The examples used in this book reflect this diversity and the potential for broad application of leadership concepts and skills.

One final comment on the practice of leadership. Many of these leadership skills and strategies are quite powerful in their effect. Instead of being used to improve working relationships, they can and have been turned around and used to increase stress and to manipulate people. The health care professional who takes advantage of opportunities to use these skills and strategies also assumes the responsibility to use them constructively.

Reference

1. TANNENBAUM, R, WESCHLER, IR, AND MASSARIK, F: *Leadership: A frame of reference.* In CATHCHART, RS AND SAMOVAR, LA (EDS): *Small Group Communication: A Reader,* ed 2. WM C BROWN, Dubuque, 1974, p 358.

Chapter *1*

Explanations of Human Behavior

This chapter and the two that follow provide the theoretical foundation on which the rest of this book is based. Chapter 1 presents the more general theories and concepts that are used to explain human behavior. These are important because a leader needs to understand human behavior in order to be able to influence it. Chapter 2 surveys the major theories of leadership, which attempt to explain what leadership is and how it acts to influence others. Chapter 3 is more specific in its application; it describes the components of effective leadership, which can be applied directly to practice.

Uses of Theory

Why have a theoretical framework? What does theory do for you? Before presenting the different theories, a brief explanation of the ways in which theory can be used will help you see the purpose of a theoretical framework.

ORGANIZATION

A theory provides a framework in which you can organize your ideas and experiences. Somewhat like a desk organizer that has many compartments to tuck things into, a theory has components or categories into which you can group your thoughts and observations. As an organizer, a theory helps you to detect similarities, differences, or other patterns in data and to provide explanations for these patterns. One way to test the usefulness of a theory is to see how it can help you organize data.

PERSPECTIVE

A theory also provides perspective or a certain way of looking at things. The particular theory you use can have a great influence on how you interpret what you see. The following example shows how á single event can be seen quite differently by people using different theoretical frameworks:

> A woman is hurling angry words at a male companion. This woman could be seen by a traditional Freudian analyst as "suffering from penis envy." In contrast, a follower of Thomas Harris and Eric Berne would describe this as an "I'm OK, You're not OK" situation. To someone using communication theory, the situation represents "a failure to communicate." To a sociologist, it may be seen as an example of "women's liberation" or someone being "aggressive rather than assertive."

The way in which you perceive a situation depends a great deal on the theoretical framework you employ (or "where you're coming from" as some people like to say). Each person in the example above was looking at the same event from a different theoretical perspective. One perspective focuses on the physical differences between the sexes, another emphasizes feelings about self and others, a third is concerned with the prevailing social climate, and so forth. In fact, the Freudian analyst, the sociologist, and the communications theorist could actually have trouble talking to each other about this situation if they did not take their differing perspectives into account. Each one might also choose a different intervention if the angry woman were a client.

PREDICTION

A theory should not only organize data but also help you to predict what is likely to happen in a given situation. For example, developmental theory predicts that certain crises will occur during adolescence, including conflicts between parents and teenagers. Familiarity with this theory enables a nurse to provide anticipatory guidance to a family with children entering adolescence. In the same way, the ability to predict people's behavior enables a leader to anticipate what will happen given a certain set of circumstances.

APPLICATION

A theory that predicts what is likely to happen in a given situation also provides some direction in regard to what action to take. This is particularly important in a practice profession such as nursing. The example in the preceding paragraph showed how theory can guide practice: the developmental theory indicates a need for anticipatory guidance. The same is true of leadership theories: they serve as guides to the selection of the most effective action for a leader to take.

Theory Selection

It is necessary to choose from among the various existing theories that explain human behavior and leadership. Just as there is no single theory of nursing accepted by all, there is no single theory to explain all human behavior. Some of the theories conflict with each other but others are complementary and together explain more than any one theory alone does.

Open systems theory is part of the selected theoretical framework for this text because it encompasses the complex interrelationships that health care professionals continually deal with, whether it is the complexity of the human being or of the organization that dispenses health care services. Maslow's Hierarchy of Needs is also used because it provides a way to bridge the gap between physical, social, and emotional needs. Attention is also given to culture, role theory, and to coping behaviors because they provide more detailed information about the way in which people interact with their environment. Each of these is discussed in this chapter. It is hoped that the reader will find them useful in perceiving and organizing data concerning human behavior and in predicting and influencing that behavior.

Open Systems: The Interaction of People With Their Environment

SYSTEMS

An amoeba, a heart, a dog, a person, a group, and a community are all systems. They are systems because you can define them as a whole entity having some kind of identifiable parts and a definable boundary. A more formal definition of a system is: *A system is a set of objects together with relationships between the objects and between their attributes.*[1]

To fully understand a system, it is necessary to look at all three aspects of a system: its parts, its attributes as a whole, and the relationships within the system and with the environment. The *objects* spoken of in the definition are the parts or components of the system. They can be almost anything: molecules, cells, organs, people, or groups of people. *Attributes* are the characteristics of the system such as color, temperature, speed, maturity, personality, and energy level. The *relationships* are what tie the system together, that is, the processes that go on between the parts, and again the possibilities are innumerable: ionization, metabolism, circulation, communication, and negotiation.

Hierarchy of Systems

There are multiple levels of systems within systems. This is called the hierarchical order of systems.[2] The smaller systems, which are parts of a larger system, are called *subsystems*. Larger systems may also be parts of an even more inclusive

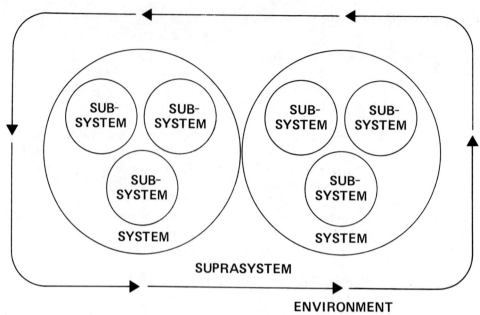

FIGURE 1-1. Hierarchy of systems.

suprasystem. Whatever is outside of the suprasystem, and which may affect the suprasystem, is referred to as the *environment* (Fig. 1-1). The explanation may seem complicated but the concept is really a fairly simple one. The following shows examples of relationships between a subsystem, system, and suprasystem:

Subsystem:	Electron	Planet
System:	Atom	Solar System
Suprasystem:	Molecule	Universe

You can see from the two examples given that the systems are named in order of increasing size and complexity. This increasing size and complexity is the basis for the ordering of systems within a hierarchy.

You might also have noticed the vast difference in size between the systems in the two examples. The choice of what level to begin with depends on your purpose in defining a hierarchy of systems and on what level is of most interest to you.[3-4] The systems of greatest interest in leadership are usually the individual, the group, the organization, and the community. Did you notice that they were listed in order of increasing size and complexity? The following examples of hierarchies are of interest in leadership and nursing:

Subsystem:	Cell	Individual	Local group
System:	Organ	Team	State organization
Suprasystem:	Individual	Agency	National organization

6

Each of the hierarchies begins at a different level but all are the same in that they follow the order of increasing size and complexity.

WHOLENESS

Another important characteristic of a system is wholeness. Wholeness means that the system is an integrated set of components (parts) with its *own* attributes and relationships that are different from those of the parts. The system as a whole has characteristics that are different from and greater than the sum of its parts.[5-6] An individual, for example, is not just a collection of bones, skin, heart, lungs, and intestines, but something quite different: a living, breathing, self-aware organism much greater than a simple sum of its parts.

Groups as Wholes

In the same way, a group as a whole has its own characteristics and relationships that are different from the characteristics of the individual members of the group. These characteristics cannot be predicted from the properties of the individual member. The following examples are ways in which the group as a whole is different from and greater than the sum of its parts (the individual members):

> A group can be dynamic and productive even if it has one member who sleeps through most of the meetings.

> Another group can consist of dynamic, high energy individuals but get nothing done because each member is caught up in competing with the others.

> Even though it is made up of mature individuals, a newly formed group will be immature until its members develop ways to work together.

The parts or subsystems of a whole system do influence the larger system, although they do not define it. For instance, in the last example given, the fact that the group's members are mature individuals will probably speed the process of developing ways to work together, yet their individual maturity does not make the group mature when it first forms. The same is true for organizations, communities, and other larger systems.

Implications of Wholeness

The concept of the whole being different from and greater than the sum of its parts has many important implications. In nursing practice, for example, its use emphasizes how important it is to assess the client as a whole being who has feelings that affect bodily functions and vice versa. The concept of wholeness also is at the root of many complaints about the use of the medical model in health care because the medical model not only concentrates on illness rather than health, but also treats lungs, stomachs, and uteri instead of people. The problem with doing this has been well documented: if you do not treat the whole person instead of just the lungs, the patient is very likely to continue smoking and make the diseased lungs worse; a stress-related ulcer will not stay healed unless you deal with the sources of stress in the environment; you have not healed the whole person by performing a hysterectomy if you have not dealt with the fact that it may have left the patient thinking she is no longer a woman.

In the same way, the concept of wholeness also has implications for leadership. Some communities as a whole are friendly; others are hostile, especially to strangers. Organizations actually take on personalities in a sense too and it makes a real difference whether you work for a progressive, growth-oriented organization that encourages innovation or for a schizophrenic one that tells you to do one thing and expects you to do another. You cannot assume that you will enjoy working within a particular organization just because you like the person interviewing you—you need to assess the organization as a whole, which may be quite different from that one individual. You also cannot predict the behavior of a group as a whole by getting to know its members individually—you need to study the behavior of the group as a whole.

OPENNESS

Open versus Closed

A system is open if it exchanges matter, energy, or information with its environment.[1] there is some disagreement on whether or not a truly closed system (which would *not* exchange any matter, energy, or information with its environment) can exist. It is difficult to even imagine a system that is totally impervious to its environment. Even a stone would be affected if its environment became warmer or colder. If you put a cold stone in hot water, the water would become cooler and the stone warmer. There is clearly an exchange of energy occurring.

Perhaps the reader can think of a completely closed system of some kind. However, it will be assumed in this book, that no matter how little exchange there may be between some systems and their environments, there are no living or natural systems that are completely closed off from their environments.

The term "closed" is used in another way that confuses the issue. Closed is often used to mean that the system has relatively impermeable boundaries or that it resists input and change. Family theorists, for example, often refer to "closed family systems." In leadership, certain types of organizations or institutions may be called "closed." These systems may be less open to their environments than others but they are not completely closed.

Interaction with the Environment

The exchange of matter, information, and energy between a human system and its environment is an active relationship. A human being is active, not passive or reactive, in relationship to the environment. At the same time that the living system

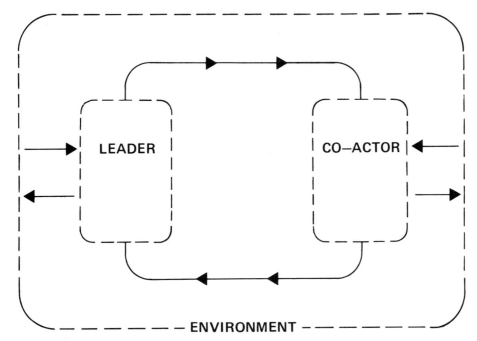

FIGURE 1-2. Elements of a leadership event.

is being influenced by its environment, it is also influencing that environment. The system uses its energies to maintain itself (as a system) in dynamic interplay with the environment. The system and its environment are continually affecting and being affected by each other.[5]

An act of leadership involves a particular kind of interpersonal exchange in which there is an attempt to influence. Whenever this exchange between people occurs, there are at least three elements or systems involved: the leader, the person or groups to be influenced (the co-actors),[7] and the environment (surroundings) in which the attempt to influence takes place. (Fig. 1-2) These can be broken down into many more elements but the leader, co-actor(s), and the environment are the most basic elements and each one needs to be considered whenever you analyze a leadership event. All these elements are important to keep in mind when taking any kind of leadership action.

A *feedback loop* has been used to illustrate this dynamic interplay.[8] A feedback loop is used to show the interrelationship of the leader, co-actor(s), and the environment. This loop is meant to represent a simultaneous interaction between the three different elements. It is not meant to represent a linear model of interaction in which the leader acts and the person or group merely reacts (that is, a stimulus-response model).

The leader and the co-acting system are both continually influencing each other even when there is no apparent action on the part of one or the other in the relationship. The following example may help to show how people can influence each other without taking any overt action:

> The team leader enters the conference room to distribute assignments for the team. The rest of the team sit silently as the leader enters. The team is usually noisy and talkative in the conference room, so the leader wonders why they are silent today. Is this silence a respectful hush so that the leader can begin talking or is it a hostile refusal to make the leader feel welcome? In either case, the silence has affected the leader.

ENERGY FIELDS

Every living system requires energy in order to grow and to maintain itself.[9] The energy may be in the form of matter, including such substances as food and oxygen or it may be an exchange of information, such as how to carry out a procedure. Economic energy in the form of money available to spend is an important source of energy for most organizations in which you may work. Other kinds of energy include measurable ones such as light, heat, or sound and the as yet unmeasurable kinds such as love, hate, fear, caring, or healing.

Energy can flow or be exchanged in different amounts and directions. There can be very small, hard-to-detect amounts or enormously explosive amounts of energy exchanged. Energy can be unused and can accumulate to the point where there is intensive pressure to release it. A balance of positive energies flowing in and out is usually a sign of a healthy system.

A system and its environment can be thought of as coextensive energy fields that exchange matter and information.[10] When you study a system, you need to look at its attributes as a whole, the attributes of its subsystems and environment, and how the system relates to its environment, that is, its energy exchanges.

GROWTH

Growth is another important characteristic of a living system. The process of growth proceeds unidirectionally; in other words, it does not reverse itself or regress back in time.[11] People do not go back to being like they were last week, last year, or when they were children. Aging, then, is not a regression but a progression to new conditions and behaviors. (You may wonder about those elderly people who have become confused and incontinent and are often described as having regressed. They have not gone back to being the same children they were 80 years ago, which is obvious from the physical size. Instead, they continue to grow and develop physically and mentally but unfortunately in a negative or pathologic manner.) Not all growth and development is in the most positive or constructive direction.

Growth in the Work Setting

Human growth and development reflect an increasing complexity of pattern and organization.[6] Orderly and sequential changes occur throughout the adult years. In order to successfully traverse the adult years, an individual must continue to learn and grow developmentally. Many of the opportunities for this learning and growth are found in the work setting. The variety of opportunities ranges from learning new technical skills to improving your ability to work as part of an interdisciplinary team. Work activities can also contribute to the accomplishment of developmental tasks such as the development of a sense of identity for the younger person or guiding the next generation of caregivers for the older worker.

A leader who is aware of these growth and development needs can organize the work of a group of caregivers in such a way that it can contribute substantially to each worker's (including the leader's) learning and growth. The following is an example of how a leader can do this:

> A staff nurse has worked in the same position long enough to know the job very well. In fact, she knows it so well that she is beginning to get bored with the job but will not be eligible for a promotion into a more challenging position until finished school.
>
> The supervisor recognized this problem and assigned the staff nurse to orient new nurses to the team. The staff nurse has gotten a great deal of satisfaction out of this opportunity to share her expertise with others and to gain some recognition for her experience. She has also had to learn new leadership skills in order to carry out this new assignment effectively.

There are many ways in which the leader can provide opportunities for learning and growth. These include problem-solving team conferences, new assignments, and seminars.

Growth in Larger Systems

There is one other aspect of the concept of growth as continuous and unidirectional in living systems that is relevant to leadership. This is the idea that not only do individuals experience growth but other open, living systems also show evidence of growth and change over time. Individuals, groups, and organizations are not static entities but open systems that change and evolve over time, either positively or negatively. Just like individuals, groups can create new behaviors and do not simply repeat old behaviors. The positive growth and development of a group or organization could include such things as successful innovations or eliminating sources of trouble for the system. These larger systems can be thought of as having life cycles too, in which they begin as immature systems with poorly defined behavior patterns and can gradually develop into mature systems with well-defined, highly functional behavior patterns. Like other living systems, their existence also has an ending at some point in time. In a later chapter, the differences between a mature and immature group will be discussed in more detail.

PATTERNS

Open systems also show some regularity and predictability over time. Any attribute or relationship that recurs at regular intervals can be called a pattern of that system.

Many patterns can be easily observed by the leader but some are more subtle and can only be detected by careful measurement.[2, 12]

Long-Interval Patterns

There are many known patterns in human systems, some vary over short periods of time and others extend beyond the life span of an individual. The unidirectionality and predictable stages of the life cycle are long-interval patterns. There are seasonal patterns to the occurrence of certain illnesses and to some kinds of destructive behavior. Seasonal variations also affect hospital admissions and agency workloads. The patterns of our clients' daily lives also affect service delivery. For example, some community health agencies extend services into the evening and weekend hours to better meet people's needs.

Short-Interval Patterns

Patterns with shorter intervals can also be significant to leadership. Many biorhythms, for example, are disrupted by rotating shifts. These disruptions leave people feeling fatigued and irritable. Although the effects are often subtle, they influence the way a person feels and behaves at work.

The patterns found in interpersonal relationships are of particular interest in leadership. Interpersonal relationships have a rhythmic nature that most people are not aware of, but which affects the way they feel about the relationship. People with the same or complementary communication patterns get along better than those whose patterns are asynchronous. Some people are quite flexible and can adjust to another's rhythms, while others can do this only within a narrow range.[13]

There are also patterns in the interpersonal relations within larger systems. Groups may have free-flowing patterns of communication or stilted patterns that discourage spontaneity. Every work group, from a small team to an entire organization, develops patterns of behavior, commonly called routines. Communities too have many patterns, including work and recreation patterns, and certain times when the people of the community gather together.

If there were no patterns, we would have chaos. The patterns of a system allow us to predict the behavior of that system with some degree of accuracy. The leader who knows the common patterns of the relevant human systems and who has observed the actual patterns of a particular system can not only better predict its behavior, but also have an influence on its patterns.

INDIVIDUALITY

Although open to the influence of their environment, living systems retain their identity and individuality. Each system has a unique pattern, organization, and behavior not like any other system. Do you remember having learned in elementary school that no two snowflakes are alike? In the same way, no two people are alike, no two groups are alike, nor are any two organizations or communities alike.

While systems do have many commonalities, each one has a unique configuration within these commonalities. For example, every person has a need for food and shelter but think of the infinite variety of ways in which these common needs can be met. In leadership, as in many other disciplines, we study the common attributes and responses of certain systems but it is important to stay alert to the uniqueness of each system. Here is an example of the difference between the commonalities and the individuality of a system:

> When something threatens the integrity of an open system (for example, a person, group, community, organization), you can expect that system to react to the threat. But without an intimate knowledge of the particular system's attributes, you cannot predict whether the reaction will be to withdraw, to resist the threat, or to attack the source of the threat.

SENTIENCE

People have the capacity for thought, abstraction, and feeling, a capacity that is termed sentience. This capacity brings into play the uniquely human importance of emotions, values, and personal and culture-bound meanings, which will affect human behavior. People are not simply aware of the world around them—they are actively involved in trying to make sense out of it and in trying to organize or influence their environment. People think, feel, reflect, and make choices in regard to themselves and their environment.[11]

The capacity for sentience is important in leadership because it affects behavior and shows how complex people are. People respond to events as totalities (wholes) so that a focus on just one aspect, such as a person's culture, values, social roles, or current emotional state, does not adequately explain human behavior. Although sometimes difficult, it is necessary to recognize the full complexity of a system as a whole in order to really understand it.

In a sense, larger human systems (such as groups) also possess this capacity to think, feel, reflect, and make choices. Evidence of sentience in these larger systems can be seen in comments such as:

> "Our group views this situation as a very serious threat to our new program."

> "The community is incensed over the new health department regulation."

> "This agency is proud of its record in delivering the highest quality care to its clients."

These larger human systems are also complex in their responses to events and must be recognized as complex wholes in order to understand them.

SUMMARY

An open system is different from and greater than the sum of its parts (subsystems). Its subsystems are related but differentiated parts of the whole. The open, human system (which may be an individual, group, organization, or community) interacts mutually and simultaneously with its environment, exchanging energy, matter, and information with its environment. It is also characterized by its patterns including growth, which proceeds unidirectionally and sequentially; by its individuality; and by its capacity to think and feel, called sentience.

Motivation and Human Needs

Maslow[14] developed a theory of motivation based on the idea that some human needs are more basic, or prepotent, than others. These more basic needs must be at least partially filled before a person has sufficient energy and motivation to work toward gratifying the higher, less prepotent (less powerful or influential) needs. These human needs form a hierarchy beginning with the lowest and most basic physiologic needs, working up through the safety and security needs, love and belonging needs, and esteem needs, and up to the highest level called self-actualization needs (Fig. 1-3).

All behavior has some purpose, reason, or meaning. Even seemingly purposeless behavior such as pacing has some meaning to the person doing it. The pacing may be a way to discharge pent-up energy. Not every behavior is constructive, however, even though it has some purpose or meaning. As you probably have observed in your own experience, even a healthy person sometimes engages in counterproductive and destructive behaviors.

FACTORS INFLUENCING BEHAVIOR

Many factors influence people's behavior. Although it may sometimes seem that a person's action was caused by a single stimulus, in fact, there are always multiple factors affecting a person's response. These include past experiences with similar stimuli, the present condition of the individual, and the environment in which this interaction takes place; all these factors influence a person's response. The following example shows how these multiple factors influence a single action:

> Miss T., a home health aide walked up the path to a client's home. The aide stopped suddenly when she found a dog blocking the path.
> The aide's action was influenced by many factors, including the size of the dog, the "Beware of the Dog" sign on the lawn, her dislike of dogs, and the way the dog approached.

HIGHEST LEVEL ↑ **Self Actualization**
Esteem
Love and Belonging
Safety and Security
LOWEST LEVEL | **Physiologic**

FIGURE 1-3. Maslow's hierarchy of human needs.

You may recall from the discussion of open systems that a person always responds as a whole to the stimulus and is at the same time influencing that stimulus or its source:

> The dog's appearance threatened the aide's feeling of safety and security. Backing away from the dog was one sign of fear. The aide also let out a startled, "Oh" when the dog approached. Backing away, the aide's adrenalin increased, her heart beat rapidly, and her whole self prepared for flight from the perceived danger of the dog in order to meet the need for safety and security.
>
> At the same time, the aide's startled response excited the dog who began barking and ran after the aide.

In the same way, one particular action can meet several needs at the same time. For example, having lunch with friends meets both the need for belonging and the physiologic need for food. As you can see, human behavior is a complex phenomenon. An accurate analysis of behavior must take this complexity into consideration.

HUMAN NEEDS

The needs dealt with in Maslow's theory of motivation may be loosely termed *intrinsic* factors because they originate primarily from within the individual. You will see, though, that gratification of these needs is certainly influenced by the environment. Hunger and thirst, for example, are influenced by the availability of food and water. The social factors that influence behavior may be thought of as *extrinsic* because they originate primarily within the environment. These will be discussed in a later section of this chapter.

Each of the levels of need from the most basic or prepotent physiologic needs up to the self-actualization needs are discussed here with emphasis on their application to leadership. Within these categories, specific needs are discussed in what is believed to be their general order of prepotency.[15] These needs do not explain *all* behavior but they do explain the intrinsic motivating forces behind people's actions.

Physiologic Needs

Some physiologic needs are constant and immediate. Any situation in which they are not met would be life-threatening—a person can live only a few minutes without adequate oxygen and blood circulation, for example. Adequate intake and output of fluids, electrolytes, and nutrients are also vital.

Because of their immediacy, when one of these needs is not sufficiently met, a person is motivated to act on meeting this need and nothing else. The person will think of nothing but this need and will focus all attention and energy on satisfying the need. The following is an example of this focusing.

> If you began to choke on a piece of steak in a restaurant, you would immediately stop whatever you were doing and try to dislodge that piece of meat. Although ordinarily not considered polite, you might put your fingers in your mouth to pull the meat out.

If this didn't work, you would probably try to get someone's attention to help you with other maneuvers.

During such an emergency, would you care about disturbing other people? Would you care about the approval of others, your dignity, or your need for independence? Not at all. Although you might care later on, at the time you were choking your main concern was air, not belonging or esteem, or even other basic physiologic needs. Ordinarily, healthy people do not think about their need for air, but when this need is not met, it becomes the central focus and motivator of behavior.

Other basic physiologic needs that are not of such an immediate nature but still necessary to maintain health include a normal temperature, adequate sleep, adequate activity and stimulation, freedom from pain, and sexual gratification. These basic needs are important to you as a leader because people will direct their attention and energy toward meeting these needs and will not be very interested in working toward higher level needs until the basic needs are at least partially met. The following examples indicate how failure to meet these basic physiologic needs can reduce people's ability to work and how the work setting can help meet some of these needs.

Temperature: If you hold a meeting in a hot, stuffy room, the people at the meeting will concentrate more on staying cool rather than on the purpose of the meeting.

Sleep: People whose sleep patterns are interrupted because they often have to work overtime or irregular hours will be tired and irritable at work.

Activity and Stimulation: Sitting at a desk in an office or classroom all day can make a person feel dull and listless. Alternating active and quiet work and allowing time for exercise breaks provide some stimulation.

Pain: A person who is ill or injured will have difficulty concentrating on work.

Sex: Opportunities to meet people may be provided in a work setting.

The leader who acts to assure that these very basic human needs are met (as much as it is possible to do in the work setting) will be helping people to free their energies for working on higher-level needs and, therefore, perform their jobs more effectively. This is also true for the next level of needs, safety and security.

Safety and Security Needs

Both actual safety and the feeling of being safe are included in this second level of needs. Physical safety is the most prepotent of these needs, followed by perceived security, stability, and dependency.

SAFETY. While work in health care settings is not generally considered dangerous, there are still some threats to safety, which should be eliminated or at least reduced by the alert leader. These threats to safety include exposure to infection, radiation, electric shock, back injuries, and potentially violent individuals. Many nurses also work in high-crime areas. The effective leader takes action to identify and minimize these and other potential threats to the safety of one's self and coworkers.

SECURITY. Providing a feeling of security is an important and challenging leadership function. People who do not feel secure in their work setting focus most of their energy on attempts to reduce the threats in order to increase their feeling of security.

Fostering security and trust is a complex task because there are so many potentially threatening situations in a work setting and also because people differ in their reactions to threats—what one person sees as a minor threat to security may be seen by another person as a major threat demanding a total response to overcome it. The following are examples of situations that may be perceived by a person as a threat.

Assignment to a task one does not feel able to do correctly.

Joining a new group.

Hearing rumors that the new boss is planning to bring in new people and get rid of the current staff.

Evaluation procedures, especially those that are inconsistent or subjective.

The hiring of a more skilled person who could easily do the present employee's job.

The above list is just a sampling of some common situations in which people's security needs become a major concern. Virtually any situation could be perceived by some person as a threat to security, so a leader needs to be alert to individual reactions as well as to responses of the group as a whole.

STABILITY. People also need some constancy in their lives. While change is stimulating and too much stability is deadening, too much change at one time can threaten the integrity of a system. It can also create a situation that is so chaotic that people cannot deal with it.

People need some regularity or pattern in the rhythms of their daily lives—in their sleep, meals, work, and play. Some predictability is needed at work. This does not mean that people need or want a rigid routine. In fact, a rigid routine is stultifying and probably impossible in a profession that has to deal with human behavior and unexpected emergencies daily. Some ways to provide stability in a work setting include:

Regular work hours and meal times.
Predictability of job expectations.
Clearly set standards for quality care.
Regular opportunities to give and receive feedback.
Preparation in advance for handling emergencies.
Continuity in patient or client assignments.

You can see from this list that there are many things a leader can do to ensure some stability in the work setting and to free people's energies to work on higher level needs.

DEPENDENCY. According to Maslow, people also have a need for dependency. This means that people need to be able to ask for help and to have someone available who can provide it. Of course, healthy adults have fewer dependency needs than young children or sick people but there are still times when they need some help from another person. The mature adult may need assistance or support when:

> Learning a new job.
> Grieving after a serious loss.
> Lifting a heavy object.
> Solving a difficult problem.
> Carrying out a complex task that requires more than two hands.

Again, the leader's function is to ensure that adequate assistance and support are available to people at work. As a leader, you may also find it necessary at times to assure people that it is acceptable for an adult to seek help or support when needed and that asking for help when it is needed is a sign of maturity, not of immaturity.

Love and Belonging Needs

People also need love and affection. They need to feel accepted, to give and receive approval, and to be part of a group (such as a family, neighborhood, gang, team, club) in which they can give and receive affection (Fig. 1-4). They need opportunities for communication and satisfying contacts with people. A person whose love and belonging needs are not met will feel lonely, friendless, rejected, or alienated.

Although it cannot meet all of a person's need for love and belonging, the work setting can be an important source of gratification of these needs. For some people, the opportunity to be part of a congenial work group and to have the acceptance and approval of this group are their major sources of satisfaction from their jobs. This is particularly true when the work itself is monotonous or unsatisfying in some way.

Unfortunately, not every work group is warm and accepting of its members. In fact, interpersonal conflict is a prime source of difficulty in work settings and it has been said that more poeple are fired because of interpersonal problems than incompetence. As a leader, you probably find that much of your energy is directed toward resolution of interpersonal conflicts and the development of warmth, acceptance, and group feeling (sometimes called ''we-ness'') among coworkers.

IMPORTANCE. Some leaders may question the appropriateness of meeting belonging needs at work. Isn't time wasted when there's too much socializing?

FIGURE 1-4. People need to feel accepted, to give and receive approval, and to be part of a group in which they can give and receive affection.

Shouldn't the leader concentrate on getting the work done? Some leadership theorists raise these same questions and conclude that attention to these needs is not important. They believe that people are motivated to work hard in order to avoid punishment such as being reprimanded or fired.

But many more theorists, including Maslow, point out that people cannot concentrate their efforts on getting their work done well unless their basic needs, including belonging, are met. People put more effort into their work when they are given opportunities to grow and develop on the job than they do if they are just avoiding punishment and giving the least effort necesary to do so. Interpersonal conflicts can paralyze a team to the point where it is nonfunctional. The effective leader will take action to reduce the conflicts so that the team can resume its function.

The importance of meeting needs, resolving conflicts, and cultivating positive feelings in order to improve the function of a work group is a theme running through this text. This can be done within a work context and does not mean that socializing per se becomes the leader's major goal. Purely social activities are beneficial but need to be kept within limits so that they enhance rather than interfere with the major goal of carrying out professional health care functions.

Esteem Needs

People need to think well of themselves (self-esteem) and to be well thought of by others (esteem from others). When the other, more basic physiologic, security, and belonging needs are satisfactorily met, then these esteem needs will emerge and become primary motivators of behavior. The work setting can provide many opportunities for filling esteem needs. Along with the next level of needs (self-actualization needs), esteem needs are frequently important sources of motivation for professional people.

SELF-ESTEEM. People need to feel good about themselves. They need to feel that they have an intrinsic worth. This feeling of self-worth is related to a sense of being useful, adequate, competent, independent, and autonomous. The alert reader may note that dependency was listed as one of the safety and security needs while independence and autonomy are listed here as esteem needs. These do not necessarily conflict with each other because a person can be independent most of the time and yet occasionally need to ask for help. The healthy adult has some dependency needs but, overall, is far more independent than dependent.

Maslow says that a healthier and firmer sense of worth is developed when it is based on what a person really is rather than on a facade or on a role into which a person has forced oneself. A person's need for self-esteem is better satisfied when worth is based on what the person is rather than on what that person could be or pretends to be. The leader needs to take this into consideration when planning ways to help staff increase their sense of worth and meet their esteem needs.

As indicated earlier, the work setting can provide many opportunities for increasing self-esteem. People feel competent when they are able to use their talents and abilities in their work and when they can do a job well. They feel useful and necessary when they are able to help others. They feel autonomous when they can make their own decisions. These are just a few ways in which self-esteem needs can be met at work and all of them can be influenced by the actions of an effective leader.

ESTEEM FROM OTHERS. Respect and recognition from others is another source of esteem. In keeping with what was stated about the preferability of esteem based on the real self, this respect and recognition from others is more satisfying if it is based on a true appreciation of the real person rather than on a facade or on the opinion of others that is not based on fact. The implication for leadership is that unearned praise is not as effective a motivation as praise that has been earned. Unearned praise may even be counterproductive because it implies that the person is not sufficiently competent to earn it.

People want others to pay attention to them. They want their uniqueness recognized and their need for dignity respected. They need to feel important in some way. They like to feel that they have some kind of status within their social groups and also that they are able to influence others. You can see that learning and practicing leadership skills is one way to increase esteem.

There are many ways in which a person's esteem needs can be filled by people's respect and recognition. Any expression of recognition or genuine appreciation helps to build esteem.

Some more specific ways in which a leader can provide opportunities to meet these needs and thereby increase staff motivation are by:

Letters of commendation.
Merit raises and promotions.
Positive and frequent evaluative feedback.
Individualized assignments that suit staff members' abilities.
Mentioning a person's positive qualities and accomplishments to that person and to others.

Several of the actions listed (raises, promotions, assignments) are dependent on the leader having the authority to grant them. But even the leader without that authority can find opportunities to influence the decisions to grant these things.

Self-Actualization Needs

Self-actualization is the next and highest level in the hierarchy of needs. Self-actualization is the growth and development of a person to that person's fullest potential. Maslow uses many terms to describe the fully self-actualized person: perceptive, accepting, spontaneous, natural, autonomous, secure, unselfish, philosophic, creative, flexible, and satisfied.

These terms offer an image of a truly mature and highly functional human being. But self-actualized people are not perfect—they can be lazy, thoughtless, or bad tempered at times. They are not always happy, either. They can feel sad, guilty, or envious. In other words, while self-actualized people are highly functional, they are not perfect.

If every human being is unique, then what constitutes a person's fullest potential is also unique. Some people have more potential capability than others. Some find expression of their fullest development in artistic ways, others in work with people, and others in work with ideas or material things. The work setting can provide opportunities to meet these self-actualization needs but other spheres, such as the family, social group, or the community can also provide these opportunities. The definition of self-actualization may also be influenced by the cultural background of the person.[16]

If you are to be an effective leader, you will seek ways to promote your own self-actualization as well as that of your coworkers. You need to know a great deal about yourself or another before you can effectively promote self-actualization.

Also, you need to remember that all the lower-level needs must be at least partially filled before people are motivated to use their time and energy working toward self-actualization.

Because of the individuality of self-actualization needs, it is difficult to describe exactly what actions will promote it. (It would be easier to say what will *not* promote self-actualization.) Some ways in which the leader may be able to provide opportunities to meet self-actualization needs are:

- Encourage innovation.
- Include staff members in planning processes.
- Provide opportunities for enhancing current skills.
- Allow the testing of new ideas in practice.
- Include staff in decisions about assignments.
- Encourage people to write their job descriptions and to set their own goals or objectives.
- Encourage staff to develop and implement new projects and programs.
- Provide resources for continued learning.
- Offer challenging work.

These suggestions may not suit everyone but they give you an idea of the ways you, as a leader, can exert influence in the work setting in order to provide opportunities for self-actualization for yourself and others.

SUMMARY

Maslow developed a hierarchy of needs that begins with the most basic physiologic needs followed by safety and security, love and belonging, esteem, and self-actualization needs. The more basic or prepotent need must be at least partially met before a person is motivated to seek gratification of the next higher needs. There are a number of ways in which the leader can help people meet these basic needs in order to free their energy to work on higher level needs.

Sociocultural Influences

There are a number of social forces within the environment that have an influence on the way a person behaves. The broad concept of culture and the more specific concept of roles and the way in which they influence attitudes and behavior are discussed in this section.

The culture of the group or society within which people live and work determines the language they speak and influences their behavior patterns—the kind of food they eat, the way they dress, how they relate to others, and their values, aspirations, and view of the world. Behavior patterns are also affected by the particular roles people play and how those roles are defined. While these sociocultural factors are not the sole determinants of behavior, they are a pervasive and often subtle influence that needs to be considered when trying to understand why people behave the way they do.

CULTURE

Culture includes all of the beliefs, values, and behavior patterns common to a particular group of people.[17] These patterns are shared by the whole group, but there are usually differences in the degree to which the patterns are evident in the attitudes and behavior of a particular individual.

Because these patterns are learned, not innate, they can differ widely from one group to another. These differences in patterns between groups are of some concern to leaders because they may result in misunderstandings and conflicts between people from different cultures.

Cultural Differences

One of the classic ways of describing how cultures differ in beliefs, values, and behavior patterns is the model developed by Kluckhohn.[18] According to this model, there are five fundamental areas in which every culture develops a set of shared meanings: (1) the innate goodness or evil of people, (2) relationship with nature, (3) time orientation, (4) emphasis on the self as being, becoming, or doing, and (5) relationships with others. These five areas and some of the cultural variations found within each one are discussed below.

INNATE GOODNESS OR EVIL. Are people thought to be basically good, evil, or neither? The Puritan ancestors of some Americans believed that people were inherently evil but that it was possible to overcome this evil nature. This point of view leads to an emphasis on the need for a great deal of discipline and control. An alternative view that people have the potential to be either good or bad is probably more common today. You can also find humanists who believe that people are inherently good and that their badness is due to environmental influences. You will see this difference in the motivational theories of leadership in the next chapter.

RELATIONSHIP WITH NATURE. Do people dominate natural forces or are they dominated by them? Those who believe that people dominate nature are likely to put a great deal of energy into altering their environment while those who believe that nature dominates them tend to accept their environment as it is. This cultural difference could lead to tremendous differences in attitudes toward work. For example, one group would accept a harsh work environment as given while another group would protest its harshness and try to change it. A third view point is to see man as part of the environment, which is closer to the open systems approach.

TIME ORIENTATION. Are people most concerned with the past, present, or future? Some groups have a great deal of respect for tradition and are likely to see change as a threat to their traditions. Others are oriented primarily to the present and consider the future too unpredictable to do any planning for it. An orientation to the future leads to an emphasis on planning ahead. People with a future orientation are more likely to see their present job as a stepping stone to better positions and to be more interested in career planning.

Another way in which time orientations can differ, which leads to some problems at work, is the definition of being on time. For some groups, a two o'clock appointment with you means that they will expect to enter your office at precisely two o'clock, even better a minute or two early. For people from other cultures, however, a two o'clock appointment means that they can expect to see you at two forty-five or so, depending on what else is happening at the time.

BEING, BECOMING, OR DOING. Which aspect is given the most attention—what a person is, what that person can be, or what that person does? People of cultures with a being orientation focus primarily on a person's present characteristics while those with a becoming orientation focus on development of the self as a whole (for example, becoming more knowledgeable, aware, or creative). The third orientation focuses on action and accomplishment. In terms of work and leadership, people with this third orientation (doing) would emphasize an individual's contribution to productivity or output and profit as measures of success. Those with a becoming orientation would look at the individual, what that individual is learning or how the person is developing, and how this contributes to the purposes of the group or organization.

RELATIONSHIPS WITH OTHERS. Which relationships are most important—lineal, lateral, or neither? In some societies, the vertical or lineal relationships, that is, who a person's ancestors and parents were, are of great importance. In others, the emphasis is on lateral relationships, that is, the members of the groups to which a person belongs including the extended family, usually with an accompanying concern for others and mutual dependency on each other. For people with this lateral orientation, group goals take priority over individual goals. A third orientation, commonly found in American business, has an emphasis on the independence and autonomy of the individual. For people with this orientation, dependence has negative connotations and individual goals take priority over group goals. People with this individualistic orientation are likely to have more difficulty working as members of a group or team than those with a lateral orientation. They are also more likely to be competitive rather than cooperative.

OTHER DIFFERENCES. In addition to the fundamental areas described, there are a number of other differences between cultures that are significant for leadership. These include differences in (1) relationship to people in authority, (2) spatial relationships, (3) the use of eye contact, (4) expressiveness, (5) language, and (6) modes of thinking.[19, 20]

Relationship to People in Authority. People in some cultural groups, for example, Asian Americans, show their respect for people in authority by remaining silent. They expect communications with people in authority, such as supervisors, to be primarily one way, from the supervisor to the employee. This respectful silence can be misinterpreted as rudeness or lack of intelligence by people from cultural groups in which an employee is expected to relate to the supervisor on an equal or near equal basis and to engage in two-way communication.

Spatial Relationships. There are significant, measurable differences between cultural groups in regard to the amount of space that feels comfortable between people in conversation. Anglo-Americans prefer to keep at least two feet between people during a conversation with a colleague, but Latin Americans and Black Americans consider this amount of space between people too distant and often try to move closer, which makes the Anglo-American feel uncomfortable. The person moving away may be thought of as cold, distant, and indifferent while the person moving closer may be thought of as pushy or inappropriately intimate.

Eye Contact. Generally speaking, Anglo-Americans use eye contact to indicate they are listening but look away frequently when they are speaking. Black Americans make greater eye contact when they are speaking and this can seem like staring to Anglo-Americans who misinterpret this nonverbal communication. In contrast, Mexican Americans and Japanese Americans may avoid eye contact to show respect.

Expressiveness. People from traditional Chinese, Japanese, and American Indian cultural groups value restraint in the expression of strong feelings or discussion of personal matters, while people from the Middle East are more likely to be loud and exuberant in expressing their feelings. Somewhere in between is the North American who values a calm, logical approach but is also learning to express feelings more openly.

Language. When people speak different languages, the communication problem is obvious. However, when they speak the same language, they may not be aware that they speak different versions of that language. For example, the use of non-standard English and regional differences in the use of certain words or expressions can lead to misinterpretations and misunderstandings. In health care organizations, the frequent use of abbreviations and shortened words can be mystifying to clients or new employees who thought they spoke the same language.

Modes of Thinking. There are a number of differences in modes of thinking among cultural groups. Some emphasize the intuitive and creative approach to knowing, others emphasize the objective, logical, and scientific method. Some people make a clear distinction between physical and mental health (a distinction that is evident in the structure of our health care system), others do not. Some people are familiar with abstract thought (such as the use of theories and principles) and comfortable with ambiguity while others prefer a concrete, structured mode that uses examples and offers specific directions. Each of these differences of information affects exchange between people from different cultures.

These cultural differences are generalizations. They are meant to stimulate your awareness of these differences and the ways in which they can affect behavior and also to increase your sensitivity to the often overlooked potential for misunderstanding between people from different cultures. Many of these differences are subtle and easily overlooked by the leader who is not alert for them.

WORKING WITH CULTURAL DIFFERENCES. Work in the health care field attracts people from many different cultures. You may work with people from your own culture or you may work with people from a culture that is entirely new and unfamiliar to you. In some situations, you may find yourself a part of the majority, in others a part of the minority culture, which is generally a more uncomfortable position.

When you are a part of the majority culture it will be especially important for you to show respect and consideration for people from different cultural groups. If you are in the minority, you may have to demand this respect and consideration from others. In either case, knowledge of both your own cultural patterns and those of other cultures is an essential first step in developing effective working relationships among people of different cultures.

There is no shortcut to cultural awareness and effectiveness in working with people of different cultures. They require some insight into your own responses to people who are in some way different and also some time to learn about these differences and develop your ability to recognize them. The following is a set of guidelines that can help you move in this direction:

1. *Learn More About Cultural Beliefs, Values, and Practices.* Knowledge comes before understanding. It may actually be more difficult to learn about your own culture than about another culture because it is so much a part of you that it is below awareness until you begin studying it or until you are exposed to other cultures.
2. *Resist Seeing Everyone in a Particular Culture as Being Alike.* If you read about your own culture, you will probably find that some of the descriptions fit you personally but others do not. The same is true for people from other cultures. Variants are found within cultures and each individual has unique characteristics that influence behaviors as well.
3. *Interpret Behavior on the Basis of Its Meaning to the Other Person and That Person's Culture.* Do not interpret the behavior of people from a different culture on the basis of your own culture. Obviously, you cannot do this effectively until you know a great deal about the other culture.
4. *Observe Different Cultural Patterns in Behavior.* If you watch the ways in which people from different cultural groups interact, you can begin to get

a feeling for the customary distance they maintain between people, the degree of expressiveness, eye contact, and so forth. This both increases your awareness and helps you to feel more comfortable with different patterns.

5. *Adjust Your Own Patterns Somewhat to Reduce the Difference Between Your Own and Other People's Patterns.* This does not mean that you must give up your culture and become the same as the people with whom you work. It does mean that you can make some accommodations, such as speaking a little softer or louder, moving a little closer or farther away, or using more abstract or concrete expressions, in order to facilitate communication and comfortable working relationships.

6. *Distinguish Between Behavior That Needs to be Changed and Behavior That can be Accommodated.* This is an especially important action for team leaders and supervisors to take. In some jobs, for example, it is necessary for an employee to arrive at exactly the agreed upon time so that people on the previous shift can leave their patients and go home. It is also necessary to learn enough of your clients' language to be able to communicate with them, especially to counsel them. On the other hand, a wide variation in such differences as preferred personal distance, expressiveness, and responses to people in authority can be tolerated in most work situations.

ROLES

Roles are social prescriptions for behavior. They specify what kind of behavior is appropriate for a person who has a specific position within a group. An alternate definition is the actual (rather than prescribed) behavior of a person occupying a specific position within a group.

Like cultural patterns of behavior, role behavior is learned through interactions with people in a process called socialization. Learning a role involves acquiring certain skills, attitudes, and patterns of behavior. However, cultural patterns are more general than role prescriptions and a person usually fills many different roles but has one or a limited number of different cultural patterns.[21, 22]

Socialization into a particular role includes changes in attitudes and behavior and an acceptance of the expectations of that role. People can become deeply committed to their roles, can get a great deal of satisfaction from them, and can suffer anger or sorrow at the loss of a role. The roles that an individual plays can affect that individual's identity and self-esteem. The roles can also help or thwart their attempts to meet the basic needs. For example, the role of nursing assistant carries little status or prestige and can fail to meet a person's need for recognition but it can help to meet a person's need for security or belonging.

People occupy different roles in different situations and within different groups. A single individual can have the roles of caregiver, colleague, friend, parent, spouse, sibling, cousin, partner, and many more. You may find yourself in the role of leader in one situation and in the role of someone responding to leadership in another situation. Both a person's understanding of a particular role and unique characteristics as an individual affect the way a person carries out that role. This means that you will find variations in the way a role is enacted. For example, although there is a great deal of similarity in the way all the critical care nurses in a particular hospital function, no two nurses will behave exactly the same way in that role despite the fact that they fill the same role within the parameters set by the hospital and by society for that role.

The existence of different roles and the fact that they influence behavior by prescribing what kind of behavior is expected helps to explain why people can be observed to act somewhat differently at various times and in various places. The person as a whole has not changed but different aspects of the self become more evident in different roles.

Role Stress Sources

There are a number of ways in which stress within a role or between roles can arise. These different sources of role stress are role conflict, ambiguity, incongruity, overload, incompetence, and overqualification. Each is explained below.

ROLE CONFLICT. Conflicts can occur within a particular role or between two or more roles. Many caregivers experience conflicts within their roles as professionals. For example, they may be expected to make independent decisions and to be accountable for their own practice and yet be expected to follow a physician's directions without questioning them.

The differences *between* roles can also be a source of conflict. For example, some people may be expected to be nurturing and supportive parents within their families but are expected to be dominant and controlling and to avoid being nurturing in their particular positions at work. This conflict of expectations can be a source of stress to people who cannot easily switch from a supportive to a domineering style as they move from home to work.

AMBIGUITY. Some roles are vague and inadequately defined. Without adequate guidelines you cannot be sure that you are fulfilling the role according to expectations. For example, you in the role of nurse are assigned to a newly formed drug treatment team. You may find that the nurse's role is ambiguous. You may not know whether you are expected to monitor drug intake, counsel individuals, be responsible for the client's physical well being, or all these.

INCONGRUITY. Some role expectations are not congruent with a person's usual patterns of behavior. For example, an experienced nurse who is asked to be a preceptor for a nursing student may find it difficult to step back and let the student give the nursing care when the nurse is used to doing it. Another common example of incongruity occurs when a person who enjoys working with highly technical equipment is suddenly promoted to a managerial position and expected to refrain from working with the equipment and to enjoy dealing with people problems.

OVERLOAD.   Some roles demand too much of the individual. For example, a nurse is expected to be an expert clinician, teacher, counselor, researcher, and leader. For some people who enter nursing, these demands constitute an overload of expectations that they cannot meet.

INCOMPETENCE.   People sometimes find that they do not have the knowledge or skills a role demands. In the example in which a skilled technician is moved into a leadership position, the technician may find that the skills needed to fulfill the expectations demanded by this new position are not the same skills the technician has acquired.

OVERQUALIFICATION.   This is the opposite of role incompetence. People some-times find themselves in a role that does not utilize all their abilities. In the drug treatment team example mentioned previously, you find the only expectation of the nurse is to monitor drug intake, much of your knowledge and skill will be unused.

Research Example 1-1 examines the frequency with which some of the different types of role conflicts are encountered by caregivers in hospitals.

Role Stress Reduction

The sources of stress just described are a matter of concern to the leader because of their potential negative effect on job satisfaction and productivity. They can be a problem for both the leader and the people with whom the leader works.

A number of ways to reduce role stress have been suggested by Hardy.[24] Most of these actions can be taken either by the individual experiencing the stress or by the leader intervening in a situation in which role stress is a problem. You will find, however, that not all of the suggestions are suitable for every situation or type of stress. The suggestions are as follows.

1. *Problem Solving.* This is usually the first step to take when trying to resolve a dilemma of any kind. The problem-solving process, explained further in Chapter 5, includes identifying the problem (in this case the kind of role stress involved) and then seeking alternative actions to take that will solve the problem. For example, if the problem is role ambiguity, it may be possible to better define the role yourself or to request clarification from the people with whom you work. The same approach can be used to resolve conflicts within a particular role.
2. *Role Bargaining.* When role stress cannot be reduced by clarification or another simple solution, then direct or indirect role bargaining can be used. In *direct bargaining,* the individual communicates the role problem to those who have established the role expectations and then negotiates a change in those expectations. For example, if on the drug treatment team, you found that your only expected duty was to monitor drug intake, you could discuss the problem of role overqualification with fellow team members or with the

Research Example 1-1. Role Conflict — A Challenge to Reality Shock

How much role conflict do nurses experience? What types of conflicts? Are these conflicts related to job dissatisfaction and turnover? Rosse and Rosse[23] questioned registered nurses, practical nurses, and aides about the types of conflicts they experienced, how satisfied they were with their jobs and the likelihood of leaving their jobs in the next six to nine months.

The role conflicts measured were role ambiguity, role overload, intersender conflict (incompatible demands from different people such as physicians and administrators), inter-role conflict (demands of multiple roles) and person-role conflict (conflict between values or beliefs and actions required by the role). For example, co-actors were asked if they ever had to work under incompatible policies, do things that were against their better judgment, or if they had conflicts with their families. The co-actors were also asked to choose one of seven faces from a scowl to a broad smile to represent their feelings about work. Altogether, 220 RNs, 188 LPNs, 78 nursing aides, and 17 nursing supervisors representing all three shifts at five different hospitals in Illinois completed the questionnaire. Their median length of employment at the hospitals was 3.5 years.

Although a high level of conflict was expected for all types listed, only intersender (incompatible demands) and role overload had means about the midpoint of the scale used. The researchers expected that role overload would be higher for those who worked in intensive and coronary care units and that intersender conflicts would be higher for RNs (especially those with higher degrees) than for LPNs or aides, but they found no significant differences on any of these variables. They did find, however, that role conflicts were related to work stress but did not find as strong a relationship to job satisfaction or to intentions to resign, as expected.

In contradiction to the concept of reality shock as a phenomenon occurring when a new, unexperienced nurse first enters the job market, increased conflicts were found in nurses who had been in their positions for a greater length of time. Head nurses and supervisors had higher levels of both role overload and intersender (incompatible demands) conflicts, probably because of their roles as mediator between nursing staff, physicians, and administration, as well as with patients.

The results of this study raise many questions about the role conflicts experienced by nursing personnel. They seem to indicate that many factors commonly believed to be the sources of role conflict—working in intensive care units, holding a bachelors or higher degree, and being a new graduate—are not as influential as many have assumed. The researchers conclude that many of our beliefs about the sources of role conflict have not been sufficiently researched.

person in authority who has limited your role and then you could negotiate an expansion of the nurse's role. *Indirect bargaining* involves the same kind of role alteration but it is done by the dissatisfied individual alone, without discussing it first. Instead, the individual simply begins to alter the role so that it better suits the individual in the hope that a gradual change will be accepted by the people involved. For example, on the drug treatment team, you could begin to gradually add to your functions without discussing the change with the team members. Although it is not appropriate for all situations, indirect bargaining is sometimes an effective way to bring about subtle role changes without provoking resistance to the change.

3. *Nonconformity.* Nonconformity is the refusal to meet unrealistic or conflicting role expectations. It is similar to indirect role bargaining in that the dissatisfied individuals proceed to carry out the role the way they want it to be. However, indirect bargaining is an attempt to gain the support of the other people involved while nonconformity is used in spite of resistance. Some nonconforming actions can produce the desired role change but involve a higher risk than indirect bargaining does.

4. *Withdrawal.* Withdrawal from the problematic role may be partial or complete. Some roles are essentially voluntary ones from which it is easy to withdraw completely but other roles have a more central position in a person's life and cannot be easily abandoned. It would, for example, be much harder to withdraw from the role of nurse than it would be to withdraw from the role of student in a recreational class after work. A partial withdrawal is accomplished by limiting the amount of time, energy, attention, and other forms of commitment to the role. For example, some people who are dissatisfied with their jobs but for some reason feel that they cannot leave them will put minimal energy into their jobs—just enough to get by— and pour the rest of their energy into roles outside of work. You can see that this kind of withdrawal can seriously affect a person's performance at work. Withdrawal is usually a last resort action taken when other actions have failed to eliminate the stress. However, it is sometimes a necessary and constructive action, particularly when the role has become highly stressful and potentially destructive for the individual.

SUMMARY

Culture includes all of the learned patterns of beliefs, values and behaviors common to a group or society. Cultural patterns vary in many ways including beliefs about the nature of people, time orientation, and relationships to nature and other people. Cultural variations of particular interest to leadership include relationships to people in authority, spatial relationships, use of eye contact, expressiveness, language, and modes of thinking. Leaders need to understand cultural differences in behavior and to learn how to work with people from different cultures.

Roles are more specific, socially prescribed patterns of behavior. Role stresses such as role conflict, ambiguity, incongruity, overload, and inappropriate preparation for the role can be dealt with by problem solving, role bargaining, nonconformity, or withdrawal.

Individual Factors

So far in this chapter, we have considered open systems theory, which applies to all people, and then Maslow's hierarchy of needs, which is meant to be a universal theory of motivation but may have some cultural biases. Then the effect of culture and the more specific role prescriptions on people's behavior were discussed. We will now consider individual determinants of behavior and the wide variety of behaviors people use to cope with the challenges of everyday living and working.

INDIVIDUALITY

Despite all of the universal, cultural, and social influences on behavior mentioned so far in this chapter, each human being is unique. Although similar to other people in many ways, every individual has distinctive characteristics and patterns of behavior unlike any other person's.

Four factors are usually cited as having a significant influence on the uniqueness of the individual pattern.[25] The first of these factors is *heredity,* the characteristics and potentialities with which a person is born. There is little argument that each person begins life with a genetic code that serves as a basic script for that person's own particular growth pattern. However, the effect of heredity on intelligence, ability, and emotional well-being throughout life is a subject of great controversy, with some saying that heredity is a primary influence but many others countering that the environment in which an individual grows and develops is the primary factor.

The second factor, *environment,* has already been discussed. The environment includes all of those forces outside the person that affect the person in some way. This includes the physical setting and its climate, topography, colors, harshness, or mildness. It also includes the social milieu, a person's parents, family, friends, neighbors, coworkers, community, and so forth. In fact, every person and every social system with which the person interacts constitute a part of the individual's environment. Every individual's interaction with the environment is unique: no two people, even siblings or twins, ever have exactly the same life experiences.

Individuals are not passive recipients of all this influence. As was pointed out earlier, people are a part of their environment and act upon their environment as well as experience its influence. For example, everyone who is a member of a particular group is partly responsible for the characteristics of that group as well as being affected by the characteristics of the group.

Individuals interpret their experiences in their own way and in light of their past experiences. For example, an unusual sight may be frightening and repellent to one person but fascinating and attractive to another person. These *differences in perception* account for much of the differences in response to a particular event found in human behavior and are the third factor contributing to individuality.

Not only do different individuals perceive events from their own unique point of view, they also have their own *particular repertoire of ways to deal with these events,* which is the fourth factor contributing to individuality. Each individual has a characteristic set of behaviors that is used more often than others. This characteristic set becomes an identifiable pattern of overall behavior similar to but not the same as any other person's. Some of the most common though often misinterpreted behaviors used to cope with daily living are discussed below.

BEHAVIOR PATTERNS

Before discussing specific behaviors, it may be helpful to consider two important assumptions about human behavior. The first of these assumptions is that all human behavior has some kind of meaning.[26] While the meaning of a particular action may be obscure or unintelligible to the observer, it is still assumed to have some purpose for that person. This purpose may be to meet a need (any of the needs in Maslow's hierarchy), to express a feeling or state of being (such as smiling, laughing, and clapping to express pleasure), or to cope with a perceived threat.

Although all behavior is postulated to have a meaning or purpose, people are not always aware of the purpose of their behavior. In fact, they may not be any more aware of the purpose than the observer is although they have the potential for developing this awareness.

It is also assumed that the present state of the individual in relation to the current state of the environment determines current behavior. How a person perceives the environment and that person's learned patterns of behavior have already been mentioned as factors influencing behavior. Another factor is the amount of energy available at the time. For example, a person whose energy level is very low may make a much weaker response to a problem than would seem justified by the seriousness of the problem, while another person who has been storing up a great deal of tension may seem to overreact to a problem. Every behavior reflects the person as a whole—one's physical state as well as one's emotional state.

Actions taken for the purpose of reducing tension or dealing with a perceived threat may be divided into three categories: reflex actions, nondeliberative mechanisms, and deliberative mechanisms.

Reflex Actions

Reflex actions are automatic responses. They occur rapidly, without any conscious or deliberate effort but are nevertheless purposeful. The purpose is usually protective in some way. People are born with many reflexes and can acquire others during their lives. Yawning, sneezing, and blinking are common reflexes. Reacting automatically to a sudden loud noise and pulling away from a source of pain are also reflex actions.

Nondeliberative Mechanisms

The term nondeliberative is used to indicate that these particular coping mechanisms seem to operate primarily below the full awareness of the individual. A person can use these mechanisms and not even be aware of doing so. Since they are below awareness, their connection to the perceived threat or problem is not always apparent. You will see that the description of these mechanisms helps to explain the often puzzling and seemingly inexplicable behavior of people, which is a subject of importance to leaders who are trying to influence behavior.

The definitions of these nondeliberative mechanisms originated with the work of Freud[27] but they have been used to explain behavior even by those who do not employ other elements of Freudian psychology. While the use of these mechanisms is generally for protective purposes, inappropriate or excessive use of any one of them is considered harmful. The most widely used of these mechanisms are discussed below.

COMPENSATION.   When people believe that they are seriously lacking in a particular ability they may try to compensate for this lack by excelling in another area. For example, a person who has difficulty with school work may make up for this deficit by concentrating on developing social skills and becoming popular at school.

REPRESSION.   Repression is a complete blocking of certain feelings or thoughts from awareness because they are unacceptable or intolerable in some way. For example, a caregiver may repress anger toward a particular patient because, to the caregiver, anger is a completely unacceptable response to patients. The result is that the caregiver is not aware of these angry feelings about the patient except perhaps for a vague sense of tension or unease when interacting with this patient.

DENIAL.   In a manner similar to repression, denial is the blocking from awareness of a painful or threatening situation or experience. Denial is a blocking of something occurring in the environment while repression refers to blocking something within the individual. A common example is the denial of a life-threatening illness. People can also deny problems at work and seem, for example, to believe that everything is going well when they are on the verge of being fired.

SUPPRESSION.   Suppression is a more deliberate form of repression. It is a temporary putting aside of disturbing feelings or thoughts until they can be handled. For example, during an emergency, a nurse may suppress emotions and act calmly but feel shaky and upset afterward.

DISPLACEMENT.   Displacement occurs when a person holds back or suppresses feelings about a particular person or situation and then later unleashes these feelings in another situation or toward a different person. For example, a coworker might be angry at the boss but is afraid to express this feeling to the boss. Later, at home, the coworker displaces the anger and yells at the spouse for leaving a pair of shoes in the living room.

PROJECTION.   Projection is another way to deal with painful or unacceptable feelings, in this case by attributing them to other people. For example, supervisors who feel anxious about the institution of a new evaluation procedure may say and actually believe that they oppose it because the people they supervise are threatened by it. Another kind of projection is to blame others for one's own failures.

WITHDRAWAL.   Already discussed in the section concerned with roles, withdrawal and thus avoidance of threatening situations is sometimes the only solution available to a person facing a problem.

RATIONALIZATION.   Rationalization is giving an explanation for one's behavior that is logical and reasonable but is not the real reason for that behavior. For example, a supervisor may deny a promotion to an eligible employee whom the supervisor dislikes intensely and say that this was done ''because the employee isn't ready to move into that position yet and will be better off staying at the present level for at least another year.''

SUBSTITUTION.   Socially acceptable energy outlets are often substituted for a less acceptable but desired outlet. For example, the urge to retaliate against an agency that has drawn clients away from a person's own agency can be replaced by a drive to improve their own agency. The substitution chosen is not always constructive. For example, some people substitute excessive eating or drinking for desired but unattainable outlets.

IDENTIFICATION.   Identification involves experiencing the same feelings as another person or behaving the same way. It is often a means of filling some lack or deficit in self-confidence or identity. People frequently identify with people they admire or with whom they have something in common. For example, a new and inexperienced nurse may identify with a head nurse whom the new nurse particularly admires and model behavior after that head nurse.

Deliberative Mechanisms

The deliberative coping mechanisms that people use more consciously to avoid discomfort, reduce tension, and solve problems are even more varied and individualistic than the nondeliberative mechanisms. Most of these mechanisms are usually helpful but they can be and are, also, misused. Unlike the nondeliberative mechanisms, most are more straightforward and self-explanatory behaviors as you will see in the examples below.[28, 29]

SEEKING COMFORT AND REASSURANCE.   Touch, hugging, and comforting words can soothe and calm people who are distressed.

USING SOUND AND RHYTHM.   Dancing, listening to music, and other rhythmic activities are a means for expressing feelings and releasing tension.

VENTILATING FEELINGS.   Crying, swearing, and laughing, to name only a few, are ways to relieve tensions and share feelings with others.

EATING.   Eating can relieve tension and substitute for other needs. When done in the company of others, it can become a time of sharing and support that contributes to well-being.

SMOKING AND CHEWING GUM.   Although not healthful, both are often used to ease tension.

ALCOHOL AND DEPRESSANT DRUGS. Both are potentially dangerous substances but are often used for their calming effect.

RELAXATION TECHNIQUES. These are nondrug methods that are often effective in reducing tension although they do not solve underlying problems.

CAFFEINE AND OTHER STIMULANTS. Again, these drugs are potentially dangerous but often used to lift spirits and reduce fatigue.

DISCUSSING A PROBLEM. Simply talking about a problem with a person who is a good listener often makes the problem seem smaller and more manageable.

PROBLEM SOLVING. Going beyond talking to thinking through a situation and seeking solutions is usually constructive.

TAKE ONE THING OR ONE DAY AT A TIME. A seemingly unmanageable problem or demand may seem less impossible to deal with if it is broken down into manageable parts that are considered and resolved one at a time. This is a kind of "tunnel vision" that may help a person get through a time of crisis.

BECOMING PASSIVE, RIGID, OR VAGUE. These behaviors conserve energy temporarily but do not relieve the stress. People using this mechanism tend to internalize their stress.

AGGRESSION. This discharges energy but often exacerbates the problem.

ASSERTIVENESS. This discharges energy, usually without exacerbating the problem, and may help resolve the problem.

TAKE STOCK OF YOUR RESOURCES. This mechanism has both a calming and strengthening effect.

SLEEP. This is a means of temporary escape but also a way to restore energy reserves.

DAY DREAMING. This is another means of escape. It relieves tension temporarily but does not resolve the problem and will exacerbate it if overdone.

PHYSICAL EXERCISE. This is a means for relieving tension and reducing stress that also can contribute to health and well-being.

REPETITIVE ACTIVITY. Seemingly purposeless, repetitive actions, such as pacing, rocking, grinding teeth, drumming fingers on a table, or swinging a leg while sitting, are used to discharge excess energy.

DIVERSIONS. Engaging in enjoyable activities can temporarily distract attention from the problem, provide pleasure, and restore energy, sometimes freeing energy for more creative problem solving.

People often engage in these activities at times when other behavior would seem more appropriate to the observer who is not aware of their need to reduce stress and tension or resolve a problem. The leader who is aware of the meaning of such behaviors can avoid misinterpretations and can sometimes help the individual resolve the problem that led to the use of these coping mechanisms.

SUMMARY

Heredity, environment, a person's unique experiences, perception of those experiences, and a person's repertoire of behavior patterns are all factors contributing to individuality. Human behavior is postulated to have meaning, although the person may not be aware of that meaning, and to reflect the present state of the individual as a whole in relation to the environment. Automatic reflex actions, nondeliberative coping mechanisms (including compensation, repression, denial, suppression, displacement, projection, withdrawal, rationalization, substitution and identification), and a large number of deliberative mechanisms are used by people to cope with the everyday challenges and stresses of living and working.

References

1. HALL, AD AND FAGEN, RE: *Definition of system.* In BUCKLEY, W (ED): *Modern Systems Research for the Behavioral Scientist.* Aldine Publishing, Chicago: 1968.

2. LASZLO, E: *The Systems View of the World.* George Braziller, New York, 1972.

3. ASHBY, WR: *Principles of the self-organizing system.* In BUCKLEY, W (ED): *Modern Systems Research for the Behavioral Scientist.* Aldine Publishing, Chicago, 1968.

4. BELL, NW AND VOGEL, EF (EDS): *A Modern Introduction to the Family.* The Free Press, New York, 1968.

5. VON BERTALANFFY, L: *Introduction.* In WERLEY, H, ET AL (EDS): *Health Research: The Systems Approach.* Springer Publishing, New York, 1976.

6. ROGERS, ME: *An Introduction to the Theoretical Basis of Nursing.* FA Davis, Philadelphia, 1970.

7. SCHEFLEN, AE: *Comments on the significance of interaction rhythms.* In DAIRS, M (ED): *Interaction Rhythms: Periodicity in Communicative Behavior.* Human Sciences Press, New York, 1982.

8. KANTOR, D AND LEHR, W: *Inside the Family: Toward a Theory of Family Process.* Harper Calophon Books, New York, 1976.

9. HANCHETT, ES: *Community Health Assessment: A Conceptual Tool Kit.* John Wiley & Sons, New York, 1979.

10. FAWCETT, J: *The Family As An Open Living System: An Emerging Conceptual Framework For Nursing.* Journal of International Nursing Review 22(July/August):113, 1975.

11. BOULDING, KE: *General systems theory—The skeleton of science.* In BUCKLEY, W (ED): *Modern Systems Research for the Behavioral Scientist.* Aldine Publishing, Chicago, 1968.

12. LUCE, GG: *Body Time.* Pantheon Books, New York, 1971.

13. CHAPPLE, ED: *The Biological Foundations of Individuality and Culture.* Robert Krieger, Huntington, New York, 1979.

14. MASLOW, AH: *Motivation and Personality,* ed 2. Harper & Row, New York, 1970.

15. CAMPBELL, C: *Nursing Diagnosis and Intervention in Nursing Practice.* John Wiley & Sons, New York, 1978.

16. SZAPOCZNIK, J, ET AL: *Cuban value structure: Treatment Implications.* Consult Clin Psychol 46(5):961, 1978.

17. LEININGER, M: *Transcultural Nursing: Concepts, Theories and Practices.* John Wiley & Sons, New York, 1978.

18. KLUCKHOHN, FR: *Dominant and variant value orientations.* In BRINK, PJ: *Transcultural Nursing: A Book of Readings.* Prentice-Hall, Englewood Cliffs, NJ, 1976.

19. HALL, ET AND WHYTE, WF: *Intercultural communication: A guide to men of action.* In BRINK, PJ (ED): *Transcultural Nursing: A Book of Readings.* Prentice-Hall, Englewood Cliffs, NJ, 1976.

20. SUE, DW: *Counseling the Culturally Different: Theory and Practice.* John Wiley & Sons, New York, 1981.

21. BIDDLE, B AND THOMAS, E: *Role Theory: Concepts and Research.* John Wiley & Sons, New York, 1966.

22. HARDY, ME AND CONWAY, ME (EDS): *Role Theory: Perspectives for Health Professionals.* Appleton-Century-Crofts, New York, 1978.

23. ROSSE, JG AND ROSSE, PH: *Role conflict and ambiguity: An empirical investigation of nursing personnel.* Evaluation and the Health Professionals 4(4):385, 1981.

24. HARDY, ME: *Role stress and role strain.* In HARDY, ME AND CONWAY, ME: *Role Theory: Perspectives for Health Professionals.* Appleton-Century-Crofts, New York, 1978.

25. JONES, KL, SHAINBERG, LW, AND BYER, CO: *Emotional Health,* ed 2. Canfield Press, San Francisco, 1975.

26. BROWN, MM AND FOWLER, GR: *Psychodynamic Nursing: A Biosocial Orientation.* WB Saunders, Philadelphia, 1971.

27. SCHWARTZ, LH AND SCHWARTZ, JL: *The Psychodynamics of Patient Care.* Prentice-Hall, Englewood Cliffs, NJ, 1972.

28. ARDELL, DB: *High Level Wellness.* Bantam Books, New York, 1979.

29. MENNINGER, K: *The Vital Balance: The Life Process In Mental Health and Illness.* The Viking Press, New York, 1963.

Chapter 2

Leadership and Management Theories

The first chapter dealt with general theories that attempted to explain human behavior. This second chapter now focuses on the more specific leadership and management theories and concepts that have been developed over the years to explain how people influence each other's behavior in work situations.

You will see that some of the earlier approaches tried to explain leadership in terms of a single characteristic or single element of a leadership situation. Some are so limited that they hardly deserve to be called theories. However, even these limited ones do have some value, although they are only partial explanations of how leaders influence people. Other later theories became more complex. These later theories attempt to account for more of the characteristics and behavior of the leader, co-actor, and environment, all of which affect a leadership situation, with more success than the earlier theories.

Becoming acquainted with these different theories helps to make you aware of some of the beliefs you may hold about leadership. Each of these theories has its supporters today and you can observe people acting on the basis of any of them, selecting leaders or trying to function as leaders on the basis of these theories.

The simplest of the leadership theories are those that focus on the personality and other traits of the leader. These will be discussed first. Then the behavioral, motivational, situational, and interactional theories, listed in order of increasing complexity, will be discussed.[1-4]

Trait Theories

If you have ever heard the statement that "leaders are born, not made," then you have heard someone expressing the fundamental belief underlying the trait theories of leadership. Trait theories assume that a person must have certain innate abilities, personality traits, or other characteristics in order to be a leader. If this were true, it would mean that some people are naturally better leaders than others.

Since trait theories emphasize given ability over the effects of learning or the development of leadership skills, they lead to the common conclusion that some people cannot be leaders, or are very unlikely to become leaders, no matter how hard they try. This approach also leads to efforts to identify people who have the characteristics of a leader rather than to the development of leader training program.

The desire to distinguish between people who have these innate characteristics and those who do not led to a search for a single trait or cluster of traits that distinguish leaders from nonleaders. Trait theorists and researchers have studied the biographies of historical leaders and the characteristics of people in positions that require leadership ability. The study of biographies was the basis of the Great Man theory of leadership.

GREAT MAN THEORY

According to the Great Man theory of leadership, the tremendous influence of some well-known people has actually determined or changed the course of history. These people are said to have possessed inborn characteristics that made them great leaders. (The opposite, determinist viewpoint would be that these people happened to be in the right place at the right time and that it was the events of their time that made them great.)

Important historical figures, such as Caesar, Alexander the Great, and Hitler, have been studied to find the characteristics that made them outstanding leaders of their time. Royalty were also of interest to trait theorists. For example, when the characteristics of the rulers of 14 European countries over 500 years were studied, it was found that the countries were strong when they had a strong ruler but that conditions in these countries were bad when they had a weak ruler.[5] It was assumed that the condition of the country was due to the influence of the abilities with which the ruler was born, ignoring the fact that the condition of the country could have affected the success of the ruler (in the manner of the feedback loop discussed in Chapter 1).

INDIVIDUAL CHARACTERISTICS

The search for a trait or cluster of traits that determines whether or not a person will be an effective leader has been the focus of many studies. So far, no single trait or characteristic has been found to be possessed by all leaders or to predict who will become a leader. In spite of this limitation, the trait approach is often used to choose people for leadership positions.

FIGURE 2-1. The tallest individual may be chosen for a responsible position solely on the basis of that supposed leadership trait.

Common Popular Beliefs

Many people believe in and try to implement a number of different—and even contradictory—popular versions of the trait theory. Certain physical characteristics are often thought to potentiate leadership ability. For example, it is commonly believed that tall individuals are better leader material than short individuals because they seem stronger and more dominating (Fig. 2-1). A tall person can literally look down on other people and can be physically imposing. A contradictory but also popular belief is that a person who was always smaller than peers has had to learn how to defend and is, therefore, a tougher fighter and potentially stronger leader than most other people.

In addition to physical characteristics, there are certain personality traits and talents that are commonly associated with leadership ability. For example, the most outspoken person in a group is often assumed to be the leader even when other evidence does not support this assumption.

Many people believe that the most intelligent or skilled person in a group becomes the leader because other group members will admire this person and will frequently come to this person for advice and assistance. Manipulative people (sometimes called ''smooth operators'' or ''wheeler-dealers'') and people who are especially courageous are also thought of as good leader material.

Despite their limitations and contradictions, these popular versions are often used as the basis for leadership decisions. For example, the most physically imposing or most highly skilled nurse in a group may be chosen for a supervisory position solely on the basis of that supposed leadership trait.

Trait Studies

The beliefs about leadership mentioned above are very subjective but even the more objective research studies aimed at finding specific traits have not succeeded in finding any one set of traits that distinguish leaders from nonleaders. When the results of different studies are compared they are found to be inconsistent. Dozens of different traits have been identified but none can reliably predict who will be an effective leader and who will not.

However, there are some characteristics that were found repeatedly in a large proportion of these studies. It is believed that these characteristics are likely to have some effect on an individual's ability to exert leadership. These characteristics are intelligence and skill, initiative, assertiveness and persistence, ability to relate to other people, a strong sense of self, ability to tolerate stress and take the consequences of a decision, originality (creativity), and status within the group. Intelligence and initiative are the two most often cited.

By themselves, the trait theories are too limited because they focus on the leader and ignore the other two elements of a leadership situation (co-actor and environment) and because they focus on the capacities a leader brings to a situation rather than on what the leader actually does in a situation. But the trait theories do contribute to our understanding of leadership by indicating those characteristics, especially intelligence and initiative, that are more likely to be found in leaders than nonleaders and would, therefore, probably be helpful to a person who wants to exert leadership. It has been said that many of these traits associated with leadership may actually be indicators of motivation or desire to lead rather than innate capacities of an individual.

42

SUMMARY

Innate capacity for leadership is the focus of the trait theories. According to the Great Man theory, important figures who influenced the course of history had innate characteristics that distinguished them from ordinary people. Popular versions of the trait theory see characteristics such as physical size, courage, intelligence, or domination as indicators that a person will be an effective leader. Research shows that traits such as intelligence and initiative are associated with leadership but also that the trait theories are too limited to determine effective leadership by themselves.

Behavioral Theories

The behavioral theories, or functional theories as they are sometimes called, still focus on the leader. The primary difference between the trait and behavioral theories is that the behavioral theories are concerned with what a leader does rather than who the leader is. These theories are far more action oriented but are still limited primarily to the leader element in a leadership situation although the co-actor is given some consideration.

In this section, we will look at one theory based on the description of leader functions and two different approaches to describing leadership styles.

AUTHORITARIAN, DEMOCRATIC, AND LAISSEZ-FAIRE LEADERSHIP STYLES

A major breakthrough came in the late 1930s when research done by Lewin, Lippitt, and White[6] on the interaction between leaders and group members indicated that the behavior of the leader could substantially influence the climate and outcomes of the group. The leader behaviors were divided into three distinct patterns called leadership styles: authoritarian, democratic, and laissez-faire (see Research Example 2-1). These styles can be thought of as a continuum from a highly controlling and directive type of leadership to a very passive, inactive style (Fig. 2-2).

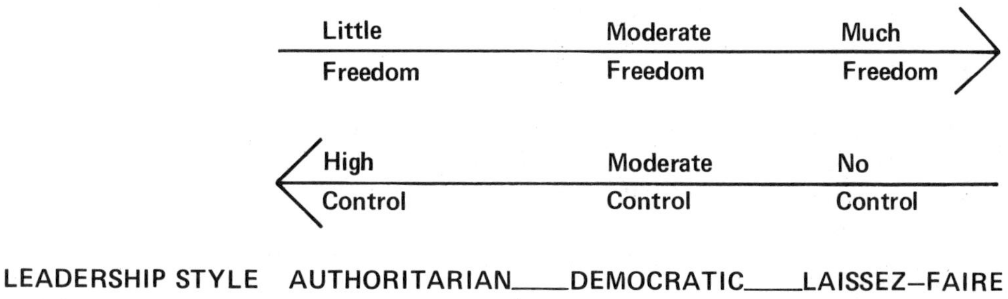

Little	Moderate	Much
Freedom	Freedom	Freedom

High	Moderate	No
Control	Control	Control

LEADERSHIP STYLE   AUTHORITARIAN____DEMOCRATIC____LAISSEZ–FAIRE

FIGURE 2-2. Continuum of leadership styles.

Research Example 2-1. Autocratic, Democratic, and Laissez-Faire Leadership

Study Design. A classic study of the effects of different leadership styles on groups was done by Lewin, Lippitt, and White in 1938.[6] Twenty 11-year-old boys (described as middle class, from the Midwest, and well adjusted) were instructed to act as either autocratic, democratic, or laissez-faire leaders.

The groups met once a week in after-school clubs in which the boys made masks, plaster molds, and other craft items. Each group was exposed to three different leaders and at least two different styles of leadership. Each leader played at least two different styles of leadership in order to control the effects of differences in skill and personal style of the individual leaders.

The autocratic leaders made all the decisions and expected the boys to obey them. When the groups had democratic leaders, the boys participated in making decisions. The laissez-faire leader avoided making any decisions and allowed the group to work or play without any supervision or direction.

The original plan was to test only the autocratic and democratic styles, but it was observed that one of the four leaders in the first series of club meetings was more anarchic than democratic and that this was having a substantial effect on his group. This leader was then encouraged to assume the laissez-faire style for that series of six meetings and another leader did the same in the second series of meetings in order to study the effects of laissez-faire leadership.

At each club meeting, an observer sat unobtrusively in the corner of the room to record the behavior of both the leader and group members for later analysis. Raw scores and percentages were reported for the behavior observed such as the number and proportion of friendly, aggressive, or dependent statements made by the boys. The differences were found to be statistically significant at the 0.05 level of confidence or better.

Results. The researchers found that the groups behaved very differently under different leadership styles. When the groups had laissez-faire leaders they were less organized, less efficient, and less satisfying for their members. Laissez-faire groups got less work done, spent more time horsing around and their work was done poorly. When the boys were interviewed later by a neutral party, all of them (100 percent) preferred the democratic leader over the laissez-faire leader.

Autocratic leadership was found to result in much more hostility (in a ratio of 30 to 1), more demands for attention, more dependence on the leaders, and other more subtle kinds of discontent in the groups. In fact, all four boys who dropped out of the clubs did so when their groups were led by autocratic leaders. It is interesting to note that autocratic groups were found to be either quite aggressive or quite submissive. The observers thought that less individuality was allowed in the autocratic groups. Motivation to work was clearly lower than in the democratically led groups—when the autocratic leader left the room, the work stopped. However, the overall quantity of work done was greatest under the autocratic leaders.

Democratic groups were more cohesive. They were described as being friendlier and more group-minded. Although they produced somewhat less work than the autocratic groups, both motivation and originality were found to be higher. Nineteen out of the total twenty boys expressed a preference for the leader who used the democratic style.

Authoritarian Leadership

The authoritarian leader maintains strong control over the people in the group. This control may be benevolent and considerate (often called paternalistic leadership) or it may be dictatorial and disregard the needs and feelings of group members.

Authoritarian leaders give orders far more often than the other types of leaders and they expect group members to obey their orders. Directions are given as commands rather than as suggestions. Criticism is more common from the authoritarian leader than from the others, though it is not necessarily frequent. Many authoritarian leaders are also quite punitive.

Decision making is done by the leader, not by the group. Some authoritarian leaders will try to make decisions that are congruent with the group's goals but the less benevolent ones often make decisions directly opposed to the group's needs or goals. Authoritarian leaders also decide how the group will move toward achieving these goals.

Authoritarian leadership emphasizes the differences in status between leader and group members. The authoritarian leader clearly dominates the group, making the status of the leader separate from and higher than the status of group members. This reduces the degree of trust and openness between leader and group members, particularly if the leader tends to be punitive as well.

Work usually proceeds smoothly under the guidance of a skilled authoritarian leader. Procedures and group actions are well defined and usually predictable, which reduces frustration and increases group members' feelings of security. Productivity is high in an authoritarian group. However, creativity, autonomy, and self-motivation are stifled. Dependency needs are usually met but growth needs often are not.

Authoritarian leadership is particularly suitable in an emergency situation when clear directions are the highest priority. It is also appropriate in situations in which the entire focus is on getting the job done or in large groups when it is difficult to share decision making for some reason. Authoritarian leadership is also referred to as a directive or controlling style of leadership.

Democratic Leadership

Democratic leadership is based on the following principles:

1. Participation in decision making by every group member.
2. Freedom of belief and action within reasonable bounds that are set by society and by the group.
3. Responsibility of each individual for oneself and for the group.
4. Concern for each group member as a unique individual.

You can see from these principles that democratic leadership is much more participative and far less controlling than authoritarian leadership. But this does not mean that democratic leadership is passive. On the contrary, the democratic leader actively stimulates and guides the group toward fulfillment of the principles listed above and toward achievement of the group's goals.

Democratic leaders rarely issue commands. Instead, they offer information, ask stimulating questions, and make suggestions to guide the work of the group, acting as catalysts rather than controllers. They are far more likely to say "we" rather than "I" when talking about the plans and goals of the group. They set limits, enforce rules, and encourage productivity. Criticism is meant to be constructive rather than punitive.

Control is shared with group members who are expected to participate to the best of their abilities. Use of the democratic style demands a strong faith in the ability of group members to solve problems and to ultimately make wise choices when setting group goals and deciding how to accomplish these goals. Not every leader can do this.

Democratic leadership is egalitarian. Equality and sharing of authority replaces the status and dominance of the authoritarian leader. Along with increasing participation in decision making, this tends to increase openness and trust within the group.

Because group members participate actively in decision making and have more responsibility for the outcomes of those decisions, dependence on the leader is minimized and independence and originality are encouraged. Participation in goal setting increases the group's commitment to those goals and motivation to get the work done comes from the entire group rather than through pressure from the leader. Group members are usually more satisfied with democratic leadership than with authoritarian or laissez-faire leadership.

Most studies indicate that democratic leadership is not as efficient as authoritarian leadership. While the work done by a democratic group is more creative and the group is more self-motivated, the democratic style is also more cumbersome than the authoritarian style. Democratic groups tend to be less quantitatively productive than the authoritarian group for several reasons. First, it takes more time to ensure that everyone in the group has participated in making a decision and this can be very frustrating to people who want to get a job done as fast as possible. Second, disagreements are more likely to arise and must be resolved, which can also require a great deal of effort.

Democratic leadership is particularly appropriate for groups of people who will work together for an extended period of time, in which case the interpersonal relationships that develop can substantially affect the work of the group. It is also appropriate when group members have to work closely together, when a great deal of cooperation and coordination between group members is needed, or when the nature of the work makes close and detailed supervision difficult or impossible, which is often true in health care.

Democratic leadership is often called supportive or participative leadership. The term *participative leadership* is used to describe democratic leadership or a style midway between the authoritarian and democratic styles in which the leader encourages input from group members and takes their views into consideration, but the leader makes the final decision.

Laissez-Faire Leadership

The laissez-faire leader is generally inactive, passive, and nondirective. The laissez-faire leader leaves all of the control and decision making to the group and provides little or no direction, guidance, or encouragement.

Laissez-faire leaders offer very little to the group: few commands, questions, suggestions, or criticism. They are very permissive, set almost no limits, and allow virtually any behavior. However, many are inconsistent in this regard and will occasionally become very directive and command group members to take a particular action. When this happens, group members often ignore the command or react negatively to the attempt to exert leadership.

Some laissez-faire leaders are quite supportive of individual group members and will provide information or suggestions when asked. The more extreme laissez-faire leader, however, will turn such a request back to the group. In fact, when the laissez-faire style of leadership becomes extreme, you could say that no leadership exists at all.

In a laissez-faire group, members act independently of each other and often at cross-purposes because there is little cooperation or coordination. In some groups, disinterest and apathy set in, in others the activity becomes chaotic and the frustration level rises considerably. In either case, the goals are unclear and procedures are confusing. Neither the task nor the relationship concerns of group members are dealt with satisfactorily. In the more fortunate groups, one or more members carry out some of the needed leader functions.

Since laissez-faire leadership is usually unproductive, inefficient, and unsatisfying, it is not generally an appropriate choice of leadership style. However, when all group members are highly self-directed, motivated, and able to coordinate their own activities with others, laissez-faire leadership may give them the freedom they need to be highly creative and productive. Laissez-faire leadership is often called permissive or nondirective leadership.

LEADER BEHAVIOR DESCRIPTIONS

When attention turned from the qualities of the person who was the leader to the kinds of behavior exhibited by leaders, it became apparent that leadership could be a shared function. In other words, there can be more than one person in the group who exerts some leadership and every member can have a leadership function in the group. For example, on a health care team each member of the team may be knowledgeable about some aspect of patient care and have some influence on patient care decisions made by the team. This does not mean that leadership is necessarily shared equally by team members but that each member can assume some leadership functions.

Beginning in the 1940s and 1950s, a large number of research studies were done to find out just what these leader functions were.[7] The purpose of these studies was to describe and categorize the behaviors of actual leaders. Unlike the subjects of the earlier trait theorists, however, these leaders were not important political or historical figures. Instead, they were supervisors or leaders of teams as diverse as Air Force crews, school personnel and, more recently, nurses.

Over 1800 different behaviors were identified. The behaviors were then sorted and put into nine categories. These categories were as follows:

1. Integration (increasing cooperation)
2. Communication
3. Production emphasis
4. Representation (speaking for the group)
5. Fraternization
6. Organization
7. Evaluation
8. Initiation
9. Domination.

These nine categories developed by Hemphill[7] were later modified and tested by Halpin and Winer[8] who finally reduced them to two major categories that are still widely used. The first of these categories is called *initiating structure* and includes task-related functions such as:

Assigns members to particular tasks.
Criticizes poor work.

Initiating structure also includes behaviors that clarify roles, organize work, define procedures, and move the group toward its goals.

The second category is *consideration* and includes relationship oriented functions such as the following:

Finds time to listen to team members.
Does personal favors for team members.[8]

Consideration also includes behaviors that build trust and show respect for the individual group members.

The initiating structure and consideration categories have been used in many research studies and in evaluations of leaders by both superiors and subordinates. Both of these categories of leader behavior seem to have a significant effect on group members and, therefore, on the leader's effectiveness. For example, when leaders are rated high on both initiating structure and consideration, their groups are more cohesive and harmonious. High consideration behavior results in increased satisfaction, lower absenteeism, fewer grievances, and lower employee turnover. High initiating structure seems to improve group productivity.

Leaders who are low in both initiating structure and consideration are usually rated ineffective by both their supervisors and the members of the group. The most effective leader is high on both initiating structure and consideration.

TASK VERSUS RELATIONSHIP ORIENTATIONS

Closely related to the initiating structure and consideration categories are the task and relationship orientations used by many leadership theorists and researchers The task-oriented leader is concerned with getting the work done and focuses on activities that encourage group productivity. The relationship-oriented leader, on the other hand, is especially concerned with interpersonal relationships and focuses on activities that meet group members' needs.

Unlike the authoritarian, democratic, and laissez-faire leadership styles, which were a continuum from highly controlling to very permissive, the task and relationship orientations are bipolar (Fig. 2-3). This means that a leader can be high or low on one or both of the scales. Blake and Mouton [9-10] have devleoped what they call a Managerial Grid to show the various combinations of high and low concern for production (task orientation) and high and low concern for people (relationship orientation). On their grid, 1 is a low score and 9 is the highest score. The leader with a 1,1 score is low on both task and relationship concerns, while a leader with a 9,9 score is high on both and considered to have the most effective style of leadership.

The 1,1 leader who is low on both task and relationship can be described as an inactive and uninvolved leader who does little planning, shows little concern for team members, and rarely takes the initiative to make changes. The high-task, low-relationship (9,1) leader can be described as a controlling, directive leader who closely supervises team members and does most of the planning. Team members

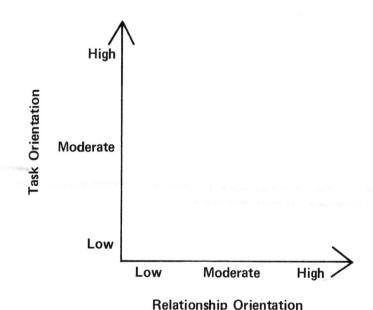

FIGURE 2-3. Bipolar task and relationship leader orientations.

are expected to do what they are told and those who do not may be punished. On the other hand, the low-task, high-relationship leader (1,9) can be described as an accepting, considerate leader who supports and encourages team members, emphasizes good feelings between people but does little planning or controlling and allows team members to make many of their own decisions.

The high-task, high-relationship (9,9) leader can be described as an active and involved leader who promotes open communication and team members' participation in setting goals. Leaders using this style also provide constructive (not punitive) criticism, intervene when a conflict arises, and introduce changes after discussing them with team members. The leader who is concerned with both tasks and relationships has been found to be the most effective leader as was the case with leaders who were high in initiating structure and consideration.

SUMMARY

Behavioral theories focus on the behavior or functions of the leader. The authoritarian leader is highly controlling and directive in comparison with the democratic leader who encourages participation in goal setting and planning. The laissez-faire leader is passive and nondirective.

Leader behaviors can also be categorized either by the initiating structure and consideration categories or as task- and relationship-oriented. The leader whose behaviors are high in both task- and relationship-oriented actions has been found to be the most effective.

Motivational Theories

The motivational theories continue and expand upon the attention given to the co-actor (team member or follower) which began with the development of the behavioral theories. In the motivational theories, the needs and motivations of the people in the group become the central focus of the theory.

Motivational theorists and researchers have concentrated on identifying the factors that stimulate or encourage people to be satisfied and productive and on eliminating those factors that inhibit satisfaction and productivity. The most effective leader is the one who can create an environment in which people are highly motivated and therefore highly productive.

Many of the motivational theories are based on a humanistic approach and you will see the influence of Maslow's theory of motivation, especially the drive toward self-actualization, in these theories. You may also notice that the emphasis on leadership of small groups and teams changes to an emphasis on leadership and management of entire organizations in which people work. McGregor's[11-12] Theory X and Theory Y will be discussed here along with two approaches that developed from Theories X and Y and one other that uses a stimulus-response approach and opposes the humanistic theories.

THEORIES X AND Y

In his 1960 book entitled *The Human Side of Enterprise*, McGregor[11] compared two different sets of beliefs about human nature and described how these contrasting beliefs led to two very different approaches to leadership and management. The first and more conventional approach he called Theory X. The second, more humanistic, approach proposed by McGregor he called Theory Y.

Theory X

Theory X is based on a common view of human nature: that the ordinary person is generally lazy, unmotivated, unresponsible, and not too intelligent. According to Theory X, most people do not really like to work so they do not care about such things as meeting the team's or organization's goals and will work only as hard as they have to in order to keep their jobs. Most avoid taking on any additional responsibility and prefer to be directed rather than to act independently. Without specific rules and the threat of punishment, most workers would come in late, goof off most of the day, and produce sloppy, careless work. Although some are intelligent, ambitious, and self-directed, the majority need a great deal of supervision in order to be productive.

Based on this view of human nature, leaders must direct and control people in order to ensure that the work is done properly. Much specific direction is needed and detailed rules and regulations need to be set and strictly enforced. People need to be told exactly what to do, and how to do it. It is also necessary to closely supervise them in order to catch mistakes, to make sure they keep working, and to be sure that rules (such as taking only 30 minutes for lunch) are obeyed.

Motivation is supplied by a system of rewards and punishments. Those who do not obey the rules are reprimanded, fined, or fired. Those who do obey the rules are rewarded with time off, pay raises, and continued employment. In many ways, emloyees are treated like children rather than adults and like creatures who have to be prodded in order to get them to work under Theory X leadership.

Theory Y

According to Theory Y, the behavior described in Theory X is not inherent in human nature but a result of the kind of leadership that emphasizes control, direction, reward, and punishment. The passivity, lack of motivation, and avoidance of responsibility are symptoms of poor leadership and indicate that people's needs for belonging, recognition, and self-actualization have not been met.

Drawing on Maslow's theory of motivation, Theory Y proposes that the work itself can be motivating and rewarding. People can become enthusiastic about their work and they will support the team's and organization's goals when these goals also meet their needs. People can also be trusted to put forth adequate effort and to complete their work without constant supervision if they are committed to these goals. Given the right conditions, the ordinary person can be imaginative, creative, and productive.

Given the Theory Y beliefs about human nature and motivation, the major function of the leader would be to provide opportunities for people to meet their needs at work. The leader cannot directly meet all of a person's needs but can provide an environment in which these needs can be met. Instead of controlling, directing, rewarding, and punishing people, Theory Y leaders are involved in removing obstacles, providing guidance, and encouraging growth. The extensive external controls of Theory X are not necessary because people can exert self-control and self-direction under Theory Y leadership.

HYGIENE AND MOTIVATION FACTORS

Herzberg[13-16] enlarged on the Theory Y approach by dividing the needs that affect a person's motivation to work into two sets of factors, one set that affects dissatisfaction and one that affects satisfaction. The first set, called *hygiene factors,* are those factors that meet a person's need to avoid pain, insecurity, and discomfort. If these needs are not met, the employee is dissatisfied. The second set, called *motivation factors,* are those that meet needs to grow psychologically. When these needs are met, the employee feels satisfied. These are two distinct and independent sets of factors according to Herzberg. Meeting hygiene needs will not increase satisfaction and meeting motivation needs will not reduce dissatisfaction.

These two sets of factors were derived from yet another set of research studies. Different types of employees, such as engineers and accountants, were asked to describe incidents at work that made them feel especially good and also incidents that were especially negative. The lists of influential hygiene and motivation factors were derived from the descriptions of these critical incidents.

The hygiene factors that meet people's needs for comfort, security, and avoidance of pain include:

1. Adequate salary
2. Appropriate supervision
3. Good interpersonal relationships
4. Safe and tolerable working conditions (including reasonable policies and procedures).

The motivation factors that meet people's needs for growth and stimulation include:

1. Satisfying, meaningful work
2. Opportunities for advancement and achievement
3. Appropriate responsibility
4. Adequate recognition.

The leader or manager's function is to ensure that both sets of needs are met, some directly and others by providing opportunities to meet them in a conducive work environment. If the hygiene factors are provided, employees will not be dissatisfied with their jobs. However, the motivation factors must also be provided in order to have highly motivated, satisfied employees.

THEORY Z

Ouchi[17] has recently expanded and enlarged upon Theory Y and the democratic approach to leadership to create what he calls Theory Z. Like Theory Y, Theory Z has a humanistic viewpoint and focuses on developing better ways to motivate people, assuming that this will lead to increased satisfaction and productivity.

Theory Z was developed in part from a study of the most successful and best managed Japanese organizations and adapted to the American culture, which is different in some ways but similar in its productivity goals and advanced technology. A number of United States organizations that are known for being well-managed, good places to work use elements of Theory Z. Many of these elements have already been mentioned but they are combined and extended in Theory Z. These elements are collective decision making, long-term employment, slower promotions, indirect supervision, and a holistic concern for employees. Each element is explained below.

Collective Decision Making

A democratic, participative mode of decision making is an essential element of Theory Z. This participation is not simply the use of a small group to make decisions but the involvement of everyone who is affected by the decision. For example, if a decision to provide a new service would affect 70 people in an agency, a small team would be assigned to talk with each one of these 70 people to reach a true consensus about offering a new service. If a major change in the decision is made at some point in this process, the team would go back and speak with everyone again. As you can see, the emphasis is on keeping everyone fully informed and gaining their commitment to the final decision rather than on the speed or efficiency with which a decision can be made.

Long-Term Employment

Movement within the organization rather than between organizations is encouraged. A substantial proportion of Japanese workers are employed by only one organization for their entire career. This is quite different from the job hopping done by many Americans, including nurses.

Despite this American tendency to change jobs rapidly, there are some Theory Z organizations in the United States in which long-term employment is the norm. Instead of moving from one organization to another, employees move around within the organization, taking on different functions and working in different departments. People who do this become less specialized but more valuable to the Z organization, which is consequently more willing to invest in training its employees and encouraging their growth. Fair treatment also becomes more important when the organization needs to cultivate the commitment and loyalty of this long-term employee.

Another advantage is that people who have worked in a particular department at some time are better able to understand how that department works and what its problems and capabilities are. This understanding results in better communications and more coordination between departments, an integration of separate units that is almost impossible to achieve when each unit's peculiarities are not understood by people in other groups.

Slower Promotions

Slower promotions may seem to be a disadvantage but there are some long-term benefits. Rapid promotions can be illusory; if everyone is promoted rapidly, your relative position in the organization does not really change. Also, rapid movement within the organization means that close working relationships within groups do not have time to develop, nor is there any incentive to develop them. Slower promotions allow sufficient time to make a thorough evaluation of the individual's long-term contribution to the organization, encourage cooperation, and discourage the kind of game playing that occurs when people try to make themselves look good by undermining others.

Indirect Supervision

Supervision of employees is subtle and indirect rather than direct. Because they are long-term employees, workers become a part of the culture of the organization and intimately familiar with its working philosophy, values, and goals. In fact, the goals belong to the workers because they are involved in setting them and decisions are made not only on the basis of what will work but also on the basis of what fits the culture of the organization. For example, employees of an agency whose primary mission is health promotion would probably decide that an anti-smoking campaign was a suitable addition to their services but that a dialysis unit would not be suitable. A person who is well acquainted with these characteristics of the organization does not need to be told what to do or what decision to make as often as a new, unassimilated employee would.

A similar source of indirect supervision is the influence of the groups in which the employee works. Employees' desire for peer approval motivates group members and supports productive behavior in a Theory Z organization.

Holistic Concern

Trust, fair treatment, commitment, and loyalty are all characteristics of the Theory Z organization. These characteristics are part of the overall consideration for each employee as a whole, including concern for the employee's health and well-being as well as performance as a worker.

BEHAVIORAL MANAGEMENT

Although a number of organizations have successfully adapted the humanistic Theories Y and Z, there are many people who believe that they are soft-hearted, unproven approaches to effective leadership. Miller's behavioral management approach is an example of this opposing viewpoint.[18]

Behavioral management is based upon the stimulus-response explanation of human behavior and uses rewards to influence and control employee behavior. For example, if an employee took too long to complete a daily report, the behavioral management approach to this problem would be to remove the distracting conditions under which the report was written, set reasonable goals for gradual reduction of time taken to write one report, and reinforce improvement by giving rewards such as intermittent praise, salary increases, free lunches, and gift items.

Proponents of this approach believe it is more suitable in a work setting than are the humanistic approaches. The following are some of Miller's criticisms of the humanistic motivational theories:

1. Maslow's hierarchy of needs simply means that people are motivated to get what they do not have.
2. Theory Y approaches demand too much of the leader or manager whose main function is to meet production goals, not to satisfy human needs.
3. An employer should be interested only in the employee's work performance. Interest in any other aspect of the employee's life is an invasion of privacy and abuse of power.[19]
4. There is little evidence that training to improve self-awareness or sensitivity to others actually improves leader effectiveness.
5. Many organizations using Theory X have prospered so McGregor's analysis of its deficiencies was wrong.

It may be that both approaches to motivation are significant and that their effects are additional rather than opposite[20] or that one approach will work better in some situations—a concept that is the essence of the situational theories (discussed below).

The reader who is interested in this conflict between the stimulus-response and the humanistic approaches may want to read about the studies done by Hall and Donnell[21] in Research Example 2-2.

Research Example 2-2. Manager Achievement: Support for Use of Behavioral and Motivational Theories

Do successful managers actually use the humanistic theories in their work? A series of five studies called the Achieving Manager Research Project was done by Hall and Donnell[21] to compare a manager's personal success and use of the humanistic behavioral and motivational theories of leadership. Altogether, 12,000 male managers in more than 50 organizations ranging from drug companies to government and nonprofit agencies were studied. Managers were divided into low, average, and high achieving groups on the basis of their rate of progress toward the top ranks of the organization.

Study I compared the managers' success with their belief in McGregor's Theory X or Theory Y. Hall and Donnell found a significant ($p < 0.03$) negative relationship between belief in Theory X and managerial achievement: low and average achievers had a much stronger belief in Theory X than did the high achievers.

Study II compared the managers' work incentives, that is, primary motivating factors derived from Maslow, Herzberg, and others, with their success. Low achievers were found to stress the hygiene and maintenance factors, especially safety and security, and virtually ignored the motivation factors of actualization, belonging, or ego status, which were emphasized by the high achievers. This emphasis on hygiene factors accounted for 77 percent of the variance between the low achievers and the others. Low achievers were also found to be more self-centered while high achievers were more other-centered.

Study III focused on the use of the participative management approach. The degree to which managers used the participative style was measured by administering a questionnaire to people who worked for them (not by asking the managers themselves). The difference in use of participative management was dramatic: as a group, the high achievers scored five times higher in participative management than did the low achievers. The average achieving group was not much higher than the low group. Managers with low and average successes offered their workers few opportunities to participate and used practices that repressed and frustrated the people in their groups. High achievers used the participative style to a much greater extent with accompanying higher levels of satisfactions in their groups.

Study IV measured the extent to which the managers disclosed or shared personal, intellectual, and emotional data about themselves and encouraged others to do the same—called interpersonal competence by the researchers. Subordinates, peers, supervisors, and the managers themselves were asked to rate these behaviors. Both self-rating and subordinates' ratings indicated that the high achieving managers were significantly ($p < 0.001$) higher in interpersonal competence measured as disclosure.

Study V measured the task and relationship orientations of the managers. Eighteen hundred seventy-eight managers and their subordinates were given a management style inventory to determine the manager's position on the Blake and Mouton managerial grid. High achievers were found to be using a collaborative, participative, high-task, high-relationship style. Average achievers tended to emphasize task over relationship and low achievers showed a preference for a low-risk, defensive style. The managers' styles seemed to be an overall summary of the individual leader's beliefs, attitudes, and practices.

The studies indicate that the successful managers apply these humanistic theories to their practices. The researchers conclude that, when taken together, the results of the five studies suggest that the use of the humanistic behavioral and motivational approaches to leadership has implications for career growth. They also hypothesize that, although the data cannot be generalized to women, the same leadership practices would distinguish female high and low achievers.

SUMMARY

There are two kinds of motivational theories: those that take a humanistic view of human nature and those that oppose it preferring the view that people are motivated to seek rewards and will avoid additional work or responsibility if possible and therefore need close supervision and control. McGregor called this opposing view Theory X and proposed a more humanistic Theory Y based on the implementation of Maslow's hierarchy of needs. Herzberg expanded this concept into two independent sets of influential factors, the hygiene and motivational factors. Theory Z extended this further, calling for collective-decision making, long-term employment, slower promotions, indirect supervision, and holistic concern for people in well-managed organizations.

Situational Theories

The behavioral and motivational theories are a significant advance over the trait theories in two ways: (1) they focus on the more measurable and observable behavior of the leader rather than on innate characteristics and (2) they include consideration of group members (co-actors) as well, especially the motivational theories. However, the third element of a leadership situation, the environment, is almost entirely missing from most of these theories, although many of the theorists have acknowledged that the environment could be an additional factor.

Recognition of this missing element has led to several more leadership theories. Of these situational theories, the contingency and path-goal theories are discussed and then some other aspects of the environment that have been found to influence leadership effectiveness.

CONTINGENCY THEORY

Participative, democratic leadership is not necessarily effective in every situation, according to situational theorists. For example, Fiedler[22] found that factors such as the nature of the task to be done, the power of the leader, and the favorableness of the situation affect the type of leadership that works best in a situation. In other words, the effectiveness of a certain style of leadership is contingent on these other factors.

Fiedler's contingency theory is less straightforward than the theories that have been discussed so far because in this approach the leader's style is determined by the rating the leader gives to the least preferred coworker (LPC). On the basis of this rating, leaders are categorized as either high or low LPC. It is not clear exactly what this LPC rating measures. It may be measuring the leader's tolerance for incompetent workers or the fact that different leaders have different types of least preferred coworkers. Most often, though, the high-LPC leader is thought of as being predominantly relationship-oriented and the low-LPC leader is thought of as being primarily task-oriented.

On the basis of extensive research over 30 years (from 1952 to the present), the low-LPC or task-oriented leader has been found to be most effective in both very favorable situations in which the leader has a great deal of power and an excellent relationship with group members and in very unfavorable situations in which the leader has very little power and poor relationships. The low-LPC leader is also more effective when the tasks done by the group are clear and structured.

On the other hand, the high-LPC, relationship-oriented leader is found to be most effective in moderately favorable situations in which the leader's power and authority are weak, the task is not clearly defined and requires creative problem solving, and relationships are good. Generally speaking, Fiedler's research seems to indicate that the most effective leaders are those who can adapt their styles to the needs of a particular situation.

PATH-GOAL THEORY

A different set of situational factors is considered in the path-goal theory developed in the 1970s by House,[23] from earlier work done by Georgopoulås and Vroom. These factors include the scope of the task to be done, role ambiguity, the employee's expectations and perceptions of the task, and ways in which the leader can influence these expectations.

The motivation to perform a certain task is based on a person's expectation that doing this work will result in a desired outcome and that personal satisfaction or reward will be achieved as a result of this outcome. In other words, people estimate their abilities to carry out the task, any obstacles to doing the job, and the amount of support they can expect. They also estimate what kind of reward (such as recognition from the group or leader or a sense of satisfaction) they can get from completing the task.

The leader who can recognize and anticipate these expectations can take such actions as providing support, removing obstacles in the way of completing the task, and pointing out the connection between doing the work and receiving the rewards. The name of this theory comes from this last leader action; the leader clarifies the relationship between the path the employees take and the goal they want to reach.

House found that when a person has a wide variety of tasks to perform, leader consideration is not as great an influence on satisfaction because the work itself is satisfying. However, he also found that all employees need recognition and other forms of consideration from the leaders. The characteristics of the employees and the number of environmental demands they have to deal with to complete their work also affect the kind of leadership needed to increase motivation.

SITUATIONAL DETERMINANTS

You may have noted that both the contingency and path-goal theories indicated that the characteristics of the tasks to be done are an important situational determinant of leadership effectiveness but that they did not agree on what the other situational determinants might be. In addition to those mentioned, there are many other determinants that have been identified in leadership research.[3,24-26] The following are samplings of these other determinants.

Group Size

Large groups need more coordination than small groups. Some research also indicates that large groups need leaders who are more task-oriented than do small groups.

Position in Group

Studies of space and territoriality indicate that the leader tends to occupy the head position at a table and that this position reinforces the leader's status. Group members tend to sit opposite the leader rather than next to the leader.

Communication Networks

Being in a central position for controlling the sending and receiving of information increases the probability of that person emerging as the leader of the group.

Social Status

People with higher social status usually have more influence on group decisions. (The effect of status may be related to ability and experiences.)

Interpersonal Stress

The existence of stress and tension between an employee and supervisor reduces the employee's ability to think and problem solve creatively. The stress of having a difficult job to do does not seem to affect thinking in the same way.

Designation of Leadership

Formal designation of a person as a leader by someone in authority outside the group reinforces that person's position as leader of the group.

Organizational Structure

Organizational structure can affect employees' satisfaction by affecting the characteristics of their jobs. The more formal, hierarchical organization tends to allow less autonomy, identity, feedback, and variety in jobs, so that jobs become routinized. In organizations with less emphasis on hierarchy, employees tend to feel more self-confident, more receptive to change, more committed to their work and less powerless.

Organizational structure also affects leader behavior. For example, leader consideration is negatively related to the size of the organization.

SUMMARY

The third element of a leadership situation, the environment, was missing from the preceding theories. A large number of situational determinants have been identified. The contingency theory identified the leader's power, relationship with the group, and clarity of the task as determinants of the most effective leadership style. The path-goal theory also identified the scope of the task as well as the individual's expectations about the difficulties of completing the task and resulting rewards as determinants of motivation. Other factors affecting leader effectiveness directly or indirectly include group size, leader status and position in the group, position in the communication network, social status, interpersonal stress, formal designation as leader, and organizational structure.

Interactional Theories

Although the situational theories contributed some needed complexity to the simpler trait, behavioral and even motivational theories, they have a tendency to treat the situation as if it were separate from the leader and each one identifies different situational determinants. You can see that no theory has yet managed to pull together all the influential factors from each of the three elements of the leadership situation (leader, co-actor, environment) into one coherent, integrated theory of leadership.

Many of the earlier theorists were aware of the need to consider other variables but ignored them when proposing effective leadership approaches. Theory Z is more comprehensive than some of the earlier theories and yet it neglects some apparently influential situational factors, such as the nature of the work to be done, and it also assumes that all group members will respond positively to the same approach. It also is not specific in distinguishing between effective and ineffective leader actions. As was mentioned above, the situational theories have similar shortcomings.

Although there is no single, fully developed theory that meets the criteria stated above, some progress has been made in the direction of clarifying and predicting the interaction between the three elements of a leadership situation. Three examples of this progress are (1) complex man and open systems, (2) elements of a leader situation, and (3) leader-group interaction.

COMPLEX MAN AND OPEN SYSTEMS

After reviewing other viewpoints on human nature, including the motivational theories, Schein concluded that they were all overgeneralized and oversimplified.[4, 27]

In their place, he proposed a model of complex man based on the following assumptions:

1. People are complex and highly variable. They have multiple motives for doing things, which vary from one person to another. For example, a pay raise can mean security to one person, recognition to another, and both to a third person.
2. People can develop new motives and their motives can change over time.
3. Goals can differ in different situations. For example, in a formal group the goal may be to get the work done, while in an informal group the goal may be to socialize and whether the work gets done or not is not important to members of the informal group.
4. The nature of the task affects people's performance and productivity. Their ability, experience, and motivation also affects productivity.
5. Different leadership actions are needed in different situations. There is no single strategy that will be effective in every situation.

Schein's assumptions synthesize trait, behavioral, motivational, and situational theories. He has also used an open-systems framework and implies its use in these assumptions. Needs, motives, abilities, the nature of the task, the work setting, the type of group and organization, and the person's past experience and patterns of relating to others all affect the leadership situation. The leader must be able to diagnose the situation and select the appropriate strategy from a large repertoire of skills in order to be effective.

ELEMENTS OF A LEADER SITUATION

Hollander[28] identified three basic elements in a leadership exchange as:

1. The leader, including the leader's personality, perceptions, and abilities.
2. The followers, with their personalities, perceptions, and abilities.
3. The situation, within which the leader and followers function, including its norms, size, density, and other characteristics.

Leadership is a dynamic, two-way process of influence. Leader and follower are interdependent; both contribute to the relationship and both receive something from the relationship (somewhat like the mutual and simultaneous interaction of the feedback loop). This model also recognizes that both the leader and followers have other roles outside the leadership situation and that they may both be influenced by environmental factors such as a hostile threat from someone in authority outside the leader-follower exchange.

According to Hollander, leadership effectiveness requires the use of the problem-solving process, maintenance of group cohesiveness, communication skills, leader fairness, competence, dependability, creativity, and identification within the group.

LEADER-GROUP INTERACTION

More attention should be paid to the interdependence between the leader and the group according to Schreisheim, Mowday, and Stogdill.[29] Many interrelated factors influence this relationship. Group cohesiveness, for example, is affected by leader behavior but it is also affected by group size, stress, relationships between group members, the nature of the task, and external pressures. Also, instrumental (task-oriented) and supportive (relationship-oriented) leader behaviors are dynamically interrelated with the group characteristics of cohesiveness and group motivation, both of which affect group productivity.

In this model of leader and group interaction, both task- and relationship-oriented leader behaviors are positively related to group motivation and cohesiveness, although the effect changes with the stage of group development (group development stages range from immature to mature). Group motivation and cohesiveness as well as the nature of the task and the group's goal in turn affect group productivity and satisfaction and also tend to reduce turnover and absenteeism. Although the relationships mentioned in this model are already complex, other factors can be identified that affect these relationships within a leader-group interaction.

DISCUSSION

These approaches have some common themes. They all recognize the multiplicity of factors affecting a leadership situation and attempt to synthesize the findings of the preceding trait, behavioral, motivational, and situational theories. Either implicitly or explicitly, they point to the need to consider the leader, the co-actor, the environment, and the reciprocal interactions among them when analyzing a leadership situation. Indirectly, they all indicate the usefulness of an open-systems framework in order to account for all of the factors that influence a leadership situation.

However, a common set of assumptions about human nature or a complete model that can explain and predict what happens in a leadership situation has not yet been developed.

SUMMARY

None of the preceding trait, behavioral, motivational, or situational theories can account for all the factors involved in complex and dynamic interactions of a leadership situation. The complexity and variability of people, use of an open-systems framework, inclusion of all three elements of a leader situation, and the interrelationships between these elements were all suggested as the basis for a more complete and integrated theory of leadership.

References

1. Heimann, CG: *Four theories of leadership.* Journal of Nursing Administration 6:18, June, 1976.

2. Maloney, MM: *Leadership In Nursing: Theory, Strategies, Action.* CV Mosby, St Louis, 1979.

3. Stogdill, RM: *Handbook of Leadership: A Survey of Theory and Research.* The Free Press, New York, 1974.

4. Wrightsman, LS: *Social Psychology,* ed 2. Brooks/Cole, Monterey, California, 1977.

5. Woods, FA: *The Influence of Monarchs.* Macmillan, New York, 1913.

6. White, RK and Lippitt, R: *Autocracy and Democracy: An Experimental Inquiry.* Harper & Row, New York, 1960. (Published after Lewin's death.)

7. Stogdill, RM and Coons, AE (eds): *Leader behavior: Its description and measurement.* Research monograph 88. The Ohio State University, College of Administrative Science, Columbus, Ohio, 1957.

8. Ibid, p 47.

9. Blake, RR and Mouton, JS: *The Managerial Grid.* Gulf Publishing, Houston, 1964.

10. Blake, RR, Mouton, JS, and Tapper, M: *Grid Approaches for Managerial Leadership In Nursing.* CV Mosby, St Louis, 1981.

11. McGregor, D: *The Human Side of Enterprise.* McGraw-Hill, New York, 1960.

12. Bennis, WG and Schein, EH (with the collaboration of C McGregor): *Leadership and Motivation: Essays of Douglas McGregor.* MIT Press, Cambridge, Mass, 1966.

13. Herzberg, F, Mausner, B, and Snyderman, B: *The Motivation to Work,* ed 2. John Wiley & Sons, New York, 1959.

14. Herzberg, F: *Work and the Nature of Man.* World Publishing, Cleveland, 1966.

15. House, RJ and Wigdor, LA: *Herzberg's dual-factor theory of job satisfaction and motivation: A review of the evidence and a criticism.* Personnel Psychology 20(4):369, 1967.

16. Locke, EA: *The ideas of Frederick W. Taylor: An evaluation.* Academy of Management Review 7(1):14, 1982.

17. Ouchi, WG: *Theory Z: How American Business Can Meet The Japanese Challenge.* Addison-Wesley, Reading, Mass, 1981.

18. Miller, LM: *Behavior Management: The New Science of Managing People At Work.* John Wiley & Sons, New York, 1978.

19. Drucker, P: *Management: Tasks, responsibilities and practices.* In Miller, LM: *Behavior Management: The New Science of Managing People at Work.* Harper & Row, New York, 1973, p 424.

20. Mitchell, TR: *Motivation: New directions for theory, research and practice.* Academy of Management Review 7(1):80, 1982.

21. HALL, J AND DONNELL, SM: *Managerial achievement: The personal side of behavior theory*. In KATZ, D, KAHN, RL, AND ADAMS, JS (EDS): *The Study of Organizations*. Jossey-Bass, San Francisco, 1980.

22. FIEDLER, FE AND CHEMERS, MM: *Leadership and Effective Management*. Scott, Foresman, Glenview, Ill, 1974.

23. HOUSE, RJ: *A path goal theory of leader effectiveness*. Administrative Science Quarterly 16(3):321, 1971.

24. FIEDLER, FE: *Organizational determinants of managerial incompetence*. In HUNT, JG AND LARSON, LL (EDS): *Crosscurrents in Leadership*. Southern Illinois University Press, Carbondale, Ill, 1979.

25. FORD, J: *Departmental context and formal structure as constraints on leader behavior*. Academy of Management Journal 24(4):274 (June), 1981.

26. OLDHAM, GR AND HACKMAN, JR: *Relationships between organizational structure and employee reactions: Comparing alternative frameworks*. Administrative Science Quarterly 26(1):66 (March), 1981.

27. SCHEIN, EH: *Organizational Psychology,* ed 2. Prentice-Hall, Englewood Cliffs, NJ, 1970.

28. HOLLANDER, EP: *Leadership Dynamics: A Practical Guide to Effective Relationships*. The Free Press, New York, 1978.

29. SCHREISHEIM, CA, MOWDAY, RT, AND STOGDILL, RM: *Crucial dimensions of leader-group interaction*. In HUNT, JG AND LARSON, LL (EDS): *Crosscurrents in Leadership*. Southern Illinois University Press, Carbondale, Ill, 1977.

Chapter *3*

Components of Effective Leadership

Many different but related concepts of leadership have been pulled together here into a simple conceptual framework for leadership that includes the most essential elements of leadership in professional practice. These essential elements, called the components of effective leadership (Fig. 3-1), are a synthesis of philosophy, theory, research, and experience in leadership.

Perhaps logically speaking, this chapter belongs at the end of the book because it summarizes the most basic principles of leadership that you need to apply to virtually any situation in order to be an effective leader. But then you, the reader, might be uncertain about what leadership is and how it can be of use to you in your professional practice. So the components are placed here, near the beginning, in order to explain and expand on the purposes mentioned in the introduction and to inform you in regard to the approach to leadership that will be taken in this book.

The components described in this chapter summarize the most fundamental concepts of leadership. Leadership in general rather than in any specific situation or with any particular person or group is discussed here. The specifics of leadership will be presented in later chapters.

Effective Leadership

An effective leader is one who is successful in attempts to influence others to work together in a productive and satisfying manner. Occasional failures are inevitable but an effective leader selects the best possible means for influencing others in

FIGURE 3-1. Components of effective leadership.

order to improve the likelihood of success well beyond what would happen by chance.

Before discussing the components in detail, an outline of the components of effective leadership is provided. An effective leader:

1. Sets *goals* that are clear, congruent, and meaningful to the group.
2. Has adequate *knowledge and skills* in leadership and in professional fields of endeavor.
3. Possesses *self-awareness* and uses this understanding to recognize personal needs and those of other human beings.
4. *Communicates* clearly and effectively.
5. Mobilizes adequate *energy* for leadership functions.
6. Takes *action*.

Each of the six components of the framework—goals, knowledge and skills, self-awareness, communication, energy, and action—contributes to your overall effectiveness as a leader.

The components can also be used to test yourself against the ideal of an effective leader. You can ask yourself to what extent you have developed your leadership potential so far within each of these components. How effective are you right now? Can you identify areas in which you can improve your leadership ability?

GOAL LEVELS	EXAMPLES
Environmental Goals	Organization Wants to Please Accrediting Agency
Group Goals	Have A Coffee Break
Individual Goals	
Personal Goals of Members	Contribute Show Conferences Are a Waste of Time
Personal Goals of Leader	Help Patient Demonstrate Leadership Ability

FIGURE 3-2. Levels of goals within a group.

Goals

All leadership acts have some kind of goal or objective. The goal is the end result desired, the reason for a particular behavior. Just as all human behavior is believed to have meaning, it is also assumed that every attempt to influence others has some kind of purpose, it is good or bad, conscious or unconscious.

GOAL LEVELS

It is unusual to find an individual who has only a single goal in mind and it is even rarer to find a group with a single clearly stated goal with which everyone truly agrees. There are three levels of goals that a leader needs to be aware of: the individual level, group level, and environmental level (which includes organizational goals).[1] These levels are shown in Fig. 3-2.

Individual Goals

These are the goals of a particular individual also called personal goals. Most of the time, there are several reasons why a person does or does not want something done. The following is an example of some individual goals that may be operating when a conference is planned.

> Let's say that you have invited several other nurses to a conference about a patient whose depression seems to be increasing. Your primary goal is to come up with new ways to intervene with this patient. There are probably some other reasons why you are organizing this conference. You may also be hoping to get the other nurses interested in holding regular conferences about patients and to show them how well you can lead one of these conferences.

There are many other possible goals, but all the goals described in the example would be your individual goals as a leader of the group.

Every person in a group will also have their individual goals and some may be quite different from the leader's as in the following example.

> Some nurses may want to contribute to the conference but others may believe that they have more important work to do and want to hurry through the conference. Some may not want to come at all. Another group member may believe that conferences are a waste of time and have the goal of seeing to it that your conference turns out the way that member predicted—a complete waste of time.

The goals mentioned in this example are only some of the possible group members' personal goals.

Group Goals

The next level of goals comes from the group as a whole. As you may recall from the discussion of open systems, the characteristics of the group as a whole, including its goals, are different from those of its individual members (who can be thought of as subsystems of the system known as the group). For example:

> When you get the group together for the conference at 10 AM, it's time for a coffee break and the group as a whole could be more interested in relaxing and idle conversation than in discussing the depressed patient.

If this is true, then the goal of the group as a whole conflicts with yours as the leader.

Environmental Goals

There is one more level of goals that needs to be considered because it will affect the outcome of your leadership actions. This is the environmental level and needs to be defined in terms of your particular situation. For instance, the most influential environment may be the climate of a particular department or team; other times it is the attitudes and goals of an entire community that will affect your activities. Referring to the conference example:

> In this particular case, the environmental setting of concern to you is the organization within which you and the rest of the group are employed. The organization for which you all work may be anticipating the visit of a national accreditation agency and so be very interested in demonstrating that patient conferences are encouraged.

This particular example shows that the environmental level may reach as far as the national or even international level. As you can see from this discussion so far, goals can be numerous, different, and conflicting within and between the different levels involved.

CONGRUENT, MEANINGFUL GOALS

In order for your leadership actions to be most effective, all goals at the different levels need to be congruent and meaningful to the group. This means that there needs to be at least enough agreement about goals so that the entire group, including the leader, can move in the same direction.

Looking back at Figure 3-2, you can see that the personal goals of the leader and the organizational goals both favor the idea of a conference although the goals themselves are not identical. The group goal and especially the goals of some individual members, however, are in serious conflict with the leader's goal. If the leader cannot change this situation, the conference will not succeed.

You will be a more effective leader if the group sees you as someone who identifies with them and has their best interests in mind.[2] For example, if the group senses that your main interest in holding a conference is your own personal goal of demonstrating your leadership ability rather than the group goal of helping the patient, their response to the conference is likely to be resistant and resentful. A leader who can identify with the group will be a more effective leader of that group. Another way of saying this is that the leader must "begin where the group is," just as in the helping relationship you begin where your client is and work from there.

Achieving Congruence

This need for agreement on goals raises some important questions. How do you increase goal congruence? Suppose you do not agree with the group's goals? Suppose their goal is unrealistic or based on mistaken ideas you could not support?

When the problem is a lack of information or understanding, simply supplying the correct information may be sufficient to change the group's goals. When there is a difference of opinion, remember that you can be accepting of the people in the group as people without accepting their beliefs. You can also show an interest in the person's or group's point of view without necessarily agreeing with it. Your interest and acceptance will encourage open discussion of goals that can lead to finding some areas of agreement that the group may be willing to begin with.

If you cannot find a common ground among the diverse goals, you may want to consider some compromise. How willing you are to compromise your goals is going to depend on you, the gravity of the situation, and the kind of compromise you would need to make. If compromising your goals is going to mean violating your own personal set of values, then you must ask yourself what you will gain by doing it. While showing some flexibility is usually productive, yielding too much is ineffective.

When the actions mentioned (supplying information, expressing an interest in the other point of view, seeking a common ground among diverse goals, and occasionally making some compromises in regard to your own goals) do not reduce the differences enough to make the goals congruent, you will need to apply change strategies (Chapter 9) to bring them into congruence. Without congruent goals, individuals or members of a group will be working at cross-purposes and are not likely to accomplish anything. But when the goals are congruent, you and your group have a starting point from which you can proceed to work together.

CLEAR GOALS

Goals need to be clear as well as congruent. In fact, you cannot be sure that the goals are actually congruent until they have been clearly stated. People often assume that everyone is on the same wave length without really checking out the validity of their assumption. For example, you often hear a comment such as "Everyone knows why we're here, let's get on with the job," at the beginning of a meeting.[3] Talking about a group's goals seems like a waste of time to many people because they assume that everyone knows what the goals are. But people may have not only their own personal goals but also individual and very different perceptions of what the group's goals are.

Group members can honestly believe that they share a common goal and yet really have diverse goals. The following example shows you how this can happen.

> A group called the "Committee to Improve Patient Care" might seem to have an obvious and self-explanatory goal. However, one member, a physician, thinks the committee's goal is to increase the hospital's medical staff. The Administrator expects the committee to endorse the building program that the Administrator proposed. The third member, the Nursing Director, expects more nurses to be hired as a result of the committee's recommendations.

A patient on that committee may not agree with any of these opinions. As you can see, every committee member interpreted the committee's goal in their own way, from their own perspectives and particular needs. Saying that the committee's goal is "to improve patient care" is obviously not sufficient.

Stating Group Goals

In order for a group to ensure that they really have a shared goal in mind, they must develop a precise statement of their group's goals or objectives. A complete statement of each of the group's goals would include:

1. The people who will be involved, that is, who "owns" the goal.
2. The target of the goal (which may be people or objects).
3. The outcome or end result desired, preferably stated in observable terms.[4]

It is important to state the end result in observable terms so that everyone can see whether or not each goal has been met. Using an action verb to begin the goal statement is an often recommended way to do this. Each goal should also be stated as specifically as possible. This statement of group goals (or objectives) does not include how you're going to achieve the results—this comes later. Using the committee example, we can see how goals can be made more specific.

It could take a lot of discussion to make the goal of the Committee to Improve Patient Care specific. Fulfilling the first criterion is easy in this case. The people who "own" the goal will be the three committee members, the physican, the Administrator, and the Nursing Director, and perhaps the groups each one represents: the medical staff, administration, and nursing service. In order to please all three members, the committee might finally decide on three specific outcomes or end results to work toward simultaneously. These outcomes could be:

Provide 24-hour medical coverage for the emergency room.
Renovate the radiation therapy building.
Supplement the work of the present home care coordinator.

Although the overall target population for the committee was *all* patients who received care in their institution, once the committee selected its specific objectives, the target could be stated more specifically. The target populations would be outpatients using the emergency room, patients receiving radiation therapy, and patients anticipating discharge. (In a self-help type of group, the group itself could be the target population.)

In order to be sure that everyone agrees on the goals, the agreed upon objectives should be as specific as possible. For example, the committee will need to determine such things as how many patients the home care program should accommodate.

After the goals are clearly stated and acceptable to all concerned, the group can then proceed to discuss how they will achieve these goals or objectives. It is often difficult to resist jumping right to this phase before clarifying goals and you may catch yourself and other group members wanting to do this.

Now the committee can proceed to a discussion of how they will go about achieving their goals. They may decide to hire more community health nurses to supplement the work of the present home care coordinator and more physicians to provide 24-hour medical coverage in the emergency room.

The feelings that arise as a group forms and evolves have not yet been discussed but these will also affect the dynamics of selecting and defining goals.

SUMMARY

Once the goals have been clearly defined, are meaningful to the group, and agreed on by all members, the group can proceed with its task. An effective leader, therefore, ensures that goals are clear, congruent, and meaningful to the group.

Knowledge and Skills

Knowledge and skills are basic requirements for leadership. They include knowledge and skills both in leadership specifically and in nursing generally, and the ability to think critically. Knowledge comes before practice: once you've learned basic leadership concepts, you need to apply them to specific situations. When you consciously apply them you can achieve more consistent results than if you used the undirected, trial and error approach of people who have not learned these concepts.

You will find, for example, that when a coworker is not doing the job, you will know some specific steps you can take to remedy the problem, instead of just complaining about it. After you have studied group dynamics, you can quickly assess what is happening in a group that seems to be stuck on a particular issue and then select a strategy from your repertoire of leadership skills for getting the group out of its doldrums.

LEADERSHIP KNOWLEDGE

What does a person need to know in order to be an effective leader? To answer this question, it is necessary to go back to the three basic elements of a leadership event from the introduction: the leader, co-actor(s), and environment (See Fig. 1-2).

As a leader you must know about human needs and motivation and how they affect behavior. You also need to be able to relate this knowledge to your own behavior, which is the *leader* element. Although leadership events can be one-to-one interactions, many of them involve far more people (for example, a health care team or a client population) so a leader needs to know how people act as a group or even as a community as well as individually. This is the *co-actor* element.

Every leadership event takes place within an *environment,* the third basic element. For example, the emotional climate in which an interaction takes place can have a tremendous impact on its outcome. Two frantically busy people are hardly likely to work out a complicated staffing schedule as satisfactorily as two calm people working without interruption. The time and the arrangement of the space in which an event takes place can also influence its outcome.

There is also the larger system of which the group is a part, another aspect of the environment to consider. For example, the event can take place in an organization that encourages growth and development of its individual members or in an organization with rigid job descriptions. An attempt to bring about a change in nursing roles would proceed very differently in those two places. In fact, you would approach the change itself differently for those two places.

Need for Leadership Knowledge

Some people seem like natural leaders and you may wonder why they would need to learn leadership theory. The theories and concepts of leadership will enhance their leadership ability and help them select actions more specific to a particular situation than they could before. Also, some of the most spontaneous-appearing leaders actually think and plan very carefully before acting; it's their flexibility in response to a unique situation that makes them seem so natural.

This emphasis on the importance of knowledge is not a denial of the value of intuition. In fact, in keeping with the open systems approach of considering the person as a whole, it would seem that knowledge, feelings, and intuition can work together synergistically resulting in creative solutions to leadership problems. If you let your knowledge and intuition work together, you will be drawing upon more of your inner resources as a leader.

LEADERSHIP SKILLS

You also need to learn some specific leadership skills and when it is appropriate to use them. Once you have analyzed the situation in terms of the three basic elements of a leadership event, you are ready to decide what action to take. There are a number of leadership skills from which you can choose. For example, there are several different ways to confront a person or to bring about change. There are also political tactics especially appropriate for the underdog, and some paradoxical ways to bring about change that may appeal to your sense of humor as well as help you become an effective leader.

NURSING KNOWLEDGE AND SKILLS

Knowledge and skills in nursing practice are also important to the leader. Planning and organizing patient care are leadership responsibilities of the professional nurse and they require accurate assessments and diagnoses based on adequate knowledge. Your peers expect you to share your expertise with them; your patients count on you to give skillful nursing care; and your assistants look to you for guidance.

It takes time to develop this expertise and you can never really be finished learning and improving your skills. Having adequate knowledge and skills gives you confidence and the security needed to try new things and to assert yourself at work. Concern about your skills can result in your focusing most of your attention on them, and this will divert energy from more productive activities. The leader who is anxious about professional skills and unsure of professional decisions will find it difficult to pay attention to the needs of co-workers or to give them guidance.[5]

Building Nursing Knowledge, Skills, and Confidence

What can you do about this need for knowledge and skills? First, take responsibility for your own education. Confidence in your ability is important and if you do not have enough of it, you need to actively seek opportunities to increase it. Your basic education provides you with the knowledge and skills needed to begin practicing nursing. But this is only the beginning of your learning and if you feel uncertain about your knowledge or skills, look for extra learning experiences wherever possible. A few ways you can continue your learning are to study on your own, attend workshops and seminars, ask for extra practice time in the laboratory or clinical area, seek out your instructor and supervisors for guidance, and let other staff members know you're interested in observing and learning.

If you really have adequate knowledge and skills, but lack self-confidence because of low self-esteem, then work on that instead. Practice might still be helpful but more general measures are probably going to be more helpful. An assessment of your strengths is a good way to begin if you follow it with a real effort to build on these. Assertiveness training is also helpful for many people, even for those who act over-assertive to the point of being aggressive, but feel uncertain behind their aggressive front. Leadership skills are surprisingly helpful in building self-esteem because they can provide a genuine sense of personal power to the individual who uses them correctly.

Getting Ahead of the Group

Surprisingly, the leader who has too much knowledge or skills may not be most effective in leading a group. This point seems to contradict the previous discussion of the leader's need for adequate knowledge and skills until you consider it in relation to another basic principle. The more effective leader is one who identifies with the group. If you know far more than the group and if you are not willing to go back to where the group is in terms of knowledge, then you will not appear to be identifying with the group and you will not be communicating on the same level as the rest of the group.

The leader who is too far ahead of the group can lose them as quickly as the leader who is not as knowledgeable as the group. A leader who is not too far ahead of the group seems to be the most effective leader.[6] This is one reason why it is important to adjust your expectations and choice of terminology to the level of the individual or group. For example:

> You would not tell a brand new aide that a child has "acute pharyngitis." Instead, you would say the child has a sore throat and, if the aide were not overwhelmed by new responsibilities, explain the technical term for future reference.

The value of leader knowledge and skills was tested in a series of studies, two of which are described in Research Example 3-1.

CRITICAL THINKING

Simply accumulating knowledge and skills is not enough. The leader is an active rather than a passive participant in the learning process. You can make choices regarding what you have learned; you can choose to accept or reject the knowledge offered to you.

UNCRITICAL ACCEPTANCE OF AUTHORITY AND ROUTINE

A leader needs to maintain an open-minded and questioning attitude. Nurses and other health caregivers frequently fail to question the validity of common practices. They are often too willing to accept the statements of authorities, particularly authorities outside of nursing, without critically evaluating their validity and usefulness in nursing. Although we laugh now at the use of leeches or the old belief that too much learning endangered a woman's health, some of our current practices

Research Example 3-1. The Effect of Leader Competence

Is a leader's perceived competence related to the leader's acceptance and influence in a group? In a series of studies, Hollander and Julian[25] tested the idea that the leader who helps the group achieve its goals acquires increased influence and esteem from the group. Two of these studies are described here.

Experiment #1: Questionnaire

Six hundred thirty-three undergraduate students in a psychology course were asked to imagine a leader of the same sex who was described as either a good or poor performer of group activities, elected or designated, and interested or not in group members. The students rated their willingness (on a scale of one to six) to have this imagined person continue as the leader, serve as the group spokesperson, be a member of the group, or be a close friend.

The greatest difference in ratings was found between the leader described as performing well (5.28) and the leader described as performing poorly (3.19) at the task of the group. A leader's high interest in group activities could raise the leader's level of acceptance when the leader was a poor performer.

The researchers also found that the respondents were more willing to accept the imagined leader as a group member or friend than as a spokesperson. The elected leaders did get a higher rating than the designated leaders but the difference was not statistically significant at the 0.01 level. The researchers concluded that the leader's perceived competence had a significant positive impact on group members' responses to the leader but that they seemed to be wary of granting someone the right to be their spokesperson as it gives the leader a position of authority over them.

Experiment #2: In the Laboratory

Eighty male undergraduate students were divided into 20 small groups. Ten of these groups held an election to determine the leader, the results of which were contrived by the experimenters, and 10 groups had a leader arbitrarily designated for them.

Group members were then given the task of judging which of three lights on the wall would go off first. Their success in making these judgments was manipulated by the experimenters. Group members were given points for correct guesses.

Again, those leaders seen as competent had significantly more influence over their group's judgments and members of groups in which the leader had been "elected" were more willing to admit that they had been influenced by the leader. Not surprisingly, the leader who distributed points on an equal basis among group members was rated significantly more fair and received a higher evaluation from the group than did the leaders who gave themselves more points. The researchers concluded that the results of this experiment supported the results of the first one in which the leader who was perceived to be competent had more influence on group members.

may seem just as irrational and unfounded 100 years from now. Many of our current nursing practices are still influenced more by ritual and tradition than by the rationale of theory and the substantiation of research.

EFFECTS OF ROUTINE

Many nursing routines may be customary habits that need critical evaluation. Having routines does increase efficiency but they can become too comfortable. You can become mechanical and unthinking about giving nursing care (especially what is called "routine" nursing care) and lose sight of the uniqueness of the individual you are caring for. People get into habits of thinking in much the same way as they develop other habits. It is easy to fall into repetitive ways of thinking and acting without realizing it.

Holt says that if we do not maintain a questioning attitude, there is a danger that we will "go stupid."[7-8] Experienced staff can be excellent resources but some of them have "gone stupid" and succumbed to the numbing of routine. An alert leader will find many examples of this in everyday practice. The following is an example of what could happen when a person develops a routine without critically examining it:

> A nursing assistant developed a time-saving routine for toileting patients in the morning and planned to share this routine with fellow nursing assistants. She systematically worked up and down the hall placing each patient, some of them frail and at great risk for developing pressure sores, on a bedpan and leaving them for as long as an hour until returning to them. The routine had become her main concern; the assistant had made it more efficient but unthinkingly also made it potentially harmful.

SUMMARY

An effective leader has adequate knowledge and skills in leadership and in that leader's own profession. A thorough understanding of leadership makes it possible to analyze all three aspects of a situation—the leader, co-actor, and environment—and to choose the most effective strategy based on the results of this analysis. A questioning, open-minded attitude enables the leader to critically evaluate information offered and to avoid the pitfall of "going stupid."

Self-Awareness

Self-awareness is one of the means by which you can increase your effectiveness as a leader. Self-awareness or self-insight is knowing yourself as a thinking, feeling being interacting with an ever-changing world. Its focus is "getting in touch with yourself" or being "open to your experience." These phrases may sound trite after being used so frequently and often casually, but it is difficult to describe in better words this state of increased sensitivity to the inner self and to your relationship with the world around you, how you respond to people and what effect you have on them.

Self-awareness in itself is not really a solution to leadership problems but a heightened sensitivity that will act as a clarifier of peoples' problems, their response to you, and your response to them. As Wicks[9] wrote rather pointedly, "self-awareness is not an end in itself. The presence of 'enlightened alcoholics' and 'aware neurotics' in the community attests to this fact."

OPENNESS TO SELF

Self-insight includes alertness to the signals your body sends you when you are anxious or have been pushing yourself too hard. As a nurse, you know that these signals can be ignored only at your peril. It also includes allowing yourself the emotions that well up—sometimes sorrow, jealousy, or anger, other times contentment, love, and joy. Self-awareness is acknowledging and expressing the full range of emotions. You probably know the symptoms of anxiety, but can you recognize them in yourself when they arise? If you do recognize the symptoms, how do you cope with them? Are you satisfied with your current coping methods? Can you recognize and constructively express anger or resentment? Can you express feelings of warmth and positive regard for other people?

It may not have occurred to you before, but it seems that there are also people who do not fully recognize their thinking side either. On the whole, our society has emphasized the cognitive aspect and rewarded cool, clear thinking rather than emotional responses. Yet some people also suppress this thinking aspect of themselves, especially women. If you get cold shivers down your spine when you hear the word "research" or are in the habit of saying, "I was never good in math," you might be suppressing your thinking side along with or instead of your feeling side.

IMPORTANCE OF SELF-AWARENESS

Self-Acceptance

People who are not self-aware or "open to their own experience," as Rogers[10] puts it, tend to define themselves as others see them. They live out their lives in response to other people's demands, including peer and parental pressures, instead of being genuinely themselves. These individuals with limited self-awareness and self-acceptance waste a lot of time and energy trying to be what they are not instead of recognizing and experiencing all that they are, including experiencing the full range of emotions. This lack of awareness tends to make a person defensive and unable to get close to others.

You cannot effectively guide and influence other people if you do not feel free to share yourself with others. Rogers believes that everyone really wants to know themselves better. Once you have experienced your genuine and unique self (the mean and nasty side as well as the good and loving side) you are less likely to act defensively and rigidly. Not only do you become more flexible but also more autonomous, which means that you are less dependent on others for approval and are able to act in ways most likely to satisfy your own needs. This does not mean that you would always be satisfied with yourself. People are forever changing and growing, whether constructively or destructively, and it is natural to experience some discomfort and even distress related to the changes you go through and about some decisions you make.

If you can accept yourself as you really are, rather than hiding from your feelings, you will like yourself better. This seems to become a self-fulfilling prophecy: people who like themselves are more likeable. On the other hand, people who feel worthless tend to get themselves in situations that will prove them worthless.[11] For example, if you are afraid that the people in a certain group will not like you, you will avoid contact with them. As a result, no one pays attention to you and you can say, "See, they don't like me." This self-fulfilling prophecy can be turned around and used to your advantage: if you think of yourself as a leader, you are more likely to be one.

Self-awareness also helps you to evaluate your abilities realistically. Being objective about your abilities enables you to identify the areas in which you need to improve and to recognize and build on your strengths. Knowing your strengths can be a useful guide for selecting leadership strategies. An example follows of how you can utilize this knowledge of your strengths and weaknesses:

> If you are afraid to speak in front of a large group, you would not plan to address the PTA about the school health program. Instead, you can involve students in putting on a health fair for their parents. Still, you also need to work on reducing your fear of talking to large groups because next time that may be your most effective strategy (for one way to do this, see the Paradoxical Change section in Chaper 9).

Building up a large repertoire of skills increases your range of effectiveness.

Responsiveness to Others

There are a number of ways in which being self-aware can help you develop more effective interpersonal relationships. If you are not aware of your thoughts and feelings, then of course you can't communicate them to others, which is a part of developing a trusting relationship. Also, if you do not see how your actions affect others, you can be badly misled in your interpretations of their behavior and in your choice of leadership strategies. Self-awareness also helps you to understand the kinds of motivations that are influencing your behavior. Are you, for example, confronting your colleagues about excuses to avoid doing care plans so that they will improve their work or are you doing it to even a score with them for pointing out something you forgot to do last week?

Self-insight helps you develop empathy. Although some psychologists suggest that you try to "get into the other person's skin" to develop empathy, you cannot actually experience or feel exactly what another person is feeling. But you can relate their experiences to your own in order to develop some understanding of what they are feeling. People always mediate what the other person says or feels through their own experience.[12] This is one reason why it is important to respond to the other person's messages and to check out your perceptions of what the other person is saying and doing, a basic and very valuable strategy in leadership discussed further in this chapter and the following chapter.

INCREASING SELF-AWARENESS

How can you increase your self-awareness? There are several ways in which you can increase self-awareness and find out how others see you. One way is to increase your understanding of human behavior, especially the roles of the emotions, human needs and motivations, and coping behaviors, there are also many other areas that could provide useful information.

Observation of people's reactions to your behavior can give you many clues as to your effect on others. One of the most important ways to do this, and one that you can do every day, is to seek feedback from others. This can be done directly and formally by asking colleagues to evaluate your performance or informally by asking them how they think you are doing. It is also interesting and worthwhile to ask your patients if you've been of any help to them and if so, to ask them to tell you in what ways—you may be surprised at some of the responses. It is worth repeating that checking out your perceptions of what the other person is thinking and feeling will increase the accuracy of your perception and of your response to other people.

Many people underrate themselves. They dwell on their negative characteristics and downplay their real strengths. If you are one of these people, you may be in for a pleasant surprise when you seek feedback from other people.

Tape recordings and videotapes are good sources of objective feedback. We do not hear our voices the same way others do and the tape recorder can supply another set of ears as well as a record of what you have said. Videotape is even better because a lot of nonverbal communication is apparent on the video screen. Both of these can be played back several times to allow you to think and analyze your behavior and your effect on others. They can also be reviewed in private, which is a comfort to some people.

Joining a group can also be a valuable experience for a developing leader. There are so many kinds of groups that you will have to evaluate both your own needs and the purpose of a group before joining one. Some groups are formed explicitly for the purpose of increasing self-awareness but in other groups, this goal is secondary or implied. You can learn something from almost any group (even if it's how *not* to conduct a group) but a group that has an open, accepting climate in which you can feel comfortable and free to be yourself is one that would be most productive. The skills of the group leader are very important in this regard.

STAGES OF SELF-AWARENESS

There seem to be stages of self-awareness. Some people do not progress beyond a limited self-awareness, which enables them to function but not up to the limits of their ability. When you first begin paying serious attention to yourself, trying to separate the real you from the roles and facades presented to the world, you can become acutely self-conscious. You may find yourself reflecting on just about every response you make to a patient or direction to a coworker. ("What am I *really* saying?") At the same time, you're probably trying to pick up more of the feeling messages in other people's responses to you. ("What are they really trying to say?") But as you become more accustomed to being open to yourself, there seems to be less self-consciousness about it. Fully experiencing your thinking, feeling, responding, and acting self becomes easier and more natural and will contribute immeasurably to your effectiveness in relating to other people.[13]

SUMMARY

Through increased sensitivity to yourself and others, you can become more flexible, open-minded and accepting of yourself and other people. Self-awareness can also improve your ability to develop close relationships with other people and to understand their behavior. As you learn more about your own unique characteristics, you can select the most appropriate leadership approaches to use and generally improve your effectiveness in interpersonal relations.

Communication

Communication is at the very heart of leadership. It is the essential means through which leadership is accomplished, whether the communication is a spoken word of praise, a written set of instructions, a frown of displeasure, or an encouraging squeeze of the hand.

Because leadership cannot occur except in relationship to others, a leadership act must include some kind of exchange. Every exchange between human beings has an element of communication in it; there is some message in every exchange. We "cannot *not* communicate" is the way that Watzlawick, Beavin, Jackson[14] have so neatly phrased it. Refusing to respond to someone sends a message indicating "I will not answer," although it does not tell the other person why you will not respond. Even a refusal to answer communicates something!

ACTIVE LISTENING

Attending and responding are basic communication skills used in virtually every leadership situation. If you do not attend to what other people are saying, that is, if you are not really listening, you will not understand them. If you do not respond to them indicating that you have listened and are at least trying to understand, they will not feel understood or valued as a person. Gordon[15] calls attending "active listening." Active listening is essential in the establishment of good working relationships. (Attending and responding are discussed in detail in Chapter 4.)

ENCOURAGING A FLOW OF INFORMATION

There are some other aspects of communication that are crucial to effective leadership. An adequate flow of information between people who are working together (the head nurse and staff nurses, for example) is necessary for smooth operation in any setting. Without an adequate flow of information, many misunderstandings and omissions can occur and people can find themselves working at cross-purposes. This is especially apparent in community settings where some members of the health team may actually never see each other. For example:

> Operating without adequate communication, a community health nurse may be gathering resources for an older woman to return home from the hospital while the social worker is checking out suitable nursing homes for her. The patient and her family, of course, would be in a state of utter confusion until someone realized what was happening and improved communications between all the people involved.

People are more likely to assume that the exchange of information is adequate when they see each other everyday. This kind of assumption needs to be thoroughly checked out by the leader before accepting it. People may literally be only seeing each other and not actively listening to each other at all.

Communication Channels

A leader uses available channels of communication and creates new ones when they are needed. A leader also encourages others to do the same. In the previous example, for instance:

> The community health nurse could arrange to meet with the social worker, the older woman, and her family to discuss discharge plans. In fact, similar mini-conferences should be held with all patients preparing for discharge. Some community health agencies have scheduled regular meetings with hospital discharge planning staff in order to create a new channel of much needed communication.

When you think about all the people who can be involved in one patient's health care, you can see why adequate communication is so important.

DIRECTNESS

A leader sends direct messages to others. A leader avoids indirect, tentative approaches such as dropping hints or, even worse, not sending any message at all and assuming that others will somehow understand what is expected of them. When the leader's messages are too tentative and indirect, the person who is expected to respond may not be at all sure what the message was. Some leaders do this even with directions for completing an assignment. For example, imagine the following being said in a very soft, tiny voice:

> Some people have told me that it is possible to do some harm, or at least no good, anyway, not to listen to a patient's complaint that something is wrong. Now, I do know that you really don't have much time, you're so busy and we've been so short-handed today, but if it's at all possible, if you could find some time somehow in your busy schedule. . . .

Do you know what this team leader wants done? Hasn't the leader wasted time hesitating and going three times around the mulberry bush to make a simple but apparently necessary request to look into a patient's complaint? Does this sound familiar to you? If you tend to be very tentative in your statements instead of direct, practice simplifying your statements so that you get directly to the point of what you need to communicate.

Some kind of uneasiness is usually related to this tentative way of speaking. People joining a new group, for instance, are often uncertain about their roles in the group and so will try to avoid making statements that may antagonize other group members or make them seem out of place in the group. Another reason people speak indirectly is that they believe that the other person is too fragile and may "fall apart" if they are not careful how they say something, particularly something negative.[16] This belief is false. People, in general, are quite resilient and will probably appreciate a direct approach. In fact, avoiding any negative responses to someone can do far more harm than good in the long run because it denies that person an opportunity to change. Negative feedback can be expressed clearly and constructively, without harm to either person involved in the exchange.

SEEKING AND GIVING FEEDBACK

Checking Perceptions

Checking out your perceptions with the other person or people involved is an important aspect of effective leadership. Doing this increases your empathic skills and helps you avoid mistaken assumptions about the reasons for people's behavior. For example:

> If someone seems angry about an assignment, you should not change it until you find out why that person is angry. The anger could be unrelated to the assignment—the individual might have gotten a speeding ticket on the way to work. Or it could be the manner in which you gave the assignment rather than the work involved that has caused the anger.

Guessing is inaccurate and you will learn more, faster by asking the right questions.

Feedback from the group can help you evaluate your effectiveness and can serve as a guide for improving your leadership skills. In fact, it is hard to imagine a leadership situation in which feedback is not useful to the leader. Another example of the way in which seeking feedback can increase effectiveness follows.

Suppose that your team members are not showing up for team conferences. By yourself, you could probably come up with 100 possible reasons why this is happening, each reason suggesting a different solution. But how could you decide which of these is the right one? To avoid making assumptions, you can *ask* your team members how they see the situation. You can first state your problem and then say to them something like "In order to avoid this happening again, I need to know why people are not coming to the team conferences."

You can see that checking out your perceptions often involves active listening in order to be productive.

Providing Feedback

Group members need feedback for the same reasons that a leader needs feedback: to increase self-awareness; to avoid operating on the basis of mistaken assumptions about other people's behavior; and as a guide for growth and change.

When you do have negative feedback to communicate to someone, it should be done without placing blame or attacking the whole person. The focus of the communication is on a specific behavior rather than on a negative evaluation of your coworker as a person. For example:

If you found an orderly feeding a patient the wrong diet, you would not say, "Hey, stupid! The patient can't eat that!" which would insult the orderly. Instead, you could say, "This patient is on a low-purine diet and can't eat liver. Let's get the patient something else to eat."

The second response is specific, it sticks to the problem and does not attack the whole person. It also allows for open dialogue that can lead to a solution of the problem (a very simple one in this case) instead of provoking a defensive response.

An important point to remember in providing feedback is the importance of respecting the rights and dignity of your coworkers as much as you do the rights and dignity of your patients. Except in an urgent situation when the correction must be made immediately, look for a way to speak to the person privately. Yelling at a person in public creates bad feelings in all concerned, including whoever happens to hear it. Many readers have probably witnessed such an incident at some time in school or at work. Doing this embarrasses people, stirs up defensiveness, increases anger, and closes off communication. It is destructive, not constructive.

LINKING

This is another aspect of communication that is especially useful but may be less familiar to you. Linking is first seeing and then expressing a connection between two separate ideas or statements. The leader can fulfill the linking function in many situations. For example, when people in a group make separate, unconnected statements at a meeting, the group will probably go in several directions at once without accomplishing anything. The following example shows how this can happen.

One group member suggests getting a TV for a bored long-term patient. The next person to speak follows this suggestion with an unrelated comment on the terrible weather. The leader then connects the two by commenting that if the weather were better, the bored patient could be taken outside everyday, but in the meantime, what else could people suggest to alleviate the patient's boredom?

When someone assumes leadership and contributes the link between unconnected statements, the discussion begins to flow in one direction building up energy as each statement is connected to the main flow of the discussion.[17]

You can also create links between people, even if they are not actually in the same place together at the time.

A colleague may complain about the number of clients the colleague visits at home who have had their food stamp allocations reduced. You can answer, "a social worker in the agency has also expressed concern about the situation, would you like to work on the problem with the social worker"?

Finding such links can be a creative endeavor. It can lead to increased group cohesion and a combining of energies to get a job done. Linking is pointing out or creating a connection where one did not exist and can be a catalyst for action in many leadership situations.

SUMMARY

A person cannot be an effective leader without adequate communication skills. Active listening, directness, checking out perceptions, giving feedback, and linking are all elements of good communication for effective leadership.

Energy

If you have ever had an exhausting exchange with an agitated individual, then you have experienced the meaning of the phrase "feeling drained." That phenomenon of which you felt drained is that elusive entity, human energy. There are times when people feel "bursting with energy" as if they had more than enough, an overflowing supply. Other times they are so low that they feel as if they are suffering an energy deficit. While we do know that a person can feel high or low in energy,[18] scientists cannot yet define exactly what this energy is or measure it accurately.

NEURAL AND EMOTIONAL ENERGY

Human energy seems to be more than a purely physical phenomenon since our feeling states have a great effect on the amount of available energy we have and vice versa. Consider, for example, how hard it is for a depressed person to just get out of bed in the morning and then compare this to a manic kind of excitement state in which a person can be active for hours and even days on end without pause.

While this energy is usually described as being either physical or emotional, these are probably manifestations of the same energy field. It is believed that some kind of energy transformation can take place in people, changing their neural (electrochemical) energy of the nervous system to emotional (psychic) energy. Gruen[19] has conducted some interesting research to test this idea.

> In a random sample of heart attack patients, the experimental group of patients who had psychotherapy during their hospital stay had shorter hospital stays, a feeling of increased vigor, and more activity with less anxiety four months after the heart attack than the control group of patients who did not have psychotherapy. The conclusion was that an increase in available energy resulted from the change in self-concept that occurred during therapy.

Gruen theorizes that somehow the person to person interaction of the therapy helped release this energy so that the patients could do more and felt more energetic—a release and transformation of energy.

ENERGY AND LEADERSHIP EFFECTIVENESS

A high energy level can increase your effectiveness as a leader. As you interact with other people, your energy level will have an influence on their response to you. For instance, one person's enthusiasm for a project can be infectious in the good sense of the term. If someone in a group gets really excited about an idea, the rest of the group often picks up the excitement and carries out the idea. The following is an example of how this works.

> A group of nurses and aides decided at a conference that one of their patients needed more social stimulation and would enjoy being with friends down the hall. The idea involved shifting several patients' units. Having to move beds around usually evokes tired groans and much procrastination but before the conference was actually over, one nurse went out and checked with the patients involved. The nurse came back saying, "Yes, they want to do it." Before the chairs in the conference room were put back in place, there was a convoy of beds rolling down the hall. In fifteen minutes, everyone was settled in their new rooms and the glow of accomplishment was visible on the staff members' faces.

Something happens when an idea catches fire like this. People involved in the interaction seem to recharge from each other's enthusiasm and the energy level of the group rises dramatically. This is called "synergic power," the surge of energy that results when people exchange positive energy with each other.[20-21] Individual energies combine synergistically and create a surge of energy that is greater than each person individually could have mustered alone.

Sharing Energy

You can share your energy with people in many ways. Information can be thought of as an organized kind of energy, which can be used and exchanged. Another possible way to share energy in nursing is the use of touch as a healing process. Krieger[22-23] believes that the touch of a healthy person with the intent to heal can have demonstrable therapeutic effects and her preliminary research supports this idea. People vary in their ability to touch therapeutically. You need to be sensitive to the needs of the person being touched because too much energy can actually produce discomfort. Although this idea may sound esoteric to some readers, nurses have intuitively been using touch to comfort and heal their patients for years.

Low Energy Levels

On the negative side, a lack of energy and enthusiasm can work in the opposite direction. If no one believes an idea will work, then it will not work!

> A favorite phrase on patient care plans is the admonition to "spend time with the patient." If you are giving such an assignment and shrug or sigh when you say it (knowing it won't be done), if you skip reading that part of the care plan or don't check later to see what the results of doing it were, it will probably not be done. But if you emphasize spending time with the patient, saying why it is needed by this patient and explaining what is meant by "spending more time" and if you are interested in the results of the interaction, you are far more likely to see it done.

The amount of energy you invest in an action, either physical or emotional energy, is positively related to its outcome.

ENERGY FLOW AND RESERVES

A leader needs to have energy available for action. If you can gauge the level of your energy reserves, then you can regulate your energy exchanges to ensure adequate reserves. Most people are at least subliminally aware when their energy reserves are low. They feel listless and weary and realize that they need to recharge. How people recharge seems to be an individual matter—the same experience can be restorative (positive) for one person and draining (negative) for someone else[24] as in the following example.

> Some people love horror movies—the more terrifying the better—while others get scared and have bad dreams for days afterward. The enjoyment recharges one person in a positive manner while the other person has stored up a negative kind of energy that needs to be released in the bad dreams. A companion of these two is just plain bored by horror movies and would not be recharged by going to the movies, but loves tennis and feels exhilarated after a good match.

Some activities like the tennis match seem to be both discharging and recharging but, as with the whole concept of human energy, this idea needs to be further researched.

The availability of human energy may be related to states of health and illness. The results of Kirlian photography indicate that there may be measurable differences in energy levels between the sick and well person. Psychic phenomena continue to intrigue people and challenge researchers to prove or disprove their existence. There is a growing sense too, that every human being has resources of personal power and energy that have hardly been tapped yet. Even if we can't actually use our psychic energy to move across the room (and who really knows for sure that we can't?) the sharing of the energy that is within each of us has a tremendous potential for impact on people.

Some people have difficulty using their energy to its best advantage. They waste their energy doing things the hard way or in a disorganized fashion. An energy squanderer like this will do 10 things to solve a single problem where one action would do just as well. Planning and organizing your activities help reduce this waste of energy.

Ineffective, unsatisfying experiences also drain your energy and leave you unprepared to meet a crisis. You can plan your activities to include more of the recharging kinds of activities. Recharging activities can be challenging, physical activity; reading; daydreaming; or satisfying person to person interaction, such as a party or a few hours with a good friend. Without a reserve of energy, you could have difficulty mustering the strength to fully handle a crisis situation or any situation really well. You need this store of energy to grow and develop not only as a leader but as a nurse and as an individual too. This also works the other way: using effective leadership techniques can reduce the number of draining experiences at work and help you keep your energy reserves up.

Energy Inventory

You might try making an inventory of your energy reserves, discharges, and recharges to see where your energy is going. List all of your activities for one day (include little things such as receiving a word of thanks from someone, and routine things such as meals). Then mark them as sources of either positive ($+$) or negative ($-$) energy and rate the amount of energy involved on a scale of 1 to 5, with 1 being very low, 3 moderate, and 5 very high amounts. A tremendously recharging activity would be $+5$ and a very draining experience would be -5. Your total would indicate a positive or negative balance for the day. Do you find yourself with a deficit at the end of the day? Are there negative sources that you could reduce or eliminate? Are there positive sources you could add or increase? Are you satisfied with the way in which you use your energy?

SUMMARY

Energy can be shared with people as information, in the helping process, and in motivating them via synergic power. An effective leader needs adequate energy reserves in order to be prepared to act.

Action

Action is the sixth component of effective leadership. All of the components that came before this one—goals, knowledge and skills, self-awareness, communication, and energy—are only of value in leadership if they are put into practice. Without action, there can be no influence and therefore no leadership.

All of the actions mentioned here will appear again in this book and some, such as confrontation and evaluation, will be discussed in detail. Describing them here will complete the components and give you a broad overview of what a leader does in order to influence others. Later in this chapter, you will find a checklist that summarizes the components of effective leadership. You can use this checklist to evaluate your own effectiveness as a leader. By now, you have probably noticed some connections between the components. You will find more here and by the time you reach the end of this book, you probably will have found many new connections between the many aspects of leadership.

INITIATING ACTION

A leader initiates action. Ideas, suggestions, and plans must be implemented in order to be effective. A good idea cannot have any influence if it remains only in your head. Even the best assessment and planning, whether a nursing care plan, community project, or some other plan, does very little good if it remains only a plan.

Many worthwhile proposals die of neglect because no one put any energy behind the proposals to bring them into the implementation stage. For instance:

> You may hear a colleague say "Whatever happened to that idea we had about getting a mobile health unit?" In response, everyone shrugs and looks around at the others. Someone had made a good suggestion, but no one had taken the iniative to pursue it any further.

A leader *confronts* himself and others. Confrontation is a powerful strategy used to present people with the way others perceive their actions. It should be a thoughtful reaction, not a thoughtless one that can degenerate into telling each other off. There are several ways in which you can confront an individual or group, ranging from very gentle to very strong confrontations.

A leader does not sit back and watch a power struggle destroy working relationships or a client being put off by one agency after another. A leader takes action to solve these problems. Timing is also important. It is true that it's sometimes necessary to wait for the right opportunity to initiate action. But what happens much more often is that people hesitate too long when initiating action. Too much delay can mean you have lost an opportunity to act decisively.

MANAGING OTHERS

A leader *plans and organizes* activities. Although the point has already been made that planning and organization without action are not sufficient by themselves, they do contribute a great deal to the efficiency and effectiveness of an endeavor. Without them, people waste energy doing useless tasks, work at cross-purposes (just as they do without goals or adequate communication) or find themselves directionless and not knowing what to do next). Without good planning and organization, a job may be done twice or not at all, a frustrating experience for everyone involved. Poorly planned meetings, too, are usually a waste of time. Good planning and organization are worth the time and effort involved.

A leader *guides* others, sharing knowledge and experience with them. The amount of guidance and direction given by a leader varies according to the needs that arise in particular situations. A new nurse would need a lot of guidance in comparison to an experienced nurse, but even the most experienced nurses benefit from some direction and from the exchange of ideas. A frequent exchange of ideas helps to prevent ''going stupid.'' This is not a one-way exchange; the leader is also open to suggestions from others and eager to learn from others' knowledge and experience.

A leader *evaluates* the actions of himself and others. This means making a judgment as objectively as possible about the effectiveness of your actions and those of your coworkers. Nursing audits and peer review are formal evaluation procedures that are becoming established parts of nursing practice. Informal evaluation should take place constantly. Is your nursing care helping the patient recover or is it adding to the patient's distress? Has your leadership made it possible for your team members to work well together or has it resulted in disruptive behavior? An evaluation of what behavior has been productive and what behavior has not been, provides you with a guide for selecting strategies in the future. Evaluation done well can be a source of increased self-insight and can stimulate personal growth and development.

CRITICAL THINKING AND PROBLEM-SOLVING

A leader *critically analyzes* beliefs and practices. Critical thinking or critical analysis is related to evaluation but has a broader application. It is an open-minded but questioning approach toward beliefs, facts, and practices. As a critical thinker, the leader recognizes that nursing practice is influenced by current beliefs and fashionable trends as well as facts. Even these ''facts'' can be inadequate or proven wrong by new evidence, as in the following examples.

> Space exploration recently showed that the planet Jupiter has more moons than the textbooks say it has. Even the order of the planets that we learned in school is going to change for the next few years.

Years ago, the germ theory revolutionized health care but now we realize that it is inadequate to explain illness in man.

What you learned in school or read in journals may also change as new discoveries are made. Even facts can be wrong and the nurse leader must be ready and willing to challenge them.

A leader *problem-solves* when confronted with a difficult situation. The problem-solving process, which consists of a series of steps (collect data, define the problem, select strategies, take action, evaluate results) serves as a guide to dealing with a problem or difficult task. Problem-solving is a systematic process that assists the leader in the analysis of a difficult situation and in the choice of actions. An effective leader usually thinks before acting.

PROFESSIONAL ACTIVITIES

A leader *develops the structure* of her own practice. Using leadership knowledge and skills is considered part of being a professional. Leaders will not wait for someone else to tell them what to do. For example, a professional nurse does not wait for a physician's order before doing some health teaching, yet there are still some nurses who do this. The following two examples are ways in which nurses develop the structure of their roles.

> A school nurse seeks opportunities for intervention, the nurse does not sit in the office hoping the teachers will remember the nurse is there.

> An infection control nurse visits the units, checks patients' charts, institutes surveys, and talks with personnel to keep on top of the situation. The nurse does not wait to be called in.

In order to do these things, a nurse must have both leadership ability and a clear idea of what nursing is. While there are many written definitions of nursing, it is suggested that the reader formulate a personal definition to live by, one you can use when someone asks you what nurses really do or why nurses should have more authority, a salary increase, and so forth.

Also, while nurses need to recognize the contributions of other members of the health team, they do not need to do this by diminishing their own contributions. Too often, nurses will refer patients to other health care workers for needs well within the range of nursing practice. For example:

> Nurses will call in a psychologist to counsel a patient for a minor problem before they try to help the patient deal with it. They will call in "experts" to teach their patients, diagnose a patient's problem, run a clinic, lead team conferences, and so forth.

Nurses can do these things and more. A leader needs a strong sense of professional identity.

A leader *interprets the role* of the professional nurse to others: coworkers, clients, and the public. This is closely related to developing structure. Developing structure emphasizes doing it, while interpreting the role emphasizes telling people about it. If you listen closely, you'll find plenty of opportunities to inform people about what nurses can do. Here are just two examples of such opportunities.

You might notice that teachers call on the school nurse to deal with head lice problems, but not with family problems that are keeping a child out of school.

You may hear a community group bemoaning their difficulties getting someone to do camp physicals and have the opportunity to say, "A nurse can do that."

Does a leader *seek recognition?* There are some questions about whether or not seeking recognition is a leadership function. A willingness to speak out in support of yourself, your group, and your profession is part of being a leader. But anyone who is obviously on an ego trip with only personal interests in mind is unlikely to be an effective leader. It seems that there are limits within which seeking recognition can be an effective leadership action.

WORKING WITH OTHERS

A leader *calls meetings* of all kinds, depending upon the particular situation. The purpose of the meeting can be to discuss plans, organize work, work out solutions to problems, ventilate feelings, or share information. Getting people together as a group rather than dealing with them individually has several advantages. First, it is more efficient, you can get the same message to everyone at once with less chance of the message being changed as it is transmitted, a situation you've probably experienced when a rumor circulated. Second, you also may be able to get that tremendous joint action effect (discussed under the Energy Section) called synergic power with a group, which you could not get if you worked with one person at a time. Communication with everyone at once, in conferences or meetings, improves coordination, saves time, and often brings greater results.

A leader *mobilizes support systems.* You are not expected to do all of these things mentioned so far alone. In fact, there are many things you cannot accomplish singlehanded. There are two kinds of support: actual assistance with a task and psychologic support. Your health care team usually provides the actual assistance with the work that needs to be done although there are many other possible sources of support. The psychologic support can come from a number of sources. These could include: administrative backing of your activities, colleagues who say, "I'm with you on this;" and your patients who appreciate your skilled care. Support can also come from sources outside work and, last but not least, from yourself.

DECIDING TO ACT

A leader *takes risks.* A leader is not afraid of confrontation; a leader is willing to make direct statements, question decisions, and, sometimes, break rules (Fig. 3-3). Leaders choose their fights, they do not get trapped in them. Leaders decide for

FIGURE 3-3. A leader takes action. A leader is willing to make direct statements, question decisions, and volunteer to take charge.

themselves when to break a rule, after weighing the consequences of breaking the rule versus obeying it.

You probably take many small risks everyday without thinking about it. Sometimes the action is so necessary that you do not even pause to consider the risk to yourself until it is all over. A leader considers the relative advantages of following the rules (taking the "safe road") versus breaking the rules and taking risks and is willing to take the risk when necessary.

Every leadership action has some risk attached to it. It takes courage to stand up and speak out, to correct people when they are wrong, and to volunteer to take charge. Some readers will find this easy to do having been accustomed to speaking up and taking charge and perhaps even taking over. The need to risk holding back and trust others to take responsibility and speak for themselves may be hard for these readers. They may need to practice weighing consequences and choosing their battles in order to avoid scattering their energies and to get the full benefit of their ability to be assertive.

Other readers may quake at the thought of confronting people and standing up for their rights. These readers may need extra practice in leadership techniques such as confrontation to build up confidence and get into the habit of speaking out. Ensuring adequate support systems and concentration on personal strengths before taking action may also increase assertiveness.

Whether you choose to act or not to act, you have made a decision. Deciding is often the hardest part. What will you gain? What will you lose? Which of these is most important to you? What are you willing to give up and what are you not at all willing to give up? When you choose to lead, you are choosing to risk challenges to your leadership, criticism, and return confrontation. But choosing not to lead also has its risks; you risk a loss of autonomy, reduced opportunities to achieve self-actualization, and a loss of self-esteem. Confronting the risks of leadership is a choice to open up opportunities for more satisfying person to person interactions and for the possibility of greater rewards in your personal life and in your career.

SUMMARY

Leadership is essentially a decision to take action. Leaders develop the structure of their practice and interpret their professional role to others. Leaders initiate actions of many kinds, which include planning and organizing work, guiding and evaluating others, calling meetings, mobilizing support systems, taking risks, and confronting themselves and others. Leaders use the basic skills of problem-solving, critical thinking, and communication to carry out these actions most effectively.

The Leadership Checklist

Each reader will find areas of personal strength and of weakness within the components of effective leadership. You may find, for example, that you are usually direct in your approach to people, but that you often forget to consider what they

	VERY MUCH	SOME- WHAT	NOT AT ALL
A. GOALS			

A. GOALS

1. Have you identified:
   Your personal goals?
   Group members' personal goals?
   Group goals?
   Environmental (such as organizational and community) goals?
2. Are your goals congruent with the group's goals?
3. Do you identify with the group, for example, use "we" instead of "I" and "you"?
4. Do members of the group see you as identifying with the group?
5. Have you clearly and specifically stated the group's goals including the:
   People involved?
   Target?
   Outcome?

B. KNOWLEDGE AND SKILLS

1. Do you have more knowledge and skill than the rest of the group?
2. Do you feel confident of the knowledge and skill in this situation?
3. Are you able to speak to the group on their level?
4. Have you identified the needs and motives of the people in the group?
5. Have you identified the sources of power and authority in the situation?
6. Have you critically analyzed the situation including the leader, co-actor(s) and environment?
7. Have you kept an open mind about the situation?

C. SELF-AWARENESS

1. Do you know what your own needs are?
   Have you found ways to meet these needs?
2. Do you know what you expect to gain from this situation?
3. Are you able to empathize with the people in the group?
4. Do you see yourself as a leader?

D. COMMUNICATION

1. Do you know what channels of communication are usually used?
   Are you using them?
2. Is there an adequate flow of information?

Continued	VERY MUCH	SOME-WHAT	NOT AT ALL
3. Have you created any new channels of communication?			
4. Are your communications open and direct?			
5. Do you attend and respond (listen actively) to what others are saying?			
6. Have you checked out your perceptions of the situation with the people involved?			
7. Do you see and point out connections (links) between the statements of different people?			
E. ENERGY			
1. Are you interested in the work of the group?			
2. Have you shared your interest and enthusiasm with the group?			
3. Do you really believe what you say to the group?			
4. Do you have enough energy for the task?			
F. ACTION			
1. Have you planned how to get the job done?			
2. Have you organized the work efficiently?			
3. Do you share your ideas with others?			
4. Do you call the group together often enough?			
5. Have you defined your nursing role and communicated it to the group?			
6. Do you use the authority you have? Do you delegate it? Have you tried to increase it?			
7. Have you mobilized support systems?			
8. Are you willing to take risks? Have you taken any risks?			
9. Do you confront when it is needed?			
10. Do you initiate action when it is needed? Without delay?			
11. Do you seek feedback? Informally? Formally?			
12. Do you provide feedback? Informally? Formally?			
13. Have you tried to improve your leadership ability?			

FIGURE 3-4. Leadership checklist.

are trying to get out of a situation (that is, what their goals are). Or you may find that you are usually very sensitive to the needs and goals of others, but tend to be so soft-spoken and indirect in your approach that people don't even know you're trying to lead them. There are as many possible combinations of these as there are readers of this book.

As you were reading the chapter, you probably thought of times you had done things described and times when you have forgotten or avoided then. Using the checklist in Figure 3-4 will help you in your self-analysis.

This is not one of those quick check lists where you add up your score and find out if you are "superior," "above average," or "fair." It is meant as a guide to serious analysis of your leadership ability. The idea is not to get a score of how effective or ineffective you are (this is better measured in terms of the results you've been getting) but to emphasize those strong points of yours that you can build on (especially those in the "Somewhat" column) and use to your best advantage and to show you where you can make some changes in your leadership in order to become more effective.

Now that you have read the chapter, think of a current or past leadership situation and analyze your actions in terms of the components of effective leadership, listed in Figure 3-4. You may want to return to this checklist after you have finished the book.

References

1. TANNENBAUM, R, WESCHLER, IR, AND MASSARIK, F: *Leadership: A frame of reference.* In CATHCART, RS AND SAMOVAR, LA (EDS): *Small Group Communication: A Reader,* ed 2. Wm C Brown, Dubuque, Iowa, 1974, p 358.

2. HOLLANDER, EP: *Leader effectiveness and the influence process.* In CATHCART, RS AND SAMOVAR, LA (EDS): *Small Group Communication: A Reader,* ed 2. Wm C Brown, Dubuque, Iowa, 1974, p 367.

3. BEAL, GM, BOHLEN, JM, AND RAUDEBAUGH, JN: *Leadership and Dynamic Group Action.* The Iowa State University Press, Ames, 1962, p 130.

4. MAGER, RF AND BEACH, KM, JR: *Developing Vocational Instruction,* ed 2. Fearon, Palo Alto, California, 1975

5. DOUGLASS, LM AND BEVIS, EO: *Nursing Leadership In Action: Principles and Application to Staff Situations,* ed 3. CV Mosby, St Louis, 1979, p 248.

6. BEAL, op cit, p 34.

7. HOLT, J: *How Children Fail.* Pitman, New York, 1964. In GREENE, M (ED): *Teacher As Stranger.* Wadsworth, Belmont, California, 1973, pp 5, 80.

8. GREEN, M: *Teacher As Stranger.* Wadsworth, Belmont, California, 1973, pp 5, 80.

9. WICKS, RJ: *Counseling Strategies and Intervention Techniques for the Human Services.* JB Lippincott, Philadelphia, 1977, p 147.

10. ROGERS, CR: *On Becoming A Person.* Houghton-Mifflin, Boston, 1961, p 108.

11. EGAN, G: *Interpersonal Living.* Brooks/Cole, Monterey, California, 1976, p 79.

12. LAING, RD: *Self and Others,* ed 2. Penguin Books, New York, 1969, p 19.

13. ROGERS, CR: *Carl Rogers on Personal Power.* Dell, New York, 1977, p 245.

14. WATZLAWICK, P, BEAVIN, JH, AND JACKSON, DD: *Pragmatics of Human Communication.* WW Norton, New York, 1967, p 5.

15. GORDON, T: *Parent Effectiveness Training.* Plume Books, New York, 1970, p 49.

16. SATIR, V: *Conjoint Family Therapy.* Science and Behavior Books, Palo Alto, California, 1967, p 15.

17. LIFTON, WM: *Groups: Facilitating Individual Growth and Societal Change.* John Wiley & Sons, New York, 1972, p 166.

18. BLATTNER, B: *Holistic Nursing.* Prentice-Hall, Englewood Cliffs, NJ, 1981.

19. GRUEN, W: *Energy in group therapy: Implications for the therapist of energy transformation and generation as a negentropic system.* Small Group Behavior. 10(1):23, Feb 1979.

20. CRAIG, JH AND CRAIG, M: *Synergic Power: Beyond Domination and Permissiveness.* Pro-Active Press, Berkeley, California, 1975.

21. CLAUS, KE AND BAILEY, JT: *Power and influence in Health Care.* CV Mosby, St Louis, 1977, p 48.

22. KRIEGER, D: *The laying-on of hands as a therapeutic tool for nurses,* speech presented at the American Cancer Society, New York City Division, Inc. In *Symposium: A Synthesis of Community Health Resources for the Rehabilitation of the Cancer Patient,* at French and Polyclinic Medical School and Health Center, New York, February 20, 1974.

23. KRIEGER, D: *The Therapeutic Touch.* Prentice-Hall, Englewood Cliffs, NJ, 1979.

24. KANTOR, D AND LEHR, W: *Inside the Family.* Harper & Row, 1975, New York, p 93.

25. HOLLANDER, EP AND JULIAN, JW: *Studies in leader legitimacy, influence and innovation.* In BERKOWITZ, L (ED): *Group Processes.* Academic Press, New York, 1978.

Chapter *4*

Communication Skills

This chapter is concerned with the whole range of communication skills from simple listening to asserting your leadership through confrontation and negotiation. The focus is on improving working relationships by improving communications. Effective communication skills are used to establish and maintain productive working relationships, to handle problems that may arise, and to encourage progress toward self-actualization for everyone involved.

Many of the same principles of communication are used in both therapy and leadership. In leadership, however, there is no implication that the person with whom you are communicating is functioning at a lower level than you. The implied emphasis in some therapy relationships is on the expertise of the therapist and the deficits of the client. This is not a relationship of equals and would not be an effective leadership approach. An approach in which the individuals involved are assumed to be equals is more effective.[1]

Communication as an Exchange

Communication is not unidirectional. You will recall from Chapter 3 that you cannot *not* communicate, which means that communication between two people always flows in both directions. Communication involves an interaction between at least two people who co-act upon or affect each other. Neither person can be left totally unaffected by the exchange. The influences are complex and no one involved in an exchange is completely passive, reflecting the basic principles of systems theory that life is dynamic, not static, and that an interaction between two people is mutual and simultaneous. Everyone involved in the exchange is somehow affected by the exchange and has some effect on it. Consider an example to show how this happens:

If you greet a friend with the ritual greeting, "Hi, how are you?" and instead of the ritual response of, "Fine, how are you?" your friend groans, "Don't ask!" your next message will be quite different than if your friend used the expected response. Your friend has jolted you out of the ritual and into concern about what is bothering your friend.

You can expect that the exchange will probably continue back and forth several more times. This exchange could be diagrammed as a feedback loop as shown in Figure 1-2.

When you send a message to someone, that person's response is influenced by the message (both verbal and nonverbal) that you sent as well as by that person's own values, beliefs, present mood, and typical patterns of responding. You, in turn, will be influenced by the way in which the person responds as well as by your own typical patterns of response, beliefs, values, and present mood. The environment will also affect the exchange. To continue the above example:

If you and your friend are standing in a parking lot and about to be late for work, then the exchange will probably be short. But if the two of you are sitting down for a coffee break, the exchange may continue for a while about what's bothering your friend.

ELEMENTS OF THE EXCHANGE

Every message has two aspects according to Watzlawick and associates.[2] The first aspect is the *content* of the message or the outward, literal information conveyed by the message. The second aspect is the *relationship* aspect, which tells you how to interpret the message. The relationship aspect is the "information about the information," also called the *metacommunication*. Going back to the ritual greeting example to illustrate this:

When your friend says, "Don't ask!" the content aspect or surface message tells you not to question how your friend is feeling. You could take this literally and not ask any more questions but this may not be what your friend wants you to do.

The metacommunication (which includes the groaning that accompanied the words) will indicate what else your friend is telling you, although not always clearly. The groan has indicated that something is bothering your friend but gives no indication of whether or not your friend wants to discuss it. If your friend puts out hands as if to stop you and continues to walk rapidly away from you, the nonverbal relationship aspect tells you this is not the right time to explore the problem. But if your friend stops with hand to forehead as if with a headache and looks at you expectantly, the metacommunication tells you something quite different: that your friend is hoping for encouragement from you to talk about the problem.

An interpretation of communications that focuses on only the content aspect or literal meaning of the message is clearly going to miss much of the message or even result in concluding exactly the opposite of what the sender intended to convey. The more of the metacommunication you can pick up and interpret correctly, the better you can understand the message sent.

NONVERBAL COMMUNICATION

There are several kinds of nonverbal communication, including body stance and position, sounds, gestures, and tone of voice and emphasis. The *tone of voice* and *emphasis* given to particular words in a statement are so closely related to the content that most of the time people do not consciously separate them when they interpret a message; they hear them together. For example:

> "*How* did you do *that*?" asked with exasperation communicates definite disapproval of your behavior. With a different emphasis and some surprise in the tone of voice, the same question, "How did *you* do that?" indicates there was some doubt about your ability to accomplish whatever is being talked about.

There are a wide variety of *sounds* that convey meaning by themselves and also serve as "information about the information." These sounds can be groans, growls, giggles, laughs, sighs, grunts, whistles, and many more. *Gestures* can do the same thing. Pointing, grimacing, smiling, nodding, shaking your head, pounding the desk, and stamping your feet all convey meaning, alone or with words. Here is an example:

> A hospitalized stroke patient would vigorously bounce the buttocks up and down on the bed if the call light wasn't answered immediately. This signal for a bedpan was unmistakable from the hallway, yet the patient could not at that time say a word.

Body stance and position within a room can also convey meaning. It is generally believed, for example, that people who sit back in their chairs with their arms folded across their chests are in a defensive or self-protecting position and will be less open to the group than the persons who lean forward and have their arms in a more relaxed position. People who surround themselves with piled-up books or other objects or who stay behind a desk are also thought of as being in a more self-protective, less open stance.[3] Those who stand behind a desk, sit in a higher chair, or walk around the outside of the group observing its process are generally maintaining their distance from the group. On the other hand, a group leader who wants to be seen as an equal in the group will select a chair within the group circle in order to avoid taking an authoritative position.

Huge desks, raised platforms, glass enclosures, and many other artifacts are signs of authority and act as distance maintainers. Such symbols are also used to designate status. In some organizations, for example, you can judge a person's rank by the size and finish of the desk:

> The person who sits at a metal desk is lower in rank than the one who sits at an imitation wood grain desk. The person with a wooden desk and a leather chair has made it to the top in such a place.

Nurses' uniforms and some pins fill a similar function. You do not have to be in the army to be aware of different ranks.

INTERPRETATION

The importance of the nonverbal aspect of a message can hardly be overestimated. Mehrabian[4] found that facial expression has the greatest impact (55 percent) and tone of voice used is second (38 percent). The words themselves have a surprisingly weak effect (7 percent). Unless your words are backed up by a congruent facial expression and tone of voice, they will have very little effect or even a negative impact on the listener. With results like these, it's no wonder that therapists emphasize the importance of being genuine or authentic in your responses. Because it is easier to control your words than your nonverbal communication, knowing your real feelings and expressing them appropriately would help to ensure congruence between your verbal and nonverbal messages.

All of these meanings inferred from nonverbal communication need to be interpreted with some care within the entire context of a situation. The group member with arms crossed might be responding to the low temperature of the room. The group leader sitting within the circle may still be exerting authority and the nurse in uniform may simply be conforming to the regulations of the employer. A person's motives and the effect on the observer may differ substantially. The meaning of a particular position or stance may not always be the most obvious one. Again, checking out your perceptions can help you avoid misunderstanding.

SUMMARY

Communication is a mutual and simultaneous exchange. There are two aspects of a communication, both of which need to be considered in interpreting the message. The first is the content aspect, which is the literal message. The second is the relationship aspect or metacommunication, which tells you how to interpret a message. This is frequently done through nonverbal types of communication that can include tone of voice and emphasis, gestures, body position and stance, sounds, and facial expressions.

Basic Communication Skills

This section describes the basic techniques for facilitating effective communication: attending, responding, clarifying, personalizing, and giving information. After presenting the basic communication skills, the more complex leadership skills of confrontation and negotiation are discussed in detail. Each of these increasingly complex communication techniques adds to the relationship to increase its dimensions and complexity.

102

ATTENDING

Reduced to its most basic meaning, attending is paying attention. In order to understand the full message being sent to you, you need to pay attention to all of its aspects: the voice tone, gestures, body language, words being spoken and often what is not being said as well. This takes concentration and a well-grounded understanding of human nature. How often do people really pay attention to what someone else is saying?

> During a research study, one of the questions asked of the adults being interviewed was how often they listened to their aging mother or father. Their answers show the difference between just hearing and listening with real interest and concentration. Many people said, "Well, I hear him, but I don't really listen," or "She talks a lot, but I guess I really listen only occasionally." What they were saying is that most of the time they do not really *attend* to what their parent is saying.

This is probably true of most people most of the time. Beginning leaders need to consciously work on increasing the amount of attending they do; experienced, effective leaders do it almost without having to think about it.

Purpose of Attending

Attending includes both observing nonverbal behavior and listening carefully in order to better understand the message and to let the other person know that you are paying attention. Think about how you would feel if you were trying to tell someone something and you get the impression that the person is not really listening to you. Attending encourages the other person to talk and to express thoughts and feelings. When you really listen, other people feel valued and begin to feel that you understand them. It conveys caring about the other person and can increase the amount of trust between the two of you or between you and a group. You can see that attending or really listening is the beginning of developing a trusting relationship.

When you do attend to what people are saying, you begin to appreciate their individuality and to understand them better. You find out their point of view, what their needs are, and how they are feeling. Part of the purpose of attending to other people is to observe and listen in order to learn more about them.[5] What you learn is needed for accurate responding, the next level of communication.

Nonverbal Attending

As with all communications, attending can be done both verbally and nonverbally. Egan[6] has a comprehensive list of ways in which you can nonverbally attend. The first way is to position yourself so that you are facing the person. This may seem obvious, but this simple technique is often ignored. Here are two examples:

If you are glancing at papers on your desk or filling out a report form while your colleague is talking to you, you are not fully attending to your colleague. The nurse who turns away to straighten up the dressing tray is also not fully attending to the patient. But if you put down your papers and your pen or your sterile dressings and turn directly toward your colleague or patient, then that person will know you are ready to really listen.

Leaning forward toward the person speaking also indicates a desire to listen, as if you want to be sure to catch every word. An open posture indicates not only attention, but receptiveness to the other person's message. In comparison, sitting back with your arms tightly crossed conveys a closed, unreceptive attitude.

Maintaining eye contact with the other person is probably the best known of the nonverbal ways to attend. When people first try to maintain eye contact, they often wind up staring down the other person, their "attentive" expression frozen on their faces. Naturally, this is not the most effective way to physically attend to someone else. A comfortable, relaxed, attentive expression and position are what you want to achieve. If you are tense or distracted, these feelings may be communicated by the rigidity of your position or penetrating eye contact even though you are in the "right" physical position.

Silence accompanied by nonverbal attending is sometimes sufficient to encourage other people to express themselves. In fact, a common stumbling block is talking so much that the other person never really gets a chance to collect thoughts and express them. Some people are just accustomed to doing most of the talking, others tend to rattle on when they get nervous or to fill an uncomfortable silence. If you catch yourself doing either, make a conscious effort to pause a little longer by taking two or three deep breaths or counting to 10 to yourself before you jump in to talk or repeat your question:

> If you are genuinely interested in what people have to say you will find that a combination of a little patience, that is, not filling in the silences too quickly, and genuine attentiveness encourages most people to amplify their answers and results in responses that go far beyond your original questions.

Not everyone needs such encouragement, however. There are times when people overwhelm you with a flood of verbalizing that you need to sort out and direct, to make it more constructive and less repetitious. Here, clarifying and focusing (discussed later) are more important communication techniques to use. Somehow, though, it is the silent individual in a group or the reluctant communicator who seems to present the most difficulty.

Verbal Attending

Attentive silence is not always enough to encourage communication and, like just about everything else, can be overdone. There are several other ways to promote communication.[7] Responses like "Uh huh, "Mm, hmm," "Yes," or "I see what you mean,'' (if you really do, that is) can be used to convey interest and encourage the person to continue. You can also reflect by repeating a key word or phrase the person has used to focus on that aspect of the conversation; you can ignore the extraneous or irrelevant parts by not attending to them.

Interpretation

You need to listen for both information and feelings, that is, to pay attention to both the content and relationship aspects of the communication. Look for patterns and themes in what the person is saying. For example, a person may repeat a particular point over and over again. Try to put yourself in that person's shoes and find out how that person feels as the same situation can provoke different responses in different people. In other words, when you want to understand what a person is telling you, try to see it through that person's frame of reference rather than through your own.

Of course, you need to pay attention to the nonverbal message as well: the tone of voice, the body position, facial expression, and so on. Does the person seem depressed when slumped in a chair or rigid with pent-up anger? Are the hands shaking or voice quivering with emotion? Is the individual drained of energy or full of vigor and functioning well? Even poor grooming can be a sign of low energy level, although you need to take culture and individual style into consideration on this point and in interpretation of communication in general. Finally, look for congruence or the lack of it between the two aspects of the communication.

Attending done with ease, warmth, and real caring can be communicated in your tone of voice, body language, and words and will help you accomplish your goal of making the other person feel accepted, valued, and at ease talking with you. Once attending becomes a natural thing for you to do, it will be most effective. This last point is true for all the other ways to improve communication as well; genuineness will improve effectiveness. As Perls once said, ''Our bodies do not lie.''[8]

RESPONDING

Responding requires a more active kind of communication than attending. Responding is done to communicate a basic comprehension of what the other person is saying and to sustain the exchange.

Responding is an accurate rephrasing of the message you received from the other person.[9] This rephrasing is not just repeating a few selected words as is done in reflecting (a way to attend) but a brief reiteration of what's been said in your own words.

You can respond to the content of the message, to the feelings communicated in the message, or to both. Two examples of responding to content are:

''In other words, schoolwork has been your major source of difficulty.''

"You're saying that your team leader doesn't seem to appreciate your needs as an individual."

Two examples of responding to the feelings conveyed by the other person in verbal and nonverbal communication are:

"You're worried about the outcome of this dispute."

"You feel great when someone recognizes your contribution."

Notice that you can respond to good feelings as well as bad ones, something people often forget to do.

There are innumerable instances in a work situation where responding is appropriate. Here are some examples of responding to content:

"You're saying that Deborah does not record everything she does for a patient."

"In other words, the staff does not really understand what a nursing audit involves."

The following are some examples of responding to both feelings and contents:

"You're upset about forgetting Mrs. C.'s extra sitz bath."

"You feel good about helping the L. family find a place for Suzie."

"You feel torn by the need to get the paperwork done and the need to spend time visiting Mr. D."

Responses that include feelings as well as content are more complete, although in work situations a response with just content may be appropriate and either can be used alone.

Pitfalls in Responding

An important stumbling block to avoid in responding is the repetition of a single phrase over and over again, especially in the same exchange, until it loses its meaning and sounds mechanical, which defeats the purpose of responding. People who are just learning to use active listening often sound like prerecorded messages (and may feel like them as well) until they get used to it.

Another pitfall is the inappropriate use of the word "feel." After reading and hearing so much about the very real importance of emotions, people begin to adopt the "You feel. . ." or "I feel. . ." messages to all occasions, which leads to absurd statements such as "I feel Mrs. P. is developing a decubitus ulcer." The word "feel" is inappropriate because this statement is a diagnosis, a factual conclusion, not an expression of emotions. It would be appropriate to say, "Mrs. P. is developing a decubitus ulcer."

ENCOURAGING COMMUNICATION WITH OPEN-ENDED QUESTIONS

Attending and responding skills are helpful in encouraging a free flow of communication but sometimes more initiative from the leader is needed, particularly in beginning the exchange. Here, open-ended questions can be very useful. They may also be used to guide an exchange, to keep it going, or both.

An open-ended question is one that cannot be answered with a single word like "yes" or "no." A question may sound encouraging and yet not be really open-ended. For example:

> If you ask, "Do you want to talk about it?" and the person responds with, "No," the exchange is stopped cold and it will be harder than ever to get a discussion underway.

Asking a truly open-ended question like "What seems to be troubling you?" or asking the person to tell you more about something will be far more likely to get a productive exchange going. This applies to all kinds of situations. The following illustrates the difference between an open-ended question and one that only sounds open-ended:

NOT OPEN-ENDED	Do you like your new assignment?
OPEN-ENDED	Tell me, how do you feel about your new assignment?

The first question encourages only a short answer while the second question allows for a much freer response and sets up expectations for a longer exchange.

There are other ways to ask open-ended questions. You can ask the person or group to give examples of what they mean, to elaborate, to describe, or to tell you more about the subject under discussion. For example:

> If a coworker describes a relationship with another staff member as "poor," you can ask the coworker to tell you what it is about the relationship that makes it poor.

As you probably have noticed from this last example, these open-ended questions also serve to encourage the other person to give more thought to the subject and to develop a greater awareness of the complexities involved in a situation. When a problem arises, it is often important to seek elaboration and explanations such as "What do you mean by. . ." or even just "Tell me what happened," in order to encourage discussion and to increase understanding.

FOCUSING

A leader may need to use several other communication techniques in order to make the exchange most helpful for all concerned. The exchange may be vague and need more focus or it may be confusing and need clarification. When you do not understand what the problem is, you may need to do more exploration of the subject.

If you have had the experience of allowing others to ventilate their feelings without making any attempt to direct the flow of words, then you will know why there are times when you need to bring more focus into some exchanges. Some people repeat themselves endlessly or they ramble when they talk even when they are not upset; they bring in all kinds of extraneous details and explanations that lead the conversation in too many directions, a lot of them dead ends. This occurs even more frequently when people are upset or anxious for some reason.

There are several ways to bring focus to an interaction. You can focus on the most pressing problem, the main point of an exchange, who owns the problem, the dominant theme that runs through a person's rambling, or the aspect of a problem for which a solution can be found. A focus on feelings may be needed in some instances. For example:

> A discussion may be centering around the difficulties your staff expect to face in implementing a new procedure but you suspect that the main difficulty is related to the anxieties aroused by the change from a familiar routine. In order to deal with the feelings aroused by the change, you need to refocus the discussion. One way you could do this would be to say, "You've all indicated in one way or another that this new procedure is going to be difficult to do. How do you feel about this?"

Focusing helps to pull seemingly unconnected statements together and to direct attention to the most important or solvable problems, or both.

To focus on the main point, you can repeat key words or phrases as questions or use open-ended questions. For example:

> Erratic behavior?

> Can you tell me more about Delia's behavior, specifically here on the unit?

> You've been talking about several things that are on your mind. Which of these concerns you the most?

When dealing with a crisis situation, you may often find it helpful to focus on the part of the problem that can be solved. This would usually be done after allowing ventilation of feelings through active listening. For example, once an accident has occurred, a focus on minimizing its effects is more productive than a focus on placing blame. Sometimes, the difficulty lies in identifying who owns the problem. For example:

> Is Delia's behavior Delia's problem or is it José's problem because it irritates him so much? Or does the problem belong to you, the leader, because your team cannot function effectively with the constant friction between Delia and José?

As you can see, open-ended questions are useful in bringing some focus to a discussion as well as in getting it started. When a person or a group experiences a general dissatisfaction or feeling of vague anxiety, they can be assisted in bringing this feeling into focus with the use of open-ended questions.

CLARIFYING AND CHECKING OUT YOUR PERCEPTIONS

It is important to ask others to clarify what they are saying when you do not understand them. If you keep on nodding your head in agreement when you really don't know what they are talking about, it will be difficult to respond when they ask, "What do you think about this?" Pretending to understand when you really do not will undermine trust and discourage further exchanges.

If you get lost and cannot follow what the person is saying, then you can say:

> I lost you there.
> or
> I'm not sure what you mean.

You can also use the focusing kinds of open-ended questions to clarify. For example:

> When a coworker is upset and repeating over and over about being continually harassed by the administration, you could ask, "Can you give me an example of what you mean by 'harassment'?"

Checking out your perceptions of what the other person is saying is also a form of clarifying. Not only do you risk undermining trust when you fail to seek clarification, you also lose an opportunity to find out more about what is on the other person's mind and to check the accuracy of your perceptions. When your main purpose is to check out your perceptions rather than to reduce confusion, what you say will give more of an indication of what you understood the other person was saying. This usually includes a rephrasing in your own words. For example:

> Did you mean that Delia's gum chewing and joke-cracking irritates the patients?

> Are you saying that my observing your work upsets you?

PERSONALIZING

As the exchange progresses, you may find it necessary to pull together what has been said and add some meaning to it, a technique termed personalizing.[10] There are two purposes for doing this. The first is to facilitate increased self-awareness and exploration of the many human factors involved in any situation. The second purpose of the personalizing technique is to facilitate progress toward a clear identification of the problem that will lead to the exploration of alternative solutions, that is, problem-solving. Of course, not every exchange involves a problem that needs to be solved. However, for those that do require a solution, especially when emotions are high, personalizing helps to set the stage for it.

Personalizing does involve some interpretation, more than the preceding actions did in most cases. It involves a response to the individual that includes a summary of the situation, a description of the meaning it has to that person and the ways in which that person has been able to cope with it and has not been able to cope with it. It is really an extension of responding, the main difference being in the added meanings you are offering. Here are some examples of personalizing:

> You feel torn by the need to do your paperwork and to visit longer with Mr. D. because you cannot find the time to do both and yet believe both are important.

> Delia's behavior upsets you because it seems to make the patients irritable and therefore harder to keep them comfortable and satisfied with their care.

When you are not certain your interpretation is correct or if you want to avoid an "I know better than you do," posture, you can put your personalizing comments in the form of a question as when you were checking out your perceptions of what the other person was saying.

Not every exchange requires focusing and personalizing, even if there is a problem being discussed. People with insight into their situations, for example, are often able to make their own interpretations. In many instances, however, you will find that focusing and personalizing are a great help in increasing a person's self-awareness and understanding and in directing energies toward the identification of the problem that needs to be resolved.

GIVING INFORMATION

Once a problem or need has been identified, a lack of information is often found to be the culprit. A professional is frequently called on to share expertise and this sharing of knowledge is an expected part of the leader's role. A formal, organized form of information giving would be teaching. The following are two examples of situations in which information giving is appropriate:

> Patients frequently are not given adequate information about their problems, about procedures that are going to be done, or about regimens they are expected to follow at home.

> Staff members are often faced with a similar lack of information about work expectations, procedures, and so forth that creates unnecessary frustrations and difficulties.

Information-giving and advice are not the same thing. Brammer[11] distinguishes between what he calls appropriate and inappropriate kinds of advice. He thinks that advice is appropriate only if the final decision is left up to the person receiving it. It may also be appropriate in times of crisis when people cannot make a decision by themselves or in a relatively inconsequential decision where the outcome is not very important. Advice is not appropriate for major life course decisions such as whether to get married or divorced, whether to move or not, what career path to take, and so on. Any kind of advice giving has its disadvantages: the danger of fostering dependency, the possibility that your advice may be wrong for that individual, and, finally, the fact that most people won't follow it anyway.

SUPPORT

Although it is more a consequence rather than a technique of effective communication, a few words about support are appropriate here. Being a trustworthy, available listener is a tremendously effective way to give emotional support.

Any assistance in a time of crisis can be very supportive and, if not continued too long, will help the person get through the crisis intact and able to function without encouraging long-term dependence. Obtaining a babysitter, finding transportation, making that difficult telephone call, or finishing that impossible report form are all examples of concrete help you can offer a client or coworker when the individual is overloaded with distressing problems.

Reassurance, on the other hand, should only be given in small doses, if at all, because it is likely to seem as if you are minimizing the problem or encouraging dependency.[12] Reassuring phrases such as, "It will all work out" or "You'll be OK" can sound false to the person who is desperately worried about something. Agreeing with the other person's statements or plans and telling that person that others have had the same problems are actually forms of reassurance also and should be used in small doses.

When a very difficult or complex problem exists, these communication techniques are only the beginning of the intervention process and are used to increase readiness to negotiate and problem-solve. But they will still help you to identify the problem (especially the focusing and clarifying techniques) and will be useful throughout the relationship to keep the negotiation or problem-solving processes going.

SUMMARY

Attending, responding, encouraging, focusing, clarifying, personalizing, and informing are techniques you can use to establish open, productive relationships with others as individuals and in groups. These techniques not only encourage a free exchange of ideas and feelings, but also help the participants in the exchange increase their self-awareness, encourage personal growth, and facilitate problem-solving.

Confrontation Techniques

PURPOSES

There are times when people will not readily participate in free and open communications. This can happen for any number of reasons: conflicts arise, trust is limited, the problem-solving process gets bogged down, and so forth. As a leader, you need to deal with these situations. They are difficult to handle but there is a group of communication skills known as confrontation techniques[13] that will help you break up these all too common interpersonal log jams.

AVOIDING CONFRONTATION

The leader should move quickly to intervene when the progress toward a goal ceases. Avoidance of the problem impeding progress is usually unproductive because many problems grow larger and more serious if you avoid dealing with them. People often think to themselves, "If I leave it alone, maybe it will resolve itself." While this is sometimes true, more often minor disagreements become major conflicts when ignored and small misunderstandings become serious communication blocks when they are not clarified.

This is true in almost every area. Former Secretary of State, Henry Kissinger, noted for his negotiation skills, expressed the same idea this way: "Competing pressures tempt one to believe that an issue deferred is a problem avoided; more often it is a crisis invited."[14] Not only do problems usually get worse instead of better when ignored, delaying a confrontation also increases the likelihood that by the time you finally do it, you and the other party involved are so frustrated and angry that your effectiveness in carrying it out is reduced.

Another drawback to avoiding confrontation is that your silence in the face of a conflict can be interpreted as approval or at least acceptance of the status quo. If you fail to confront when situations call for it, you will have lost many an opportunity for open communication and growth. Behavior can be misinterpreted, stereotypes prevail, and misunderstandings continue unless you confront what is happening. The following story is an illustration of what can be lost if you fail to confront when this action is needed:

> A student in a community health nursing course visited a young mother (about 15 years old) every week to see how she and her infant were progressing. Every week the mother undressed the baby and every week the student did a complete physical assessment of the infant's condition. The student was going on another assignment and would no longer be visiting the young mother and informed her of this. The mother then asked if the student had found her care of the infant satisfactory. This question led to a more open discussion than had occurred before and some surprising discoveries.
>
> The young mother thought the student was checking the infant for signs of neglect and abuse because the student had been sent by a governmental agency, and the student had thought that the mother wanted the infant checked every week to see if the infant was all right. The mother feared that any negative evaluation from the student would result in the baby being taken away from her. The student had been aware of the fact that there was little trust between them but had failed to confront the problem until the client did so at this last meeting. What a loss for both of them that the misperception of each other's motives wasn't dealt with sooner.

Many writers have been critical of nurses' tendency to avoid confrontation. Nurses, they say, lack assertiveness and prefer to use the softer, more therapeutically oriented strategies in their attempts to resolve conflicts and bring about change. This tendency is attributed to a caring, humanitarian set of values and also to the habit of over-classifying people as "sick" and in need of help rather than as well and able to handle a confrontation.[15] The fact that most nurses are women who, in the past, have been taught traditional ideas of what is "ladylike" behavior is also blamed. This situation is changing rapidly for some nurses and gradually for others.

Your colleagues can handle an objective and appropriate confrontation. So can your employer. In fact, when you go too far in being helpful and protective of them, you wind up violating your own rights. The following is an example of how this can happen:

> Imagine that your employer has refused to consider your request for a salary increase and tells you how much the agency would like to give you a raise but cannot because of its terrible financial troubles. If you are prone to using the soft, unassertive approach, you could find yourself reassuring your employer that it's all right and you understand the problem. This is an inappropriate use of reassurance; you are trying to help your employer feel better when in fact by doing so, you will feel worse, or at least poorer. A more appropriate initial response would be to describe your accomplishments and your value to the organization.

Some people avoid confrontation because they fear retaliation. This fear is not always unreasonable; in fact it may be realistic in some instances. Bennis[16] provides an example of a situation where retaliation is a possibility:

> Samuel Goldwyn (the movie producer), a notorious martinet, called his top staff together after a particularly bad box-office flop and said, "Look, you guys, I want you to tell me exactly what's wrong with this operation and my leadership—even if it means losing your jobs."

If you are unfortunate enough to work for a "notorious martinet" you should consider retaliation a possibility. But in most cases, a confrontation well done is much more likely to improve your work situation, not remove you from it.

CONFRONTATION DEFINED

Confrontation is a direct approach to a problem or conflict, an act that challenges others, pulls them up short and directs them to reflect on their behavior and, as a result, change that behavior. People often don't realize how their behavior affects others until they are confronted with these effects. Walton[17] defines it as the "process in which the parties directly engage each other and focus on the conflict between them." Confrontation is not "telling someone off." Correctly done, it is not a hostile attack on another person.

Anyone in a group or organization can confront an individual or a whole group. In fact, the newest member of a group may be the one with the most objective view of the situation and can be the appropriate person to initiate a confrontation. One organization may confront another organization. For example, a state nurses' association may confront a hospital on employment issues or another professional organization on encroachment into nursing functions. The special logistics of this kind of organizational confrontation will be dealt with as a political strategy and as collective bargaining. Smaller groups can also confront each other, such as the nursing staff of one unit confronting the pharmacy over medication distribution problems or the dietary department about the adequacy of nutrition education for their patients. Aides may confront nurses, the medical staff may confront administration, and so on. These groups can confront each other as a whole or they can each designate representatives to confront and then negotiate with each other.

There are several confrontation strategies that differ in content, in method and, perhaps most important, in strength. We will begin with the most common, confrontation through information, and then look at several of the more useful variations of this basic type of confrontation.

CONFRONTATION THROUGH INFORMATION

Confrontation through information is one of several strategies suggested by Egan[18] and probably the most common confrontation technique. This kind of confrontation is frequently delivered as an "I" message, to use Gordon's[19] term. It is an honest, open, and direct communication of the way you are experiencing a situation. Its purpose is to foster openness in the relationship, especially to stimulate a reciprocal open response to you in order to improve the interpersonal relationship involved. Indirectly, it is a challenge to the other person. The following are some examples of confrontation through information:

> I was embarrassed that the lounge was dirty when our visitors came through today.
>
> I have been assigned the last minute tasks every day this week.
>
> I'm afraid that we're not going to get done on time.

Inappropriate Confrontations

Confrontation is a powerful form of communication that should be used with respect for its force.[17] *Do* confront—and do it with care for the other person or persons as human beings. But there are several *don'ts* that are important to keep in mind. First, do not make the confrontation message a put-down of the other person. Messages that begin with "you" instead of "I" tend to put all the blame on the other guy. For example:

> You didn't clean up the lounge after your break.
>
> You've been picking on me, giving me all the last minute tasks every day this week.
>
> You're running late again today.

These "you" messages usually provoke defensive responses such as:

If it's so important, why didn't *you* clean it up?

I couldn't help it.

No I'm not!

The fact that a message begins with "I" is not enough if a put-down or blaming message is hidden in the confrontation. For example, "I am really disappointed in you," is a put-down even though it looks like an "I" message. A little more subtle but still negative is, "I feel that you have been careless." You can be sure that these disguised blaming messages will be recognized for what they are by the person receiving them. As a rule, you want to put the emphasis on your feelings in these messages and to avoid criticism of the other person.

A second important don't is do not use confrontation to make blanket negative statements about the other person or group such as "You are so lazy," or "You never get your work done." It is also important to avoid psychoanalyzing, which is almost guaranteed to provoke a defensive response. Here are some examples of psychoanalyzing statements:

You have trouble relating to patients because you're always on an ego trip.

Your insecurity is at the root of all your problems here.

Your hostility is showing.

How would you feel if someone said those things to you? How would you react?

Direct challenges to shape up also provoke more defensive than honest attempts to improve. Some direct challenges are:

Why don't you pay more attention?

Pull yourself together.

When you look at the examples of inappropriate confrontations, you'll notice that they often contain a ready-made solution devised by the confronter. All the non-recommended forms of confrontation show more concern for the confronter than for the confronted and a lack of faith in the confronted person's or group's ability to make constructive decisions to change. Direct challenges are strong mesages, usually stronger than they need to be and are likely to stimulate a return challenge, which is not what you want.

Confrontations have a powerful impact. Because of this, another important consideration is that the importance of the contents of the message to the person or group receiving and responding to it can vary from person to person. A message could stir a painful memory or hit an Achilles heel (that is, a particularly vulnerable spot). For example, a joking comment to a colleague who forgot a meeting saying,

"You're getting so forgetful; it must be hardening of the arteries," might sound funny to a younger colleague but hurtful to an older colleague who is fighting mandatory retirement.

These inappropriate confrontations are often done in anger. Gordon[19] has some interesting comments about anger as an emotion. He believes that it is a secondary response following an earlier primary reaction of something like fright, embarrassment, or disappointment. For example, anger at a coworker's rough handling of a patient with multiple myeloma is the secondary result of your fear that the patient will be hurt. Or anger at a friend who reveals a confidence may be secondary to the embarrassment you feel. If this is true, then it is the primary reaction you should express in a confrontation, not the secondary anger that will probably have a blaming message attached to it.

This caution applies only to anger and negative feelings such as wanting to get revenge on someone. Ordinarily, you do not want to be hesitant or timid about expressing your feelings. If you are very disturbed about a particular situation, then say so rather than minimizing it so much that no one recognizes your concern. You can see that composing and sending "I" messages helps increase your self-awareness too.

All the examples given in this section are inappropriate kinds of confrontations for some very specific reasons. They are inappropriate either because they provoke defensive or angry responses, imply a lack of trust in others abilities to find their own solutions, reinforce feelings of inadequacy, or emphasize your needs at the expense of the other person or group. In other words, they are not constructive.

Responses to Confrontation

It is possible for a confrontation through information to be ignored. Usually this happens when you have understated your own feelings regarding the situation. If this does happen, Gordon[19] suggests telling the other person how you feel about being ignored—this usually gets through to the other person.

When you confront someone, be prepared to be confronted in return. This is far more likely to happen than being ignored. In fact, a whole lot of issues may arise as a result of a confrontation, issues that had not been confronted in the past and so were left to develop and grow more serious. This multiplication of issues is called issue proliferation and will be discussed further in this chapter in the section on confrontation meetings.

Frequent confrontations through information and the fostering of an open climate will help prevent issue proliferation from becoming an inevitable result of confrontation. When you are confronted in return, use your attending, responding, and other communication skills to clearly identify the problems that exist in the relationship between you and the other person or group you confronted. The return confrontation may be in the form of "you" messages and direct challenges so try to avoid the defensiveness that could turn the confrontation into an exchange of put-downs or into an argument.

Confrontation through information is the basic form of confrontation. All the considerations suggested above for the best use of confrontation through information hold true for the variations that follow.

CALLING THE OTHER'S GAME

Calling the other's game[18] is a confrontation strategy that can be adapted to many situations once you learn how to identify games. We all find ourselves getting caught up in "games" with other people such as "Let's keep talking about the weather and avoid the problems we face," or "I won't mention any of your shortcomings if you won't mention any of mine," or "If you yell, I'll yell louder," and many others. There is a whole series of these games given humorous titles in transactional analysis.[20, 21] People can get caught up and sometimes stuck in these games without realizing it.

Breaking Up A Game

The leader with a heightened consciousness of these games will be able to spot them and take action to break up the game. To do this, the effective leader makes an unexpected response that breaks up the game by refusing to play it. For example, social chatter or joking is sometimes used to avoid getting down to work or facing an unpleasant decision. The following demonstrates how the leader can call such a game:

SOCIAL CHATTER Staff 1: Did you hear that M got a new sports car?
Staff 2: No, where did you hear that?
Staff 1: Well, I was down in the cafeteria getting some coffee and Danish when. . . .
BREAKING UP THE GAME
Leader: Let's get started on that report.

While this game is a time waster, it is otherwise harmless. Some games can be far more destructive but they are still broken up by simply refusing to play them.

Karpman Triangle

There is a game that is peculiarly appealing to members of the helping professions called the Karpman Triangle.[22] Nurses are expert players of this game. There are three roles to choose from in the triangle. They are victim, persecutor, and rescuer, shown in Figure 4-1. Participants switch from one role to the other around the triangle to play the game. To break up the game, participants must refuse to play *any* of these roles and must instead give a nondefensive and nonhostile adult response.

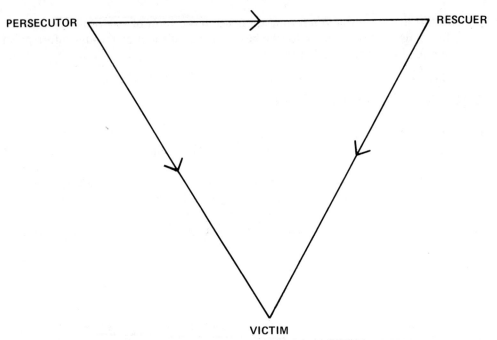

FIGURE 4-1. The Karpman triangle. A game in which players frequently switch roles. (From Karpman, SB: *Fairy Tales and Script Drama Analysis.* Transactional Analysis Bulletin [now TA Journal] 7:26 [April 1968] p39.)

To illustrate this, we can return to the brief example given earlier in this chapter about asking for a raise.

> Saying no to you makes your employer feel like a persecutor so your employer switches into the victim role by telling you of all the budgetary woes and saying that it is impossible to give you a raise. If you respond by telling your employer you understand the trouble, you've been sucked into the game in the rescuer role. Responding in a nondefensive, adult manner by describing your contributions to the organization is one way to avoid getting trapped in the game.

Nurses can get caught in this particular game with their patients or clients too. The following is a common example:

> Let's say you have a patient who has missed three important appointments in a row. When you visit the patient at home to find out what the problem is, she tells you she is really sorry but she has to babysit her sister's kids all day so she can't get out to the clinic. Your patient has moved into the victim role. You have several choices for a response, all common responses from caregivers:
>
> 1. You could scold her for missing the appointment and tell her not to miss the next one.

2. You could offer to babysit the children while she goes to the clinic.
3. You could ask her how she plans to solve her problem.

Which one of these would you choose?

1. If you chose the first one, you would have moved right into the persecutor role in response to her victim role, giving her a good excuse not to go to the clinic where those heartless people are who want her to leave her sister's babies alone or take them out with her in this cold weather.
2. If you chose the second, you would be rushing into the rescuer role and leave her expecting to have you babysit the next time she has to go to the clinic. If you do this, you have also lost an opportunity to help her problem-solve, a skill many people have not learned very well.
3. The third choice speaks to the responsible adult your patient is and gives her credit for being able to handle everyday problems herself or at least to make her own choices among the alternatives that you can help her come up with.

You can see that breaking up the game with a client is in keeping with the notion that clients should be treated as partners in their care and as responsible adults capable of varying amounts of self-care.

TAPE RECORDINGS

Videotapes and tape recordings are objective confrontations in which an individual or group can see themselves almost in the same way that others see and hear them. Tapes are a "clean" confrontation according to Egan[18] because they are not filtered through another person's perceptions of a situation.

The purpose of these recordings is to create a permanent record of performance that can be objectively analyzed to improve performance. So much goes on at one time in a group that you frequently see things on the videotape that you didn't even realize were happening in the midst of the interaction. Videotapes can be used to evaluate nurse-patient interactions and the correctness of technical procedures as well as interviews, staff conferences, and the like.

Tapes are especially useful in analyzing the effectiveness of a leader, the responses of a group to its leader and the responses of individual members to each other. Group members can see the roles they are playing within the group and their effect on others. On the tape, you can see how a number of people are responding simultaneously, which can be difficult to pick up during the actual group process. Tapes can also be used to illustrate different leadership approaches for educational purposes.

Knowing that they are being taped tends to increase self-consciousness in many people. Sometimes they concentrate so much on the tape that the other purposes of their actions are forgotten. Making the recorder unobtrusive helps to keep the focus on the other processes going as does the use of tapes only for self-improvement rather than for grading or job evaluation purposes. This does not apply to everyone. There are many "hams" who love to be on videotape and there is no need to persuade them or make them feel at ease.

One more point about using tapes. They are an excellent way to confront yourself and other people with an objective record of behavior, however, they should be used only with the knowledge and consent of those who are being recorded.

PROCESSING

This is another form of confrontation described by Egan.[18] Processing is a direct commentary on the group process. The degree of directness can vary. To illustrate this, let's say that you are working with a group of parents that is not making any progress at all and you want to get the group moving again:

> One way to do this is to stop the group interaction and ask the group to evaluate what has been happening within the group. In a more direct way, you can point out that the group seems to be getting nowhere and ask group members if they agree or why they think this is happening, or both. Most directly, you can point out the hidden agenda that is blocking the group's process and say, "None of you really wants a sex education program and that's why we're not getting anywhere."

This last very direct type of processing is getting close to being a direct challenge and may provoke more defensiveness than real progress. However, there will be times when this much directness is the only way to break up a real stalemate and, while you risk having people becoming defensive, you might also get a direct response in return such as:

> "You're right. We have been dragging our feet on this. Let's get going."

Changing Routines

An indirect way to confront a group or individual through processing is to change some aspect of their routine function. Both individuals and groups get into routines that they find hard to break. There are many ways in which you can alter the routine. Just rearranging the chairs in a circle so that no one can hide in the back can change group interaction (and indirectly confronts those who were hiding in the back). Did you ever wonder how a class would react if a professor began the lecture standing in the back of the room? You can also introduce new members into a group to change the dynamics. You can bring staff from other units or from other disciplines into meetings and conferences. Inviting patients and their families to a patient-centered conference makes it much harder to talk about the patient as a nonperson when the patient is sitting right there (although some caregivers manage to do so anyway, especially on rounds in a hospital). Any strategy that points out or changes the status quo will confront the individual or group with the way in which they have been behaving.

Pros and Cons of Processing

Rogers[23] says that he does not like to use the direct kind of processing because it makes the group too self-conscious, slows down its processes, and makes its members feel that they are being observed and analyzed, all of which destroy spontaneity. If comments are needed, it is best to have them come from the group, Rogers says. He tends to avoid probing into what's behind behavior (that is, interpreting or psychoanalyzing) because it can never be more than an educated guess in any circumstances.

There is some validity to Rogers' criticism. If direct processing is used too often the group process would almost inevitably become stilted and self-conscious. Also, if it is done too directly and the group is not ready for an indepth analysis, it could discourage openness, particularly when it involves interpretation. Because interpretive challenges tend to evoke defensiveness, they could result in reinforcing the old unproductive patterns.

Despite these limitations, processing has some real benefits. Rogers' groups generally had more time available to them to deal with a situation than the work groups that a nurse leader encounters every day. While open communication and increased group awareness are important goals for work groups too, you cannot always wait for the group to achieve them spontaneously. The less directive kind of processing strategy in which you verbalize your observations of group process without interpreting the reasons for the behavior can be very useful in stimulating group awareness and in getting the process going, both of which are part of the leader's role. In fact, you will probably find group members agreeing with you that they had also noticed what you are pointing out to them but had not acted upon it. Rogers' criticism of processing demonstrates a difference in viewpoint on how active and directive a role the leader should take, a question that comes up often in leadership

THE CONFRONTATION MEETING

The confrontation meeting[24] is a dynamic, powerful form of confrontation. A large number of people can be involved. The leader may confront the group or vice versa, or an individual member of the group may initiate the confrontation. It can be an effective way to bring about change if you can handle it. The confrontation can also happen spontaneously, usually as the result of an accumulation of unexpressed feelings or unresolved conflicts.

In a productive confrontation meeting, the group as a whole can quickly assess its own conflicts and within hours negotiate a plan for resolving them. A confrontation meeting (Fig. 4-2) usually has a high degree of open communication and mutual confrontation. The information exchanged during the meeting is current and subject to validation by those who are present. The release of unexpressed feelings and expression of unresolved conflicts means that emotions will be high, even intense. This sharing of feelings and information serves to increase the level of trust

FIGURE 4-2. A confrontation meeting.

NURSING LEADERSHIP

within the group when communications are kept on a mature, constructive level. During a confrontation, a skilled leader is needed to:

1. Make sure everybody is heard.
2. List or at least keep track of everything that is said. (This task can be delegated to a responsible individual.)
3. Guide the group toward using "I" messages and constructive criticism rather than direct challenges and blaming, destructive kinds of criticism.
4. Use attending and responding skills to keep communications flowing; focusing, clarifying, and sometimes informing skills to set the stage for negotiating a settlement of the differences.

During the confrontation meeting, intentions and procedures are clarified, issues needing attention are brought out, and plans are made for resolving the conflicts. Negotiation is usually needed to devise a plan agreeable to all and to bring the meeting to a satisfying conclusion.

Before reaching the negotiation stage, attitudes and feelings need to be explored. Participants describe how they see themselves and how they see the other party during a confrontation. This brings out the misunderstandings and misinterpretations of each other's behavior that have been operating and the stereotypes people have been using. Often at this point explanations of the real motivations behind the behavior and increased ability to see each other as individuals rather than as stereotyped roles can resolve the conflict that led to the confrontation.[25]

Issue Proliferation

A whole host of issues may arise during a confrontation meeting including numerous criticisms, negative feelings, and many other conflicts besides the one that sparked the confrontation meeting in the first place. This is called issue proliferation.[17] There are several reasons for this occurrence. It can be an attempt to save face on the part of the confronted person or group, it can be a counterattack, or it can be the result of the unleashing of pent-up emotions.

If these new issues that come out are symptoms of the basic conflict and fairly easy to resolve, you may want to deal with them first in order to interrupt the continuing build-up of negative feelings and to demonstrate the possibility of constructive action. If they are either not easily resolved or serving to sidetrack the group away from the basic conflict, you will find it more productive to lead the discussion back to the main issue. Sometimes, the proliferating issues will indicate that there is a far more basic conflict operating than the one that had begun the confrontation meeting. If this happens, the more basic conflict should become the major focus of the discussion and of the negotiations that follow.

Tension Control

An increase in tensions usually accompanies issue proliferation. When this happens, you will find it necessary to set some limits in order to reduce and control the tension. Walton compares this to the use of boxing gloves in a fight: it softens the blows.[26] Openness shoud be encouraged; power plays should be discouraged. Putting all the blame on one person should not be allowed; destructive criticism and name calling should also not be allowed. Allow only constructive criticism and suggestions for improvement that are both specific and concrete ways to improve whatever is criticized.

A moderate level of tension sustains the confrontation although too much will increase the hostilities and may become intolerable to some people. Humor is an excellent tension reliever. Occasionally, a cooling-off period or pre-meetings with individuals can be used to reduce tensions if they are severe but they should not be used to avoid confrontation.

Listing the issues that are in conflict helps to keep the confrontation in focus and under control. This can be followed by asking for alternative solutions, which usually succeeds in creating a more cooperative atmosphere. However, you do not want to cut short the discussion of the problems by doing this too soon. Negotiation is usually needed to devise a plan agreeable to all and to bring the meeting to a satisfying conclusion.

A confrontation meeting is an efficient, effective way for you to determine the sources and extent of a conflict and to come up with ways to resolve the problems involved. If you plan such a meeting, it is essential to approach it with a willingness to be confronted as well as to confront. to handle the intense feelings, to listen, to change yourself as well as others, and, perhaps more important in the long run, to follow up on the resulting plans made. Failure to follow through on the plans made will negate the entire process, close off communication again (probably more than before) and reduce trust dramatically. But if you are prepared to do all these things, a group of people can accomplish more in one intensive confrontation meeting than they ordinarily would do in months otherwise.

If you fail to confront when the situation calls for it, you will have lost many an opportunity for communication and growth. A leader confronts both individuals and groups in order to remove communication blocks, solve problems, and resolve conflicts. Once a problem has been successfully confronted by those involved, negotiation is the next step in the communication process.

SUMMARY

The different types of confrontations, confrontation through information, calling the other's game, taped recordings, processing, and confrontation meetings, are appropriate for various kinds of conflicts and communication blockages. When embarking upon a confrontation, you need to evaluate the strength of the confrontation in terms of the need for confrontation, quality of your relationship with the person or group and the psychologic state of the confronted individual or group of people. You also need to be aware of your motives for confronting: getting back at the other person is not an acceptable motive for the leader but resolving conflicts, improving relationships, and furthering individual and group growth are valid reasons to confront. Finally, you need to be aware of your individual capabilities for carrying out a confrontation and the subsequent negotiation.

Negotiation

Negotiation is a give-and-take between individuals or groups during which the parties involved try to come up with a resolution of their problems that is acceptable to all concerned. Negotiation is needed to resolve complex problems, especially conflicts, once they have been adequately identified and explored. Much more has been written about facilitating open communication and confronting problems than about negotiation, almost as if it could be assumed that once you have an agreement with the other person or group on what the problem is, you will also agree on the solution. Such an assumption is false.

A lot of questions can arise during the negotiation. Should you compromise? If you're willing to concede something should you do it immediately or wait until the negotiations get bogged down? Should you start out tough or try to sound reasonable? Who wins? Most of the literature concerns union-management relations but negotiation can be necessary in any interpersonal relationship and will be discussed in this more general sense of resolving interpersonal conflicts here.

SETTING THE STAGE

There are several conditions that set the stage for negotiation.[27] First, of course, there must be a recognized conflict of interest or incompatibility between the people or groups involved. Those involved in the negotiation must be prepared (usually by using some form of confrontation) to enter into the exchange of offers and counter-offers that constitute the negotiation process.

Another condition that is often overlooked is that the relationship must be voluntary. This means that the people involved must want the relationship to continue but have the option to withdraw from the relationship. In fact, it is the existence of this option to withdraw that motivates both sides to seek a resolution that will allow the relationship to continue. In an employment relationship, for example, as an employee you have the option (however reluctantly you might exercise it) to quit and your employer has the option (again however reluctantly) to fire you.

Win-Win Not Win-Lose

Negotiations should end in an agreement that satisfies everyone involved. Negotiation should be a win-win proposition, not win-lose. Ideally, both sides should feel as if they had won; neither should feel as if they had lost or even had to compromise something important to them. But realistically, some negotiations will turn out to be win-lose situations in which at least one party has to compromise. This usually happens when the distribution of power is unequal. Telbert King, an expert union negotiator, recommends that you always try hard not to compromise your fundamental position in any negotiation.[28]

Identify Key Issues

The key issues must be identified at the beginning of the negotiation. These are the issues that are of primary concern to the people involved in the negotiation. You need to find out as much as possible about the other person's or group's position on the key issues during the confrontation and the discussions that follow. You also need to get at those underlying emotional issues that may be disguised as disagreements over policies. Your knowledge of human motivation and behavior is very useful in doing this.

The key issues may be divided into two categories: emotional issues and substantive issues. *Emotional issues* may revolve around different kinds of negative feelings such as fear of rejection, anxiety, or personal need deprivation. *Substantive issues* are those concerned with such things as policies, rules and regulations, differing concepts of roles, role invasion, salary, and other questions about the work being done and the way it is organized.[29] Any situation that has created enough conflict to require negotiation usually has a mixture of both the emotional and substantive issues. Actually, considering the holistic nature of human beings, both cognitive and affective needs will always be operating at any given time. But separating the issues into emotional and substantive helps you to identify all the major issues and identify which is primary in a given situation.

THE OPENING MOVE

The opening move in a negotiation is considered a decisive point by most negotiators because it sets the climate or tone for the rest of the negotiation. "Extreme but not ridiculous," seems to be the best description of the general rule for making your opening move. In other words, you should begin the negotiation phase by informing the other person or group of the full extent, unmodified at all, of what it is that you want. Here is an example:

> Let's say that you are negotiating for a new position. If you think $25,000 is a reasonable beginning salary but really want $29,000, then begin the negotiations by asking for the upper limit of your expectations, which in this instance is $29,000. If you begin by asking for $25,000, you really have very little chance of getting $29,000 and in the negotiating you are likely to come down a little in your demands.

Beginning wth the upper limit of your wishes makes you more likely to get what you think is reasonable. Do not worry too much about seeming unreasonable—you will have an opportunity to demonstrate your reasonableness later in the negotiation. To reiterate, avoid the absurd demand, but inform the other party of the upper limit of what you want from the negotiation in the crucial opening move.

It is far harder to escalate your demands later than to moderate them. Moderating your demands in a later move makes you seem more cooperative. Also, the extreme (but within reason) opening move sets the tone of the negotiation. It allows you room to negotiate without having to compromise your needs and gives you time and space within which to move and to find out more about the other person's or group's preferences and intentions. It also communicates that you will not allow yourself to be exploited, which may be even more important. It is an assertive position that has proved to be the most effective way to begin negotiations. At least one research study indicated that it is by far the most influential factor deciding the outcome of negotiations. The extreme opening move followed by gradual concessions results in far more satisfaction with the outcome than a moderate stance held firmly.[30]

The recommended pattern for a negotiation, then, is a tough opening move followed by willingness to make some concession but, as Telbert King advised, not to give in on the basic needs that led you into the negotiation process in the first place. The effect of a strong opening move in collective bargaining was tested in the experiment described in Research Example 4-1.

CONTINUING THE NEGOTIATION PROCESS

Following the opening moves from both sides, the rest of the negotiation is a series of offers, counteroffers, and elaborations of each side's position until an agreement is reached. Too many concessions made too quickly will weaken your ability to get any concessions from the other side. Since negotiations proceed most effectively under conditions of relatively equal power, making concessions too quickly would be giving too much of your power to the other side. It is more effective to pace your concessions in order to appear cooperative but firm.

As the negotiation process proceeds, each side is trying to do several things. Each side will still be seeking to find out the real preferences of the other side. They will also be attempting to communicate more clearly their own positions. Most important, each side will be trying to influence the outcome of the negotiation. In order to show how events lead up to this point and then proceed to a series of offers, counteroffers, and elaborations, an example of a common staffing problem will be used:

> A group of staff nurses has confronted their head nurse because they are dissatisfied with the organization of nursing care on their unit. As a result of their confrontation meeting with the head nurse, the group concludes that the main conflict is over the way in which each nurse is assigned a different set of patients daily. The result of this assignment procedure is that continuity of care on the unit is minimal; the satisfactions that result from continuity have been drastically reduced; the staff nurses feel that they have no autonomy; and the head nurse feels that the staff has been uncooperative.
>
> In their opening move, the staff nurses declare that they should be allowed to choose their own patients and be assigned the same patients every day. The head nurse responds that this is impossible. Suppose some patients were not chosen? How will they provide for continuity on their days off?

Research Example 4-1. A Simulated Negotiation

Is a tough initial stance more effective than a soft one in the opening move of a negotiation? What effect does mediation or arbitration have on the course and outcome of negotiations?

A simulated collective bargaining game was used by Bigoness[31] to compare the effects of taking a hard or soft initial position and the effects of anticipating mediation, voluntary arbitration, or compulsory arbitration on a negotiation. In order to provide some incentive to bargain seriously, game players were paid on the basis of their success in bargaining for wages, fringe benefits, and cost of living increases.

Game players were divided into pairs, one of the pair represented management, the other represented the union. Each was instructed to take a hard or soft initial position. For example, a soft management position was to offer a 6¢ increase while the tough position was to offer a 2¢ increase. On the other side, the soft union position was to demand 10¢ more and the tough position was an opening demand for a 20¢ increase. Pairs of players who were assigned to mediation or arbitration were told to accept a 12¢ increase for either if they had not reached an agreement on their own after 15 minutes of play.

When analyzed, the results showed that the total amount eventually conceded by management was significantly less under a tough initial stance than under a soft one. The difference was not significant for the union side. However, less issues were left unresolved at the end of the game when management began with a soft stance.

The least number of issues were left unresolved when straight bargaining without mediation or arbitration was done. Compulsory arbitration left fewer issues unresolved than mediation or voluntary arbitration. Mediation was not usually successful. The researcher found that the players were most likely to reach a successful agreement when they could not anticipate having any outside assistance. Straight bargaining was the most successful when management took a tough initial stance but arbitration was more effective when a soft stance was taken. Parties who entered into negotiations with less distance between their initial positions were most successful in reaching an agreement. It was concluded that the threat of outside intervention may facilitate agreement under low-conflict conditions but may be detrimental under high-conflict conditions.

Then elaborations of positions follow:

> The head nurse must assure that the patients receive the best nursing care possible and is responsible for the care given to all patients. The staff nurses agree but point out that the present system is not doing this well.

At this point, if a competitive or hostile atmosphere prevails, both sides can become entrenched in their positions. Both sides can refuse to budge and the negotiations would then be likely to be concluded with a power play from either side:

> The head nurse could declare the staff nurses' plan unworkable, assert authority, and insist that they continue with the old assignment method. The staff nurses, on the other hand, can refuse to work until their proposal is accepted.

However, if a cooperative mood prevails, either side can suggest a workable alternative:

> Either the head nurse or a staff nurse can suggest that they find a workable way to provide better continuity of care and increased satisfaction for the staff while ensuring quality care for all patients over the whole week. The group can then proceed with suggestions from both sides and further elaborations of what exactly each one wants and why certain conditions are particularly important to them.
>
> For instance, a set of criteria to be used by the head nurse in making patient assignments could be agreed upon by the whole group so that it would satisfy everyone (including the patients). The head nurse would retain authority to assign staff and gain by increasing continuity and staff cooperativeness. The staff would gain increased continuity and satisfaction in their work as well as from having had input into the way they are assigned.

A poor compromise leads to one or both sides feeling they have lost in the negotiation. A good agreement results when both sides feel they have gained something important to them and has the added benefit of leading to increased cooperation in the future.

STRATEGIES TO INFLUENCE THE PROCESS

There are a number of factors that will influence the negotiation process and outcome, some of which you can use to your benefit[31] in a negotiation if you are familiar with them.

Cooperation and Concessions

The majority of the research studies done on the subject indicate that a cooperative orientation will result in more satisfactory outcomes than a competitive orientation. It would seem, then, that it is worth the effort to try to establish a cooperative climate and to encourage cooperative efforts. This does not mean that you should make a lot of concessions or compromises.

Change Strategies

There are several other ways you can influence the other side. You may notice as you read that each one is a form of change strategy and that some are power tactics.

The first of these strategies to influence the negotiation process is by *emphasizing the similarity* between your demands and theirs, pointing out that you really want the same thing or have the same need (as occurred in the example of the staff nurses above) or that you have a common enemy. The latter is a popular political strategy, by the way. You can also *supply information* that supports your proposal as the head nurse in the example did by pointing out the need to account for days off in making patient assignments.

Appeals to fair play are often persuasive. For example, the head nurse in the example could point out the responsibility they all had to provide quality care to every patient, not just those selected by individual staff members, while the staff nurses could point out that an arbitrary method of making assignments does not divide the work fairly.

Rewards

Promising some kind of reward is another way to influence the outcome. This can be used occasionally, depending, of course, on your ability to actually provide one. In the example given, neither side had much capability for providing tangible rewards. But the head nurse could write favorable evaluations or grant time off and the staff nurses could make the work climate more agreeable when they are satisfied with the work assignments. Both could provide general satisfaction for each other from a job well done but this is really an outcome of the process, not a specific reward that one side could promise the other.

If overdone, promises can make you seem too anxious to concede. They can seem like bribes in which case the other side may begin to demand bribes in all subsequent negotiations. Used sparingly, promises can increase the cooperative climate of the negotiation. If they are used too much or too often, they can weaken your position.

Threats

Threats do just the opposite of rewards: they increase the competitive climate of the negotiating process. Also, if the threat is too small, it can be seen as an insult. If it is too large, the threat will increase hostility to the point where effective negotiation is not possible. To return once more to the example given, the head nurse could have threatened to fire the nurses and the nurses could have threatened to walk off the job, either of which would have increased the tensions tremendously.

Even if it is left unspoken, both sides are aware that the other has these ultimate weapons, such as the ability to quit or fire. Any statements regarding this kind of ultimate weapon are going to be perceived as threats. When the problem is solvable by other means, the threat is better left unstated. Threats are out of place in a cooperative, effective negotiation process.

There will be some occasions when a person or group refuses to enter into cooperative negotiations despite your confrontations and attempts to influence the negotiation process. If this happens, you have two choices: you can concede or you can use the more powerful political strategies that will be discussed in Chapter 9.

This chapter on communication skills has emphasized the interpersonal aspects of working with people: how to encourage them to communicate more clearly and openly, how to remove blocks to open communication in order to improve the effectiveness of working relationships and how to deal with interpersonal conflicts all the way through the confrontation and negotiation phases. Each of these serves to create and sustain cooperative working relationships, one of the major goals of leadership. You may notice at times later in this book that the use of good communication skills will be assumed in order to concentrate on other processes involved in solving leadership problems. In real life, however, the effective leader never stops using good communication skills.

SUMMARY

Negotiation is a give-and-take between individuals or groups aimed at coming up with a solution that is acceptable to everyone involved. The opening move is considered to be a crucial point in the negotiation and should be used as an opportunity to inform the other party of the upper limits of your demands. This is then followed by a series of offers, counteroffers and elaborations of each side's positions. A cooperative atmosphere, emphasizing the similarity of each side's demands, supplying information, and appealing to fair play positively influence the negotiation process. Threats and competitiveness generally have a negative influence.

References

1. EGAN, G: *Interpersonal Living.* Brooks/Cole, Monterey, California, 1976, p 92.

2. WATZLAWICK, P, BEAVIN, JH, AND JACKSON, DD: *Pragmatics of Human Communication.* WW Norton, New York, 1967, p 52.

3. LIFTON, WM: *Groups: Facilitating Individual Growth and Societal Change.* John Wiley & Sons, New York, 1972, p 50.

4. MEHRABIAN, A: *Silent Messages.* Wadsworth, New York, 1971.

5. CARKHUFF, RR, PIERCE, RM, AND CANNON, JR: *The Art of Helping.* Human Resources Development Press, Amherst, Massachusetts, 1977, p 40.

6. EGAN, op cit, p 97.

7. BRAMMER, LM: *The Helping Relationship: Process and Skills,* ed 2. Prentice-Hall, Englewood Cliffs, New Jersey, 1979, p 67.

8. BRAMMER, op cit, p 166.

9. CARKHUFF et al, op cit, p 69.

10. CARKHUFF et al, op cit, p 110.

11. BRAMMER, op cit, p 95.

12. BRAMMER, op cit, p 105.

13. TAPPEN, RM: *Strategies for dealing with conflict: Using confrontation.* Journal of Nursing Education 17:5 (May 1978) p 47.

14. KISSINGER, H: *Crisis and Confrontation.* Time (October 15, 1979), p 82. (Excerpted from his book *White House Years.* Little, Brown & Company, Boston, 1979.)

15. SMOYAK, SA: *The confrontation process.* Am J Nurs 74:9 (September 1974) p 1632.

16. BENNIS, WG: *Post-bureacratic leadership.* In LASSEY, WP AND FERNANDEZ, RR (EDS): *Leadership and Social Change.* University Associates, La Jolla, California, 1976, p 186.

17. WALTON, RF: *Interpersonal Peacemaking: Confrontation and Third-Party Consultation*. Addison-Wesley, Reading, Massachusetts, 1969, p 84.

18. EGAN, G: *Face to Face: The Small Group Experience and Interpersonal Growth*. Brooks/Cole, Monterey, California, 1973, p 107.

19. GORDON, T: *Parent Effectiveness Training*. New American Library, New York, 1970, p 125.

20. BERNE, E: *Games People Play*. Grove Press, New York, 1964.

21. BERNE, E: *What Do You Say After You Say Hello?* Grove Press, New York, 1972.

22. KARPMAN, SB: *Fairy Tales and Script Drama Analysis*. Transactional Analysis Bulletin 7:26 (April 1968) p 39.

23. ROGERS, CR: *Carl Rogers on Encounter Groups*. Harper & Row, New York, 1970, p 57.

24. BECKHARD, R: *The Confrontation Meeting*. In BENNIS, WG, BENNE, KD, AND CHIN, R (EDS): *Dynamics of Planned Change,* ed 2. Holt, Rinehart & Winston, New York, 1969, p 478.

25. FILLEY, AC: *Interpersonal Conflict Resolution*. Scott Foresman & Co, Glenview, Illinois, 1975, p 79.

26. WALTON, op cit, p 90.

27. RUBIN, JZ AND BROWN, BR: *The Social Psychology of Bargaining and Negotiation*. Academic Press, New York, 1975, p 2.

28. Personal Communication. TELBERT KING, 1982.

29. WALTON, op cit, p 73.

30. RUBIN, op cit, p 267.

31. BIGONESS, W: *The impact of initial bargaining position and alternative modes of third party intervention in resolving bargaining impasses*. In KATZ, D, KAHN, RL, AND ADAMS, JS (EDS): *The Study of Organizations*. Jossey-Bass, San Francisco, 1980. (*Reprinted from Organizational Behavior and Human Performance*. 17:1976, 185.)

32. RUBIN, op cit, p 198.

Chapter *5*

Decision-Making Skills

Problem-Solving

The problem-solving process is simply a series of steps designed to help you organize your thoughts in order to come up with the best possible solution to a problem (Fig. 5-1). It is a deliberate, thoughtful way to deal with a situation that is creating some kind of difficulty for which there is no ready-made solution. Instead of reacting to a problem without thinking, problem-solvers try to first sort out the complexities of the situation and then to bring some kind of thought-out planning and organization to their actions.[1-2]

PURPOSES

Problem-solving itself does not supply the answer. It is only the *process* through which you arrive at an answer. Its major usefulness is in providing some guidelines or structure for you when you are faced with difficulty. Problem-solving is also the basis of the nursing process, which is probably quite familiar to you. If you look at the comparison between the nursing process and the problem-solving process in Figure 5-1, you will see that problem-solving is simply the more general application of the same familiar steps. The term nursing process refers to the use of these steps in relation to a patient, client, or group that requires specific nursing intervention while problem-solving refers to any kind of problem, whether it's related to your patients, coworkers, or to repairing your car.

As you read the steps in problem-solving you may have noticed that they are also used in crisis intervention. The deliberateness of the process can help the

	I	II	III	IV	V
PROBLEM—SOLVING	Collect Data	Define Problem	Select Strategies	Take Action	Evaluate Results
NURSING PROCESS	Assessment	Diagnosis	Plan	Implementation	Evaluation

FIGURE 5-1. Comparisons of the problem-solving and nursing processes.

person or group undergoing a crisis to bring some order to what seems like an uncontrollable situation. By listing everything that was wrong, then trying to formulate a statement summarizing the problem, and then listing every possible alternative solution, the crisis begins to seem more manageable and less overwhelming. By the time a person in crisis reaches the listing of solutions, that person will begin to feel at least partially in control of the situation again and able to respond more constructively.

Use of the problem-solving process can have a calming effect. "Let's problem-solve," is very often a useful response from the leader when a person or group is angry, upset, or confused about how to handle a problem. You can help a client problem-solve, you can lead a group through the process, and you can problem-solve for yourself.

A common source of stress in a work situation is used to illustrate how to use each of the steps in the problem-solving process:

> Imagine that you find yourself in the following stressful situation at work. Several incidents in the past two weeks have given you the impression that your supervisor is unhappy with your work. Because you're a new employee and have heard fellow nurses describe past incidents saying "You haven't been here long enough to see how fast the heads roll," you're afraid you may be the next to be fired.

In such a situation, the most difficult thing to do may be to remember to problem-solve. It may seem that the problem-solving would be too slow when quick action is required to save your job, but quick action without thought sometimes has worse consequences than no action. What is needed is action that is both quick and deliberate. This is one reason why a leader or facilitator is so valuable in getting people to begin problem-solving in a high anxiety situation. We will work through this stressful situation as we proceed with the discussion of problem-solving.

STEP 1. ASSESSMENT: COLLECT DATA

List as much data as you can. You may not have all you need to complete the process, but can and should seek more as you proceed through the process. If your data at this point are unreliable or too incomplete to define the problem, you will have to get more before proceeding. Sometimes you can continue through the problem-solving process and include getting more data as one of your selected strategies for resolving the problem. For example, the data list for the stressful work problem could include:

The supervisor frowns at my charts.

The supervisor does not make eye contact with me.

Other nurses are given special assignments, I have not been.

A coworker overheard that I was "being observed," and told me.

I have not been evaluated since I began this new job.

No one has told me that I am doing a good job. (You should also note that no one told you the opposite either).

I believe I am functioning adequately but feel anxious about the extent to which my performance is seen as satisfactory by the supervisor.

It is also important to put the data list in as objective a form as possible. You can do this by listing observed behavior instead of your interpretation of that behavior. For example, one of the incidents in the imaginary job problem that led you to believe your work was considered unsatisfactory was that your supervisor frowned when checking the charts of your patients. The following statements illustrate the difference between an interpretive and objective data listing:

INTERPRETIVE   The supervisor does not like the way I chart.
OBJECTIVE   The supervisor frowned when reading my patients' charts.

STEP 2. DIAGNOSIS: DEFINE THE PROBLEM

Once you have collected a reasonably adequate amount of data, you need to analyze it. Look especially for patterns in the data as well as for clues to the underlying dynamics of the situation. Then prepare a summarizing statement of the situation in which you define the problem as specifically and objectively as possible.

This summary (or diagnosis of the problem) should not include the solution to the problem. The differences between the two statements are illustrated below:

SOLUTION STATEMENT (Premature)   Patient J. needs more therapy.
PROBLEM STATEMENT (Appropriate)   Patient J. is still withdrawn.

Jumping to the solution is a trap many people fall into. It keeps you from exploring new avenues and from selecting the very best one or combination of the available alternatives.

EXAMPLE. To return to the stressful work situation, your data so far, although stated objectively, are still vague. But there is evidence of several patterns running through the data. The first pattern is a general sense of your being concerned about your position. There are also clues that point to some kind of dissatisfaction from your supervisor. The second pattern is a vagueness in the data. Almost all the information is indirect and open to different interpretations. From this analysis, the problems may be defined as follows:

1. Possible supervisor dissatisfaction with my work. Insufficient data to confirm or deny this possibility.

2. Feeling of concern related to my impression that the supervisor may be dissatisfied and to lack of evaluative feedback.

STEP 3. PLAN: SELECT STRATEGIES

When you first make the list of possible strategies, write down every appropriate action you can think of. Do not discard any of these strategies irrevocably until you've considered *all* the possibilities. This is a form of brainstorming (a term used to describe the approach of making every possible suggestion whether wild, weird, or brilliant without judging how good they are until the brainstorming is over).

After listing all the possible actions, go through the list and select the most effective and appropriate strategies for the situation. Effective means the ones most likely to work. Your leadership skills and experience will help you make this decision. Appropriate means the ones that best fit the particular situation. For example:

A strike could solve a disagreement with administration over where nurses can park their cars, but it is too strong a measure, while a memo, although also appropriate, is too weak, that is, not effective.

It would be inappropriate to tear down defenses a colleague needs in the midst of a crisis—there is a better time to confront someone with their use of defense mechanisms.

These are obvious examples; more subtle distinctions usually need to be made in real life.

EXAMPLE. Here is a list of possible strategies to resolve the stressful work situation:

1. Resign before I'm fired.
2. Demand an evaluation as my right.
3. Ignore the problem; it might go away.
4. Transfer to another unit.
5. Try to improve my performance.
6. Compliment my supervisor so my supervisor will like me.
7. Ask my coworker what was meant by saying I was "being observed."
8. Seek feedback from coworkers on my performance.
9. Request an evaluation from my supervisor.

After comparing the list you need to analyze the potential effectiveness and appropriateness of each strategy:

1. Resigning is too drastic a move at this time.
2. Demanding an evaluation is also too strong because no one has refused yet.

3. Ignoring the problem is ineffective because it will neither reduce your anxiety nor tell you where or what the problem is.

4. A transfer is a milder form of withdrawal from the problem but you will still not learn as much about yourself or others if you do not explore the problem before requesting a transfer. Because you do not know yet why this problem has occurred, you would not have learned how to handle it if it happened again.

5. Trying to improve your performance would probably not solve the problem at this point because you do not know exactly how it needs to be improved. This strategy could be effective later if you determine from further data collecting that your performance was not yet satisfactory. A self-evaluation might provide some reassurance and would also prepare you for a formal evaluation.

6. Complimenting the supervisor might help but if it is too obvious it may alienate your supervisor or your coworkers and it will not resolve your anxiety. Flattery is an inappropriate strategy.

7. Since part of the defined problem was insufficient data, talking to your coworker, seeking feedback, and requesting an evaluation from your supervisor can all help fill this need. An evaluation can take some time so talking with coworkers and requesting feedback from your supervisor can provide you with more immediate information and perhaps reduce your anxiety level, another part of the defined problem, enough so that you can function well in the meantime.

In this example, a combination of strategies looks like it will be most effective.

STEP 4. IMPLEMENTATION: TAKE ACTION

Now you are ready to act. You have selected the strategies that in your judgment are most likely to be effective and appropriate for resolving the problem. As you put your plan into action, the responses you get will tell you whether to proceed or to go back and think through the process again. The results can be surprising.

EXAMPLE. Gathering more data is a common strategy and one that is needed in this work situation. In the example, you planned to get more information and evaluation feedback from your coworkers, to do a self-evaluation, and then to ask your supervisor for an evaluation.

Although you can't be certain that the supervisor will see it the same way, you conclude from your self-evaluation that you have done well the last three months. A list of your strengths will also be a good selling point during the formal evaluation process.

The next day when you go to work, you talk to some coworkers and find out that they think you've been "making waves." They point out that you've been adding to the patient problem lists in the charts and only physicians do that here. You've also been consulting with other departments about your patients' problems, which has traditionally been the team leader's role. Your coworkers suggest that you keep the team leader better informed about your activities but indicate they approve of your patient advocacy.

Your request for more feedback from the supervisor results in some clarification of what you thought was happening. The supervisor frowns at your charting because your handwriting is so small the supervisor can't read it. You have not been given a special assignment because you're still new, but so far you are performing well. A formal evaluation is usually done after six months but the supervisor agrees to prepare an interim report and share it with you next week. You feel relieved, promise to write more legibly, and decide to tell the supervisor that you are ready to take on special assignments along with the rest of your colleagues.

The formal evaluation confirmed that you are doing above average work. Your list of strengths not only gave you confidence, but were also added to the evaluation form by the supervisor.

STEP 5. EVALUATION: EVALUATE RESULTS

Although it is listed as the last step, you cannot wait until you are all done to begin evaluating the results. At each step you need to critically analyze the data you are collecting or evaluate the responses you are getting, or both. Thinking about what you are doing and what results you are getting should be a continuous process so that you can revise your plan where needed as you go along. The evaluation can be subjective as well as objective, including not only the measurable results but also your feeling of accomplishment and satisfaction from having resolved the problem successfully. Your evaluation should also provide clues for future action. For example:

Will you proceed the same way next time?
Did you find a better way?
What did you learn from this experience?

EXAMPLE.   To return to the experience with the supervisor, one more time:

Your original diagnosis was an inaccurate but adequate guide to action because you tried to avoid interpreting the data and kept an open mind despite some anxiety. The selection of strategies was correct. If you had resigned or transferred to another unit, you would probably have heard how satisfied the supervisor was with your work when you left the unit. If you had ignored the problem, your anxiety might well have eventually interfered with your performance. It turns out that while there is still plenty you can learn about your work, you are doing well, and can feel satisfied with both your performance and your evaluation.

In the future, you will ask people right away to explain what they mean when they use a vague term like "being observed," instead of worrying about it. You will also confront a problem sooner but feel that you used this strategy quite skillfully this time.

SUMMARY

The problem-solving process is a more general version of the nursing process. It serves as a guide to help you organize data and find the best solution to a problem. The steps in the process are collect data, define the problem, select strategies, take action, and evaluate results.

Critical Thinking

PURPOSE

Critical thinking is an attitude and an approach; it is a willingness to give fair consideration to every idea but to accept an idea only after you have thought about it. It is an inquiring way of looking at the world.

The purpose of this section is to assist you in the development of this spirit of open-mindedness. A leader cannot be dogmatic. A person with a closed mind, sometimes described as having a "mind like a steel trap," misses many opportunities for positive growth by rejecting all new ideas. On the other hand, a person who is gullible, that is, open to anything offered, accepts the useless along with the useful idea. You could compare this gullible type to an old-fashioned grain sifter that keeps the chaff and lets the wheat (the good part) through.

Leaders need to have what could be called semi-permeable minds when accepting new ideas: open to possibility, not to certainty. In this spirit, leaders ask, "Why?" when no one else does. Leaders also ask, "Why not?" when everyone else fails to see a possibility.

Complex Judgments

You may be asking yourself, "What has this to do with being a nurse?" Like other professionals, nurses make many decisions and judgments for which there are no simple answers. Nurses deal with complex human beings and work in or with some very complex systems. Neither are simple or completely predictable. The uniqueness of each person and of each interaction with people demands a newly formulated response.

Selective Attention

A second reason why critical thinking is important to professionals is the vast number of messages directed at them through television, radio, newspapers, books, and journals as well as in person. People today are bombarded with political promises, bureaucratic doubletalk, Madison Avenue hype, bandwagon propaganda, and meaningless verbiage mixed in with useful facts and thoughtful discussions. It can be difficult to decide what to accept and what to reject as many of the biased, misleading messages sound very convincing. An example of this kind of message follows. Try reading the next paragraph quickly and see if you can make any sense out of it:

> In particular, initiation of critical subsystems development presents extremely interesting challenges to the subsystem compatibility rating. In this regard, an overview of the entire installation performance is further compounded when taking into account the philosophy or commonality and standardization. On the other hand, any associated

supporting element presents extremely interesting challenges to the philosophy of commonality and standardization.[3]

Did the difficulty of the paragraph puzzle you or make you feel slow-witted? If it did, you were not using critical thinking. That paragraph is all chaff and no wheat; it is a sample of computer-generated sentences put together in a completely random fashion. It is nonsense. You need to be able to separate the wheat from the chaff in any information you receive and critical thinking can help you do this.[4]

Making Choices

Nurses make choices constantly and cannot avoid them in their practice. For example, the use of triage in an emergency room is realistically based on the assumption that someone has to decide who to treat first. The staff nurse has to decide which call light to answer first many times a day; the community nurse often must decide what to tell a patient and the family about the illness and prognosis. Nurses speak of protecting the comfort and dignity of the patient but many procedures threaten both for the sake of physical recovery.

Health care professionals also confront people with their avoidance of an issue in order to bring about greater health in the future, even though this may make people temporarily uncomfortable. They do this based on the belief that it is worth it to suffer some temporary discomfort in order to ensure future health and well-being. Philosopher Maxine Greene points out the assumption behind these confrontations when she asks, "Who has a right to make other human beings 'likeable and happy and productive'?"[5] But which is more important, the present reality or the uncertain future? Isn't this a choice you have to make in your practice?

MAKING CONNECTIONS

Critical thinking has a creative side to it; it is far more than simply being critical. Have you often noticed relationships between different pieces of information or between different experiences? Greene calls this *making connections*.[6] When you look for these relationships, you will begin to see new connections between ideas, theories, isolated facts, and everyday experiences. Doing this brings more meaning to what you observe and learn. It can also lead you to the discovery of new meanings, for example:

> Physiology, sociology, and pyschology may seem like separate worlds, but they are all attempts to explain the same phenomenon—man—that becomes more apparent when you look for connections. Listen to a person's heart beat and at the same time watch that person's expression and body language. If you listen too long, the expression may become worried, the body position less relaxed, and the heart beat more rapid. A connection between concepts in physiology, sociology, and psychology can explain what has happened but each one separately will not provide a complete answer.

Making connections helps to eliminate the feeling that you have learned a lot of little bits of unrelated information. When these bits become related to each other and to your experience, they then become more meaningful and easier to remember. It also can lead to completely new connections that no one else ever saw before. Many important scientific discoveries, such as the recent revelations about the role of interferon in fighting cancer, were made this way. Not every new connection is quite this momentous, of course, but new connections add creativity to your practice and are worth sharing with your colleagues. They can lead to exciting new discoveries that will improve the whole profession.

TAKING A STRANGER'S VIEWPOINT

Thinking critically and creatively is what Greene describes as taking a stranger's viewpoint. She compares it to the way you look at familiar surroundings after being away from them for a long time. When you first come back, you see more details and more features, and are much more aware of routine then you usually are. Greene describes this way of seeing things:

> To take a stranger's vantage point on every day reality is to look inquiringly and wonderingly on the world in which one lives.[7]

When you compare the idea of taking a stranger's viewpoint to a reflexive acceptance or rejection of every idea that comes your way, you can see how much of a difference this can make in your approach. You can use the information in the next section on critical analysis as one way to take a stranger's viewpoint and see your world in a different, more creative perspective.

CRITICAL ANALYSIS

The term "critical thinking" refers to the questioning, open-minded approach discussed so far. "Critical analysis" is a related term used to describe a set of questions you can use to apply critical thinking to a particular situation or idea. It is a process that will guide you in separating the wheat from the chaff.

The set of questions involved is more a set of criteria for judging an idea rather then sequential steps like those in problem-solving. You may not need to use each question or criterion every time you apply critical analysis as you needed to use every step in the problem-solving process in order to adequately problem-solve.

USES

Critical analysis is useful in a variety of different situations. You can critically analyze any of the following:

Nursing Practices of all kinds, whether it is preoperative teaching, stoma care, contracting with a client, or virtually any other practice.

Nursing Issues, such as continuing education, career ladders, institutional licensure, and so forth.

Research Reports, especially in deciding if the results are applicable to your practice.

Rumors, Gossip, and Advice. While not ordinarily listed together, all need critical analysis before you accept or reject them.

Journal Articles and other written materials.

Evaluations of coworkers, nursing outcomes, and so forth can be made more objective and creative if you use critical thinking.

THE QUESTIONS

Several scholars have developed schemes to help people think critically. Two of these schemes, one from Ennis[8] and one from Dressel and Mayhew[14] have been combined into a set of questions and criteria that will help you progress along the road to being a critical thinker and a sharper, more aware, and effective leader.

These questions may seem abstract and unrelated to everyday experience to you until you engage yourself in the process of critical analysis. In order to do this, it is suggested that you choose one or two nursing practices or beliefs that disturb you in some way and test them with each critical analysis question as you read the rest of this section. In this way, you can see how critical analysis can work for you.

Question 1. What is the central issue?

To get at the meaning of the central issue, try to restate it as a pro and con in your own words. If this is difficult, it may be easier to identify a main theme. Even when there are no pros and cons given, there is always at least a hypothetical opposing viewpoint. You can also try reorganizing the ideas into a new pattern. A creative reorganization often results in new insights and new perspectives on an issue.

EXAMPLE.   Prison reform is a good example of the need to search for the central issue.

> Actually, there seem to be several underlying issues operating in debates about prison reform. One of these issues is the question of whether the inmates are "bad" or "sick." If you assume that they are bad, then they should be punished and prisons should be miserable places to be (and most are). But if you think of the inmates as sick or troubled, then they should be given treatment that requires a therapeutic environment.

A major theme or issue in prison reform, then, would be punishment versus treatment.

Question 2. What are the underlying assumptions?

Some underlying assumptions are personal, others are culture-bound. In either case, these assumptions are unstated beliefs that influence conclusions. People make assumptions all the time and often act on them without realizing it. Greene says that you can't really be self-aware until you examine your preconceptions (assumptions).[9] She especially emphasizes the need to be aware of the models or paradigms we use in constructing our world.

EXAMPLE. This book can be used as an example of the way in which models are used to construct our world.

> This book is based on the open systems view of the world and on a concept of people as holistic beings who strive toward growth and self-actualization. This is an optimistic view of human beings and you could find many people who disagree with this way of looking at people.

Question 3. Is the evidence given valid?

Most of the time, some kind of evidence is given to support a point of view. This evidence can be fact or opinion and in either case can be accurate or inaccurate. Stereotypes, clichés, biases, appeals to emotion, and obvious contradictions are clear warning signals that you'd better look closely at the evidence given. On the other hand, relevant, verifiable, and consistent evidence given to support a clearly stated conclusion are signs that an argument is well supported. These points are summarized in the following six criteria to be considered when judging how valid the evidence is.

Are stereotypes or clichés used?

Every time phrases that overgeneralize about people such as "the bored housewife," the "rebellious teenager," "middle-aged man" or "cancer patient" are used there is the danger of stereotyping. When this is done, you lose sight of the uniqueness of the individual who happens to keep house, be an adolescent, middle-aged, or stricken with cancer. Nurses are, fortunately, working on becoming more aware of cultural, racial, and other stereotypes, but there are still many of them in use.

Clichés are overused expressions. People tend to use them without thinking about what they mean or imply. "You're old enough to know better," and "Why don't you take it like a man," are clichés that could be counterproductive if directed to a distressed client or colleague.

Are emotional or biased arguments used?

An emotional appeal can be very persuasive and so it is often used. Even professional issues have their emotional component. Arguments are biased when they present only supporting evidence and none of the opposing viewpoints. A long-standing issue in nursing shows how emotions and biases are frequently used:

> The reaction of some nurses to proposals that the bachelor degree (B.S.N.) be required for licensure in the future was one of anger and anxiety because they were afraid that they would find themselves treated as second-class nurses if such a requirement were approved, even though the grandfather clause protected their licenses. The argument that the proposal is unfair to nurses who do not have B.S.N. degrees has a strong emotional component.

The biased nature of evidence or the emotional appeal may be quite subtle and hard to detect. While a biased or emotional appeal is often effective, a critical thinker is alert to their presence in order to avoid being persuaded for the wrong reasons.

Are the data adequate and verifiable?

First, you need to judge whether the data given consist of fact, opinion, or a combination. Often the information and research available on a subject is inadequate. When this happens, it becomes necessary to rely on judgment. Even so, you can distinguish between a heavily biased opinion and a well thought-out judgment based on a combination of experience and whatever knowledge is available. While you can have more confidence in the second case, it is still important to keep an open mind on the question because future data may contradict even the expert's best judgment. For example, hypertension used to be called the executives' disease but statistical analyses have shown that it is also a poor man's problem and is related to other factors besides occupation.

Even research is not always conclusive. The artificial sweetener controversy is a good example of its inconclusiveness. Although the evaluation of research is too complicated a subject to go into here, it is safe to say that most research findings are tentative (often raising more questions than answers) and subject to error even though there are statistics used to estimate the amount of error that is likely to have occurred.[10] Probably the best questions to ask in considering the acceptability of research findings are; 1) whether or not you could repeat the investigation and get the same results, 2) whether or not the design allows for collection of the data that are really needed to answer your question, and 3) are the results applicable to your situation?

Are important terms clearly defined?

Have you ever had an argument with someone only to find that the main disagreement was in the way you each defined a term? The following story is an example of how important clear and mutually agreed upon definitions can be:

> A clinical nurse specialist proposed to begin a cardiac rehabilitation program on two cardiology units. Coworkers in several departments assisted in the development of the

plan and agreed to participate. The Director of Nursing and Medical Chief of Cardiology approved the plan.

The clinical nurse specialist prepared the educational materials and protocols for gradual increases in activity just before implementing the program. At this point, the Hospital Administrator approached the specialist and stated that the rehabilitation program could not begin without the approval of the Board of Trustees.

Upon hearing the term cardiac rehabilitation, the Administrator had pictured a large outpatient clinic with elaborate exercise equipment and its own new staff. In contrast, the clinical nurse specialist had actually planned an inpatient program designed to assist patients with cardiac problems to improve their level of function and prepare for discharge using existing staff and equipment from several departments under the clinical nurse specialist's supervision. Neither the specialist nor the Administrator had clearly defined for the other person what they meant by the term cardiac rehabilitation.

Health caregivers use a lot of jargon, often without being aware that they are using it. Not only do they abbreviate everything from OB to CVPs, there are also words that are currently in fashion.[11] For example, the term client is currently preferred by many people because it implies more health and less dependence than the term patient does.

Many nursing terms are vaguely defined. A classic example of this is the term *nursing need*. Is a nursing need something that nurses need or is it an identifiable need for nursing care?[12] Another example is the term *assessment,* which is used to refer to the collection of data, the diagnosis of the problem, or both. When terms are clearly defined, it becomes much easier to determine the relevancy of the data, which is the next criterion for judging the validity of the data.

Are the data relevant?

An argument may be so persuasive that you don't notice that the evidence given is not directly related to the question at hand. While you might think that this is a rare occurrence, actually it is not too unusual. Arguments are often illogical and emotional. In fact, side issues or irrelevancies may be brought up purposely to draw your attention away from the main point, especially when the side issues are more likely to be persuasive.

People can also get so involved that they do not realize they are getting sidetracked into side issues and irrelevancies. For example, a student might be interested in exploring the relationship between the Director of Nurses and the Hospital Administrator and then start asking questions related to the medical staff because that is also a very interesting subject, although irrelevant to the planned project. The same irrelevancy of the data collected shows up in many different situations. Another example:

The major objective of a class for people with hypertension would be to help them control their high blood pressure by means of diet, medication, exercise, stress reduction, and so forth. Yet, at the end of class, participants are asked if they enjoyed the class and to define such terms as systolic and diastolic. Neither of these factors is relevant to control. What is relevant is whether they can carry out their treatment program correctly and whether this results in a lowering of their blood pressures.

Is the problem or issue correctly identified?

This last criterion of validity is related to the previous two, which were concerned with the relevance of the data and the clarity of the definitions. All three of these are also important points to consider in assessing and diagnosing a problem when working through the problem-solving process. The following is an example of a problem that may need to be redefined:

> Both professional caregivers and parents have been trying to find ways to slow down hyperactive children. But Rogers[13] believes that the hyperactive child is an evolutionary emergent, that is, the next step in our evolution as humans, and actually more in tune with the rapid pace of change than the rest of us are. If she is correct, we have been working on the wrong problem.

Problems and issues may also have been oversimplified. While people often prefer to reduce a complex issue to a question that can be answered with a simple yes or no, there is a danger that in doing this, important aspects of an issue will be ignored. The following is an example of a frequently oversimplified issue:

> The shortage of nurses is a perennial question that needs continual redefinition. "Do we need more nurses?" is too simple a question to emcompass a complex situation. There is, for example, a difference between counting the number of actively employed nurses and counting every nurse in the country including those who will never return to nursing practice.
>
> Is there a shortage in one part of the country and a surplus in another? Is "need" measured by the number of job openings or by the number of nurses who could be utilized to improve the current standard of health care?
>
> These and other questions need to be answered before deciding whether or not we have a real shortage of nurses.

Question 4. Are the conclusions acceptable?

There are three parts to this question of acceptability: accuracy, applicability, and value stance. Each of these is an important part of the final decision to accept or reject and each represents a different perspective on the question of acceptability, as you will see.

Is the conclusion accurate?

The first concern is with the correctness or accuracy of the conclusion. Is the conclusion based on the facts given? Sometimes a conclusion ignores the facts. For example, a researcher asked families if they would take care of an elderly family member who became ill. Almost exactly half of the families said they would not, the other half said they would. The researcher, who believed that *every* family should be willing to help, concluded that *most families will not* take care of their elderly family members if they become ill. The researcher's conclusion was not based on the facts. You also need to ask if facts or supporting arguments are sufficiently valid. The criteria in question 3 will help you make this decision.

Is the conclusion applicable?

Second, you need to ask if the conclusion is applicable to your situation. Sometimes an idea or solution will fit only one situation; other solutions can be adapted to a variety of circumstances. You will need to decide if the solution or conclusion will work for you. For example:

> An experimental drug treatment project may be successful primarily because the clients were handpicked or had volunteered for the program and because the staff was so enthusiastic about the new treatment. If this is true, how well will this treatment work in your agency when it becomes an ordinary routine used for a wide variety of drug problems?

Is there any value conflict?

The third aspect of the question is the extent to which the conclusion or solution conflicts with your personal and professional values. To take an extreme example, a lobotomy may effectively calm certain highly agitated individuals but can you accept it as a treatment of mental illness if you believe in the right to self-determination and free will?

Restraints, total life support systems, abortions, withholding diagnosis of a terminal illness, and fostering independence are just a few of the issues that can arise in your professional practice that may challenge your values and beliefs. The accuracy, generalizability, and value stance of a conclusion are all important aspects to consider in deciding its acceptability. A critical thinker considers each one of these before accepting a conclusion.

SUMMARY

Critical thinking is defined here as an inquiring way to look at the world. This approach includes such actions as seeking new connections between ideas and using a set of criteria to judge the acceptability of an idea. The criteria include identifying the central issue and underlying assumptions, analyzing the validity of the evidence given, and deciding whether or not the conclusion is acceptable, applicable, and congruent with your value system.

References

1. KAUFMAN, R: *Identifying and Solving Problems: A Systems Approach,* ed 2. University Associates, La Jolla, California, 1979.

2. GOLIGHTLY, CK: *Creative Problem Solving for Health Professionals.* Aspen Systems, Rockville, Maryland, 1981.

3. *Scientific Report Writer,* a computerized nonsensical report writer, origin unknown.

4. GAY, JT AND EDGIL, AE: *Critical reading.* Nursing and Health Care 3(5):(May) 266, 1982.

5. GREENE, M: *Teacher As Stranger.* Wadsworth, Belmont, California, 1973, p 56.

6. GREENE, op cit, p 159.

7. GREENE, op cit, p 267.

8. ENNIS, BH: *A Concept of Critical Thinking.* Harvard Educational Review 32, Winter 1962, p 81.

9. GREENE, op cit, p 80.

10. THOMAS, L: *The art of teaching science.* New York Times, March 14, p 78, 1982.

11. INGLE, DJ: *Is It Really So?* Westminster Press, Philadelphia, 1976, p 19.

12. BLOCK, D: *Some crucial terms in nursing: What do they mean?* Nursing Outlook 22(11):689, 1974.

13. ROGERS, M: *An Introduction to the Theoretical Basis of Nursing.* FA Davis, Philadelphia, 1970.

14. DRESSEL, P AND MAYHEW, LB: *Critical thinking in social science.* (From a mimeo, no date.)

Chapter **6**

Groups

Small Groups

This chapter deals with the basic dynamics of the small group, especially the growth and development of a group, common patterns of interaction within a group, and common blocks to group interaction and growth. The following two chapters will then look at specific kinds of groups—teams and conference groups—and how the leader can facilitate their development and function.

GROUP DEFINED

A group is an open system composed of three or more people who are held together by a common interest or bond. The individuals who make up the group are its subsystems.

The number three was used deliberately as the minimum to constitute a group because it is only when there are three or more in the system that the complex set of relationships develops that characterizes a group. When there are three or more people in a group, any interaction is affected by the presence of other people and you can identify a group climate or emotional state in which the exchange takes place.[1]

COMMON BONDS

The common interest or bond mentioned in the definition of a group is the relationship that holds people together as a group. This bond may be either physical proximity, a shared purpose or goal, a special meaning that has been attached to the group, or a combination of these factors.

Physical Proximity

Sharing the same physical space is one common bond that can bring people together to form a group. For example, five people who get caught in a sudden rain shower and huddle together under the same awning to keep dry form a temporary group. If they had not been caught by the rain, they probably would not have become a group but remained an aggregate because they would have had nothing to hold them together even temporarily. An aggregate is a number of people who do not have a common bond. In other words, people in a group have developed some kind of relationship with each other, people in an aggregate have not.

Living or working in the same physical space increases the number of contacts between people and the likelihood of their developing a common bond. People who live near each other form social groups such as neighborhood clubs or block associations. People who are in the same class or work together in the same office often form groups because they spend so much time together in the same place in addition to sharing many common experiences.

Shared Purpose

Many groups are formed primarily to accomplish a specific goal or purpose. For example, people may form groups to protest budget cuts, to preserve the environment, to fight crime in their neighborhood, or for any number of other reasons.

For most groups in the work setting, a shared purpose or goal is the strongest bond. The shared purpose of a work group could be to survey the needs of people living in a designated geographic area or to provide nursing care for a given number of patients. These work groups are often referred to as teams.

Other work groups, such as task forces and committees, are formed to accomplish more limited goals. Committees may, for example, be formed to develop a new protocol for hyperalimentation or to carry out a peer review procedure. The variety of purposes for which a group can be formed is almost endless.

Special Meaning

Some groups are formed primarily because of the special meaning they have for their members. This kind of group holds some special significance or meets some basic need of its members. The meaning of the group itself is the common bond that holds people together. Most religious and social groups fall into this category.

Even work groups originally formed to accomplish a specific goal can develop a special meaning or symbolic importance to its members. The following are two example of work groups that have developed a special meaning:

Membership on the peer review committee may become a desirable position because of the power of the committee and the qualifications for membership. The committee then becomes a symbol of power and prestige to its members.

A team that was formed to provide rehabilitative services may become a source of satisfaction and support for its members. The team may also develop social significance if team members find that they enjoy spending time together after work.

THE GROUP AS AN OPEN SYSTEM

Like other open systems, groups evidence wholeness, pattern, growth, individuality, and sentience. Groups also exchange energy with their environment and are continually affecting and being affected by their environment. These basic concepts of open systems theory were discussed in Chapter 1. A few additional points are mentioned here to focus on the group as an open system.

Wholeness

The group as a whole has its own unique characteristics that are different from the characteristics of the individual members. A group has its own identity, its own rhythms, growth patterns, and interactions with the environment. You cannot accurately predict the behavior of a group from an assessment of the individual members. One group theorist pointed out that a group can act completely irrationally even though its members are rational people.[2] It is also interesting to note that people act differently in different groups.

In leadership, we are interested in both the group as a whole and the individual as a whole. Both the patterns of interaction that characterize the group as a whole and the patterns exhibited by people when they are acting as members of a group are important to the leader. An assessment of only one or the other would be inadequate in a situation involving more than two individuals. For many people, this consideration of the group as a whole is a totally different focus, one that requires a real change in perspective.

Growth

There is a regular and predictable sequence to the development of a group. While not every group will be able to complete this sequence successfully, those that are able to do so will proceed through identifiable stages in their evolution. When these stages are discussed later in this chapter, you will see that there are very evident differences between an immature group in the early stages of development and the mature group that has progressed to the later stages of development.

Interaction with the Environment

Groups exchange energy in the form of information and matter with their environment. There is an ebb and flow of energy both within the group and in its exchange with the environment. There are high and low energy levels in groups as well as in individuals.

A group may take action to change its environment or it may make a decision based on the expectations or demands of people outside the system. Environmental influences may be as subtle as the effects of spatial arrangements or they may be as obvious as a directive from the administration telling the group how to function. This influence is not a one-way exchange—the group may also make demands of the administrator and its very existence can subtly effect those who are not members and see themselves as "outsiders." These influences and exchanges will be discussed further in later chapters on teams, conferences, and organizations.

Pattern

As open systems, groups have common patterns of behavior that can be identified, analyzed, and influenced by the leader. There are different patterns of interaction that are likely to appear in groups and tend to change as groups mature. The way in which a group responds to its members, the way a group makes decisions, and the way a group handles conflicts are just a few examples of these patterns. Some of these patterns promote group development but other patterns are indications of group disharmony and immaturity.

Individual members of the group also have common patterns of behavior that can be identified, analyzed, and influenced by the leader. Some of these patterns are functional within the group while others tend to disrupt the group and delay group progress. These patterns will be discussed later in this chapter.

SUMMARY

A group is an open system consisting of three or more people joined together by either physical proximity, a shared purpose, a special meaning, or a combination of these common bonds. As open systems, groups have their own characteristics and identifiable patterns, are open to and exchange energy with their environments, and may grow and evolve over time.

Stages of Group Development

Years of observation by group theorists as well as a number of research studies indicate that groups go through predictable developmental stages in the course of their existence. Groups evolve over time from an immature stage to a mature stage of development.

Of course, not every group achieves maturity just as not every individual successfully fulfills the developmental tasks of each stage of life. Also, like individuals, groups may proceed to the next stage without completely accomplishing the task of the earlier ones and may need to go back to complete them later. A group may terminate before it has progressed through all of these stages.

FIVE STAGES

Tuckman and Jensen[3] call these five stages of group development forming, storming, norming, performing, and adjourning. While a number of other different terms are used to describe these stages, there is agreement on a general pattern and order to the evolution of these stages.

Groups first go through a formation stage characterized by the uncertainty felt by group members about their place in the group. This is followed by a stormy period in which there is a great deal of conflict and emotions are high. The group must find a way to deal with these conflicts and develop a functional pattern of interaction. If the group succeeds, it then matures into a highly functional system abundantly able to perform its tasks and meet the relationship needs of its members as well. At some point, the group finishes its task or is no longer of use to its members and ends.

These stages describe a general pattern followed by most groups as they form and develop. The course of the group's development will be affected by the purpose of the group and the setting in which it functions as well as by the internal dynamics of the group.

Each of these five stages is described in more detail below. For each stage, the tasks of both the group as a whole and the individual members will be mentioned and the characteristic group climate and behavior during the stage and leader actions to facilitate group development are discussed.[4-9]

Stage 1. Forming

This is the stage in which the group forms and begins to develop an identity as a group. By the end of this stage, the group will have enough of a sense of self that it can at least define a boundary between itself and the environment. In other words, people in the group will be able to say who is and who is not a member of the group but will not yet know exactly what being a member entails.

In this first stage, the group is very immature. In fact, when people first come together they can barely be called a group because they have just begun to identify their common bonds and have not yet formed any relationships within the group. Group members will also have differing perceptions of the purpose and goals of the group and will be uncertain about their position within the group.

INDIVIDUAL TASKS. Members of a new group do not know yet what the group will be like or what will be expected of them within this group. The first individual task, then, is to learn about the group and to find out what will be expected, that is, what roles and responsibilities they will be fulfilling in this particular group.

Along with this need to become acquainted with the group and its expectations comes the need to deal with individual feelings about entering a new group. These feelings include uncertainty, mistrust, and anxiety related to the unknowns of the group.

A certain amount of stress can be expected to accompany the change in pattern required when entering a new group. The amount of stress can vary a great deal according to the demands of the situation and individual response to these demands. For example, joining a group similar to one you've enjoyed working in before would be less stressful than joining a group in which you will be asked to carry out an entirely new task that you do not feel prepared to do.

GROUP TASKS. The group as a whole also has two tasks to accomplish in the forming stage. As was mentioned earlier, the first task is to establish its identity as a group. This is done in several ways. One way is by defining who is and who is not a member of the group. Another is to define and to talk about what members of the group have in common with each other (for example, went to the same school, are all new in their jobs, have the same problem, and so forth). This discussion will eventually lead to a definition of group expectations in later stages. A third way to establish group identity is to give the group a name and to decide on a time and place to meet again. This last activity also extends the existence of the group beyond the initial encounter.

The second group task is to provide support for individual members who in this formative stage are experiencing varying degrees of discomfort. This task is difficult for the immature group to achieve. Introductions and discussion of common bonds help to provide some support. Avoiding conflict and direct confrontation is also a temporary means of providing support. As the group matures it is more capable of meeting its members' basic needs and can therefore allow more open communication and confrontation.

GROUP CLIMATE AND BEHAVIOR. Uncertainty and insecurity characterize the forming stage of a group. Members' basic needs for security and belonging have not yet been met within the group, therefore much of their behavior is aimed at meeting these needs. More specifically, behavior in the group at this time is aimed at assuring acceptance, avoiding rejection, increasing feelings of comfort, reducing anxiety, reducing ambiguity, and attempting to clarify roles and expectations.

People tend to feel anxious when facing a new situation in which they do not know how to respond. Members of a forming group do not yet know how they are expected to behave or what to do to avoid rejection. At this point, they do not know whether or not they will be accepted by the group and so are cautious in their behavior. For some people, this uncertainty and anxiety become so intolerable that they literally flee from the group.

From what was just said about acceptance and rejection, it is clear that the level of trust within the group is low at this stage.[10] This low trust coupled with unmet needs for security and belonging, results in numerous attempts to bring some order and structure to the group and also results in guarded, nonconfronting, non-revealing communications. Typically, conversation is somewhat formal and very polite. People will talk about safe, familiar subjects (such as the weather, the traffic, or a current item of general interest) and try to conceal their feelings and personal concerns. These maneuvers keep other people at a safe distance and prevent open confrontation, retaliation, or rejection.

A new group lacks form and organization; it hasn't had time yet to develop regular patterns of interaction or other kinds of behavior and so is very unpredictable even to its members. The politeness and formality used for self-concealment also serves to structure and pattern communication.

Another way the group can increase structure and predictability is to set limits on each other's behavior. For example, members will control participation by having each one take a turn to speak or by interrupting those who stray beyond the limits set saying, ''Let's stick to the subject.'' Other ways to set limits are by setting up an agenda for the meeting and by designating not only a specific time and place for the next meeting but also a specific duration and restrictions on who is welcome to attend.

Several other behaviors are common at this stage. One is an almost total concentration on the task of the group in order to avoid dealing with feelings. Another common occurrence is for the group to get stuck on a minor point and spend the whole meeting squabbling about it, this way the group doesn't even have to deal with its major task. Or the forming group may take a different approach and try to rush through too many decisions at the first meeting in order to reduce tension. However the group first approaches these issues, it usually has to return to them later and resolve them in a more mature manner.

Despite these uncomfortable feelings and the concentration of energy on limiting them, there is usually an underlying tone of optimism within the new group. People who enter a new group usually bring with them the expectation that the group will somehow be able to accomplish its purpose. While it does need to be kept within realistic bounds, this optimism helps to keep the group together through its difficult early stages.

LEADER ACTIONS. You can see by now that a newly formed group needs a leader. In fact, the group can easily become too dependent on the direction of a strong leader, which would hinder group development over the long term. The leader's actions, then, need to be aimed at providing support and structure without encouraging dependence.

As the leader of a forming group, you will experience some of the same feelings of uncertainty and insecurity that the rest of the group does. Recognizing that these feelings are related to the formation of the group can help you deal with them constructively. One way to do this is by helping the group accomplish its developmental tasks and complete this stage successfully.

It is important to be alert to the individual needs of group members. For example, some people may prefer to remain silent at this stage rather than taking their turn to speak and the leader can encourage the group to allow them to "skip their turn for now." Other people may need recognition in order to feel comfortable in the group and the leader can supply some of this recognition.

As leader you can also be a role model for mature group behavior by engaging in more open communication than the rest of the group. This encourages others to speak more freely. You can provide more direct reinforcement of mature group behavior but only indirect, low pressure kinds of confrontation should be used at this stage.

You can also help the group develop the needed group identity, structure, and some clarification of purpose. Simply using the word "we" in referring to the group helps to promote a group identity. Giving the group a name, using this name, and distinguishing it from other groups also reinforces the groups identity.

While some structure is needed, it should be flexible in order to allow for growth. A rigid structure will retard further development. The following is just one example of the difference between a flexible and rigid approach to structuring group behavior:

Flexible   Encourage the group to discuss when they want to meet next time and to decide what they want to do or discuss.

Rigid   Ask the group to make a list of each separate item to be discussed at the next meeting and allow no deviation from that list no matter what comes up.

The group leader can suggest constructive approaches and encourage the group to keep things flexible and yet predictable enough to make members feel comfortable.

A real clarification of the group's goals is not a realistic expectation for most groups in the forming stage. Firmly set goals would be premature and probably have to be renegotiated later on, which frustrates and discourages those who are very task oriented. But a general statement about the reason why people are getting together as a group would be appropriate and reduces ambiguity to a more tolerable level. Group members can also be assigned to some general responsibilities such as taking minutes or thinking about the group's goals and bringing some information or ideas with them to the next meeting.

The leader's function in a forming group is to encourage optimism, flexibility, and open communication and to provide support, some clarification of purpose, and some guidance to promote accomplishment of the individual and group tasks of the forming stage. Failure to complete these tasks means that the group either remains at this low level of function or that it will have to return to them and deal with them later.

Example. There is no substitute for real group experience in which you can actually be involved in the complex interactions and changes that take place and to feel the tensions rise and fall as the group moves through the stages of development. The example given here will illustrate the way in which a group changes from stage to stage but it cannot do justice to the full complexity of group dynamics.

> An outbreak of meningitis in a grade school upset many parents in the district. Three parents, two from the affected grade school and one from the middle school, met with the School Superintendent to express their concern and to demand that action be taken to improve school health services. The Superintendent suggested that they meet with the District Coordinator of Special Services who is responsible for health services in that district.
>
> The following evening, the three parents and the Coordinator met at the grade school. The Coordinator expected that the blame for inadequate health services would fall on the Coordinator and was apprehensive about the meeting. Each of the parents was very anxious to see some action taken and had a list of suggested actions. Each list was different from the others.
>
> After everyone arrived and had been introduced to everyone else, the Coordinator read a long report (which the Coordinator had written for the school board) to the parents. When the Coordinator finally finished, the parents took turns asking questions about the way the outbreak had been discovered and handled. They gradually realized that the person who had been most actively dealing with the outbreak was a nurse from the health department. Someone suggested they speak with the nurse. The parent whose children attended the middle school offered to call the nurse and ask the nurse to meet the group at the same time next week. Since it was very late by then, the meeting broke up after this.

Not a single item on any of the three lists was accomplished at this meeting. The Coordinator was expected to attend another meeting despite the Coordinator's hope that the parents would be satisfied by the report and drop the whole thing. You may have noted that only the Coordinator felt any real anxiety and insecurity about the formation of the group in this particular example. The Coordinator's maneuver of reading the long report succeeded in protecting the Coordinator from attack but did not help the group make any progress toward a goal. A real leader has not yet emerged in this group. The example will be continued at the end of the discussion of Stage 2.

Stage 2. Storming

It would seem that after the relative uneasiness of the first stage the group would move into a calmer phase next but it does not. While group members usually feel a little more comfortable with the group by the end of the first stage, the group soon moves into the second stage, which is characterized by an increase in tension and conflict.

This stage is a difficult, stormy one. It is probably the most stressful and unpleasant for everyone in the group. This tension does have some value, however, since it eventually pushes the group to work on resolving those problems and issues that were evaded in the first stage but move to the forefront of the group's awareness in the second stage.

INDIVIDUAL TASKS. As the group rearranges and reorganizes itself throughout this stage, the main task of the individual member is to find a position in the group. This includes defining what one is able to contribute to the group, the degree to which one can fulfill group expectations, and whether or not that individual member will remain a part of the group.

In order to do these things, the group member needs to develop more connections with other group members and some idea of the purpose of the group and its probable objectives (the objectives are not usually clarified until the next stage). Group members frequently test several different roles and options available to them before the conclusion of this stage.

GROUP TASKS. The tasks of the group as a whole in this second stage are to resolve the conflicts that emerge and to begin reorganizing itself into a more functional whole. These conflicts were avoided in the first stage but now emerge and demand almost the total energy of the group to resolve them.

In order to successfully reorganize, the group must develop more common bonds between its members and further develop its identity beyond the simple naming and defining of boundaries. The minimal structure developed in the first stage is usually challenged and often reworked. While the purpose of the group becomes clearer by the end of this stage, specific objectives are usually established in the next (Norming) stage.

GROUP CLIMATE AND BEHAVIOR. As the name of this stage implies, the climate of the group is unstable and emotional. When previously hidden conflicts emerge, the tension level rises rapidly. Group members find themselves feeling frustrated, tense, and sometimes overwhelmed by these conflicts. Trust is still low and the group is clearly still immature although struggling to mature.

People who are not familiar with group dynamics are often suprised that decisions made in the first stage are either ignored or completely changed in the second stage. This seemingly irrational behavior is necessary if the decisions were made hastily or based on a superficial consensus that was concealing serious disagreement.

In some groups, communications become openly hostile and attacking in the second stage. Angry individuals may stomp out of a meeting when they don't get their way. The noise level can rise dramatically and shouting matches may occur. In other groups, the hostility may be more restrained and covert but still evident to the alert observer and still felt by members of the group. People who fear open hostility may withdraw from the group, temporarily or permanently.

The conflicts that arise in the group stem from an increased awareness of the differences and disagreements among group members. The conflict can be over such trivial matters as the way to pay for refreshments or whether or not minutes of the meetings should be kept or the conflicts can be over such serious issues as the purpose of the group. Personal conflicts are also common. For example, one group member may become irritated by another's mannerisms; another may become upset or sulky when criticized. When a group focuses too long on a trivial disagreement, it is usually because it is avoiding or unable to deal with more substantial issues such as the group's purpose or its inability to meet members' individual needs.

Differences between individual members become much more apparent than they were in the first stage. As these differences appear, individual members begin to develop affiliations with other members who seem to agree with them or share their interests. *Subgroups* or factions may form out of these affiliations. Within the subgroups, members begin to show more interest and concern for each other than had been shown earlier. Any sharing of personal concerns is usually superficial but subgroup members do begin to listen to each other more than they had before.

As these subgroups form, people begin to take sides on issues and to support those who agree with them against those who disagree. Sometimes, the conflicts between these subgroups can escalate into serious battles. To an observer, the subgroups may seem to literally be at war with each other. At times, the group may seem ready to split into two or more separate groups and this does occasionally happen when the differences cannot be reconciled.

Those members who do not join the subgroups or do not commit themselves on a hot issue are often pressured to choose sides. Sometimes, a member is singled out for criticism and blamed (unfairly) for the problems of the group. This is called scapegoating and the leader of the group is often the target.

Power struggles may erupt as people try to maneuver themselves into favorable positions within the group. For example, two or more people may try to designate themselves as leaders of the group or subgroup at the same time or they may try to remove the already designated leader by calling for a vote, by constantly challenging the leader's actions or by simply taking over. These power struggles often develop over control of group functions. For example, one group member might try to impose a set of rules on the group and in response, a second member will demand that the group accept the second member's own completely different rules. The struggle over whose rules will be accepted can quickly turn into a shouting match or can become an endless argument unless someone intervenes.

LEADER ACTIONS. There is much the leader can do to channel the energies released during this stage into constructive activity. These actions include the use of confrontation and negotiation, linking, testing for consensus, encouragement, and reinforcement.

Confrontation is an appropriate kind of communication at this stage. It can be used, for example, to get things moving again when the group gets stuck on a trivial matter and is avoiding more substantial issues. Both *confrontation and negotiation* together are useful in the resolution of the many conflicts and power struggles that emerge in this stage.

Along with using confrontation, however, it is very important to lay down ground rules for confronting the issues, using "I" messages and not attacking the person or by using "you" messages (this was discussed in Chapter 4, in relation to confrontation meetings). These ground rules may need to be repeated and violations pointed out until the group becomes accustomed to following the rules. The purpose of emphasizing these rules is not to suppress open expression of feelings but to keep these expressions from feeding the tension that already exists, to avoid provoking more hostility, and to avoid driving anxious members away from the group, that is, to keep emotions and tensions within reasonable bounds.

As the leader of a group in the second stage, you can also point out the commonalities that exist and can be further developed between individuals and subgroups. This is the linking function. *Linking* can help strengthen group identity and assist people in making connections with each other and in clarifying the purpose of the group.

Also important in clarifying the purpose of the group is encouraging free discussion and then *testing for consensus*. Once some commonalities have been found, the leader can ask, "Do we all agree that . . . ?" When it seems that the group has reached some agreement on purpose, the leader can then test for agreement on a general purpose. When there have been disagreements, testing for consensus may be used to identify what commonalities do exist.

During the second stage, the group may not be ready to come to consensus on every question that is raised and may have to vote on some issues. The problem with voting is that some people (the minority) will lose to the majority and this can polarize the group even further into competing factions. Voting is preferable, however, to autocratic decisions by the leader or another member of the group. On some points it may be necessary for group members to agree to disagree to avoid splitting the group permanently.

There are several different ways in which the leader can *encourage and reinforce* positive group action. Encouragement of open discussion of issues has already been mentioned. The leader can also point out to the group that it usually takes a long time to get organized and to get to the planning stage, which restores flagging optimism. The leader can also reinforce positive action by recognizing contributions and pointing out ways in which individual members have been helpful to the group such as being a conflict resolver, a good listener, or the expert who shares needed information with the group.

Many of the leader actions from the first stage are still helpful here. The leader can continue to use open communication and to provide support for individual members when others in the group do not. You can also continue to use "we" to refer to the group and to point out features indicating group identity. At the same time, however, it is important to allow the group to grapple with its own problems and to resist trying to impose your own solutions in an autocratic fashion.

Example. Let's return to the group of three concerned parents and the school district's Coordinator of Special Services as they come together for their second meeting and the second stage—storming:

> As the group members sat down around a table, the parent who had offered to call the nurse was asked when the nurse was coming. "The nurse couldn't come this week due to a previously scheduled conference. The nurse will be here next week" was the reply. The other group members looked annoyed and said, "Why didn't you tell us!

We wasted our time coming tonight." The first parent responded that they could use the time to decide what questions to ask the nurse.

Although everyone thought they had agreed on the questions, when people began bringing up questions, each one was different. One parent wanted to ask how meningitis spread but another one said they knew that already. When the third parent suggested that they ask the nurse how the problem could be handled better next time, the Coordinator took offense and said, "No one said it was badly handled this time." Almost in a chorus, the three parents said, "But that's why we're here! Our children were dangerously exposed." Again, the Coordinator said that everything possible had been done and anyway, the Coordinator didn't think that parents should get involved in administrative decisions. While saying this, the Coordinator started to put papers away as if getting ready to leave.

As the Coordinator finished packing up the papers, a parent said coldly, "If you don't want to cooperate, we'll be glad to tell that to the Superintendent" and the other parents nodded in agreement. The Coordinator backed down from the aggressive stance and said, "Well, I do want to be cooperative." The first parent said, "I know the Coordinator is concerned and we all want the children to be healthy."

The group then decided that each person could ask the nurse questions, but should try to keep to the subject. Everyone agreed to return the next week.

The first parent (who called the nurse) is emerging as the leader of this group. At one point the parents sided together against the Coordinator and the group nearly split apart. But the meeting ended with a positive although vague agreement that they were all concerned about the children's health. The group now has a defined purpose though it still has no specific objectives.

Stage. 3 Norming

In this stage, the group experiences some relief from the anxieties and tensions of the first two stages. Conflicts are resolved, positions and responsibilities are defined, and plans are made. Confrontations become less hostile and actions are more productive. The group begins to establish more predictable patterns that will be carried over into the next stage.

The group is more relaxed in the norming stage and participation in the group is less stressful than it was in the first two stages. By the end of this stage, group members are beginning to feel a sense of really belonging to the group and of progress being made. The group is clearly maturing.

INDIVIDUAL TASKS. The main tasks of the individual group member at this stage are to clarify one's position in the group and to develop one's ability to be a fully functional group member. By this stage, the individual has made a decision to remain a member of the group and has begun the task of defining a position for oneself in the group. In the norming stage, the members have an opportunity to test and refine their positions and to begin functioning as an integral part of the group as a whole.

Interactions with others in the group are more purposeful and constructive now. The individual member can practice such actions as confronting, disagreeing, and collaborating within this more predictable group and should be contributing to accomplishment of the group's task (which is setting goals in this stage) and offering support to other group members.

GROUP TASKS. A major task of the group in this third stage is to decide on the specific goals or objectives that it will carry out in the next stage. If the purpose was not clearly defined during the second stage, it will need to be defined now in order to develop objectives. After developing its objectives, the group also needs to decide what has to be done and who will do it, that is, select tasks and assign them to people.

Two other tasks of the group at this stage that are related to each other are to develop cohesiveness as a group and to establish functional patterns of behavior. The group needs to complete the tasks of working out its own constructive ways to resolve conflicts and to meet individual members' needs.

GROUP CLIMATE AND BEHAVIOR. This third stage is characterized by a gradually increasing feeling of progress, openness, and relatedness among group members. Both, group members and the leader feel a sense of relief after having made it through the storms of the second stage.

This change in group climate is not quite as radical as it may seem. Although unnoticed because of the tension and conflict of the second stage, some positive steps were being taken that finally bear fruit. For example, you'll recall that there were instances of mutual support and developing connections especially between subgroup members in the second stage. These are now extended to the rest of the group as the conflicts are resolved and the hostilities decrease.

Also, as connections developed, group members felt less isolated and more related, which contributes to the development of cohesiveness. Finally, as group members take more active roles in the group they usually feel less threatened and become more comfortable with communicating openly in the group. All these gradual changes prepare the group to complete the tasks of Stage 3.

Exchanges between group members are freer and more open in the third stage. People are more likely to share their personal concerns than they were before and, when they do, the group is more likely to respond with support and helpful suggestions.

Responses from the group are now more predictable. This does not mean that people do or say the same thing over and over again. It means that if a group member offers a constructive suggestion, someone will at least acknowledge the contribution. Or, if someone makes an insulting remark, this violation of the ground rules will be pointed out in some way. In neither case will the people be completely ignored or attacked for making a comment as they might have been in the storming stage.

Discussion turns away from conflicts over trivial matters to the sharing of ideas and suggestions. As the discussion proceeds, the group is able to finally decide on its purpose and begin planning how it will carry out this purpose. By the end of this stage, the plan should include objectives, activities to carry out the objectives, and decisions on how the work will be shared by the group. When this is done, each group member will know what will be expected of each individual.

Decisions are made in a more democratic manner now. Reaching consensus on an issue is not only possible but happens more frequently. Voting is much less common and autocratic decisions are no longer acceptable to the group.

Cautious optimism about the outcome of the group replaces frustration and discouragement. The group has finally proved it can get something done such as developing a plan of action but has not yet proved its ability to carry the plan out to completion successfully.

LEADER ACTIONS. The group becomes more autonomous and less likely to look to the leader for assistance that now comes from other group members. In fact, you could say that as each member of the group learns more about effectively influencing other group members, the leader becomes more like just another member of the group.

As the leader, you can help to guide the group through the planning process by doing such things as keeping the group from getting sidetracked, testing the feasibility of suggestions, and encouraging the use of consensus in making decisions. At the same time, it is important to avoid the temptation to give advice. The group should assume the responsibility for doing the planning and will, therefore, feel that it owns the final plan and be more committed to it.

Again, some of the actions taken in previous stages are still appropriate. It is still helpful to encourage debate on issues that arise, to test for consensus, and to use confrontation and negotiation when needed. There should be less need to provide support or to enforce the ground rules for confrontation except for an occasional reminder.

Example. At the third meeting, the three parents and the Coordinator met with the nurse from the health department to discuss the meningitis outbreak:

> Each group member brought a new list of questions to ask the nurse and was surprised that the others had also done so. Most of the questions were about the handling of the meningitis outbreak. The discussion flowed freely. The Coordinator seemed less defensive and more relaxed than at the second meeting. The parents were attentive and impressed with the nurse's thorough knowledge of the situation and the way the nurse had dealt with the problem.
>
> As they neared the end of their questions, one of the parents said, "I guess we were fortunate to have you on hand when this happened." "Yes, it was very fortunate because I only visit the school once a month" said the nurse. The parents gasped and asked the nurse to explain. The nurse described the way in which nurses were assigned to schools in the district. The nurse was only able to provide minimal services to the school because that's all the district contracted for.
>
> Another parent asked the nurse what services should be available and the discussion of this subject took up the rest of the meeting time. When it was time to end

the meeting the first parent thanked the nurse for coming, said some notes were taken and that the nurse had given them something to think about. The others agreed and asked if the nurse could return to consult with their committee in the future. The nurse agreed. The group left after agreeing to meet the next week.

At the next meeting, the group discussed the nurse's suggestions for a comprehensive health service. The Coordinator pointed out that such services would be expensive. The parents agreed but said it would be worth the cost.

By the end of the meeting, the group had decided to propose an improved health service for the district but also agreed that they needed much more information first.

The Coordinator was asked to look into the costs and feasibility of improved services. The first parent volunteered to speak with other health department officials and the other two parents offered to do some library research. Each member would bring their information back to the group in two weeks.

Not every group progresses as rapidly through the stages of development as this one. It may take many weeks for some groups to even enter the second stage. The group in the example has matured substantially; note how differently the Coordinator's disagreement was handled in this stage.

Stage 4. Performing

This is the most productive and enjoyable stage in the life cycle of a group. By this stage, the group has clearly defined its purpose and agreed on its objectives and on a plan to achieve them. Each member also feels a part of the group; knows what behaviors are expected of individual members in the group and knows what one can expect from other members of the group. In other words, the group has finally reached maturity and is ready to perform at a fully functional level in this stage.

INDIVIDUAL TASKS. During this stage, individual members carry out the roles and responsibilities that were gradually defined over the course of the last three stages. The two developmental tasks of the individual member can be described in terms of those two familiar aspects of leadership style—tasks and relationships. The first task of every individual member is to carry out their part of the work that was planned by the group. Attempts to do this are usually made during earlier stages but it is not until Stage 4 that group members have sufficient energy free to concentrate on performing the work of the group.

The second task is to relate to both the group as a whole and to individual members. Group members now address their messages to the group as a whole as well as to other individuals. For example, a characteristic of the mature group is the degree to which a group member who is unhappy about a group action discusses that displeasure with the group (mature group behavior) rather than to another person outside the group (immature group behavior). In a mature group there should be few barriers to communication between individual members. While there may still be a need to have subgroups within the group in order to divide up complex tasks, communication between these subgroups should flow freely and openly.

GROUP TASKS. The tasks of the group at this stage are to move toward its goals by engaging in productive behavior and to maintain relationships within the group and with the environment. As you can see, these tasks are closely related to those of the individual group member. This happens because the needs and goals of the group as a whole are much more congruent with those of the individual members now than they were in earlier stages.

In order to fulfill these tasks, the group must now function as a whole whose members are functionally interrelated. The following description of a group exercise may help to illustrate this functional interrelatedness:

> Six or seven volunteers are asked to stand together in a group and link arms with each other. Then each person is asked to select a point somewhere in the room. After each person indicates that they have decided on a point in the room, they are told to move toward that point.
>
> Of course, with their arms linked, everyone finds themselves pulling against the others and the group goes nowhere. The people in the group become frustrated (Fig. 6-1 A). Finally, they realize that they can't all reach their different points at once and begin to move together from point to point in the room until each point has been reached. As this is done, the people in the group usually begin to smile and laugh with pleasure at their accomplishment (Fig. 6-1 B).

You can see in this example how the climate changes as the group moved from unproductive to functional behavior.

GROUP CLIMATE AND BEHAVIOR. The climate of the group at this stage is open, pleasant, and relaxed. Most behavior is purposeful and constructive. The level of trust among group members is high and each member has a sense of involvement in the group. Cooperation has replaced conflict. Participation in a mature group is usually a satisfying experience.

The pleasant, cooperative climate does not mean that differences among group members no longer exist. The differences do exist but are handled in a different manner in a mature group. In fact, the leader should be suspicious of a group that claims it never has to deal with differences or disagreements among its members. When a group presents a totally harmonious, unanimous front, it may mean that it has set up rigid norms that prohibit disagreement. Beneath this surface agreement, members are concealing their concerns and opinions for fear of rejection by the group. The harmony is an illusion and those members who believe in it are deceiving themselves.

In contrast, the mature group recognizes that each member is a unique individual who is likely to disagree with some of the things that are said or done in the group. The mature group can tolerate individuality and disagreement. Each member's abilities are recognized and utilized. Individuality is appreciated rather than suppressed. The mature group is also capable of openly confronting conflicts that may arise from disagreements and of negotiating their resolution when necessary.

FIGURE 6-1 Functional interrelatedness in a group. *A,* In the immature group, all members try to meet their own individual needs, thereby opposing the other members; nothing is accomplished. *B,* In the mature group, the members work together as a whole toward the group's goal, thereby accomplishing the goal of the group and meeting the needs of the individual.

Since group maturity is finally achieved in this performing stage, it seems appropriate to summarize the characteristics of the mature group here.[2] The following list compares the characteristics of mature and immature groups:

Mature	Immature
Definite boundary	Indefinite, shifting boundary
Defined purpose	Vague purpose
Common, shared goals	Conflicting or no goals
Strong identity as a whole	Uncertain identity threatened by gain or loss of members
Relaxed, informal	Rigid and formal or chaotic
Open, confronting communications	Closed, concealing communications
Accepting	Rejecting, indifferent, or hostile
Tolerates differences	Suppresses or is disrupted by differences
Flexible, predictable norms	Rigid or inconsistent norms
Cohesiveness	Few connections between members
Deals with both tasks and relationships	Ignores relationship concerns, focuses on tasks
Recognizes and responds to member's input and needs	Often fails to recognize or respond to its members
Feedback is constructive	Feedback is minimal or destructive, or both

The group that has achieved all of the characteristics of maturity listed above is not perfect but it is far more functional and effective than the immature group.

LEADER ACTIONS.   The effective leader acts as a group facilitator in the performing stage. Group members, even more than in the last stage, can assume many of the early leader functions but they can still benefit from the additional guidance of the leader during this stage.

The leader is still a valuable resource for the group. Groups in the performing stage still need feedback on their progress. In addition, they often need refocusing on objectives when they are sidetracked, support when they face a particularly difficult task, and guidance for such things as how to delegate responsibility, make assignments, and revise their plans when necessary.

It is important to avoid being overprotective during this stage because protectiveness is not only unnecessary but counterproductive with a group that is able to confront and resolve problems. At this stage, the activities involved in working out a problem contribute to the cohesiveness of the group and to its general development. The overly helpful leader can inhibit the group's continued development.

Example. The school health committee, composed of three parents and the Co-ordinator of Special Services, met again after gathering some data needed to develop a proposal:

> Committee members shared their findings with the rest of the group. As they discussed their proposal for improving health services again, they began to realize how many people would be affected by this change and decided that they needed more input. They decided to survey not only school and health department officials but also the students, parents, and teachers in the entire school system.
>
> At the same time, they also planned to find out how other school systems designed and financed their health services. To do these tasks they formed two subcommittees. During the survey, two more parents and a school principal joined the committee and became involved in the surveys.
>
> The group as a whole met regularly to discuss their progress and share the results. Some of the ideas presented to the committee by the members were too ambitious; others were too limited. Many disagreements arose as discussions of the proposal progressed. Finally, the committee worked out a realistic proposal that satisfied each member and was feasible financially.
>
> The survey activities had generated much community support for the proposal by the time the committee presented the proposal to the school board. The board conducted public hearings on the proposal and finally approved it after making some minor changes in it.

The group in this example completed its work successfully, but not every group is able to do this. Some fail to progress this far in their development as a group and either abandon their objectives or work ineffectively on them. Even those who do reach this stage may find that their project can't be completed or will not be accepted for some reason that wasn't apparent when they began their work. If this happens, the group has to decide whether to give up its objectives or revise its work plan and continue working.

Stage 5. Adjourning

In this fifth and last stage, the group comes to some kind of closure and ends. Closure should include a summary of the events that took place over the life of the group and an evaluation of both the group process and the degree to which the group fulfilled its purpose and met its objectives. The evaluation part of this stage, especially evaluation of the relationship aspects of the group process, is often overlooked or avoided by groups coming to a close. When a group fails to complete closure, its members are left with an unsatisfied, unfinished feeling.

INDIVIDUAL TASKS. The task of the individual member in this stage is to evaluate both the process and the outcome of the group to complete the group experience. All members both give and receive feedback on their own roles, other members' roles, and on the group as a whole. Group process, achievement of group objectives, individual members' contributions, productive and unproductive behaviors, and ways in which all these could have been improved should be included in the evaluation.

GROUP TASKS.   Two tasks of the group are to support a thorough evaluation of the group's processes and outcome and to continue to foster an open climate in which the evaluation can take place. Without this support, individual members will not be able to engage in objective, worthwhile evaluations.

A third task of the group in this last stage is to obtain or provide some recognition of the group's work and achievements. This recognition can be in the form of an announcement of the group's success, a recounting of what has been attempted and accomplished, or a celebration of some kind.

GROUP CLIMATE AND BEHAVIOR.   This stage is characterized by mixed emotions: relief that the work is done, satisfaction from a job well done, sadness that the group is coming to an end. Of course, not every group succeeds but even if it does not, its members can get some satisfaction from having at least attempted to reach their objective. They can also still evaluate how well they worked together and how well they planned their approach to the task.

As was mentioned before, groups often omit or rush through this last stage. Some of this behavior is due to avoidance of a potentially threatening situation. Some of it is also due to a failure to appreciate its value in terms of learning and increased self-awareness.

Evaluation promotes learning and increased awareness in several ways. It can make the group more aware of how it has changed since its first meeting, which is something many people are not aware of unless it is pointed out to them. Evaluation also increases self-awareness as people receive feedback on how they have influenced others. Sharing feedback also provides information on how others feel and respond to things that happen within a group.

LEADER ACTIONS.   As a member of the group, the leader should expect to both give and receive feedback. An important function of the leader at this stage is to encourage this sharing of feedback. Since many groups are reluctant to do this, the leader can initiate the process by asking the others to evaluate the leader's role. Another way to do this is to ask group members to fill out questionnaires or checklists and then share the results with the group. For example, you could give group members the list of characteristics of the mature and immature group and ask them to rate the maturity of the group on each characteristic.

As was done with other confrontations earlier in the group's development, the leader can also set ground rules for constructive rather than destructive evaluation. (Guidelines for giving and receiving constructive feedback can be found in Chapter 7.) Independence can still be encouraged by refusing to do all of the evaluation even if the group requests this.

In this last stage, the leader can also challenge the group to face the reality that it is coming to an end. You can encourage the group to recognize and validate members' contributions to the process and achievement of goals. It is also important to ensure some expression of appreciation of the group's efforts and a celebration of the group's accomplishments so that its members can leave the group with some feeling of satisfaction from having completed what they and their fellow group members set out to do.

Example. With the acceptance of their proposal by the school board, the school health committee had met its primary objective:

> All seven members of the committee gathered after the school board meeting and a reporter took a picture for the local newspaper. They decided to celebrate their success by meeting for lunch at a favorite restaurant the next day.
>
> Over lunch the next day, committee members reminisced about all the meetings they had had and the work they had done. The newer members expressed surprise over the difficulties the committee had in getting started. One of the parents from the original group said to the Coordinator, "You seemed to think we were out to get you at first." The Coordinator responded, "Yes, it did seem that way. None of you realized how little money we had to work with. I thought I was doing the best I could." The other parents agreed and shared how angry they had felt at first about the poor health service and how their feelings changed as they began to work on ways to improve the services offered.
>
> At the end of lunch, one of the newer members expressed some regret that the committee would no longer meet. "We could meet once in a while to check on the progress of the proposal" said another parent. "No, it's up to the school board now and it's our job as individual citizens and parents to check their progress" said the parent who had been the informal leader of the group. The others agreed somewhat reluctantly, congratulated each other on a job well done and left the restaurant.

SUMMARY

The evolution of a group can be divided into five stages: forming, storming, norming, performing, and adjourning. Each of these stages has a characteristic emotional climate, group behaviors, and specific individual and group developmental tasks. Different leader actions are appropriate for each of these stages. The group reaches maturity by the fourth or performing stage and is a far more functional and effective system at this point than it was in the earlier stages during which it was likely to be disorganized, inflexible, unresponsive, and uncertain of its purpose or goals. During the fifth stage, the group reaches closure by reviewing prior events, evaluating both the process and achievements, and celebrating its achievements.

Patterns of Interaction

A number of different patterns can be found in the interactions of a group whenever its members gather together. Some of these patterns, such as the functional and nonfunctional group roles played by group members, are primarily patterns of individual behavior. Others, such as the communication patterns, hidden agendas, and dominant synchronizers, are patterns of the group as a whole.

GROUP ROLES

Group roles are descriptions of the behavior of individual group members in terms of their effect on the group. With this definition in mind, the various roles can be divided into two categories: functional and nonfunctional roles. Behavior that contributes to the completion of a group task are called *task roles;* those that encourage or support group function are called *group building roles.* Both task and group building roles are functional roles to play within a group.

Roles that meet the needs of the individual member, but not of the group are called individual roles. Most of the time these individual roles, aimed at meeting individual rather than group needs, are nonfunctional or at best neutral in terms of group progress.

An individual can play any number of different roles within a single group meeting. Some people will restrict themselves to one or two roles while others may play many different roles. Each time a person interacts with the group, that member is playing at least one and sometimes several of these different roles.

People tend to play different roles in different kinds of groups but there is usually an identifiable pattern of roles within the same group over a series of meetings. While there is some relationship between personality and the roles a person is likely to play in a group, it is important to remember that when you describe the roles played you are not describing the person but the effect the person's behavior is having on the group process. For example, a person's objections to a decision may be blocking group progress but this does not mean that this person is always a blocker.

The functional task roles are listed first below, then the group building roles, and finally the nonfunctional roles.[11] Examples will be give in Chapter 7 in the analysis of a problem discussion.

Functional Task Roles

The following roles contribute to the completion of a group task:

Initiator/Contributor—makes suggestions, proposes new ideas to the group. The suggestions may be ways to solve a problem, a new way to approach a problem, or a new way for the group to proceed in its work.

Information Giver—offers pertinent facts from personal knowledge or experience that might help a group in its deliberations.

Information Seeker—asks for pertinent information or clarification of facts or suggestions.

Opinion Giver—offers opinions, judgments, or feelings on suggestions. May comment on their appropriateness in terms of a particular set of values.

Opinion Seeker—asks for opinions, judgments, or feelings of other group members; seeks clarification of values.

Disagreer—points out errors in information given or takes a different point of view.

Coordinator (Linker)—points out relationships between suggestions and statements that have been made.

Elaborator—expands on suggestions or ideas made and gives examples or rationales.

Energizer—stimulates the group; encourages activity and movement toward group goals.

Summarizer—pulls together all the ideas or suggestions from the group; briefly restates or outlines what the group has accomplished.

Procedural Technician—performs needed mechanical tasks such as setting up chairs, running the video camera, passing out papers, or serving refreshments.

Recorder—writes down ideas, suggestions, or decisions made by the group; may also diagram group interaction.

Functional Group Building Roles

The following roles encourage and support group development and function:

Encourager—responds to others warmly; accepts and sometimes praises contributions of others.

Standard Setter—expresses standards or guidelines for the group to use in its deliberations.

Gatekeeper—elicits contributions from other members; sometimes suggests limits or ways to make sure everyone has a chance to speak.

Consensus Taker—tests group opinions and decisions by stating them and asking whether or not members agree.

Diagnoser—determines and points out blocks to group progress.

Expresser—describes feelings, reactions, and responses of self and others; expresses feelings of the group.

Tension Reliever—provides an outlet for tensions built up in the group through use of humor, conciliation, and mediation.

Follower—accepts group decisions; goes along with the group without initiating or taking other active role.

Nonfunctional Individual Roles

The following roles are played to satisfy individual needs rather than to promote group development or progress toward a goal:

Aggressor—makes hostile, attacking remarks, criticizes others; is overly assertive.

Recognition Seeker—does things to call attention to oneself; uses the group as personal audience.

Monopolizer—talks so often or so long that others do not get a chance to speak.

Dominator/Usurper—tries to take over leadership of the group; wants to have own way and tells the group what to do.

Blocker—obstructs progress of the group by making unconstructive contributions, being very negative, and resisting beyond a reasonable point.

Playboy—makes irrelevant and silly comments; whispers, plays around, and does not take the group task seriously (Fig. 6-2).

FIGURE 6-2 The playboy makes silly and irrelevant comments and does not take the group task seriously.

FIGURE 6-3 The zipper mouth does not participate, even nonverbally, demonstrates no acceptance of the group, and may sulk.

Zipper-mouth—does not participate even in nonverbal manner; demonstrates no acceptance of the group (as follower does); may sulk (Fig. 6-3).

Analyzing Roles

Identifying the group roles played by individual members is a useful way to describe what is going on within the group. When you can quickly recognize the effect certain behaviors are having on the group you can take action to encourage the productive behaviors and to redirect or discourage the nonfunctional behaviors. You can also analyze your own behavior within a group in terms of functional and nonfunctional roles you play in that group.

An analysis of group roles can point out the need for further diagnosis and intervention. When there is a high proportion of nonfunctional individual roles in comparison to task and group building roles, this is an indication of either group immaturity or of a more specific problem. The specific problem may be low morale, lack of cohesion or agreement on group objectives, poorly defined tasks, or a leadership style that is either too controlling or too laissez-faire.

COMMUNICATION PATTERNS

While there will be some unique characteristics about the communications in each group, the overall patterns of verbal communication can usually be compared to one of five common patterns found in groups.

These patterns are best identified by observing and recording who speaks to whom in each interaction during a group meeting. While casual observation will pick up the extreme patterns of communication, written, audiotape, and videotape records are more complete and pick up the less extreme patterns more accurately and objectively.

Five common patterns of verbal communication in groups will be described here. They range from the very formal one-way communications to the completely chaotic patterns found in some disorganized groups. In between these extremes are the stilted, limited, and open patterns of verbal communication.[2] Diagrams showing the flow of communications in these five different patterns are shown in Figure 6-4.

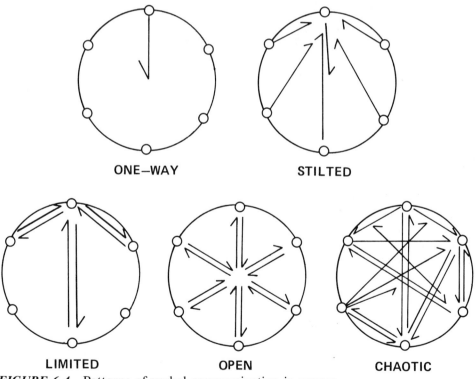

FIGURE 6-4   Patterns of verbal communication in groups.

FIGURE 6-5   In the one-way pattern, verbal communication moves in one direction from the leader to the rest of the group.

One-Way

Verbal communication moves in only one direction in this pattern: from the speaker (or leader) to the rest of the group (Fig. 6-5). The formal lecture is the best known example of this pattern but it can also be found in other situations. The one-way pattern can be compared to a live performance in a theater in the sense that the speaker is performing and the rest of the group acts as the audience.

The one-way pattern is a highly organized form of communication controlled by the leader or speaker. Although the leader seems to have total control in this kind of group, it is important to note that the group has placed this control in the hands of the leader or at least not tried to take control away from the leader.

The extreme form of one-way communication allows no verbal feedback from the group but the leader is still influenced by the nonverbal responses of the group, which can be surprisingly powerful. Boos, hisses, laughter, and clapping from an audience all tell the performer how well the performer is doing. The more subtle

176

smiles and nods of agreement from a group listening to a lecture positively reinforces the speaker while frowns or yawns can discourage the speaker. Despite the highly controlled nature of this communication pattern, the principle that you cannot *not* communicate still holds true.

In less extreme forms, the speaker will recognize people in the group and let them ask questions or make comments. The speaker responds to the questions and comments but retains control of participation. This allows for some clarification and disagreement, which the most extreme form does not.

The one-way pattern is appropriate for a performance or for transmitting information to a group. It is an efficient way to communicate information to a large number of people in a short time, but it is not necessarily the best way to facilitate learning (Chapter 8 discusses other ways). It is an authoritarian approach that sets the leader apart from the group and allows little or no group interaction. It is not an appropriate pattern for group problem-solving, decision making, sharing feelings, confrontation, evaluation, and other processes in which people need to reflect on and respond to each other's input. A group cannot mature when a one-way pattern is continued.

Stilted

Verbal communication flows in both directions in the stilted pattern but the pattern is still stiff and somewhat formal. The most common type of stilted pattern is one in which each member takes a turn to speak, usually going around the circle or up and down rows in order. In the most stilted version, all communication is directed at the leader but in the less formal version, communications may also be addressed to the group as a whole.

Though less controlling than the one-way pattern, the stilted pattern still imposes a great deal of structure on the group's interaction. Discussion is not likely to be lively or animated so long as the stilted pattern continues.

The stilted pattern is very common in new, immature groups and can be helpful as a temporary way to impose some order or to make sure that everyone has a chance to speak. Insistence in continuing this pattern would retard the development of the group. It is also used for introductions and for "show and tell" presentations, even with adults. When all communications are to the leader, it may be due to the authoritarian style of the leader or because group members are not yet comfortable with each other. Members can simply be asked to talk to the whole group to make the pattern less stilted but it usually takes more than a simple request for members to relax enough to move from this pattern into the open pattern of communication.

Limited

In the limited pattern of communication, some group members communicate with the leader and with each other, but other members of the group do not. When these interactions are animated or relaxed, it may seem to the casual observer that the group has an open pattern of communication but careful observation or recording of the interaction reveals that the communications are limited to some members of the group and that other members are not a part of the interaction.

This limited pattern can be the result of increasing dominance of the subgroup that is controlling communications within the group. It may also be due to the leader's and group's inability to prevent some members from monopolizing the discussion. Monopolizers are not always seeking dominance—some people mask anxiety by hyperactivity while others may withdraw and become isolated.

The silent members in the group must also be considered. Their silence may indicate disapproval of the group's actions or feelings of discomfort within the group. Silent members may be interested followers who simply need some encouragement or an opportunity to participate more actively or they may be zippermouths whose negative feelings about the group need to be dealt with by the group. Leader intervention should be directed at diagnosing the reasons for the pattern and at promoting group progress toward maturity.

Open

This pattern is characterized by free and easy exchange between all members of the group including the leader. It is the kind of communication usually found in mature groups. Each member of the group has an opportunity to speak, to be heard, and to receive some kind of response. The leadership style is usually democratic, but it could be laissez-faire in a mature group.

An open pattern of communication is flexibly organized. It is predictable in the sense that members know what they can expect of each other. This underlying order may be hard for an observer to detect in a very open pattern.

The open communication is appropriate for most group interactions. However, it is not the most efficient pattern for completing a simple task or the fastest way to make a decision so it is not appropriate when speed and efficiency are of the highest priority. It is effective for meeting most other leadership goals.

Chaotic

The chaotic pattern goes beyond the free and easy exchange of the open pattern to an exchange that is disorganized, unpredictable, and uncontrollable. Side conversations between two members are common. Group members interrupt each other, ignore each other, or talk at the same time, sometimes shouting to be heard. The group may be relaxed as people are at a party or it may be tense with openly warring factions. The leadership is usually laissez-faire and almost completely lacking in control by either the leader or group members.

The group with a chaotic pattern of communication is as immature as those groups that have one-way communication but it is usually less productive. The open pattern may seem to approach chaos at times but careful analysis of its interactions reveals the predictability and organization that the chaotic pattern lacks, somewhat like the difference between a three-ring circus and a rioting mob. Anything accomplished by a group with a chaotic pattern of communication has happened by accident.

The chaotic pattern is not appropriate for any group that has a task to accomplish. Leader intervention should be aimed first at bringing some order into the communication pattern and secondly at increasing group maturity.

PUBLIC AND HIDDEN AGENDAS

As they form, groups develop some kind of stated, evident reason, goal, or objective for meeting. This stated reason for the group is called the public or official agenda. Below the surface, however, there are usually other goals operating that influence the group process even though they are not openly acknowledged. These unannounced underlying goals are called the hidden agenda.[11]

Unless called to the group's attention, hidden agendas operate below the surface of the group's awareness. Although their existence is not recognized, they can be strongly felt by group members and can greatly influence the outcome of the group process. The following is an example of how a hidden agenda can affect a group's process and outcome:

> A task force was formed to develop a peer review procedure for a community health agency. However, the caregivers appointed to the task force found peer review threatening. As a result of their feelings about peer review, a hidden agenda of avoiding the implementation of peer review developed and operated below the surface in this group.
>
> While this hidden agenda operated, the task force employed an astonishing variety of delay tactics in the course of its discussion of peer review. At the end of a year of meetings, the task force was still unable to find or develop a working definition of peer review that satisfied everyone in the group.

A leader should have intervened with this group long before a year had gone by. You can see from this example that hidden agendas can prevent a group from making any progress at all if they are not dealt with in some way. Groups will react the same way to a goal they do not accept (such as staffing changes) or to a goal they think is not worthwhile. The common sources of hidden agendas and their effect on the group are discussed next and will be followed by some suggested leader interventions.

Sources

An individual group member, several group members, the leader, or the group as a whole can have a hidden agenda. Sometimes, the individual or group is aware of having a hidden agenda, but often the hidden agenda is outside the awareness even of those who are its source.

Some hidden agendas arise from individual needs that are not met within the group. For example, individual group members may feel threatened by something that is happening in the group and may act to reduce this threat. Other people may have feelings of dependency or hostility toward the leader, which affects their behavior in the group. Some people try to dominate the group while others are very hesitant about participating.

Preconceived ideas about how the group should function are often the source of hidden agendas. One or more people may come to the group with a ready-made solution to the problem the group is trying to solve. Their hidden agenda would be to convince the group to accept their solution and to block acceptance of any other solution.

A similar kind of hidden agenda occurs when one or more group members have a special interest or a strong loyalty to another group. Either of these can influence behavior in the group. The following is an example of their effect:

> Two nurses were appointed to an interdisciplinary committee that was responsible for screening research studies proposed in their institution. Both nurses worked on the unstated goal (hidden agenda) of assuring that all proposals submitted by nurses would be approved.

Conflicting loyalties to several different groups often lead to hidden agendas in such groups as the committee described in the example above.

The leader may also bring hidden agendas to the group. Leaders too have individual needs that can be threatened in a particular group. They can also have conflicting loyalties to several groups. More often, leaders find themselves wanting to present the group with a ready-made solution to the group's problems. Even when they resist the temptation to share their solution with the group, it can be difficult to keep it from operating as a hidden agenda. Some leaders also find that they enjoy being dominant or having others dependent on them and unwittingly encourage dependence even though they say publicly that they want group members to be independent and assertive.

Some of the hidden agendas held by groups have already been mentioned. A common occurrence is the group that gives lip service to a goal that it does not genuinely accept. This lack of acceptance may be due to the fact that the goal was imposed on the group by the leader or by an outside authority; the group may have chosen a goal that sounded good, but really was not important to the group; or the group may be working on a goal that is no longer relevant to the group.

Another kind of hidden agenda found in groups is the unspoken agreement to behave in a certain way. For example, you may recall that immature groups frequently have an unspoken agreement that members will be polite and not confront each other. This agreement is not discussed but it is understood by group members. Groups may also have an unspoken agreement to ignore certain behavior (such as the acting out of a particular member) or they may agree to attack certain behaviors.

Other hidden agendas in groups may be to avoid discussing certain subjects or to deliberately slow down work on stated (public) goals.

Leader Action

The purpose of leader intervention when hidden agendas arise is to help the group work out the conflicts between goals so that the group's and members' goals are congruent and genuinely accepted. Because they conflict with the stated goals, hidden agendas usually impede the group's progress and keep the group from meeting its stated goals. Also, because they are hidden, their existence tends to restrict open communication and to support immature rather than mature group behavior.

The first and most important leader action is to recognize when a hidden agenda is operating in the group. Self-awareness is needed to help the leader recognize one's own hidden agendas. Some hidden agendas are easy to recognize once you're aware of the possibility of their existence. Others are much more subtle and are detected only when the group fails to make progress.

Once the hidden agenda has been identified, the leader must decide how to deal with it. Hidden agendas are not entirely negative. Some of them reflect attempts to meet real needs that have been ignored in the public agenda. Others provide a needed defense against a perceived threat. When these situations exist, finding a more direct way to meet these needs is usually preferable to confronting the individual or group about the hidden agenda.

When the hidden agenda seems to reflect the real goals of the group or to be a sign that the group cannot or will not work on the publicly stated goal, an open discussion of both public and hidden goals is usually appropriate.

The leader needs to judge how much confrontation the group is ready to handle. A mature group that is accustomed to evaluating its process would be able to handle a confrontation with information about the hidden agenda. However, making a direct statement that a hidden agenda is operating is offering a diagnosis or interpretation and is likely to provoke a defensive response even from a mature group. A more acceptable form of confrontation would be to present the information without the interpretation. For example, if the group is avoiding dealing with staffing changes that have to be made, you could say either of the following:

We have been talking more about problems on units than about staffing changes.

What kinds of problems do you think these staffing changes will cause on your units?

When dealing with hidden agendas, you will also find that it is helpful to recognize the legitimacy of the needs or problems reflected by the hidden agendas and to avoid implying that anyone should feel bad or guilty about their existence. The achievement of congruent, acceptable goals can have a dramatic effect on the group's ability to progress toward maturity and work on fulfilling its objectives.

Dominant Synchronizers

DEFINITION

Dominant synchronizers are the primary forces affecting the group at a given time. These forces may be within the group or in the environment of the group.

As with other open, living systems, there are identifiable rhythms and patterns in the behavior of a group. Synchronizers are any forces that influence the rate, character, or recurrence of these patterns. The degree to which the synchronizer influences a pattern depends on both the strength of the force and how sensitive the group is to that particular force. Those that have a major influence, of course, are the dominant synchronizers.

You may find that the concept of a dominant synchronizer is difficult to understand at first, partly because the manner in which these forces influence the group cannot be observed directly. It may also be partly due to the fact that the concept has not yet been fully developed in regard to its application to groups and much more research is needed yet on this subject.

Even though the concept may be hard to grasp in its present stage of development, it has some value in the analysis of group dynamics. The concept is valuable because there is so much happening in a group at one time—and so much to analyze—that if the leader can identify the primary or major forces affecting the group, the leader can concentrate on influencing these forces rather than on trying to influence every aspect of the group's functioning, which may be too complex a task.

EXAMPLE. If you would like to see how a group behavior pattern can become synchronized, you might want to try the following experiment:[12]

> A fairly large group is best for this experiment but a minimum of six or seven people may be enough to demonstrate the effect.
> Everyone in the group needs a large coin (such as a quarter) and a hard surface on which to tap the coin (such as a table). When everyone is ready, ask them to close their eyes and begin tapping the coin on the hard surface.
> At first, the tapping noises made will seem random or out of synch but as the group continues to rap their quarters on the table, the tapping noises begin to come closer together until the whole group is rapping their coins in unison.
> Groups differ in the rhythm that results. Some rhythms are slow; others are loud and insistent. They may even be more complex or syncopated in some groups. The character of the rhythm seems to reflect the climate of the group at the time this experiment is done.

The pattern of behavior in the example given was the eventually rhythmic tapping of coins. The dominant synchronizer in this case was the actual noise made by tapping the coin, not the behavior itself as group members had their eyes closed. Hearing when others tapped their coins influenced the timing of the next coin tap by each group member.

Chapple's[13] description of the way in which synchronization occurs in a group helps to explain how the noise of the tapping quarters set up a new pattern of behavior within the group:

> If one person initiates and several others respond, in *that* interaction sequence their interaction rhythms have become synchronized with one another, even though there may not be perfect synchronization with the initiator. So doing, their *orientation system* is no longer random. . . . When set (group) events become repetitive and the group initiated to responds in unison, they share a common rhythm. . . . It is well known from practical experience that once such group response patterns are established, they generate a powerful influence on the emotional states of the individuals participating.

Although Chapple is describing a situation in which there is a single initiator, the noise of the coins worked the same way to synchronize the group's behavior. Many other dominant synchronizers are more subtle in their influence and harder to detect than the noise of the coins, but the way in which they influence the flow and movement of the group is the same.

TYPES OF SYNCHRONIZERS

A number of forces can be identified as potential dominant synchronizers. These forces may be physical or interactional in nature and they may originate in the group or in the group's environment. Since each group's situation is unique in some way, it is not possible to provide a comprehensive listing of all the forces that could affect a group but a sampling of the most common ones is presented here.

A group can be strongly influenced by the amount of heat, light, or humidity in its immediate environment. For example, it is very difficult to concentrate on a lecture if you're sitting in a near-freezing classroom. A darkened room may evoke a feeling of intimacy as it does in a candlelit restaurant but it could also inspire fear or put people to sleep under different circumstances and in combination with other forces. In either case, however, the darkness can have a real effect on the group and can be a dominant synchronizer of that group.

The time of day, noises in a room or outside, colors, textures, and furnishings may also influence the group. For example, a formal arrangement of hard chairs in straight rows create an air of formality and can reinforce polite, formal behavior while soft couches and chairs evoke a casual feeling and encourage more casual behavior. Serving refreshments can have the same effect.

Each of these physical forces mentioned so far may be strong enough to influence the group but often the character of the interpersonal relations outweighs their influence. For example, a group that is exhilarated over the successful completion of a long campaign is likely to respond enthusiastically to a suggestion for a new project despite fatigue or a physically uncomfortable environment. The force of the emotion of exhilaration can predominate over the fatigue or the environment at least temporarily.

·Another common example of social interaction as a dominant synchronizer is the effect of the hidden agenda. A strong hidden agenda that everyone must be serious and formally polite to one another can overcome the informality of a setting and the serving of refreshments.

Social interactions within the group's environment can also become dominant synchronizers. For example, if a large number of people are fired in an apparently indiscriminant manner when a new administration comes into an organization, the resulting climate of fear and tension is felt within the group and will affect the group's ability to function, especially in regard to the degree of trust between members, openness of communications, ability to make decisions and willingness to take any risks at all.

LEADER ACTION

As mentioned before, one of the main reasons for identifying the dominant synchronizers of a group is to bring some focus to the analysis of the group's dynamics. This does not mean that less dominant forces influencing the group can or should be completely ignored, but because it is difficult or impossible to deal with all these forces at once, the leader can identify those that predominate and concentrate efforts on them.

The specific action taken by the leader is dependent on the types of forces predominating. For example, if a physical force dominates, the appropriate action may be to change the temperature or lighting in the meeting room. If a hidden agenda is operating, the appropriate action may be to confront the hidden agenda that is influencing the group's behavior.

Those dominant synchronizers that have a positive effect on the group can be continued and encouraged. If a new seating arrangement seems to encourage participation in discussions, then the leader would want to continue using that arrangement or perhaps to improve on it.

When the force is outside the control or influence of the leader, the major action would be to increase the development of relevant coping skills. For example, if the organizational climate is tense and fearful, the leader would work on keeping the fear and tension in the group limited and within bounds. You would also want to avoid actions that may escalate the tension and encourage the use of the group as a support system for individual group members and perhaps as a force to change the climate of the organization.

SUMMARY

Several patterns of interaction were discussed. On the individual level, group members may play functional or nonfunctional roles. Functional task roles include initiator/contributor, information giver, information seeker, opinion giver, opinion seeker, disagreer, coordinator, elaborator, energizer, summarizer, procedural technician, and recorder. Functional group building roles are encourager, standard setter, gatekeeper, consensus taker, diagnoser, expresser, tension reliever, and follower.

Nonfunctional roles are aggressor, recognition seeker, monopolizer, dominator/usurper, blocker, playboy, and zipper mouth.

On the group level, patterns of communication may be one-way, stilted, limited, open, or chaotic. Hidden agendas are unacknowledged goals that operate below the surface but can exert a great deal of influence on the group. Dominant synchronizers are the primary forces affecting the behavior patterns of the group. These forces may come from within the group or from the environment and may be physical or interactional in nature.

References

1. SAPIR, E: *Group.* Group Process 5(2):105, 1973.

2. BION, WR: *Experiences in Groups and Other Papers.* Basic Books, New York, 1961.

3. TUCKMAN, BW AND JENSEN, MAC: *Stages of small group development revisited.* Group and Organization Studies 2(4):419, December 1977.

4. BRILL, N: *Teamwork: Working Together in the Human Services.* JB Lippincott, Philadelphia, 1976.

5. HILL, B, LIPPITT, L, AND SERKOWNEK, K: *The emotional dimensions of the problem-solving process.* Group and Organization Studies 4(1):93, March 1979.

6. BRADFORD, LP (ED): *Group Development,* ed. 2. University Associates, La Jolla, California, 1978.

7. BENNIS, WG AND SHEPARD, H: *A theory of group development.* In BRADFORD, LP (ED): *Group Development,* ed 2. University Associates, La Jolla, California, 1978.

8. NEILSEN, EH: *Applying a group development model to managing a class.* In BRADFORD, LP (ED): *Group Development,* ed 2. University Associates, La Jolla, California, 1978.

9. BRAATEN, LJ: *Developmental phases of encounter groups and related intensive groups: A critical review of models and a new proposal.* Interpersonal Development 5:112-129, 1974-5.

10. GIBB, JR AND GIBB, LM: *The group as a growing organism.* In BRADFORD, LP (ED): *Group Development,* ed 2. University Associates, La Jolla, California, 1978, p 104.

11. BRADFORD, L: *The case of the hidden agenda.* In BRADFORD, LP (ED): *Group Development,* ed 2. University Associates, La Jolla, California, 1978.

12. BUCK, J AND BUCK, E: *Synchronous fireflies.* Scientific American 234(5):74, May 1976.

13. CHAPPLE, ED: *Culture and Biological Man: Explorations in Behavioral Anthropology.* Holt, Rinehart, & Winston, New York, 1970, p 225. (Reprinted as The Biological Foundations of Individuality and Culture. Robert Krieger, Huntington, New York, 1979.)

Chapter *7*

Leading Meetings and Conferences

This chapter continues the study of groups. It focuses on the types of meetings and small conferences in which health care professionals are most often involved. This includes meetings to discuss problems and ventilate feelings, conferences designed to solve problems (especially those concerned with the delivery of care), and conferences designed primarily for sharing information.

*Problem Discussion Meetings**

It is often necessary to bring people together for a meeting to find out what is bothering them and to provide an opportunity for them to express their feelings.[1] This kind of meeting is a problem discussion.

There is no universally accepted term for this type of meeting. It has been called a feelings conference, a confrontation, a feedback meeting, and a discussion of issues. It bears some resemblance to encounter and sensitivity groups because they both deal with feelings. But the primary purpose of a problem discussion is to deal with a work-related problem, while encounter and sensitivity groups are formed primarily to explore the self and emotions in depth and this is not appropriate for a work group meeting in which everyone is expected to participate.

A meeting to discuss problems is often necessary before problem-solving can be done. Feelings can be so strong on an issue that they block group progress until they are dealt with in some way. Also, when emotions are high it is often not clear

---

*Written with C. Daubman.

exactly what the problem is and different group members can have very different perceptions of the problem. When this happens, the problem discussion is an effective way to confront the issue and clarify it before it can be resolved.

Preparing for this type of meeting will be discussed as well as points to consider in conducting a problem discussion and analyzing it afterward. The script of an entire problem discussion is included in this chapter so that you can see how a meeting like this could actually be conducted. You will see that there are flaws in the way the meeting proceeded—these are to be expected in any real meeting.

PREPARATION

Thorough preparation results in a more effective meeting and better use of everyone's time. There are many things to consider in preparing to lead a meeting including your purpose; the presentation; the date, the place, and time of the meeting; publicizing the meeting; refreshments; providing staff coverage; and reducing any possible threat the meeting may be to those who are invited to attend it.

Purpose

You need to think about why you are having the meeting and to decide whether or not the problem discussion is the right approach. If your purpose is to encourage more open communication between group members and ventilation of feelings in order to confront an unresolved conflict or identify the problem, then a problem discussion is appropriate. However, if the sharing of information or the solving of a known problem is your primary purpose, then a problem discussion is not appropriate.

As usual you need to thoroughly assess the situation. A good way to do this is to write down what you have observed. Be sure to separate your observations from your interpretations since your interpretation may differ from those of the group. You will be sharing some of these observations with the group in your opening statement and throughout the meeting. Your observations will also be the basis upon which you decide who should be invited to the meeting and what needs to be accomplished at the meeting.

Usually, only one subject or problem is dealt with in the meeting. This is done to keep the meeting to a reasonable length of time, to keep the meeting focused, and to deal with the subject of concern adequately. For example, the problem discussion script is taken from a meeting of nursing staff that was held to encourage the staff to express their feelings about caring for a particular patient and to critically evaluate the care they gave in order to improve it in the future:

> The subject of the meeting was how the staff felt about caring for patients like Mr. C. Mr. C was an older man who had been on the unit several months before he died (his death occurred one week before the meeting). Mr. C. had had an extensively gangrenous foot that was hideously decayed but could not be treated surgically because he was considered an extremely poor surgical risk.

Mr. C. also had many decubiti, was contracted into a fetal position, and was unable to care for himself at all. He did not respond verbally to the staff and his level of awareness fluctuated. Most members of the staff found it extremely distasteful to care for him because of the odor and horrible condition of his foot and his complete dependence. The leader had observed several staff members expressing their distaste in Mr. C.'s presence. The leader also noticed that they spent as little time as possible in his room although he had been there a long time and had few visitors.

When Mr. C. died, the staff felt a mixture of relief from the horror of his physical condition and guilt for the feelings they had had about caring for him. The meeting could have focused on the staff's feelings about his death but the leader believed it was more important to deal with their feelings about giving care to patients in this condition.

Plan the Presentation

It is important to have a design for the meeting, one that is flexible enough to accommodate the needs of the group but with enough structure to guide the group toward the accomplishment of the meeting's purpose. There are two aspects to consider in this design: your opening remarks and pertinent comments and questions to guide the group through the rest of the discussion.

The leader's presentation at the beginning of the conference should be brief. The purpose of the conference, the subject to be discussed, and the ground rules for the discussion (like those for confrontation) are included in the opening remarks. A few words of welcome and comments designed to help people feel at ease are also included.

If you have looked ahead at the script, you may have noticed that the leader of the meeting about Mr. C. did not directly confront the staff with their specific behavior toward this patient. Based on the leader's knowledge of the staff, the leader judged that such a strong confrontation would have been difficult for some to handle and might have provoked anger, denials, and defensiveness, which would not have been productive. Instead the leader took a less direct, more general approach and encouraged the staff to discuss their experiences with Mr. C. and how they felt about caring for him. If the members of the group had not brought up some of these behaviors, however, the leader probably would have had to introduce them in order to achieve the purpose for the meeting.

It is also helpful to write down some questions, preferably open-ended, that would help to move the group along during the discussion and some additional points or observations that you want to bring up in the course of the discussion. For example, the leader of the problem discussion about Mr. C. prepared and used the following list of questions and points to bring out during the meeting:

1. How did you feel about him? How did you feel about caring for him? About the condition he was in?
2. Do you think that he was suffering?
3. Toward the end, was he conscious of anything?

4. When caring for a patient like Mr. C., put yourself in the patient's place.
5. How do you deal with suffering? Is it difficult?
6. Can nurses become desensitized to others' pain?
7. Was it worthwhile to speak to him?
8. What was the likelihood that Mr. C. could still hear you and understood how you felt about him?
9. How should we deal with patients who are suffering, someone like Mr. C. who is comatose part of the time and aware some of the time?

Choose a Date

Each situation must be assessed separately to decide the best time for the conference. You may want to allow time for people to think about a problem before they discuss it in the group or you may want them to share their thoughts and feelings immediately after something has happened. For example, if a patient on the unit commits suicide during the morning, the head nurse may call a meeting for just after lunchtime. This allows time for the commotion surrounding the actual suicide to settle but it does not allow much time for unexpressed feelings of guilt, grief, and anger to build up in the staff. In this case, the conference needs to be held quickly in order to deal with the emotions aroused by the traumatic event.

On the other hand, if the administrator announces that the agency will be changing over to management by objectives (which is explained in Chapter 10), the supervisor may wait until staff members have attended some inservice programs on management by objectives before calling a meeting. This could provide staff members with an opportunity to acquire some knowledge of the subject before the meeting is held to discuss how they feel about the change. In this second instance, staff members are not as likely to have strong feelings on the subject and can discuss it more intelligently after they know more about it.

Two other considerations in choosing a date are avoiding conflicts with other scheduled conferences and events and choosing a day when most staff members are able to attend.

Choose a Place

Convenience, comfort, and atmosphere need to be considered when deciding where to hold a meeting. The place you choose should be a convenient location so that it requires the minimum of time and effort to get to it. This is true whether or not members of the group are all from the same organization. Most health care professionals are quite busy and consideration of their need to make the best use of their time is usually appreciated.

The room you select should be comfortable. It does not have to be luxurious but it is important to avoid any discomfort great enough to distract group members from the discussion: too hot, too cold, chairs too hard, or insufficient seating so that some have to stand. Lighting that is too harsh or too dim is also distracting; so are loud noises and harsh echoes in a room.

The atmosphere or climate of the room can also have an effect on the group. For example, the meeting room used by the board of directors may be too formal or forbidding for some people in your group while sitting outside under a tree may be too much like a picnic to keep others serious. The size of the room can also affect the group. A small group feels lost and often uncomfortable in an auditorium while a room that's too small and crowded makes people feel constrained from moving freely because they might bump into someone. In between these extremes, the size, color, and style of a room may have a more subtle effect on the group. The personal and cultural preferences fo people in the group will also affect their response to the place selected.

The arrangement of furniture in the room is another consideration. For most meetings and small conferences it is preferable to arrange the seating so that everyone can see each other and so that there are no obviously designated status positions in the group. A classroom with desks that are bolted to the floor would not meet these criteria as well as a circular table with chairs around it. You can see that it is much more difficult to achieve this seating arrangement for a large group.

Set the Time

The time for which the conference is set should also be as convenient as possible for both the leader and the members of the group. For example, staff working the day shift often find a relative lull in the day's activities just before and just after lunch. On the other hand, people who have to travel to a meeting often prefer to have it either at the beginning of the day or late in the afternoon in order to reduce the degree to which it interrupts their day.

Publicize the Meeting

The people who are invited to the meeting should receive adequate notice of the time, place, and purpose. This allows them to arrange their work schedules so that they can attend the meeting and also gives them some time to think about the subject of the meeting. Reminders are also a good idea. They reduce the possibility of a busy person forgetting the meeting, communicates the importance of that person's attendance, and eliminates that familiar excuse for absence from a meeting—"I forgot."

Provide Coverage

Unless meetings are held before or after the usual work day, staff members must be assured that their responsibilities are being taken care of while they attend the meeting. This may necessitate having someone take telephone messages or having several staff members remain on the unit in order to provide adequate care. Unless this coverage is provided, staff members will not be able to focus their full attention on the subject of the meeting and may have to run in and out of the meeting to attend to other responsibilities, this is very distracting for all concerned.

FIGURE 7-1 Refreshments are not necessary but can add a feeling of warmth, sociability, and informality to a meeting, which is often desirable.

Refreshments

Refreshments are not necessary but they can have a positive effect on the climate of the group. They can add a feeling of warmth, sociability, and informality to the meeting that is often desirable. The activities surrounding the distribution of refreshments can help relieve tension and restlessness when they are present (Fig. 7-1). The refreshments themselves are sometimes welcome simply because they meet a basic need when staff have not taken time out for meals (a pattern that should be discouraged because it affects people's ability to function). Refreshments should not be so elaborate, however, that they draw the attention of either the leader or the group away from the purpose of the meeting.

Reduce Threats

Unless you know the people and the group as a whole it is difficult to estimate how much of a threat a particular problem discussion poses for them. The meeting can be perceived as a welcome break from work or it can be a dreaded source of fear and anxiety. Because people differ in their responses, each situation and individual will have to be assessed separately in order to effectively reduce the threatening nature of a problem discussion. Some of the most common reasons for seeing it as a threat are mentioned below.

The unknown is often a source of anxiety. People who are not familiar with this type of meeting will wonder what's going to happen during the meeting and what they'll be asked to do. Some may feel threatened by the anticipation of any kind of confrontation. Others may be worried about being criticized or embarrassed in front of the group. An explanation of the meeting and its ground rules and prior positive experiences in problem discussions will help to reduce this threat.

People who are not used to expressing any kind of feelings in such a group may need extra support before they are comfortable in any problem discussion. Those who are uncomfortable being the center of attention need to be treated differently from those who feel threatened when they are not the center of attention. You can adjust your actions and expectations accordingly.

People who hold low status positions (such as aides or orderlies) may feel uncomfortable when asked to give their opinions in front of the professionals on a health care team. Other people with higher status and authority within the organization may see the meeting as a threat to their authority when they are not leading it. In the meeting about Mr. C., the leader asked Mr. C.'s primary nurse to describe his condition to prevent the primary nurse feeling usurped.

IMPLEMENTATION

Opening the Meeting

There are several things you can do to get the meeting off to a smooth start. The furniture can be arranged ahead of time and any equipment (such as a taperecorder) can be in place and ready to use. If refreshments are being served, they should be ready and can be offered to people as they arrive. Greeting each person by name as they arrive makes people feel that they are welcome and important members of the group.

It is important to start on time. Some people may have left work incomplete in order to get to the meeting on time and will resent being kept waiting. Also, if you start late, people will arrive even later for your next meeting. Those who have time to socialize can do so at the end of the meeting, so you do not have to hesitate about breaking into social chatter that is going on before the meeting.

The leader opens the meeting by welcoming the people as a group and briefly stating the purpose of the meeting. A short description of the problem to be discussed and the ground rules for the discussion is then followed by an open-ended question that will open up the discussion to the rest of the group. The first page of the script is an example of the way one leader opened a meeting.

Guiding the Meeting

One of the leader's primary responsibilities during the rest of the meeting is to foster open communication within a nonthreatening environment. A statement at the beginning of the meeting that all group members should recognize and respect the personal and subjective natures of the feelings expressed will help to establish an accepting climate within the group. The leader can also stress that no contribution should be attacked or labeled as a "wrong" feeling or "wrong" thought. Any contribution should be accepted as stated and not judged by the group but it may be further explored and discussed by the group.

During the course of the discussion, the leader can remind the group of the ground rules when it is necessary. The leader should also cut off any personal attacks and point out the difference between constructive and destructive statements and confrontations.

The leader can confront any nonfunctional behavior. For example, you can ask someone who is monopolizing the conversation to give someone else a chance to speak. Confrontation is also appropriate if the group evades the issue or denies having any problem when it is evident that a problem exists.

When the group is not sufficiently mature to recognize the needs of group members, the leader can meet some of these needs, especially for support and recognition. This can be done nonverbally by nods, smiles, positive voice tones, and eye contact, as well as verbally. It may also be necessary for the leader to encourage contributions from the silent members. This can also be done verbally or nonverbally by looking in their direction when asking a question.

Another responsibility of the leader is to keep the discussion focused on the subject of the meeting. This can usually be done by asking pertinent questions but sometimes it is necessary to remind the group of the problem under discussion or to point out that they are getting off the track.

The questions and pertinent comments prepared ahead of time by the leader have two other purposes. They can be used as a stimulus for discussion when the conversation lags. The leader's evident interest and concern about the problem also acts as a stimulus to keep the discussion going. Once group members become actively involved in the discussion, they can also act as energizers.

Another use of those questions and comments is to guide the group toward some kind of closure at the end of the meeting. The kind of closure needed depends on the purpose of the meeting: it may be agreement on what the problem actually is, it may be the resolution of a conflict, or it may be primarily a sense of having shared feelings and supported each other. In the example given here (of the meeting about Mr. C.) the leader tried to guide the group toward an evaluation of the care they were giving and a commitment to improve it in the future.

Summarizing

At the end of the discussion the leader summarizes the points of view offered and identifies any closure that has been achieved by the group. It is often helpful to take notes during the conference or ask someone else to do this in order to be able to quickly and accurately summarize the results for the group at the end of the meeting. Meetings that end abruptly without a summarizing statement about the resolution of differences or consensus on how a situation can be improved are apt to leave people feeling that nothing has been accomplished.

SCRIPT

The following script of an actual meeting in which the nursing staff discusses their problems caring for a patient shows the leader carrying out many of the actions discussed above but omitting some others. Some comments about the leader's actions and the roles played by various group members are given alongside the script. An analysis of this meeting follows the script.

PROBLEM DISCUSSION SCRIPT

Script	*Comments and Roles Played*
Leader: I'm really happy that you're all taking time out to do this today, 'cause I know it's time out of your really busy schedules. We've been talking a little about what a feelings conference is. A feelings conference is when you take a subject and examine your own feelings about it and share with others your feelings and perhaps things that influence your thoughts—maybe something in your background, your past experience, or your training that influences your feelings about a certain person or a disease—something to do with nursing. And, hopefully, the goal of this is to understand your fellow team members, and to promote communication. The end result is better patient care.	*Role: Initiator* The leader sounds uncertain about staff members' interest in attending the meeting. The leader could have been more positive and assertive about the value of spending time at the meeting.
This is the ideal. Would you like to try this for the next fifteen minutes? (pause) OK. I would like to talk about Mr. C. Even though he passed away about a week ago, I thought we still might discuss him because we might have patients now who are like him. Or in the future, you'll most likely run into patients like him again.	The words by themselves do not convey the nonverbal interest in the meeting evident in the leader's voice, which had staff members nodding their heads in agreement at this point.
Would someone briefly like to run over his problems—what his condition was?	Here the leader looked at the primary nurse, encouraging this individual's participation and showed a willingness to share leadership of the meeting.

Primary Nurse: Mr. C. was a cardiac patient. His problem was that he was such a poor surgical risk that he was not operated on. He had gangrene of the foot, and it got worse. He had contractures of both arms and legs, in fact, he was almost in the fetal position. At first he was unable to speak to us.

Roles: Information Giver, Contributor

Leader: How many people here came in contact with him or cared for him?

Role: Information Seeker

Nurse 2: I think all of us did at one time or another.

Role: Information Giver

Leader: How did you feel about him?—About caring for him?—About the condition he was in?

Note how every other sentence is spoken by the leader here. This is a stilted pattern that gradually changes as the conference progresses.

Primary Nurse: Sorry for him. So sorry that someone would have to suffer like that.

Role: Expresser

Leader: Do you feel that he was suffering?

LPN 2: Oh yes, because he knew what was going on for a long time. Like, when you were doing anything to him, when he'd had enough, he'd pat you on the arm. That was for a long time. Well, toward the end it was like he wasn't a person. I mean, he was a person, but it was like he was already dead but still alive.

Roles: Information Giver, Expresser

Leader: So, toward the end, do you think he was conscious of anything?

Not an open-ended question. Note the response.

LPN 2: Yes.

Leader: Why do you think so?

LPN 2: Because I still think Mr. C. responded to pain. When you did his dressings he certainly indicated his discomfort. When you spoke to him and managed to get through his subconscious, I think he sort of acknowledged the fact that you were there. The response of his eyes. But even the last days it seemed he was aware.

Roles: Information Giver, Opinion Giver

Leader: How did you feel when you cared for him? Was it something you liked doing because he was suffering, or was it distasteful to you?

LPN 2: I found it unpleasant. With Mr. C., I just felt like I could pick him up and hold him. You just felt empathy and I never minded being assigned Mr. C. I mean it was distasteful, *yes.* But he was just so dear. When he was himself he used to squeeze your hand and his eyes would just twinkle. And I think when you remember these things about a patient. . . . When you had a patient for so many weeks, I don't think anybody could enjoy doing the dressings because it was an almost insurmountable task. Sometimes, we ended up with the dressings looking less than desirable. It was a difficult chore. Speaking for myself, I never minded doing Mr. C. I just thought he was the sweetest thing.

Role: Expresser

Nurse 3: I feel pretty much the way LPN 2 did. I have my own personal problem with odors. I had to leave the room many times and come back because I really got kind of nauseated at times. I'd walk away for a minute, but I came back. But I just felt he was a patient who needed a lot of care, the basic needs. I think he was very much aware that you were taking care of

Roles: Expresser, Elaborator, Contributor
This group member is openly sharing a reaction to the patient, which is what the leader had hoped to elicit from the group.

him. That we did care, that we'd do anything we could to keep him comfortable. I do feel he had pain, and more could have been done in that area. We could have stressed that he should have had something for pain, which he did not have. He was a real challenge to do, but I think he was very much aware of what was happening in his room, and who came and went.

Leader: How do you deal with a patient who's suffering?—Someone like Mr. C. who is comatose some of the time, aware some of the time.

Roles: Information Seeker, Gatekeeper

LPN 2: I don't think Mr. C. was ever what you'd call "comatose." He was, I think, deep in sleep quite a bit, but we could always manage to reach his subconscious.

At this point, the leader had to decide whether to clarify these terms for the LPN or to continue the focus on feelings—a difficult decision.

Leader: Do you think it was worthwhile to speak with him, to him?

Role: Opinion Seeker
Not an open-ended question. Could have stifled discussion but it did not.

LPN 2: To him, yes.

Nurse 3: Oh, definitely, yes. Because he was aware that we were in the room. They don't have T.V.'s, they don't have radios, and I think a lot of the patients really look forward to whatever reason we come in. That's a couple of minutes they can talk to somebody. Because I think it's extremely lonesome for these patients and I really think that's a very important part of our nursing care, that you do talk about the weather or what's in the headlines. To talk to them— some kind of interaction—it keeps them in touch with reality.

Roles: Elaborator, Contributor

LPN 2: I know in orientation classes, they tell us that we are to keep a patient in contact with time and place and even though the patient is unable to respond to you, you should still treat the patient as somebody with a mind that is still functioning whether we're aware of it or not. No matter how comatose a patient is, that's always the proper thing to do.

Role: Information Giver

Nurse 2: I had what would be termed, I suppose, a real awakening. I know when I was at another hospital we had a young man, not Mr. C., but I think it is a good simile. This young man had been in a motorcycle accident. He was only married about three months. I think he was about age 25. He was on a Stryker frame, fully paralyzed, totally unresponsive, with a tracheostomy tube, foley catheter, and the whole bit. And yet his wife—it was almost eerie, and it sent shudders up and down your spine to walk past the room and hear her, day after day, reciting her marriage vows, for richer and poorer, in sickness and health. She and his whole family came in and would tell him what happened in church today, and do you know that boy came around. He walked out of that hospital and went home. And I think it's because his family kept his brain alive. As a matter of fact, even when he had the tracheostomy, we had to caution his wife against feeding him whole pieces of turkey that she had prepared at home and we'd end up suctioning. But I mean, they would not give up on him. And I'm glad they didn't. I'm not going to say that his mind was as healthy as we would have liked it to have been; he was rather

Roles: Elaborator,   Recognition Seeker
The example given here generally supports the idea that it's important to give good care to a comatose patient but is getting off the track and could divert the group from the subject of the meeting.

juvenile. But at least he was a functional human being. So we can't ever say that they don't hear you and that it's not going to be worth the effort.

Leader: So you feel even if they can't respond to you in some big way that they still can hear you and understand you and get your vibes and feel how you're feeling.

Role: Consensus Taker.
The leader is bringing the discussion back to the subject.

Nurse 2: Hearing is supposed to be one of the very last senses to leave the body. And this is something we have to caution our visitors about repeatedly. Visitors will come in and they'll even talk about funeral arrangements right over a patient. And we always have to caution them, "You know, the patient may not be talking to you but is listening to us."

Role: Information Giver

LPN 3: Some things, even to say, "Gee, he must be so uncomfortable"—at least that person may hear what you're saying and at least know that you're trying to understand he's uncomfortable. Those things, I feel are right to be said. It's a real situation to them, it's a real situation to us. And I think we should be factual, and if he's uncomfortable, let's do something about it.

Role: Opinion Giver

Leader: When you're caring for a patient who is in very sad condition, like Mr. C., or someone who really wins your heart, do you feel sorry for those patients, do you ever put yourself in their place?

Role: Opinion Seeker

LPN 2: I think that's a good idea, to put yourself in another's place, because then you would be gentler with them. And you wouldn't want some-

Roles: Encourager (accepting another's idea), Opinion Giver

body to be rough with you if you were a patient.

Leader: Is it difficult to deal with suffering?

Again, this question could have elicited a deadening "yes" or "no" answer but the group is moving along well enough that it did not have this effect.

LPN 2: Yes, it always is if you have compassion for someone. We had a Nursing Arts Instructor who told us whenever we enter a room we are to consider a patient's age. And if the patient is 25 years old and you are 24, you can consider this your husband, brother, sister, or whatever the case may be. If the patient's twice your age you can say, "this could well be my father or mother, and I intend to take care of the patient as I would for grandparents and so forth." I think this is something everybody should do. Aside from putting yourself in that person's position, just to think in terms of this person belonging to you in some relationship.

Roles: *Information Giver, Contributor*

LPN 3: Just in terms of interaction between one human being and another. If you were very ill, and some stranger came in to care for you, you'd hope that that stranger would treat you like a human being. The family concept I was also taught— person to person, stranger to stranger. You walk into that room and consider how you'd like to be cared for by a stranger.

Role: *Elaborator*

Leader: Do you feel that a nurse can be desensitized to pain? Can you be bombarded with people who are suffering so much that you might forget?

Role: *Consensus Taker*

Nurse 3: I think you can be too busy sometimes, for the moment, to stop and think, but I don't think you could ever be really desensitized.

Role: Opinion Giver

Nurse 2: You build up certain protections for yourself, because you are around them so much. You have to protect yourself—we'd be drained, thoroughly drained, if we didn't. But myself, no. I would never be completely desensitized.

Roles: Elaborator, Opinion Giver

Leader: So, summing up, if we were to walk into a patient's room who couldn't communicate with us, or else that patient's communication was minimal, and it was evident that the patient was suffering a great deal— and needed total care—and you had to give the patient a bed bath, what kinds of things would you consider or should do or think of while you were caring for the patient, knowing that the patient is suffering?

Role: Coordinator and Information Seeker, not Summarizer
The leader is not really summarizing as stated but is guiding the group toward moving on to the second purpose of the conference, which was to critically evaluate the care they give.

LPN 3: Be gentle, don't take too long, just straighten the patient out, wash, turn, and position the patient. Just to remember the patient's a human being. Every patient's different and you see so much suffering. And I really felt terrible for Mr. C.—it was terrible to see someone have to die like that, and see that gangrene every day. And then we had a Mr. H. here and I found that very bad. That was enough to break your heart, watching that man suffer.

Role: Contributor, Expresser

LPN 2: They both had the problem, too, of loose bowels. I know I will certainly admit to being guilty of saying, just after getting Mr. C. repositioned and dressed, "Oh, no, not

Role: Information Giver, Expresser

again!'' I would voice what crossed my mind because all of a sudden it was running all over and we had to begin from scratch again.

LPN 3: What could you talk to the patient about when you were going to give the patient a bath?—If you had to move him into the portatub?

Roles: Information Seeker, Gatekeeper
Nonverbally, the LPN looked around the group while saying this.

Nurse 2: You're supposed to tell your patient, ''Now, Mr. C., we have to move you, and pick you up. It's going to hurt.'' Let them know what's being done. You're not supposed to pick the patient up and just suddenly put the patient in the middle of the air even though they're supported by strong arms. They should know where they're going and why.

Roles: Information Giver, Opinion Giver

LPN 2: I don't think any of us do that. We all talk to them—we all say, ''OK, you're going to get a bath and have to roll over. We all talk to them. That would be scary. . . .

You can see that the meeting has become much less stilted here. This is a common pattern as people relax and become more involved in the discussion.

Nurse 3: Even a patient that you're not sure what they're hearing and seeing or how much they're aware of, if we say our name to them, ''I'm S.T., and I'm going to take care of you and give you a bath,''—a voice and a name. They remember good things and bad things, so, if they're waiting for that one person, it must drive them crazy when we don't say our name! Even though they can't say, ''Good morning, I'm Mr. C.,'' we should still say, ''Good morning, I'm S.T.''

Role: Elaborator

LPN 1: He didn't want to be touched. He just wanted you to leave him alone and let him die.

Role: Blocker
The tone of voice and body language strongly communicated negative feel-

ings from this group member who only spoke once. If it were not for the nonverbal negativism, the role would have been *disagreer.*

LPN 2: I know, especially when you were doing his mouth and suctioning and so forth, he just sort of looked up annoyed. I think sometimes they just wish you wouldn't show up on the scene when they're bubbling froth and so forth. I got that impression.

Role: Elaborator

Nurse 2: I think we were with him the last day, and LPN 2 you were doing him up and we rolled him over. He ceased breathing. We suctioned him and he went on for another 12 hours.

Role: Information Giver
This group member is getting off the track again.

Leader: But you felt he communicated with his eyes.

Again, the leader is bringing the group back on the track by restating what LPN 2 had said. This is also a good way to support what people have said.

Nurse 2: I think he certainly did, and with his hand, too. There would be pressure from his hand. When I spoke to him and asked if he could hear me it was like he was really trying to communicate. The reason we knew he was in pain, too, because when you were dressing him, and he was turned to his side, his arms were extremely long and he had seven-inch fingers, and he'd be doing this, trying to grasp your bottom or your waist or your back, just to let you know that you were hurting him. I mean I don't think it was any other sense, it was just his way of reacting. You don't often see, thank goodness, challenges quite like Mr. C. Most of them never get to that stage. He was an elderly

Roles: Expressor,   Information Giver, Opinion Giver
Note that this response is back on track.

man, but he had an extremely strong heart. He had pneumonia three times while he was here.

Leader: Is there anything else any-one would like to say?	*Role:* *Gatekeeper*
Leader: Well, thank you all very much for taking time out. I really am very appreciative of it.	The summary belongs here but was omitted by the leader.
LPN 2: Thanks a lot. I learned a lot from you.	*Role:* *Encourager*

ANALYSIS

The number of factors that can be included in the analysis of a conference is almost endless. For the most part, the ones included here are those that have been emphasized before in this book: the seating arrangement, the communication pattern, roles played by each group member, maturity of the group, the course of the discussion, the decision-making process and outcomes of the conference, the dominant synchronizers, and the leader's style and effectiveness. In addition to all of these, a sociogram that illustrates the pattern of the group interaction has been included.

Sociogram

A sociogram[2] (Figure 7-2) is simply a diagram that illustrates the seating arrangement of the group, the number of contributions and side comments each member made, and to whom they were directed: the leader, a group member, or the group as a whole. The sociogram can be drawn during the meeting by someone who is willing to record the group interaction or it can be done afterward from a videotape of the meeting. The leader of the group is usually too involved in other activities to make a sociogram during the meeting.

To draw a sociogram you begin with an outline of the room and a schematic representation of the furniture arrangement. As people take their seats their names are placed on the diagram. When the meeting begins, the recorder draws a line from one group member to another to indicate who spoke to whom. An arrow to the center of the diagram indicates a comment made to the group as a whole. The slashes on these lines indicate how many times a message was sent in this same direction.

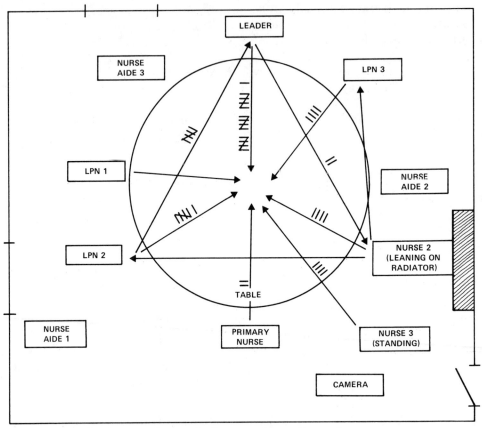

FIGURE 7-2 Sociogram drawn during a problem discussion.

When it is done, the sociogram tells you who the most active contributors were, who was the recipient of most of the comments, and who did not participate. The pattern of interaction can be seen from the lines and direction of the arrows and it may also show how the seating arrangement influenced the interaction. A sociogram is a helpful tool for analysis of group dynamics but it cannot tell you what the climate of the group was, what roles were played by group members, or the value of the contributions made.

Figure 7-2 shows the sociogram drawn for the problem discussion relating to Mr. C.'s care. You can see that the leader spoke much more often than anyone else and that none of the nurses aides spoke at all. Note also that Nurse Aide 1 was voluntarily positioned outside the group. LPN 1 spoke only once but the other two LPNs were more active contributors. Nurse 2 directed comments to several different people as well as to the group and this active role would lead you to look at the script to see if Nurse 2 dominated the group or tried to usurp the leadership of the group, which was not done in this case.

Seating Arrangement

The number of chairs available was inadequate, leaving two people standing throughout the meeting. One of the people began shifting from one foot to another as though getting tired of standing.

The arrangement of the chairs was an informal circle and allowed each member to make eye contact with everyone else who sat in a circle. Those who stood and the aide who moved to sit in the corner could not do this as well as the others.

Communication Pattern

You can see from both the sociogram and the script that the overall communication pattern was somewhat stilted. This is especially true for the beginning of the meeting, when every other contribution came from the leader. Later in the meeting, the spontaneity of the group increased considerably. The presence of the videotape camera may have had some influence on the initial lack of spontaneity.

Roles Played by Group Members

The majority of roles played by group members were functional ones as you will see in the following review of the roles. You will also notice that nonverbal behavior, which cannot be communicated well in either the script or the sociogram, is an important component of the role played.

1. The *PRIMARY NURSE* played the roles of *Information giver, contributor, expresser, and follower.* At the beginning of the conference the primary nurse reviewed Mr. C.'s condition and the information this group member gave served as the basis for further discussion. Throughout the rest of the meeting the primary nurse remained silent, not a disinterested or sulky silence, but one that communicated an attentive attitude as this member looked at each speaker with an expression of interest. The primary nurse also indirectly encouraged others to feel free to say what they really felt by having done so early in the conference.

2. *NURSE 2* played the roles of *information giver, recognition seeker, elaborator, and opinion giver.* Once nurse 2 played a nonfunctional role and twice this group member's contributions tended to get off the track but nurse 2's overall contribution to the group was not really negative because this member generally supported the purpose of the meeting and other people's comments. Due to the lack of chairs, this group member stood leaning against the radiator through the whole meeting.

3. *NURSE 3* played only functional roles. Nurse 3 shared feelings near the beginning of the meeting about caring for Mr. C. and how odors were offensive. Nurse 3 acted as an *elaborator, contributor, opinion giver, and expresser* several times. This member's overall contribution was very positive and with frequent participation

nurse 3 helped to keep the discussion moving along. This group member stood through the whole meeting and seemed to get tired and restless near the end.

4. *LPN 1,* in contrast played only nonfunctional roles. LPN 1 was a *blocker and a zipper-mouth.* Except for one comment, which was negative, this member sat silently throughout the conference, looking around the room and not making eye contact with any of the speakers. A slight scowl and peeved expression was evident on this member's face.

Apparently, LPN 1 came to the meeting because this member felt pressured to attend after being invited by both the leader and the primary nurse, not due to a desire to attend. Before the meeting LPN 1 said, "I can't be in two places at one time. Someone has to stay on the floor!" in an angry voice. During the meeting, LPN 1 sulked and LPN 1's overall contribution was negative because this member's behavior could not have helped but have at least some dampening effect on the group.

5. *LPN 2* was an *information giver, opinion giver, expresser, contributor, elaborator, and encourager.* The roles LPN 2 played were as functional and positive as those played by nurse 3, except that some of what LPN 2 said was not entirely accurate. LPN 2 sat at the table actively listening and making eye contact with each speaker, sometimes frowning with concern when Mr. C.'s suffering was mentioned. LPN 2's contributions and voice were warm and friendly in tone, which indicated this member's willingness to support the stated purpose of the meetings.

6. *LPN 3* played the roles of *opinion giver, elaborator, contributor, expresser, information seeker, and gatekeeper.* LPN 3 responded positively to other people's contributions and expressed some feelings about Mr. C. This group member sat at the table and remained silent at the beginning of the meeting, seeming to need time to warm up.

7. *NURSE AIDE 1* played only the role of the *zipper-mouth.* Nurse aide 1 did not say one word during the conference but sat in a corner, removed from the group physically as well as socially. This member seemed completely inattentive, looking down frequently, and had a bored facial expression. This member's yawn was an indication of lack of interest. Nurse aide 1 enjoyed the provided refreshments and seemed to regard the conference as a chance to sit down and get away from the unit for a while.

This group member's effect on the meeting was mostly neutral. Nurse aide 1 neither added nor detracted, this member's presence was barely felt. This member was like an object that was simply present, just like one of the lockers.

8. *NURSE AIDE 2* acted as a *follower.* Although nurse aide 2 did not say a single word, this member sat up straight and made eye contact with each speaker, occasionally, nodding in agreement. Nurse aide 2's contribution to the group was positive in the sense that this member nonverbally supported the others when they spoke.

9. *NURSE AIDE 3* was also a *follower* during the meeting. Nurse aide 3 sat at the table near the leader and watched with wide-eyed curiosity. This member had never attended a problem discussion before and was attentive throughout the meeting. Nurse aide 3's contribution was positive in the sense that this member acted as an attentive audience.

Maturity of the Group

The somewhat stilted communication pattern is one indication that the group had not achieved maturity. Much of the discussion had an air of politeness and restraint (noted also nonverbally) and there were no confrontations except from the leader. Several group members were quite open about their reactions to Mr. C. but others seemed to hold back and did not share their feelings. Still others contributed nothing and the group made no attempt to include them, which would have been another sign of a mature group.

This group was composed of people from the same patient care unit. They work together on a regular basis but evidently have not developed into a mature group yet. They certainly have not completed the performing stage and are probably working on some of the tasks of the norming stage of group development.

Course of the Discussion, Decision-Making, and Outcome

There were only two minor instances in which members of the group began to get off the track. With the exception of these two, the discussion remained focused on the subject introduced by the leader in the opening remarks.

Although the discussion became less stilted and more relaxed as it continued, there was little change in the way group members dealt with the subject. In fact, there really wasn't much more sharing at the end of the meeting than at the beginning nor was there any increase in the depth or strength of the feelings shared or of the emotions aroused during the meeting. This indicates that an unspoken agreement, that no group member would confront another member about their feelings or about the care they gave to Mr. C., was probably operating as a hidden agenda. In spite of this hidden agenda, there was some discussion of the ways in which patients such as Mr. C. should be cared for, which was something the leader had hoped to accomplish.

It is interesting to note that all of the nurses and most of the LPNs participated verbally in the discussion but not the aides. The reasons for their lack of verbal participation needs to be explored before the next staff problem discussion in order to increase their involvement in the group. The aides could have been uncomfortable with the subject of the meeting or with expressing negative feelings in a group that contains people who have some authority over them, or both. Because the aides did not participate verbally, any decision made by this group would have come from the nurses and two of the LPNs and would not have been a true consensus of the group as a whole.

Actually, the design of the meeting was not meant to lead to any specific decisions about actions that the group would take in the future. These decisions would probably have been premature at this point and so would probably not be carried out later. The group did come to some agreement on the fact that a patient such as Mr. C. can suffer terribly, can understand and respond to their communications, and is greatly in need of good nursing care. Also, the meeting did increase the staff's awareness of the needs of patients such as Mr. C. and supported those who tried to give them good care. However, they did not directly confront the fact that their care of Mr. C. had been lacking in several respects or that they needed to improve in the future. Nor did they commit themselves to an improved standard of care in future for patients with similar conditions, which was the leader's hoped for outcome of the meeting. Additional meetings with a deeper exploration of the issues could eventually lead to such a commitment from the entire group.

To summarize the outcomes, the first purpose of this meeting, to encourage a sharing of feelings about caring for Mr. C., was fairly well accomplished although the depth of the sharing could have been greater. The second purpose, to critically evaluate the care they gave, was partially met and the hoped for commitment to improve care in the future was not achieved.

Dominant Synchronizers

The hidden agenda to avoid confrontation was the most apparent dominant synchronizer of this group, from the very beginning of the meeting right to the end. The leader's evident concern for the needs of patients such as Mr. C. was a second influence throughout the discussion but it did not overcome the force of the hidden agenda.

Leadership Style and Effectiveness

The leader's style during the meeting was clearly democratic but the leader was more directive (authoritarian) in the preparation of the meeting, especially since the leader chose the subject without input from the group. However, the choice was appropriate because the leader's observations had substantiated the need to discuss this subject.

The leader's preparations for the meeting were thorough in some respects but not in others. Everyone invited to the meeting was given adequate notice of the date, time, and place and they all knew what the subject of the meeting would be. Everyone who was invited attended, although one did so under protest and this member's needs were clearly not met by either the leader or the group. The meeting started and ended on time and the refreshments were simple and ready when people began to arrive. The seating was inadequate and this could have been avoided. The leader prepared some helpful questions and comments ahead but the opening remarks did not explain the ground rules clearly and apparently, the leader did not take notes or have anyone record comments during the meeting to use as a summary at the end.

Comments have already been made about the effectiveness of most of the leader's actions during the meeting so they will be summarized here. The leader's questions, though not always open-ended, were pertinent and helped to keep the discussion moving along in the right direction. The group was kept on the track most of the time (which is not always easy to do) and did share some feelings. The leader's verbal and nonverbal behavior was supportive, encouraging, and nonjudgmental throughout the meeting, which is especially important during a problem discussion.

No meeting or conference is perfect. The flaws that are pointed out in this analysis of the problem discussion about Mr. C. do not reflect any serious errors in judgment or failure to take action on the part of the leader. Instead, they reflect the ordinary ups and downs of leading meetings and conferences that you can expect to encounter in your practice of leadership.

SUMMARY

Problem discussions are a type of meeting designed to allow ventilation of feelings and confront issues and clarify them before problem-solving can be done. Preparation for such a meeting involves consideration of the purpose and the potentially threatening nature of the meeting, the leader's presentation, and coverage for the staff as well as deciding on the date, time, place, seating arrangements, and refreshments. The opening remarks by the leader should include greetings, the purpose of the meeting, the ground rules, and a brief description of the problem. The main responsibilities of the leader during the rest of the meeting are to enforce the ground rules, keep the discussion focused on the subject, provide support, encourage participation, confront when needed, guide the group toward closure, and summarize accomplishments at the end of the meeting. The script of an actual problem discussion meeting was included followed by a detailed analysis of the group dynamics and the leader's actions.

Problem-Solving Conferences

Problem-solving conferences are meetings held for the purpose of finding solutions to the numerous problems encountered by people at work.

Although many problems can be solved by an individual using the problem-solving process described in Chapter 5, group problem-solving has several advantages over the individual approach. Group problem-solving brings together the expertise and diverse viewpoints of several people. Combining the energies of group members may have a synergistic effect and may result in more inventive, creative solutions to problems. In addition, people who are actively involved in the whole process are far more likely to be committed to carrying out the solution than are people who have been handed a ready made solution to a problem.

Many different types of problems can be raised and dealt with in a problem-solving conference. These different types of problems include procedural problems, difficulties in relationships within the team or with other departments and agencies, and problems encountered in working with patients or clients. Patient-centered, client-centered and family-centered conferences are all types of problem-solving conferences concerned with working out better ways to help people receive proper care.

The term *problem* is used in the broad sense here to mean any kind of difficulty, dilemma, or complex situation in which careful thought and planning is needed to work out the best way to approach the situation. The problems can be minor ones that are dealt with within a few minutes or they can be major ones that require a series of meetings for their resolution.

A format for problem-solving conferences is described in this section. This is a suggested format that should be adapted to your own particular needs and situation. Many of the considerations in preparing, implementing, and analyzing the problem-solving conference are the same as those for leading problem discussions, so the areas in which there are differences between the two types of meetings are those that are emphasized here.

PREPARATION

Purpose

A problem-solving conference is held for the purpose of proposing alternative actions that can be taken in a particular situation and then weighing each of these alternatives and deciding which ones to implement after the conference. In other words, it is a group approach to the problem-solving process.

The problem discussion type of meeting is held primarily to allow the ventilation of feelings and to clarify issues. Once this is done, problem-solving can take place but it is not always necessary to hold a problem discussion first. When the subject is not an emotional one and the problem can be readily identified and agreed upon by the group, you can proceed directly to problem-solving with the group.

Problem-solving conferences are most effective when they are an integral part of your team's or department's regular functions. These conferences are designed to bring together the knowledge and skills of all teams members to deal with the regularly occurring perplexities of providing high-quality health care services. They are not meant to be held only when something has gone wrong or when students are assigned to the team.

When problem-solving conferences are regularly scheduled, team members can anticipate these meetings and plan their work schedule to include the meeting time. These conferences can also increase the cohesiveness of the team by providing opportunities to share ideas and experiences. When staff members are accustomed to the conferences, they are more likely to suggest subjects to be dealt with in the meetings and less likely to be threatened by them, provided they are conducted in a nonthreatening manner.

Plan the Presentation

Problem identification and clarification are done before the conference, so that the group can move quickly into generating solutions. The extent to which group members need to be involved in this part of the presentation depends on how well the leader knows the group and how much clarification of the problem is needed.

In order to set the stage for problem-solving, it is important to gather all information available on the subject and to present a clear picture of the problem to the group. This usually requires more extensive fact gathering than is necessary in preparation for a problem discussion. If this preparation is not done well, the group will spend too much time adding information or disagreeing with your initial presentation of the problem and little or no problem-solving will be done.

Usually, there are several sources of information to tap for the needed data including the people who will be invited to the conference. Thorough preparation requires the use of all these sources. For example, if you were planning a family-centered conference you would use your own observations, agency records, other agencies who were involved with the family, the family itself, and each participant in the conference as sources of information. Consulting with conference participants not only supplies information but also gives you an opportunity to find out their opinions, identify potential blockers (and prepare for them), and recognize the importance of each group member's participation.

When the fact gathering has been completed, the information is summarized in a brief but complete description of the situation and statement of the problem. The emphasis should be on the most pertinent facts and the current picture rather than on the past history except when the past history influences the current problem. This is especially important when preparing a summary about a client with a long and complicated health history.

When the problem concerns a client, it can be stated in terms of a theoretical framework. For example, if the conference is about a family about to be evicted from their apartment, the problem can be stated as a threat to the family's basic physical need for shelter, using Maslow's hierarchy of needs as the theoretical framework. The use of a theoretical framework may help to prevent participants from restating the problem in terms of their own framework, especially in an interdisciplinary conference where people from different professions often use different terms and concepts to describe the same problem.

Reduce Threats

Since current situations and alternative actions are discussed more than personal feelings during a problem-solving conference, the meeting itself is not as likely to be threatening as a problem discussion, even to those who are not accustomed to attending them. However, the unfamiliar is always potentially threatening to some people, so the leader needs to be alert to this response to the conference.

There are several other ways in which a problem-solving conference may pose a threat to people. Some people are uncomfortable about having their work discussed in a group and may be anxious about the possibility of being criticized or embarrassed during the meeting. Others, especially ancillary personnel, may be afraid of saying something stupid or of not having anything to contribute. Also, if you are recording the conference in order to analyze it later, some people may feel self conscious or uncomfortable about being recorded or about having their participation evaluated later.

Most of the time, these feelings of anxiety or insecurity are not strong enough to keep people from attending the conference but you need to be aware of the fact that this can and does happen. The leader who is alert to this potential can take action to reduce the threat sufficiently that people feel comfortable enough to attend and participate in the meeting.

Choosing a date, time, place, providing coverage, seating arrangements, and refreshments are virtually the same for problem-solving conferences as they were for problem discussions with one exception. Problems discussions are held when the need for them arises but problem-solving conferences can and should be a regularly scheduled part of any work group's activities. The scheduling is based on the same considerations as those for a single meeting. Additional problem-solving conferences can also be held as needed.

IMPLEMENTATION

A problem-solving conference begins with opening remarks, a description of the problem, and a statement of the problem. This is followed by discussion of alternative actions that can be taken to solve the problem and a decision by the group on which actions will be taken. Finally, the conference is summarized and the decisions made are carried out.

The leader of the conference makes the opening remarks, describes the problem, and then turns over the discussion to the group. The leader guides the discussion, summarizes the results of the meeting, and ensures that the decisions are followed up after the meeting.

Opening the Meeting

A few words of welcome from the leader are a good way to begin any meeting. These greetings are followed by a brief explanation of the purpose of the meeting. Reminding people about the ground rules for confrontation is not as vital to the success of a problem-solving conference as it was for the problem discussion but it is helpful to remind the group that time is limited, ask them to keep to the subject, and encourage contributions. In some situations, it may be a good idea to also remind the group of the difference between constructive and destructive criticism.

The description of the problem is probably the most important part of your opening remarks because it sets the stage for the rest of the meeting. After describing the problem (a helpful rule of thumb is to limit yourself to five minutes for doing this), you open the floor for suggestions from the group. For example, you can say, "How can we as a group (or team) help the family meet their need for adequate shelter?" This statement, or one similar, serves to summarize the problem and encourage contributions. It also fosters group feelings and emphasizes the responsibility of the group members rather than the leader to generate suggestions for solving the problem.

Once the leader has asked this question, the leader remains silent in order to allow group members to get involved in the discussion. Remaining silent can be difficult to do if you are anxious to have the meeting go well. While the period of silence may seem like an eternity to the leader, it is usually only a matter of seconds before someone in the group begins the problem-solving.

Guiding the Meeting

There are two things to accomplish during the main part of the meeting. The first is to generate alternative solutions to the problem. The second is to decide which of the solutions will actually be implemented by the group after the conference.

Once you've opened the meeting and presented the problem, most or all the suggestions should come from the group. The leader's role is to encourage and recognize these contributions and keep the group focused on the subject of the meeting. If the group gets stuck, you can suggest that they try brainstorming to come up with a solution. At other times during the meeting, it may be necessary to restate the problem if the group gets off the track. If restating the problem does not help, you can point out to group members that they are getting off the subject.

A climate of acceptance encourages creative suggestions, so you also need to ensure that people are not criticized or attacked for making a contribution. Verbal or nonverbal attention from the leader also stimulates contributions. Every suggestion should be responded to in some way so that people are not discouraged from making further suggestions. The suggestions should also be recorded so that none are forgotten and all are recognized.

When the group has finished generating alternatives, the leader guides the discussion into the decision-making phase of the conference. Both a selection from among the alternative actions and a commitment to carrying out the actions are needed to fulfill the purpose of the conference.

While the suggestions were being made, there may have been some spontaneous evaluative comments and some mature groups will progress to a consensus without guidance. But most conference groups will need some direction from the leader in order to reach a consensus on which of the suggested actions they will actually take after the meeting. If the group comes to a decision too quickly, it may be necessary to test and challenge their commitment to the decisions made because a superficial agreement will quickly fall apart after the conference.

There are several common problems with group members that you are likely to encounter when leading problem-solving conferences.[3-4] These are problems with group members who talk too much, do not talk at all, or who try to take over the leadership of the group.

These nonfunctional behaviors usually reflect an unmet need of some kind. For example, aggressive and monopolizing behavior can be the result of frustration from not being able to achieve a desired goal. Feelings of insecurity may also be manifested by aggressive behavior. When these needs cannot be met within the group or by other actions of the leader, other measures must be taken to reduce their disruptive effects on the group. In this case, the leader can encourage contributions from others and avoid making eye contact with the monopolizer. A person who continually monopolizes the discussion can also be asked to give someone else a chance to speak. Direct statements about expected behavior in the group may be necessary in dealing with a person who attacks others. Group pressure can also effectively restrain attacking behavior.

Lack of participation may be the result of fears of being ridiculed, hurt, or embarrassed by the group. It may also be the result of disinterest, sulking or simply having nothing to say. Although the nonparticipant is not disruptive, this member's silence is usually not functional and does affect the group; imagine an entire group of zipper mouths and you will see why.

Assertive behavior on the part of the leader is necessary when faced with attempts to usurp that leadership. The democratic leader shares leadership with the group but does not abdicate the leadership role. Weak, laissez-faire leaders leave a leadership gap that others will try to fill. People who are accustomed to the leadership role may find it difficult or uncomfortable to allow someone else to act as the leader of a conference in which they are participating. Active, assertive leadership behavior in preparing and leading the conference is an effective way to counteract this. Other times, however, the usurping of leadership is a conscious power play and the leader needs to confront this behavior or counter it with a stronger power play. It can become necessary to use power tactics to overcome an attempt to take over your leadership.

Summarizing

Summarizing the results at the end of a meeting is a good way to review the conference, ensure that everyone agrees with the results and remind everyone of what they have agreed on during the conference. Every suggestion offered by a group member should be mentioned in the summary in order to provide recognition for participation and to avoid anyone feeling that their contribution was worthless. This listing is followed by a statement of the actions that the group has decided to take to resolve the problem.

Follow-Up

Unless the actions chosen by the group are actually implemented, there is little reason to hold the conference and go through the problem-solving process. For this reason, the leader's responsibility extends beyond the end of the conference to following up and ensuring that these actions are actually carried out. Even when the group seems to be highly motivated to carry out its decisions, you cannot assume that these will actually be done. If the decisions are not carried out, the leader's and group's time and energies expended in planning and attending the meeting are wasted and future problem-solving conferences are likely to be viewed with disinterest and even apathy or resistance.

ANALYSIS

Decision-Making

A participative, democratic, decision-making process is vital to the successful outcome of a problem-solving conference. The active participation of every member of the group is sought in problem-solving conferences because each participant will be expected to carry out the decisions made by the group. Decisions made by the leader or by only a few group members will not get as much support from the rest of the group as would decisions based on a true consensus of the group. In fact, when the leader or a subgroup dominates the decision-making during the meeting, the rest of the group may simply ignore the decisions after the conference (See Research Example 8-1).

Outcomes

The decision made should effectively resolve the original problem as well as being a consensus from the group. For example, if the group decides to continue an action that has not been helpful in resolving the problem so far, the meeting probably did not accomplish anything even if a consensus was achieved. On the other hand, if the group has come up with a well-conceived, creative solution and is committed to carrying out the solution, then the meeting was worthwhile.

With the exception of the decision-making process and outcomes discussed above, the analysis of a problem-solving conference should look for the same elements as the analysis of a problem discussion: the sociogram, seating arrangements, pattern of interaction, group roles, course of the discussion, dominant synchronizers, and leader style and effectiveness, all discussed in the previous section on problem discussions.

SUMMARY

Problem-solving conferences are meetings held to work out ways to resolve the many procedural, interpersonal, and client care problems encountered by work groups. The preparation, implementation, and analysis is similar to the problem discussion except that a more complete presentation of the problem is made; the conference may threaten participants in different ways and the purpose of the meeting is to generate a list of alternative solutions and to obtain a commitment from the group to carry out the selected actions after the conference. A successful conference results in a consensus on taking action that will effectively resolve the original problem.

Information Conferences

DEFINITION

An information conference is the sharing of knowledge, skills, and experience with others. The conference can be on almost any subject: it can be a review of an aspect of nursing care for coworkers, a report about a new nursing service to other caregivers, a class for patients preparing for discharge, a mini-workshop in health prevention strategies for the community, and so forth. The information conference usually has a more general application than the problem-solving conference, which focuses on a specific situation.

The information conference is essentially a short-term, teaching-learning situation. Even though it is brief in comparison with formal courses and seminars, the design of such a conference still needs to be based on an understanding of the teaching-learning process. The basic principles of teaching and learning that will be discussed here can be adapted to almost any group of adults so long as you keep their special characteristics and needs in mind as you plan the conference.

DESIGN PHASES

The design of an information conference has nine important phases (or steps) according to Kemp.[5] These phases are summarized in Figure 7-3. The leader first must have an idea of the general purpose of the conference and of the concepts on which the conference will be based. You will also need to assess the characteristics and needs of the people who are attending the conference and the setting or environment in which the conference will take place. Once you have decided on these general outlines of the conference, you can then write specific objectives for the conference and assess some more specific characteristics of the learner. The content of the conference and the way in which it is presented should be based on your assessment and your objectives. At the same time, you also need to provide a comfortable, facilitative setting for the conference. Finally, after the conference is given, its effectiveness needs to be evaluated.

The planning of information conferences and other informal teaching is often haphazard and incomplete. These phases of instructional design, from stating the purpose to evaluating the outcome, provide a clear guide for systematic planning and implementation that will increase the effectiveness of your information conferences by directing your attention to the many aspects of the situation that need careful consideration. Each of these phases will be discussed in the following sections. It is important to note that the environmental aspects of planning an information conference (selecting a convenient time and place, creating a climate of trust, and so forth) are virtually the same as for the problem-solving conference except as noted. These aspects will only be mentioned briefly here, although they are equally as important for information conferences as they are for other types of conferences.

State the general purpose within a conceptual framework.

Identify relevant characteristics of learners and environment.

Write specific behavioral objectives.

List content areas for each objective.

Assess learner's pre-instructional level of achievement for each objective.

Select appropriate teaching/learning activities.

Provide a facilitative environment.

Implement a teaching plan.

Evaluate outcomes and revise as needed.

FIGURE 7-3   Phases in the development of an information conference.

STATE THE GENERAL PURPOSE WITHIN A CONCEPTUAL FRAMEWORK

Purpose

At this point in planning, you can state the purpose in broad terms. The purpose is the reason for or the goal of the conference and should be a simple general statement. The following are examples of general purposes for information conferences:

> To inform other agencies about our new pilot program for families of brain-damaged children.
> Improvement of our crisis intervention techniques.
> Increase staff understanding of the new hyperalimentation procedure.

Being concerned about writing specific objectives or using the correct form or correct wording is not necessary at this point. In fact, being so specific may be premature since you have not yet found out the needs of the group. Specific objectives can be written after you have done your assessment.

You also need to decide whether or not an information conference is the most appropriate approach. Why are you planning an information conference? Do you want the staff to figure out why a patient is suddenly confused or do you want to improve the staff's ability to intervene with confused patients? In the first case, which involves an individual patient, a problem-solving conference would be more appropriate; in the second case, which has a more general perspective, an information conference is appopriate.

Conceptual Framework

A concept is a statement describing a common property of several facts or pieces of information.[6] It is a classification of things, ideas, or relations. A conceptual framework serves the purpose of organizing or unifying the information you plan to present. Using concepts rather than separate pieces of information organizes the content to make it more meaningful and easier for people to remember. Higher level principles and theories that predict or prescribe may also be used as a framework, of course, but at least a conceptual level is needed for a brief session.

The following is a sampling of some commonly used concepts in nursing. They are offered only to clarify what a conceptual level of organization for a conference could be, not to tell you what concepts to use.

Crisis Intervention	Nursing Process	Body Image
Sensory Deprivation	Grief Work	Self-Actualization
Developmental Tasks	Hope	Support Systems
Regulatory Mechanisms	Immobilization	Isolation

EXAMPLE. In order to illustrate how these phases can be applied to the planning of an actual information conference, the pilot program for families of brain damaged children will be followed through each phase.

> For the Family Project pilot program mentioned above, the conceptual framework could be networking (increasing the network or number of supports available to a person or family) to increase support systems for families with brain-damaged children.

IDENTIFY RELEVANT CHARACTERISTICS OF LEARNERS AND ENVIRONMENT

For whom are you planning this conference? Who needs this information? In order to write appropriate objectives for your conference, there are a number of things you need to know about the group. Although what you need to know about the group varies somewhat according to the purposes of the conference, the following list includes the characteristics and needs that most often influence the outcome of an information conference.

Goals: What does the group want to accomplish? What do they need to know? Are their goals congruent with yours?

Motivation:	What incentives are there for the group? Does the group have a need for the information? Other sources of motivation include expectation of some kind of reward, career achievement goals, general desire to improve skills and upgrade knowledge and the satisfaction inherent in mastering new skills or acquiring more knowledge.[6]
Abilities:	People differ in academic ability, knowledge, and skill already gained from other learning situations and on the job. For some groups, it is important to find out if everyone in the group is able to read because people rarely volunteer this information.
Learning Style:	Individuals and groups learn at different rates and approach learning in different ways. For example, some prefer a step-by-step explanation while others prefer open-ended discussions and use of general principles.[7]
Maturation:	The adult learner tends to prefer self-directed activities and is able to assume responsibility for one's own learning. As with any authoritarian style, a "teacher knows best" attitude is likely to elicit resentment and resistance.[8]

ENVIRONMENTAL CHARACTERISTICS

Setting

The setting in which you hold your conference can either facilitate learning or it can be a barrier to learning. As with any group, an open, accepting climate facilitates group process and learning. People need to feel free to make comments and ask questions. For some people, an informal arrangement is much more comfortable than a classroom setting. This is especially true for people who have had negative school experiences or who feel that classroom education is only appropriate for the young. Also, the social attitude that education ends in the early twenties and the myth that the ability to learn declines as people grow older still influence the way some adults feel about learning something new.

A comfortable physical setting facilitates learning. When you are too hot, too cold, or sitting on a hard chair, your discomfort can distract your attention from the conference. An inconvenient time and place can often keep people from attending even a worthwhile conference.

Organization or Community

The organization or community, or both within which you are working must also be considered in assessing the environment. Will people be rewarded for attending your conference and using what they have learned there or will they be penalized for "taking time off from their work" or for bringing back new ideas? For clients, in particular, a lack of support from family or friends can discourage them from attending a conference and can also undermine their efforts to implement what has been learned. Resistant coworkers can have the same effect on staff. Potential conflicts with socio-cultural values is of special concern with patient or health education but needs to be considered with staff as well.

EXAMPLE. To continue the Family Project example:

> Based on your past contacts with the agency personnel involved, you can conclude that they are able to understand the relatively basic level of information you plan to present (Ability). However, you will need to find out if they are familiar with similar programs and the services they offer because you'll need to offer more details if they are not. On the other hand, if the agency personnel are familiar with a similar service, you can compare and contrast the two. (This refers to Specific Achievement, which will be discussed after the Objectives Section.)
>
> The group's goals and motivation may be important: if the group is not interested, they may not even come to your meeting unless you build up their interest, perhaps by indicating how the new service can be of use to them (Motivation). Finally, how do these people from other professions feel about your agency beginning such a program? Do they, perhaps, see it as an invasion of their turf? (Goals and Sociocultural Factors)?

WRITE SPECIFIC BEHAVIORAL OBJECTIVES

Now that you have a clear idea of the purpose of the conference and of who the participants will be, it is time to be more specific about what you hope to accomplish. A brief description of goal setting and objective writing can be found in Chapter 00 on Components. To summarize, the objectives should begin with an action verb and should include a description of the behavior you expect of the group members at the end of the conference. Your purpose, conceptual framework, assessment of the group and environment, and knowledge of the subject are your guides in selecting appropriate objectives for your information conference. Two examples of objectives that could be used in a leadership course might be to:

> Compare the primary and team methods of delivering nursing care.
>
> Plan an information conference based on principles of teaching and learning.

Many people find it difficult to write objectives at first, partly because they get hung up on the correct form, but also because objective writing demands a very clear idea of what outcomes you expect from your teaching. However, it is this demanding nature of correctly written objectives that makes them worth writing down. Clearly stated objectives reduce much of the vagueness of purpose that can plague any planned learning situation.

Common Mistakes

There are several mistakes people make when they are learning to write objectives. A common one is to write the objectives in terms of the teacher or group leader rather than in terms of outcomes for the group as the following example shows:

| TEACHER OBJECTIVE | Show a film about insulin injections |
| LEARNER OBJECTIVE | Select appropriate site for insulin injection |

There are times when you will write objectives for yourself such as in a job description or in an independent learning situation, but when planning a learning experience for a group of people, objectives are written as the specific behaviors you expect the group to be able to do at the end of the conference or series of conferences.

Objectives should also be as specific as possible. Notice in the above example that the second objective is also more specific than the first one is. Another common mistake is to begin the objective with a vague verb such as "understands," which is difficult to define in terms of how you will observe that the group has actually accomplished the objective.

As much as possible, it is important to use observable behavior in your objectives. However, you will probably find that many equally important objectives related to attitudes and expression of feelings are difficult to measure directly although observable behavior can usually provide you with some indirect indications of a change in attitude. For example, acceptance of a diagnosis of cancer might be measured indirectly by a person's willingness to discuss the fact that one has cancer and by the kinds of future plans one is making. It is preferable to include a hard-to-measure objective than to leave out an important goal of your conference because measurement of the outcome will be difficult.

There is also a tendency to write more objectives for the lowest, more simple kind of learning (such as knows, defines, names, recognizes) than for the more complex kinds (such as use, apply, analyze, compare, design, plan, appraise, evaluate)[9] and yet these more complex objectives are often important goals of a conference. For example, in a class for people with diabetes, you would not want the people to only know what the symptoms of impending hypoglycemia are, but also how to differentiate these from hyperglycemic symptoms and to be able to take appropriate measures to raise their blood sugar level. The following example illustrates the difference between the lower and higher level objectives:

| LOW LEVEL OBJECTIVE | Defines hypoglycemia |
| HIGHER LEVEL OBJECTIVE | Distinguishes between symptoms of hypoglycemia and hyperglycemia |

Categories of Objectives

One additional point about behavioral objectives that you may have already gathered from the preceding discussions; there are three different categories of objectives, cognitive, affective, and psychomotor. *Cognitive* refers to the knowledge type of objective; *affective* refers to attitudes (such as accepts, defends, challenges, supports); and *psychomotor* refers to skills (such as injects, bathes, communicates).

The names of each of these types of objectives is probably not as important to most readers as is the fact that these categories help to remind you to consider using objectives from all three areas as appropriate.

Sharing Objectives

Educators usually recommend sharing your objectives with the group. From a leadership point of view, this recommendation does not go far enough. Objectives are essentially specific statements of a group's goals for learning and you will recall from the components of effective leadership that congruence of goals between the leader and members of the group influences the leader's effectiveness with a group. It was also recommended that the group be involved in goal-setting.

The effective leader includes group members in the planning of an information conference. You may not want to ask group members to actually write the objectives because it is a demanding and time-consuming task, but group members should participate in setting goals for the conference. Involvement of group members in goal-setting for an information conference will both increase goal congruence and increase group motivation to participate in the conference and to support the objectives of the conference. A set of objectives for an information conference about the Family Project pilot program could be stated as the following::

> At the end of the conference, participants will be able to:
> Describe the goals of the Family Project.
> Explain the services of the Family Project to their clients.
> Make appropriate referrals to the Family Project.
> Support the Family Project's goals.

LIST CONTENT AREAS FOR EACH OBJECTIVE

The objectives you wrote with the participation (or at least with the input) of the group can now serve as your guide in selecting content and then later in planning and evaluating the actual activities of the conference. The content includes whatever information the group needs in order to accomplish the objectives. It should also include the concepts that provide the framework for the conference and principles or theories that can be applied to the particular subject of the conference. If you have psychomotor objectives, you may include demonstration and practice of some skills. To achieve affective (feeling or attitude) objectives, you can include discussion of common myths, of positive and negative experiences, and of people's reactions or feelings about the subject.

Need to Know

Probably the most common mistake in selecting content for any kind of learning experience is to confuse what is "nice to know" with what people "need to know."

It is very tempting to throw in some interesting facts about the subject or a few anecdotes that are amusing but not really pertinent. For example, this happens in patient education where patients are told the intricate details of the surgery that is going to be performed or how a new valve or joint replacement was invented, but not how they are going to feel during the procedure or what they will need to know to care for themselves when they get home. Relating the content to each specific objectives will help you avoid falling into this trap.

Sequencing

Regarding the sequence or order in which to present the content, it is usually helpful to begin with content that is familiar to the people in the group and then proceed to the unknown. Another useful sequence is to begin with the simple or concrete and proceed to what is complex or abstract. Some content has a logical order to it such as a procedure that you would probably want to demonstrate step-by-step from beginning to end.

EXAMPLE. Let us look now at what kind of content would be appropriate for the information conference about the Family Project. In order to see how the content flows from the objectives, the objectives will be repeated and the related content listed alongside each objective.

Objective	Content
1. Describe the goals of the Family Project.	1. Briefly describe the assessed needs of the families and how the Family Project is designed to meet these needs.
2. Explain the services of the Family Project to their clients.	2. List and describe each service offered: family support groups; telephone networks; counseling; legal consultation; financial assistance; health guidance; respite care.
3. Make appropriate referrals to the Family Project.	3. Specific procedure for referral; who to contact; eligibility requirements (need, financial, residence).
4. Support the Family Project's goals.	4. How the agencies represented plan to use the service; what the group thinks of the project; how the project can meet the needs of the agencies.

ASSESS LEARNERS' PRE-INSTRUCTIONAL LEVEL OF ACHIEVEMENT FOR EACH OBJECTIVE

The main reason for doing this specific assessment of previous achievement in regard to each objective is to avoid wasting time, both yours and the group's. There are two aspects to this assessment. The first is the *prerequisite knowledge and skills* that are needed to begin the learning experience. These prerequisites could include background knowledge in math, psychology, nursing, or previous practice and experience. If the group members have this background, then they are ready for your conference.

The second aspect of this assessment, *specific achievement,* is the extent to which members of the group have already achieved specific objectives. You can find this out by using a pretest, a questionnaire, or by informal questioning and discussion before the conference. This specific assessment will also help you to apply another important leadership principle: begin where the group is. The pretest may have a useful side effect—it can arouse interest and awareness of the need to learn if presented in an effective manner.

In the Family Project example, you would need to assess the following:

Prerequisites:
　　Ability to assess clients' needs.
　　Experiece in making referrals.
　　Some familiarity with networking.
Specific Achievement:
　　Experience using the agency's referral procedures.
　　Extent of information already received about the Family Project's goals and services.
　　Attitudes toward the Family Project.

Avoid Assumptions

The emphasis here on a thorough assessment may seem excessive when you are simply planning a short, information conference or a series of informal classes. But a thorough assessment can save time and increase the relevance and effectiveness of the conference. There is a saying, often related in patient education, that may be appropriate here: *Assume nothing.*[10] Failure to do a complete assessment has led to many poor conferences, where information is presented that the group already knew or that the group could not comprehend because it was assumed that they had the prerequisite knowledge or skills.

Every person and every group has different characteristics, needs, and past experiences, so assessment is always an important part of planning an information conference. For example, caregivers frequently assume that their well-educated clients understand what is happening to them. Yet in hospitals that do not provide adequate patient teaching, many cardiac patients leave unable to even list the risk factors associated with their heart disease. The community nurse might be surprised to find that even a well-educated client thinks it is OK to share an insulin syringe with another family member. An inservice educator might find that many nursing assistants do not know the location of many vital organs in the body.

SELECT APPROPRIATE TEACHING/LEARNING ACTIVITIES

Unfortunately there is no formula for selecting the appropriate strategy. But there are some specific factors to consider in making your choice from the almost infinite variety of ways in which you can structure a learning experience. To help you select strategies for your conferences, a list of some basic, generally accepted principles of learning will be presented and then the most common approaches to presenting content will be considered.

Basic Principles of Learning

The following list is not exhaustive, but it includes some of the most commonly agreed upon principles or recommendations for facilitating learning. The first four have been mentioned already, others may already be familiar to you:

1. Begin where the learner is.
2. Stimulate motivation to learn.
3. Make a thorough assessment: assume nothing.
4. Allow for individual differences in abilities, style, and sociocultural background.
5. Vary the rate of presentation according to the abilities of the learners and the difficulty of the material.
6. Provide opportunities for success.
7. Present challenging materials and activities to stimulate interest.
8. Provide sufficient repetition and emphasis of main points to promote remembering.
9. Provide opportunities for practice and for application of learning to new situations to promote transfer of learning.
10. Provide feedback as close to the event as possible.

While these principles are easily understood, it takes throrough preparation and often some ingenuity and creativity to actually apply them to a specific conference.

Presentation of Content

There are many different ways to present content. These are divided into three broad categories: autotutorial, presentation to the group, and active interaction.[5] A discussion of each of these follows.

AUTOTUTORIAL. Autotutorial literally means self-teaching. Most adults can assume responsibility for their own learning. They are able to make decisions about what it is they need to learn and can seek opportunities to fulfill these needs. This does not mean, however, that guidance and feedback are unnecessary; both are helpful to even the most skilled and autonomous person or group.

There are many ways in which people can learn on their own. Television, films, books, modules, and programmed instruction are all forms of autotutorial learning. The content can be fed into a computer, printed in a book, put on film or tape, put into a notebook format, or a combination of these. Preplanned autotutorial programs usually include objectives, pretest, exercises and other learning activities, and then a post-test.

Advantages. One particular advantage of autotutorial learning is that it can be highly individualized because it allows as many opportunities for repetition and review as are needed by each learner, and each learner can proceed at one's own pace. It is also efficient in terms of the leader's time. For example, an inservice instructor can put together a learning module explaining the use of a new crash cart. Then staff members can work on the module whenever they have the time and the instructor only needs to be available to answer questions that may come up and to administer the post-test.

Disadvantages. In completely autotutorial learning, the person interacts with the material, but not with other people. This means that there are no opportunities provided for sharing ideas with others. These opportunities are not only stimulating, but also reinforce learning. Discussion is also particularly helpful in bringing out feelings and attitudes. Some programmed materials become monotonous after a while (this happens with other methods also). Unless sophisticated equipment is available, learners cannot get frequent feedback on the quality of their work or the accuracy of their skills as they are learning or can they get a question answered readily, which can be frustrating.

PRESENTATION TO THE GROUP. Probably the first method you thought of in this category is the lecture, one of the most popular and yet most maligned of all teaching strategies. A lecture can be virtually one-way communication (but not *actual* one-way communication because you cannot *not* communicate) from a speaker to a passive listening group. But it can also be made more interactive through the use of question and answer sessions and discussion.

Lecture. A lecture is particularly useful when you want to introduce a subject, to clarify and explain a complex subject, or to share your experiences with a group. You can present a large amount of information quickly using the lecture format. When giving a lecture, it is especially important to pay attention to feedback from the group because the feedback is likely to be more subtle (unless they fall asleep) than with other approaches. Audiovisuals of all types from the use of a blackboard to films and videotapes can be used for visual stimulation but you need to keep in mind that they are also relatively passive modes.

Demonstration. A second popular form of presentation to the group is the demonstration. Here, instead of talking, the group leader shows a group how to carry out a skill. This skill could be anything from an aseptic technique to a client interview. Although demonstrations are usually interesting to watch, you need to be aware of the fact that the group is still relatively passive unless you provide opportunities for practice and return demonstrations.

ACTIVE INTERACTION. In this mode, the learner interacts with both the learning materials and with other members of the group. The leader's role in active interaction types of learning is to facilitate learning, focus attention on the objectives, challenge assumptions, provide feedback, and summarize learning. As you can see, the leader's role is still an active one, but less controlling than in the presentation to the group mode. The learner becomes an active participant in the learning experience.

Discussion. Open discussion is one of the most common ways to encourage active interaction. Discussion is useful in encouraging expression of feelings and attitudes, stimulating creative and divergent thinking, and for group problem-solving.

Role Playing. There are many other ways to provide active interaction even when equipment and facilities are limited. Role playing, games, and exercises are some of the many possibilities. An example of an active interaction mode for a leadership course would be to hold a mock conference with learners taking the roles of different staff members and then analyzing the mock conference dynamics and outcome.

Simulations. Simulations are another form of active interaction in which learners try out their skills in an imitation of life-setting. The almost life-like simulators called "Annies" used in CPR instruction are a well-known example of simulation. Simulations are an effective way to promote active participation and transfer of learning, especially for complex psychomotor skills, but they tend to require more equipment.

Each of the three modes—autotutorial, presentation to the group, and active interaction—has its advantages and disadvantages. A combination of two or all three is sometimes the most effective way to allow flexibility for different learning styles and to accomplish all the objectives of an information conference.

Example. To return to the Family Project example, the following teaching strategies could be chosen from the three modes:

Distribute written materials to participants before the conference (Autotutorial).
Briefly tell the group about the project's services and referral procedures (Presentation to the Group).
Give participants case study examples and ask them to determine eligibility and to fill out actual referral forms (Active Interaction).
Discuss the group's reactions to the program and how they think it will be of use to them (Active Interaction).

PROVIDE A FACILITATIVE ENVIRONMENT

A facilitative environment is just as important for an information conference as it is for a problem-solving or confrontation conference.

Adequate, well-prepared materials and functional equipment are especially important for learning situations. Inadequate or broken equipment creates frustration, wastes the group's time, and reduces learning. The well-prepared leader checks all these things ahead of time in order to ensure a smooth running conference.

Provision of comfort, psychologic security, and sometimes privacy, all make group members feel at ease. Setting a convenient time and place make it easier for people to attend the conference and show the leader's consideration for group members. Stimulation of motivation, including a supportive organizational or community climate, will also encourage people to attend the conference. The leadership activities involved in these facilitating conditions were included in the discussion of problem-solving conferences and will not be repeated here.

All of the factors mentioned under characteristics of the environment need to be considered in providing an environment that facilitates group process and learning during an information conference.

IMPLEMENT TEACHING PLAN

As with providing a facilitative environment, the leadership skills required to implement an information conference are similar to those needed for other conferences. Among the most important points to consider in conducting an information conference are the following, which are drawn from the components of effective leadership.

GOALS:	Be sure that the leader's and group's objectives are congruent.
KNOWLEDGE:	Know your subject well.
SELF AWARENESS:	Be yourself; do not try to mold yourself into a teacher role (especially the role of authoritarian expert) that does not suit your personal style or the style of the group.
COMMUNICATION:	Use language that people can understand; watch the use of jargon or technical terms. Encourage feedback from the group; provide frequent feedback to the group.
ENERGY:	Share your interest and excitement about the subject with the group.
ACTION:	Start the conference on time. Engage the group in the purpose of the conference by stimulating moti-

vation. Guide the learning process; keep group members on the track. Keep the pace lively but not so fast that you lose people. Encourage the active participation of *all* group members. Summarize at the end of the conference.

EVALUATE OUTCOMES, REVISE AS NEEDED

The evaluation serves several purposes: it is a measure of your effectiveness as the leader of the conference; it measures the extent to which you and other members of the group achieved your objectives; and it provides some direction for changes and improvements for your next conference. The obejctives you wrote in the planning stage will now serve as your guidelines in evaluating the conference. To the extent possible, the outcomes of the conferences should be measured in terms of the observable behaviors defined by the objectives.

A careful analysis of the objectives will tell you what behaviors need to be evaluated. Then you need to decide how you are going to evoke the identified behaviors, record them in some way, and then analyze the results.[11] Each of the steps will be discussed briefly.

Identify the Behaviors to be Measured

The more specific your objectives were, the easier this step will be now. If, for example, the objective was concerned with selecting the appropriate site for insulin injection, it is clear that asking for a return demonstration of an insulin injection by the client is one way to meet the objective.

However, a more general objective like one of those in the Family Project example about making appropriate referrals is more difficult to evaluate. To evaluate this more general objective, it will probably be necessary to observe a cluster of behaviors including the ability to determine need and eligibility and the ability to fill out the referral form correctly.

Evoke the Identified Behaviors

Paper and pencil tests are the most common ways to evoke the identified behaviors. There is a tendency with these tests to measure more lower level objectives such as defining terms or recalling information.

> An example of this would be to ask a person to list the appropriate sites for insulin injection. Asking that person instead to point out the appropriate site on a diagram or on oneself would test a higher level objective and an important ability for a person with diabetes to have.

Tests are usually more relevant when case studies or other ways to apply knowledge are used rather than simply asking for definitions or recall of facts.

When you need to find out not just what a person knows, but whether or not a person can actually perform in a given situation, other ways to evaluate achievement may be more appropriate.[11] Just as with the presentation of content, simulations of various kinds can be set up to measure the degree to which the objective was met. There are many ways to do this. You can ask people to react to a problem situation, select the correct procedure, perform in a laboratory simulation, or evaluate a videotape performance, to name a few.

There are two other ways that are often used to evaluate learning. The first is to ask for a *final product* such as a project report, a case study, or a videotape. The second is to test people in *real-life* situations. This has the advantage of high relevance but errors in performance can be more serious.

Affective objectives, those looking for changes in feelings or attitudes, are measured indirectly. Some ways to do this include the use of opinion surveys, questionnaires, and interviews. Another way is to keep anecdotal records of comments or actions.

> For example, one way to judge whether or not patients have accepted their diagnosis is to note whether or not they ever talk about their diagnosis. Another way, also indirect, is to observe the degree to which patients are following the prescribed treatment plan.

RECORD THE BEHAVIOR.   Some kind of permanent record is needed in order to share the results of the evaluation with others. A written test or final product provides its own record. Other ways to record behavior include videotapes, audiotapes, behavior checklists, and anecdotal notes. The last two (checklists and notes) are harder to keep objective.

ANALYZE THE RESULTS.   Grades are not usually needed or relevant for information conferences. What is needed in the evaluation of an information conference is a clear idea of what behaviors would indicate to you that the objectives have been met. Objective criteria that define what constitutes adequate performance are often important.

There are several approaches to determining the outcome. You can write out the correct answers to the test questions; write a model answer to a case study question; or produce a tape of an acceptable performance for comparison. Another approach is to draw up checklists that provide detailed descriptions of acceptable performance. For example, you can list each step in giving an insulin injection (draws up correct dose, cleans site before injection, and so forth) and then check that each step is done correctly.

Often the outcomes defined by the objectives are more general. For these outcomes, you can describe the behavior in more general terms and, if possible, specify a frequency. For example:

> You may decide that hearing a patient mention the diagnosis only once is not adequate evidence of acceptance of that diagnosis but that the patient mentioning it on three occasions to three different people would be acceptable evidence.

232

USE THE RESULTS.   The purpose of evaluating an information conference is to find out whether or not you've achieved your original goals for the conference. The evaluation will tell you how much has been learned and whether or not you need to hold another conference on the same subject. It will also tell you where your instructional design was well done and where it was weak and needs improvement. You can see that being involved in the evaluation process can contribute to your growth and development as a leader.

Evaluation has a use for the people attending the conference too. It provides them with important feedback about their behavior. By asking for some kind of return performance, evaluation also reinforces learning.

Example.   One of the objectives of the Family Project was to enable people from other agencies to make appropriate referrals to the project. This includes the ability to determine need, to determine eligibility, and to fill out the forms correctly.

> Presenting a case study of a client applying to the project for assistance would be an appropriate way to evoke most of these behaviors (except the ability to elicit the necessary information from a client during an actual interview). Group members could be asked to evaluate the hypothetical client's need and eligibility and then to fill out a referral form.

The answers could be compared to a model evaluation and referral form you prepared before the conference. Any discrepancies between the model and the group's answers could be discussed with the group to determine what people had learned and what further information was still needed. The discussion should also give you some indications of the strengths and weaknesses of your design of the conference as well as the degree to which you fulfilled your own objectives.

SUMMARY

The planning and implementation of an effective information conference includes a number of steps. The leader begins with an idea of the general purpose of the conference and then identifies an appropriate conceptual framework within which to organize the information to be shared. An assessment of the characteristics of the group members and the environment is the next step. Then the leader is ready to write specific objectives for the conference.

Once the objectives have been determined, the content for the conference can be outlined and a more specific assessment of the learners can be done. Selection of appropriate activities completes the planning process. The leader then implements the conference, keeping in mind the factors that facilitate learning and applying the components of effective leadership. An evaluation based on the degree to which the specific objectives were met provides useful feedback to both the leader and to the other members of the group.

References

1. DOUGLAS, LM AND BEVIS, EO: *Nursing Management and Leadership in Action,* ed 3. CV Mosby, St Louis, 1979.

2. BEAL, GM, BOHLEN, JM, AND RAUDABÁUGH, JN: *Leadership and Dynamic Group Action.* The Iowa State University Press, Ames, Iowa, 1962.

3. BRADFORD, LP: *Making Meetings Work: A Guide for Leaders and Group Members.* University Associates, La Jolla, California, 1976.

4. HAIMAN, FS: *Group Leadership and Democratic Action.* Houghton Mifflin, New York, 1951.

5. KEMP, JE: *Instructional Design: A Plan for Unit and Course Development,* ed 2. Feron-Pitman, Belmont, California, 1977.

6. GAGNÉ, RM: *Essentials of Learning for Instruction.* Dryden Press, Hinsdale, Illinois, 1975, p 58.

7. BIEHLER, RF: *Psychology Applied to Teaching,* ed 3. Houghton Mifflin, Boston, 1978.

8. VACCA, R AND WALKE, JE: *Androgogy: The Missing Link in College Reading Programs.* Lifelong learning: The adult years Vol III, No 6 (February 1980), p 16.

9. BLOOM, BS ET AL: *Taxonomy of Educational Objectives. Handbook I. Cognitive Domain.* David McKay, New York, 1956.

10. GULKO, CS AND BUTHERUS, C: *Toward better patient teaching.* Nurses' Drug Alert Vol I, No 8 (March 1977), p 52.

11. GRONLUND, NE: *Measurement and Evaluation in Teaching,* ed 3. Macmillan, New York, 1976, p 197.

Chapter *8*

Teamwork

Teams are groups of people who work together. In this chapter we look at some of the different types of teams commonly found in health care organizations, including interdisciplinary teams, and at the advantages and disadvantages of working in teams. Then the major leader functions of team-building, delegating responsibility, and providing feedback will be discussed.

Teams

Teams are working groups. In order to be considered a team, a group must have some stability of membership and a common purpose. The people who are members of the team work interdependently, that is, they function as interrelated parts of the whole team. People who work independently of each other, with little communication, coordination, or shared responsibility, are not working as a team.

TYPES OF TEAMS

Teams can be classified according to their composition, purpose, leadership, and function. These categories are not mutually exclusive; teams can be described according to any or all of these categories.

Composition

The skills and experience of the people who make up the team are an important characteristic of any team. Some teams, such as the medical team, are made up of people in only one profession though members often have different specialties. Others, such as the nursing team consisting of registered nurses, practical nurses, aides, and orderlies, are made up of people at different levels within a particular health profession. Another example is the dental health team, which includes the dentist, dental hygienist, dental assistant, and sometimes a dental health educator.

Another type of team of increasing importance in health care is the interdisciplinary team made up of people from two or more different professions. The various combinations of disciplines are almost endless. The following description of a team is one example:

> A team formed to design a cardiac rehabilitation program could include a physician cardiologist, an exercise physiologist, a physical therapist, nurses specializing in cardiology and rehabilitation, a patient educator, a community health nurse, dietitian, social worker, and a psychologist specializing in stress reduction and biofeedback. In addition, the team would probably consult with others including administrators of the organization supporting the program, community health educators, public relations experts, and other specialists in cardiology, rehabilitation, and health education.

These combinations on one team create some additional difficulties and challenges to effective team functioning due to the additional differences between members of the team.

Purpose

The purpose of the team or the kind of work it does is often indicated by the team's name. There are surgical teams, IV teams, primary health care teams, and cardiac care teams. There are also teams with vague names such as project teams or management teams. Having such a name, however, does not guarantee that the team's purpose and goals are clearly defined or even that it really does the type of work implied by its name in some cases. You can find project teams that never complete a project and primary care teams that rarely give real primary health care.

Leadership

The leadership of most teams can be divided into three categories according to the way in which a person became the leader of the team: designated, emergent, or situational leaders.[1] One or more such leaders can exist at any one time in a team.

The *designated leader* is one who has been deliberately chosen either by the team or by an administrator or someone else who has some authority over the team. The leader chosen by the team itself is more likely to have the respect and support of the rest of the team but may not have as much delegated authority as the one who was imposed on the team by an administrator or other authority. The designated leader has clearer roles and responsibilities and usually a more permanent position as leader of the team than the emergent or situational leader. Most immature groups seem to need and prefer having a designated leader because it offers some structure to the group.

The *emergent leader* is one who evolves from the group by acting as the leader consistently enough to become the actual leader of the team. Emergent leaders often arise when the designated leader is weak and ineffective. They also arise when the team has no designated leader.

The *situational leader* emerges from the group in response to a particular situation or need. This leader is far more temporary than either the emergent or designated leader. The situational leader's role is limited to situations in which that person has the best skills or experience to guide the team's work. This switching of people in and out of the leadership role allows a great deal of flexibility as the team responds to different demands, but it can create some difficulties with continuity and coordination except in mature teams whose members can handle the frequent changes and are able to move in and out of the leadership position without friction or power struggles over the leadership position.

Teams can also be described in terms of their predominant style of leadership. For example, some teams have a strong preference for the participative or democratic style of leadership and will resist any attempts on the part of their leader to be too directive or autocratic. This is especially true of mature groups. Other teams have a nondirective or laissez-faire style, which can characterize both members and leader. Still others are very task oriented and have leaders who are controlling, allowing team members little or no say in the decisions made. Conflicts within teams often arise from a mismatch between the leader's style and the needs and developmental level of the team.

Function

Teams can also be categorized according to the way in which they function. Teams evolve and develop in identifiable stages just as other groups do. They can be classified according to their stage of development (forming, storming, norming, performing, or adjourning) or degree of maturity in the same way.

Another classification of function that is closely related to the style of leadership is the classification according to the way members of the team relate to each other. When the relationships are collegial, every member is accorded equal worth as an individual and recognition is based on their contribution to the team, rather than on their status and position within the team, larger organization, or in the community. In other words, all team members treat each other as equal and worthy colleagues.

In contrast to the collegial type of relationships, hierarchical relationships are based on each team member's status and position. Individual team members are not accorded equal worth. Recognition given to team members is based on their status rather than on their ability to contribute to the team. For example, on a team with a hierarchical pattern of relationships, the recommendations of a social worker would automatically take precedence over the recommendations of a home health aide. When strictly adhered to, the hierarchical pattern of relationships discourages free exchanges between team members of different status and results in team meetings dominated by higher status members. At team meetings, the lower status members would typically remain silent or go unheard when they try to contribute their ideas during a meeting.

ADVANTAGES AND DISADVANTAGES OF TEAMWORK

Leading teams and working as a member of a team presents a number of difficulties and challenges as well as benefits.[2-4] While they can't actually work in total isolation from other people in any health care setting, there are people who prefer to work independently rather than interdependently on teams. Some of the reasons for this preference will be mentioned in the listing of the disadvantages of teamwork. As you will see from the list of advantages, however, many types of health care can be delivered effectively only by well-functioning teams.

Advantages

The following are some of the advantages of using teamwork. This listing indicates some of the reasons why teamwork is often the preferred mode for carrying out organizing work on complex demanding tasks, including the delivery of health care:

Best Use of Skills.　When people with complementary skills are brought together on a team, each one is able to contribute their own special skills, experience, and viewpoint to the task at hand. With the right combination of skills, a highly functional team can manage more complex situations, provide more comprehensive care, and produce more creative ideas than any individual alone could do. Teams also allow greater use of paraprofessionals by providing the close supervision from the professionals on the team as is done in team nursing.

Coordination.　Teamwork demands that team members communicate with each other about the work they are doing. Effective communication among team members reduces duplication of effort and the possibility that people are working at cross purposes. For example, clients who receive uncoordinated health care often find that they are given conflicting advice from health care givers; one advises more rest, another advises more exercise, and clients do now know what change to make in their activities.

Synergy.　When people work well together, combining their energies to complete a task has a synergistic effect in which each one stimulates and reinforces the other. This synery contributes to the development of a highly motivated group of people committed to producing high-quality work.

Flexibility. A team with its combination of talents and skills is able to handle a greater variety of situations competently. When they have been working together for a while, team members are also able to help each other and to substitute for each other in an emergency so that the team is more flexible and responsive than individual workers can be.

Support. Team members can provide emotional support for each other as well as actual assistance with work. Effecive teams can help manage the anxieties and release some of the tensions that build up in many health care positions. Teams are also a source of collective strength and can supply a small power base and political support for its members when needed.

Increased Commitment. When individual team members have been involved in setting the team's objectives and deciding how they will be met, the team is usually much more committed to the successful completion of these objectives. The support from other team members and the effect of synergy reinforce this commitment.

Evaluative Feedback. When people work together on a team, the quality of their performance is more apparent and their team members can serve as valuable sources of helpful feedback.

Opportunity for Growth. In addition to being a valuable source of feedback, the team provides other opportunities for growth, especially for the development of interpersonal and leadership skills. Because people work more closely together and share more of their experiences with other team members, teamwork also provides an opportunity for members to expand their knowledge and skills in areas outside of their specialties.

Disadvantages

You may have noticed that many of the advantages of teamwork occur only when the team functions well. Likewise many, though not all, of the disadvantages arise when the team functions poorly.

Demands Interpersonal Skills. People often assume that you can simply put people together and they will function as a team. Of course, this does not happen. Effective teamwork requires a considerable amount of interpersonal skill from team members as well as the leader. Without these skills, teamwork can be a frustrating, discouraging, energy-consuming experience. In addition, people who prefer to work by themselves may find the continued interaction and demands for sharing among team members quite uncomfortable.

Conflicts. Differences in personality, culture, professional experience, norms, education, skills, status, and pay are all potential sources of conflict among team members. If you consider the fact that many teams work together eight hours a day, you can see why the tensions and conflicts can build up to an intolerable level if they are not dealt with effectively. Conflicts also arise when the goals of the team are not well defined and when the roles and responsibilities of individual team members are not clearly defined and differentiated.

Time Demands. Even the most ardent supporters of participative or democratic management cannot claim that it is a faster way to make decisions than the autocratic approach. An autocratic leader can make an instantaneous decision and communicate it to the group later but it takes more time to bring team members together and ask for their input or ask them to make the decision.

Reduced Autonomy. The person who values independence and autonomy over opportunities for feedback, support, and sharing of experience may feel a sense of loss when assigned to a team. Some caregivers find it difficult to "share" their clients with others and prefer to think of themselves as able to provide all the care needed. Others find it difficult to compromise or to go along with the team's decision when it is not in agreement with their own opinion on a subject.

Increased Scrutiny. A person who works alone can hide mistakes and inadequacies better than the person who works on a team. Being put in a position where these flaws will be revealed can be threatening to many people, especially to professionals who feel they should be perfect and not make mistakes.

Uncertainties and Diffusion of Responsibility. Because of the differences and uniqueness of each team member, teamwork demands flexibility and a tolerance of uncertainty about the way work will be done by different team members. This can be a source of frustration and stress for people who have a great need for structure and predictability. Also, when responsibility for patient care outcomes is shared by all team members, each member has to be able to trust the skill and judgment of other team members.

SUMMARY

Teams are groups of people who work together for a common purpose over a given period of time. The many different types of teams can be described according to their composition, purpose, leadership style, manner in which the leader evolves, degree of maturity, and pattern of relationships within the team. Advantages of teamwork include the best use of skills, improved coordination, synergy, flexibility, support for members, increased commitment, availability of evaluative feedback, and opportunities for growth. Disadvantages include the increased demand for interpersonal skills, conflicts, time demands, reduced autonomy, increased scrutiny, and increased uncertainty and diffusion of responsibility.

Team-Building

Effective teams do not just happen. Team-building requires specific knowledge, skill, and work.[5-6] In this section, steps used to build a team into an effective functioning unit and some problems encountered in team building are discussed. These include selecting team members, setting goals, defining roles, developing team identity, guiding decision-making, influencing group norms, encouraging open communication, and managing conflicts.

SELECT TEAM MEMBERS

Although you will not always be free to choose the people who are on your team, you will frequently have an opportunity to influence the selection. Ability to contribute to the work of the team and to work as a member of the team, or at least the potential to do these things, are both important considerations in selecting team members. Neither one alone is sufficient qualification to be a valuable team member or leader.

A third consideration in selecting team members is an appropriate mixture of people and skills on the team. For example, some nurses are especially good at responding quickly but calmly in emergencies while others have more skill in gaining the trust of a new client. Or you might find that your team needs a bilingual member in order to communicate more effectively with some of the clients served by your team. The need to achieve the right combination of skills has led to many different types of specialty and interdisciplinary teams.

SET GOALS

The need to clearly define your purpose and objectives or goals is one of the components of effective leadership and a common theme throughout this book. While this need may seem to be a relatively simple and basic principle of leadership, it is often violated.

Many teams are formed with only the vaguest idea of what they are actually expected to do. In fact, teams are often formed to deal with a problem that has not been effectively handled in the past and for which there is no clear solution. In this case, the team's purpose is to determine a solution and then implement it. Unfortunately, this is often not clearly spelled out and the team flounders trying to resolve the problem before the solution has been worked out.

Even when the purpose is almost self-evident, as would be the case with a surgical team or a home care team, there often is a lack of clarity and agreement on the specific objectives of the team or on the way the team is expected to meet these objectives. The following is an example of the questions that can arise:

The home care team has obviously been formed to provide health care in the client's home. However, many questions about the team's specific objectives can arise. Is the purpose of the home visit to enable the person to stay in the home rather than be hospitalized or is it to encourage hospitalization for a serious illness? Will the team meet only physical needs or will it also provide psychosocial support and counseling? Will the team help a client with housework and repairs, make referrals to meet these needs, or not deal with them at all?

You can imagine the number of possible conflicts and instances of team members working at cross purposes if these and similar questions are not answered before the team begins to provide home care.

DEFINE ROLES

As with the purpose and objectives of the team, the roles of individual team members are often not clearly defined. This ambiguity can lead to many conflicts; especially, on an interdisciplinary team where there are even more opportunities for confusion and misunderstandings about others' roles than on a single discipline team.

Role clarification is essential to smooth team function. Definition of roles is related to the purpose and objectives of the team. The following is an example of roles that need to be clarified in terms of what best meets the team's purpose and objectives:

A question arose at a planning meeting for the home care team: Will the physician and dentist on the team visit people in their homes or will the team's clients have to travel to the hospital for medical and dental care? Because most physicians and dentists do not make home visits, some team members assumed that their clients would travel to the hospital for these services. However, if two of the team's objectives are to avoid hospitalization and to reduce the necessity of travel as much as possible for their homebound clients, then the physician and dentist would be expected to provide as many of their services as possible in the home.

It is difficult to overstate the importance of clarifying such expectations as the one described in the example above. Conflicts over differing expectations can immobilize the team and even contribute to its demise if they are not resolved.

Even when the team's objectives are clearly spelled out, role negotiation among team members may be necessary since there is often more than one team member who can and wants to do a specific task or fill a certain role. For example, there are many overlaps between the usual functions of people in different health care professions. Nurses, social workers, psychologists, psychiatrists, and chaplains on a team may all see themselves as counselors or group therapists. Physicians, physician's assistants, pharmacists, and nurses are all likely to consider themselves prepared to develop and dispense information about medications to their patients. When this overlap occurs, a decision must be made whether to share the task, divide it, or designate who will do it. This decision needs to be made in such a way that it does not turn into a power struggle and that each person's ability is recognized by the team.

DEVELOP TEAM IDENTITY AND COHESIVENESS

In order to mature as a group and to encourage cooperative efforts among team members, people must first identify with the team. The team needs to develop a sense of itself as a functioning whole. In order to develop commitment to the goals of the team and the willingness of team members to engage in the sharing and support functions of the team, cohesiveness is also needed. There are a number of actions the leader can take from the very beginning of the team's formation to develop team identity and eventually cohesion within the group.

Definition

The team first needs to be defined. The more team members know about their team and its functions, the more they can identify with the team. They need to know who is and who is not a member of the team. If the team has not been given a name, you can do this or encourage team members to come up with a name that reflects the purpose or function of the team. Using the term "we" to refer to team members and yourself emphasizes the unity of the team as a functioning whole. A well-defined purpose and clearly stated objectives also assist in reinforcing the development of the team's identity.

Territory

A new team needs to stake out its territory; an established team holds and often expands its territory. This territory is not only geographic but also functional and psychological.

The influence of geographic territory on a team should not be underestimated. The team needs a place to meet, a place that is sufficiently quiet, comfortable, and private so that team matters can be discussed freely. Also, if the work spaces of team members (such as offices, examining rooms, or patient rooms) are physically close together, there are more opportunities for informal exchanges during the course of the work day. When the team has acquired work space, its territory can be identified and personalized by signs, arrangement of furnishings, and verbal statements of ownership, such as "This is our team's conference room but you may use it for your meeting tomorrow."

The team needs to acquire a functional and psychological space as well as physical space in the organization or community within which it functions. This means that in addition to team members having a clear conception of its identity and purpose, other health caregivers must also recognize and accept the functions and purposes of the team. In order to develop and maintain its identity and cohesiveness, it is important to have people outside the team respect its territory. Here is an example:

If you were the director of the inservice education department, you would want your team (department) to be involved in the development of all the inservice programs given within your organization. You would not necessarily insist that members of your team actually conduct every inservice but if you are to hold on to your territory, you would want all inservice programs to be coordinated through your department.

Maintaining your functional and psychological territory within the organization is necessary to maintain the identity and existence of the team.

Connections

Cohesiveness in a group is developed by increasing the number of connections between team members. Simply holding team meetings increases these connections. Every time team members interact with each other as members of the same team, their sense of being part of the team can be strengthened.

There are many other ways in which the leader can carry out this linking function. For example, whenever something exciting happens, the leader can make sure the experience is shared with the rest of the team. When someone on the team needs help solving a problem or getting work done on time, the leader can ask another team member to offer help. When a job is done well by the team, the leader can point out how cooperation between team members contributed to its successful completion. Each of these actions and other similar actions build positive connections among team members and increase team cohesiveness.

Esprit de Corps

Esprit de corps is a shared spirit, a feeling of enthusiasm that characterizes the team as a whole. The leader's own energy and enthusiasm can suffuse the entire team. It is also developed when members' needs are met within the team.

Setting some worthwhile but fairly easy goals helps to develop an esprit de corps because success can increase the team's motivation. But even failure can be used by the resourceful leader to show how team members need to work together in order to overcome the failure along the lines of that famous saying "We must hang together or we will all hang separately." Competition between teams can be used the same way. The power tactic of identifying a common enemy can also be used if needed to develop cohesiveness and esprit de corps. However, competition and working against an enemy must be used with care because they tend to set the team up in win-lose situations. Leaders can also become overly dependent on these more negative approaches when they are not necessary.

GUIDE DECISION-MAKING

The different ways in which decisions are made by a group can be divided into six categories. Decisions can be made by default, authority, minority, majority vote, consensus, and unanimous consent.[7]

Default

A decision by default is actually a nondecision by the group. The silence or lack of response from the team is taken to mean consent.

An idea is proposed to the group and when no opposition to the idea is expressed, it is assumed that everyone accepts it. This assumption is often false—team members may actually be strongly opposed to the ideas but for some reason have not expressed their opinion. A lack of response is usually a sign of withdrawal or apathy on the part of team members and also a symptom of some serious problems in team relationships. A team in which people feel restrained from speaking or are too apathetic to speak cannot function very effectively.

Authority

A decision made by authority is one made by a single person who has some authority in the group, usually the leader. This method is faster than having the whole team make the decision but it fails to use the expertise of other team members in making the decision and does not encourage the professional growth of individual team members or the maturing of the team as a group. It may also reduce the team's motivation to carry out the decision.

There are times, however, when decision by authority is the most appropriate method. For example, in an emergency situation the speed and accuracy with which the decision is made is more important than either the team's growth or motivation. There are also some administrative decisions, such as the firing of an employee, which are usually done by someone in authority rather than by a team, even a top management team.

Minority

Decisions made by a minority are those made by a small number of people on the team, usually a dominant subgroup. When a decision is "railroaded" this way by a small number of people, it is often resented by the rest of the group. This kind of decision-making occurs when the rest of the team either feels powerless to oppose the subgroup or when withdrawal, passivity, and apathy on the part of the majority of the team results in decision-making by a minority.

There are occasions when the team may decide to designate a subgroup to make certain decisions. This would be appropriate when only the people in the subgroup are affected by the decisions or when they are the only ones with sufficient information to make the decision. However, when the decision affects the whole team it is preferable to at least present a summary of the information with recommendations to the team and ask for a final decision from the team as a whole.

Majority Vote

Decisions made by taking a poll of the entire team is a method that is acceptable to most people. It has the advantage of soliciting everyone's opinion on an issue and of recognizing the desires of the majority of the group. However, decisions made by majority vote often leave the minority who voted for the losing side feeling somewhat dissatisfied even though they usually accept the decision (Fig. 8-1).

While voting has the advantage of fairness, it sets up a win-lose situation in which the majority wins but anyone who disagrees with the majority loses. It can also lead to some serious battles to gain the majority vote, which can be divisive and even disruptive if opponents begin attacking each other. Voting is particularly appropriate in a large group where it is difficult to give everyone a chance to speak on every issue or in an immature group that is not ready to come to a consensus on an issue.

Consensus

Decisions made by consensus are those in which the team seeks to gain every member's agreement on an issue. Decision by consensus is based on the prior understanding that everyone will go along with the final decision even if they are not completely satisfied with it. Members of a mature group are willing to do this because it is also understood that the team will attempt to resolve any differences of opinion in order to come as close as possible to a decision that satisfies every team member.

Decision by consensus recognizes both the right to disagree and the necessity of having some basic agreements in order to work well together. It also avoids setting up a win-lose situation and makes the achievement of a win-win situation possible. True consensus decisions demand that all members be willing to openly express their opinion and be willing to negotiate their position when there is some disagreement in the group. Although other groups can try using the consensus type of decision, a true consensus on a difficult issue requires substantial maturity on the part of the group.

Unanimous Consent

Unanimous consent is the genuine agreement of every team member on an issue. Although it is usually a sign of a mature group, unanimous consent can be reached on noncontroversial questions even by immature groups. However, when unanimous consent is reached too easily the agreement may be a superficial one covering underlying disagreement and a lack of open communication. For this reason, the leader should test the unanimity of a decision particularly in an immature group or when it is reached too quickly. Unanimity is not always possible on an issue and it is preferable to agree to disagree and try to resolve these differences enough to work together, rather than to press for unanimous consent and force team members into hiding their disagreement.

FIGURE 8-1 Making decisions by majority vote has the advantage of soliciting everyone's opinion on an issue but often leaves the minority who voted for the losing side feeling dissatisfied.

Selection

The type of decision, maturity of the group, and the effect on the team of the particular mode of decision-making should all be considered when guiding your team in regard to their choice of decision-making method. Most teams will not actually discuss their choice of decision-making method unless the leader brings up the subject, so you will probably have to initiate the discussion when a decision is about to be made rather than wait to be asked about it. The positive effects of including team members in decision-making are described in Research Example 8-1.

While each of these six ways to reach a decision are used by teams, some are more appropriate than others. Consensus and unanimity on a difficult issue require more maturity from the group than voting does. Decisions by authority may be necessary at times but decisions by default should be avoided as much as possible. Minority decisions are occasionally appropriate but often cause problems when the decisions affect the team as a whole.

Research Example 8-1. A Case Study of Participative Decision-Making

Bragg and Andrews[8] reported the results of an 18-month study of the implementation of participative decision-making in a hospital laundry. They compared the outcomes with two control hospital laundries. They defined participative decision-making as an approach in which the decisions about the way work is to be done are made by the same people who will carry out those decisions.

The administrator of the experimental hospital was in favor of participative decision-making but the laundry supervisor used an effective authoritarian style of leadership and was doubtful about the experiment at first, though the supervisor did agree to try it. The union also approved but provided no active support.

The 32 workers in the laundry who would be affected by this change were told that the goal was to make their work more interesting, not to increase their already high level of productivity. To implement participative decision-making, a total of 28 meetings were held in which the employees made suggestions for change. The supervisor changed roles, from direction-giver and overseer to one of being available, being a good listener, and sharing expertise with others.

At one of the early meetings, the employees suggested beginning and ending work two hours earlier. This suggestion was implemented in less than two weeks, as was done with other suggestions when it was possible to act quickly. By the fifth meeting, the supervisor was no longer an active moderator for the group but did continue to schedule the meetings, set the agenda, and assist in the implementation of suggested changes. As the group's climate became more cooperative and supportive, even the most reticent members began suggesting changes. Although the researchers anticipated that the older workers would resist the most, it was actually three younger employees who strongly resisted for a long time.

The implementation of participative decision-making resulted in increased employee satisfaction, increased productivity, and a total of 147 suggested changes. Eleven of these changes involved working conditions (such as the change in working hours), 44 involved equipment changes, 90 involved work methods, and 2 were concerned with safety. The score on an employee attitude scale rose from 62 percent at the beginning of the project to 90 percent near the end. The already low absentee rate improved even more during the experiment (from 1791 hours to 1194 hours of sick time) and productivity increased significantly resulting in a cost saving to the hospital of about $1000 per employee a year. These results did not occur immediately but happened gradually over the 18-month implementation period and they did not occur in the control groups. One of the reasons that productivity increased over an already high level was that most of the employees' suggestions were technical and measurably improved the work flow of the laundry. The researchers concluded that the employees had begun to adopt the organization's goals (for example, increased productivity) as their own when they were included in the decision-making process.

Postscript:
After the success of this experiment, participative decision-making was also implemented in the hospital's medical records department with a resulting decrease in a high employee turnover and in the number of union grievances. However, implementation of participative decision-making on a nursing unit was a failure due to a lack of administrative support and the strong resistance of the head nurse. The appointment of a supportive head nurse helped considerably but continued resistance from medical personnel kept it from doing as well as it had in other departments.

INFLUENCE GROUP NORMS

Norms are those unwritten rules that prescribe acceptable behavior in the group. Since they are often unspoken as well as unwritten, these norms can develop in a team virtually unnoticed and yet their influence on what happens within the group is significant. For example, norms that support creativity and flexibility over rigidity and resistance would affect the way the team responds to a new assignment. Norms supporting open communication over the suppression of feelings and disagreements would affect the way conflicts are handled. Norms can support arriving at work on time, working at a steady pace, and getting finished on time or they can support arriving late, doing the least amount of work possible, and leaving early.

Once a norm is established within the group, it can be difficult to change. The following is an example of a norm that developed unnoticed within a team and eventually led to a serious conflict before it was changed.

> When the IV team was first established, team members often finished their work early and were allowed to leave at 3 o'clock although their work day actually ended at 3:30. Over the next year their workload increased gradually but team members were still able to finish by 3 o'clock. The team coordinator (leader) usually stayed until 3:30 to provide coverage until the evening shift came in but rarely experienced any trouble doing this and felt that the team would appreciate the coordinator allowing them to leave early, although the coordinator did not actually verbalize any of this to the team.
>
> The team's work increased more rapidly the next summer and team members worked hard to be finished by 3 o'clock. One Friday, the team had a particularly heavy work load and had twice the usual number of emergency calls. By 3 o'clock, the emergencies were over but much of the routine work had not been finished. When team members began putting on their coats at five minutes to three, the coordinator asked them what they were doing and they responded that it was time for them to leave. The coordinator pointed out that there was a lot of work left and a team member said, "Well, you usually do the leftover work because you work later than we do." The coordinator told them it was too much for one person to finish and that they would have to stay. The same team member said "Sorry, but we leave at three," and the entire team walked out leaving an angry coordinator with several hours of work to complete since the evening shift team was a small group that could barely handle their own work.

In this example, the norm had developed to the point that team members actually believed they had the right to leave at 3 o'clock and felt that the coordinator's request was unreasonable. As you can imagine, there was a great deal of tension between the coordinator and the team the following week until the differences in expectations were clarified and the norm was changed.

The leader who is alert to the development of norms within the team can reinforce those norms that support effective working relationships and challenge those that would reduce effectiveness, preferably before the latter become well established. You can identify and question ineffective norms that are developing and discourage their use. You can support effective norms by pointing out their positive effects, encouraging and rewarding their use, and also by being a role model for effective working relationships. If these actions fail to change an established norm that is interfering with team function, stronger measures including confrontation, negotiation, and change strategies would be needed to modify that norm.

ENCOURAGE OPEN COMMUNICATIONS

Within the Team

Open communication is essential to the development of effective working relationships. It leads to the kind of understanding that promotes positive relationships and helps to prevent duplication of effort and working at cross purposes. It is the means by which purposes and objectives are clarified, roles defined and negotiated, conflicts dealt with, and decisions are made. Leader actions to encourage open communication within the team are the same as those used to foster the development of a mature group.

Written communications are also important, especially when team members are not in frequent personal contact with each other. They need to be direct, clear, concise, and free of jargon and abbreviations that are likely to be misunderstood by people with different backgrounds, education, and experience. Also, if written communications are to serve any purpose, they must be actually read by other team members and this cannot be assumed, it needs to be encouraged and verified.

With Other Teams

Although the focus here has been on what happens within the team, teams do not operate in a vacuum. They do operate within a particular environment and they have to deal with other individuals and groups within that environment.

Relationships between teams can be cooperative and productive or they can be unproductive, full of conflict, and even hostile. There is often some interdependence between teams such as having similar objectives, experiencing the same problems within the organization and community, or having overlapping work responsibilities. When these areas of common interest and concern are discussed openly, the potential for understanding each other and developing cordial working relationships is increased. The team needs to know what type of work is being done by other teams in order to prevent the problems of duplication of effort and working at cross purposes, which are even more likely to occur between teams than within a single team. Even teams with similar or overlapping functions can be widely separated and isolated from each other so the leader may have to deliberately plan meetings between the teams. Stronger measures may also be necessary when conflicts with other teams arise.

MANAGE CONFLICTS

Conflicts within a team are inevitable and sometimes necessary. While they can raise tensions and disrupt team functioning, they are not necessarily harmful. In fact, they can stimulate creativity and provide opportunities for growth.[1] They can be an opportunity to learn and improve interpersonal and leadership skills and to develop a deeper understanding of other people.

As a general rule, conflict is neither to be avoided nor stimulated, but managed. Too much conflict, or conflicts that are not resolved, reduce the team's effectiveness and eventually immobilizes the team. On the other hand, suppressed conflict continues to grow underground and is more difficult to resolve when it eventually surfaces because people have had time to harden their positions on issues and to become increasingly bitter or angry about the continuing conflict. Too many conflicts at once can overstress team members so it is sometimes necessary to wait until the most immediate problems are taken care of so that there is enough available energy to deal with the remaining conflicts facing the team.

Sources of Conflict

The conflicts experienced by a team can arise from any number of sources. These sources are usually related to an incompatible difference, a dispute over the allocation of resources, or a perceived threat to an individual member or to the team itself. Many incompatible differences can arise in a team. These differences may be due to culture, values, beliefs, language, education, experience, skills, professional values and norms, behavior patterns, status, pay differentials, and many others. Cultural differences, for example, can be related to differing concepts of work, change, and openness. Work may be seen as a means to an end or as satisfying in itself. Change may be seen as progress or as an unfortunate disruption in the present order of things. Some cultural groups value individuality and autonomy while others place a higher value on families and other social groups. Revealing personal feelings may seem natural to some people but inappropriate to others. Some of these differences can be profound. Adaptation is slow and often resisted as a dilution of a valued cultural heritage so these differences are often resolved by agreeing to accept and live with each other's differences.

The resources over which conflicts can arise are equally numerous. Resources that frequently are the source of conflicts within or between health care teams include work space, budgetary allocations, promotion to positions of higher activity, salaries, equipment and supplies, and recognition from administration or from the community. When resources are plentiful, an equitable sharing and negotiation for highly prized resources usually resolves the conflict. However, when resources are scarce or inequitably distributed, those with a greater share are very resistant to reducing their share and conflicts can be long and acrimonious.

There are also many instances in which an individual team member or the team as a whole becomes involved in a conflict in an attempt to reduce or remove a perceived threat. For example, some people perceive teamwork as a threat to their professional identity and to the territorial rights of their profession. There can be conflicts over who can change treatment orders, who tells the patient the diagnosis, who teaches the patient how to manage problems, who counsels the patient, who orders the lab tests needed, and so forth. Role clarification and role negotiation may help resolve this type of conflict.

Conflict Resolution

Conflict resolution begins with preventive measures to reduce the number of conflicts facing the team. Conflict resolution proceeds through accepting that a conflict exists, identifying the source of the conflict, seeking areas of agreement, and generating a solution.

Even before a conflict arises, there are some actions a leader can take to prepare for conflict resolution. It is especially helpful to create a climate in which individual differences are considered natural and acceptable. Although this does not sound difficult, there are often strong pressures for conformity to counteract in establishing this climate, especially in immature groups. Encouraging open communication and developing skills in confrontation and negotiation prepares the team to handle conflict constructively. Leader and group efforts to meet the needs of team members before a conflict arises helps to reduce the occurrence of the type of conflicts that are perceived to be threatening.

The existence of a conflict within the team should not be interpreted as a symptom of serious malfunction but rather as a sign of a problem that needs to be resolved. It is also helpful to maintain a realistically optimistic attitude that the conflict can be resolved. When team members refuse to accept the fact that a conflict exists, either because they can't handle it or because of accepted norms for ignoring and suppressing conflict, you may stay at this stage of conflict resolution for a considerable length of time.

Once the team has accepted the existence of the conflict, the conflict is analyzed to determine its source and who is involved in the conflict. If the source is not clear or emotions are too high to move into problem-solving, a problem discussion type of meeting devoted to ventilation of feelings and clarification of the problem is needed. During this whole process, a high level of leadership skill is needed to keep the conflict from escalating.

The next step is to discuss areas of agreement. This helps to reduce the gap between the opposing sides in the conflict and also serves to make the conflict appear a lot smaller and more manageable than it did when the focus was on the areas of disagreement. When the areas of agreement have been mapped out, the core conflict is more apparent and may actually be different from what is first appeared to be. Once the core of the conflict is evident, the team can generate alternate solutions. It may take a great deal of confrontation and negotiation to finally arrive at an acceptable resolution of the conflict.

SUMMARY

Team-building involves many actions aimed at developing effective working relationships. Team members are selected on the basis of their ability to contribute to the team. The purposes, objectives, and team members' roles need to be clearly defined and often negotiated. The team needs to define itself, stake out its territory, develop connections, and build a team spirit to achieve identity and cohesiveness. The leader also guides the team in decision-making, influences the establishment of

252

norms, encourages effective communication, and manages the resolution of conflicts within the team and with other teams.

Staffing Decisions: Delegating Responsibility

The delegation of responsibility and assignment of work is a basic leader function that may be more complicated in the health care field than it is in some other fields. This complexity is due to the great number and diversity of caregivers, the vast amount of knowledge from a number of different fields needed to provide comprehensive, high quality care, and the numerous interrelationships between staff members, clients, and the environment, which must be considered when delegating responsibility and delivering care.[9]

In this section, the many factors that need to be considered when delegating responsibility will be listed followed by a discussion of ways to communicate assignments and some problems and issues faced by the health care team leader in carrying out this necessary function.

CRITERIA FOR MAKING ASSIGNMENTS

As you read about these factors—and especially when you try to implement them—you will find that it is not always possible to fulfill every one of them. This means that a great deal of judgment on the part of the leader is required to make assignments that are as appropriate and fair as possible in a given set of circumstances.

There are two criteria of paramount importance in the delegation of responsibility, one primarily related to the task, the other to team relationships. The first is the ability of the individual to carry out the task. The second is the fairness of the assignment not only for the individual but also for the team as a whole. Effective delegation requires that both of these criteria are met as well as all or at least most of the others listed.

Task-Related Factors

The primary task-related concern in making assignments is that the person assigned to the job has the ability to carry it out and that you have chosen the best person available for the job. Priorities, efficiency, and continuity also need to be considered.

Ability. In order to make appropriate assignments, you need to know the customary knowledge and skills, legal definition, and job description for each health care discipline represented on your team. It is also necessary to be able to differentiate between the different levels of caregivers within each discipline since the amount of education and ability to assume responsibility can differ widely. This is particularly important because in addition to being accountable for your own work, you are also accountable for work that is delegated to others.

Not only are there many different kinds of caregivers, there are also many individual variations in work-related abilities. Every individual has their own particular strengths and weaknesses. A careful assessment of these differences is needed before making individual assignments.

Individuals should not be assigned a task they cannot do, not even the highest level professional. At any level many people are reluctant to admit that they cannot do something. Instead of telling you that the assignment is inappropriate they may avoid doing it, delay getting started, try to look as if they've begun the task but not actually get any work done, or, perhaps most dangerous, try to bluff their way through the task.

Orientation is necessary before assignment to a new task. The orientation may be a brief explanation, short demonstration and return demonstration, referral to written information or to someone who has done the task well, or a formal educational program—the choice depends on the need. While this is especially true for the new employee who is likely to feel a little lost and confused anyway, you cannot assume that present employees necessarily have the needed education, skill, or experience to complete a task correctly.

Priorities. Although ideally the team would be able to complete all of its work in a given time, the reality is that there is often less staff than needed and that the course of most work is rarely so predictable that it is always done exactly as planned. With this in mind, certain tasks or projects are given priority over others.

The priority rating is based on client needs, team needs, and organizational and community demands. For example, counseling an anxious parent would take priority over completing paperwork. Or an immunization clinic may be set up before a parents' group is started because both meet equally important client needs but the community is more interested in obtaining the clinic.

Determining priorities can be very difficult as the values of the client, caregivers, organization, and community may be quite different, even diametrically opposed. All of these needs and values should be discussed with team members so that they can participate in making a knowledgeable decision on the team's priorities.

Efficiency. Although other care-giving values may take precedence over efficiency, the cost of health care in terms of time and money must also be considered. The time and money available for health care are often limited resources that need to be allocated wisely. For example, you would avoid having two nurses travel to the same distant location if one could handle both of the tasks well. Or, if a telephone consultation can meet a client's needs as well as a home visit, then the telephone consultation is the better choice since it is far more efficient. If the travel time saved is used for giving care to someone else, then more health care has been offered at the same cost by using the more efficient method. Another example: if two professionals can perform physical examinations equally well, then efficiency dictates the use of the lower paid team member for doing physical examinations. Attention to the comparable costs of different work methods and assignments can sometimes appreciably increase the team's efficiency without reducing the quality of the care given.

CONTINUITY. Continuity is related to efficiency, quality of care, and client and staff satisfaction. Every time a new person takes over a task from an experienced person some time must be spent in familiarization before the task can be done efficiently. Clients appreciate having the same caregivers for several reasons: it reduces the number of times they have to repeat the same information, it increases the opportunities to develop a personal, trusting relationship with caregivers, and it makes their experience more predictable, which increases their feeling of security. Continuity also makes a more holistic approach to care possible and gives caregivers an opportunity to see the client's progress over a period of time. For these reasons continuity of care should be considered when making assignments.

There are some drawbacks to an emphasis on continuity of assignments, however. Some tasks are monotonous and if repeatedly assigned to the same person they lead to too much routinization and boredom. There are times when either the caregiver or the client wants a change from the same people. Also, it is helpful to have more than one person on the team able to carry out a task so that adequate substitutes are available during absences or vacations. You can see, then, that continuity has to be balanced against the problem of monotony, desire for change, and need for prepared substitutes.

Relationship Factors

Fairness is the second major concern in delegating responsibility to staff members. Fairness includes an evenly distributed work load, equal consideration for each team member, and avoidance of favoritism. Other relationship factors include opportunities for learning, health needs, compatibility, and staff preferences.

Fairness. There is probably no faster way to alienate team members than by making assignments that are not fair or that seem to be unfair. Fairness means evenly distributing the work load so that no one has substantially more or less work than the others. As the workload is not completely predictable, what began as a fair assignment may have to be adjusted in order to balance the changing work load.

Fairness means distributing the work so that no one gets all the enjoyable tasks or all the unpleasant tasks. For example, if one aide is always cleaning the supply rooms or bathing all of the incontinent patients, the aide may begin to wonder about being singled out for punishment even if the aide has no more work to do than anyone else.

Fairness also means an equitable amount of consideration for each team member. This includes consideration of requests for special assignments or vacation time. It also includes adequate recognition for the contributions of each team member and an equal sharing of rewards as well as sharing the hard work.

When special consideration or an assignment that could be interpreted as favoritism is given to a team member, it is a good idea to discuss this with team members so that they understand your reasons for doing it. Misunderstandings and resentments are likely to build up if this is not done. Also, when team members actively participate in making the decisions regarding distribution of assignments they are more likely to cooperate when the assignments are difficult.

Learning Opportunities. Although the assignments given must be within the capability of the individual, another factor to consider is that challenging assignments stimulate motivation and learning. Carefully planned assignments can promote the professional growth of individual team members and the team as a whole. The effective leader also seeks stimulating new tasks and projects for the team to provide additional opportunities for challenge and learning.

Health. The health and well being of team members is another factor to consider in making assignments. Certain jobs are very stressful and, while it may be preferable to learn how to reduce this stress, team members may need to be rotated through these assignments in order to keep their stress at a tolerable level. Another health consideration of frequent concern in hospitals is the effect of rotating shifts and frequent overtime that disrupts body rhythms and increases fatigue. There may also be individual health needs such as a family crisis for which additional time off is needed or special physical problems (such as back problems) to consider in making assignments.

Compatibility. Even when every effort is made to develop effective working relationships within the team as a whole, there may still be some individuals who do not work well together. For example, the highly task-oriented nurse may have a great deal of difficulty working alongside an empathic colleague who spends much more time interacting with both clients and staff. An experienced, aggressive, and impatient physician would not be an appropriate partner for an inexperienced, timid technician. Given sufficient time and effort these people can learn to work together but there may be instances, especially when the team is new or in the midst of a crisis, when the frictions of incompatible work relationships are better avoided.

This does not mean that you should try to put people who are alike together. A complementary blend of skills, talents, and personalities is desirable. Mixing people on this basis creates opportunities for sharing and learning from each other and can increase the overall effectiveness of the team.

Preferences. When they do not conflict with the other criteria for delegating responsibility, the preferences of individual team members should also be considered when making assignments. Often these preferences will reflect the ability and learning or health needs of the individual and so will be congruent with other criteria. Considering these preferences demonstrates a respect for the person as a unique individual and often meets a very real need of that team member.

COMMUNICATING ASSIGNMENTS

Even when team members participate in deciding how to delegate responsibility, the leader still needs to make sure that each team member knows what to do. Assignments and directions must be clear and concise so that all individuals know exactly what is expected of them and they can plan their work schedules accordingly. The assignment and accompanying directions also need to be complete so that team members have all the information they need to begin the assigned task.[10]

In order to ensure that team members understand and remember their assignments, both written and verbal means of communication are used. The written form can be used for later reference and evaluation as well as for a reminder. Long-term assignments are often written in the form of objectives (as described in Chapter 10) to facilitate later evaluation. Verbal communication of the assignment is done in addition in order to: encourage comments about the assignment; verify that it is understood by asking to have it repeated, if necessary; add further explanation when needed; and answer any questions the team member may have about the assignment.

ISSUES AND PROBLEMS IN DELEGATION

There are several very common problems and issues encountered in the process of delegating responsibility, which are discussed below. When you have adequate staff and satisfying work to delegate to them, assigning people to different tasks is usually not too difficult but when the staffing is inadequate or the work difficult and unpleasant, the decisions are much harder to make. Delegators themselves may also have some problems with the role.

Difficulty Delegating

The reasons people have difficulty delegating responsibility are varied but the outcome is generally predictable. The following is an example of what happens:

> Leaders who cannot delegate responsibility to their team members are always very busy. They usually need to be in three places at once and are often seen rushing from one crisis to another because they do not have time to deal with a problem before it becomes a crisis. Perhaps because they have so much practice, they are very good at dealing with crises but they do not do much planning.
>
> These leaders are frequently heard saying how busy they are and it is hard to make an appointment with them. When they are away from work for more than a day or two, the teams falls apart because no one else on the team knows how to handle many of the team's regular functions. Team members don't know anything about these routine tasks because the leader always does them.

The leaders who have difficulty delegating responsibility end up taking on most of the team's responsibilities themselves. This limits the amount of work that can be done by the team, limits team members' contributions to the team, and reduces their opportunities for growth.

Why do some leaders have this difficulty? First, some do not even realize that this is what they are doing. They believe that they are hardworking, dedicated people (which they are) and do not realize how much they limit the effective functioning of the team. Others simply do not trust their team members and believe that old saw "If you want a job done well, you have to do it yourself." For others, the need to retain control or to dominate others is so strong that they cannot let other team members share the leadership role or even become proficient in too many of the team's tasks. Consciously or unconsciously, they withhold needed information from team members as a means of control.

If you see yourself in the description of the leader who does not delegate responsibility, you need to begin working on sharing responsibility with others. It may be easier for both you and the rest of the team to do this a little at a time so that things do not become chaotic in the transition, which would reinforce your reasons for maintaining control. Team members can help by assuming more responsibility and reducing their dependency on the leader, at the same time offering support to the leader who may feel threatened by the loss of control. Team members' actions to assume more responsibility and, with this increased responsibility, some of the leadership functions within the team may lead to a power struggle between the team and the leader if the team moves too quickly or if the leader refuses to share control.

Manager or Specialist or Both?

This problem in defining the role of the team leader is common on health care teams and frequently occurs on teams of professionals in other fields too. The manager versus specialist problem is essentially a role conflict that arises from the way responsibility is delegated to the leader and the conflicting expectations of the leader, the team, the administration, or all three.

The following is an example of this role conflict as it arose between a number of leaders and an administrator:

> When the new Chief Administrator reorganized the administrative structure of the hospital, the head nurses were told that they were now expected to be the managers of their units. They were given courses on communication skills, group dynamics, and evaluation procedures. They were also given additional responsibility for doing their own budgets and staffing schedules, and told that they were now "part of the management team." Although some head nurses resisted the change, most liked the feeling of having a higher status and more management responsibility and so they assumed their new roles willingly.
>
> About a year later, the Director of Nursing decided to expand primary nursing from three demonstration units to the entire hospital. Although some of the head nurses felt that their staff was inadequate for full implementation of primary nursing, most of them supported the concept. However, after they accepted the plan, they were informed that head nurses would now become the clinical specialists on their units and their

major functions would be to act as expert consultants to the primary nurses and to provide highly skilled care to patients with particularly complex problems. The title head nurse would be eliminated and those head nurses who did not qualify as clinical specialists (and many did not) would be able to apply for any primary nurse positions that were open. No mention was made of budgeting, staffing, or evaluation and it was not clear who would perform these functions.

The head nurses rebelled. They refused to implement primary nursing until their roles were renegotiated. Most of the staff nurses and ancillary personnel supported the head nurses; primarily because they felt the need for the kind of leadership the head nurses had been providing. The Director of Nursing finally agreed to suspend the plans to implement primary nursing until the head nurse role was redefined. Eventually, the head nurse title was retained and a separate clinical specialist position was created. Head nurses were expected to be well qualified in their field of nursing and also to fulfill a reasonable number of management functions but they were not required to be clinical specialists nor were they expected to be administrators. A council of head nurses and supervisors was reorganized and given more influence over future decisions affecting their units including the implementation of primary nursing and the evolution of the head nurse role on primary nursing units.

Expectations regarding the manager versus specialist roles will differ according to the policies and norms of various health care organization. However, if you recall the components of effective leadership, you will see that an emphasis on either role to the complete exclusion of the other is less effective. The effective leader needs both an adequate expertise in the team's work and the ability to communicate, delegate, energize, support, and evaluate this work. While in some situations a greater emphasis on one or the other may be needed, both are necessary for the most effective leadership of the team.

Inadequate Staff

Inadequate staff is a common and often chronic problem in the health care professions. There are several ways in which staff may be inadequate: the total number of staff; staff members' level of education, skills, and experience; and the mix of disciplines represented on the team. While some of these may be more serious problems than others and each has a slightly different effect on team function, they all have the same general result—the team cannot fulfill all of its responsibilities effectively if the staffing is inadequate.

Providing adequate staff for each team is primarily an administrative responsibility but there are several actions the team leader can take to encourage administrators to fulfill their responsibility to provide adequate staff. The leader can ensure that the people in administration are aware of the inadequacy and of the effects of this inadequacy in detail. For example, you can point out the losses to the organization in terms of lower quality care, reduced efficiency, poor public relations, failure to meet legal requirements or accreditation standards, and inability to expand operations that result. The more specific, emphatic, and persistent you are, the more likely you are to be heard. If the administration does not respond, it may be

FIGURE 8-2 Fairness in delegating responsibility to team members means evenly distributing the work load so that no one member has substantially more work than the others.

necessary to make the public and the appropriate regulatory agencies aware of the problem. Although recruitment is also primarily an administrative responsibility, the leader can be alert to opportunities to attract potential team members with the needed qualifications.

When staff deficiencies are minor, careful consideration of priorities and use of staff to their optimum level can make up for the deficiency temporarily. However, when there are major staff deficiencies, it becomes necessary to reduce the team's work load to a safe level and to refuse to take on any additional responsibilities. For example, you might have to refuse new admissions to your unit or to stop opening new cases in your agency because the team cannot deliver safe care to any more clients. The extremeness of these measures may also be necessary to call attention to the staff inadequacies and elicit a helpful response from your supervisors and administrators.

Assigning Undesirable Work

There are always some tasks that are more desirable than others and preferred by most team members. It usually isn't too difficult to distribute these pleasant tasks equitably. But it can be much more difficult for leaders to decide how to distribute the unpleasant tasks that teams also have to complete. Some leaders succumb to the temptation to give these jobs to the willing team member who rarely complains but this violates the criterion of fairness and also inadvertently rewards the less cooperative team members who avoid doing their share of the unpleasant work (Fig. 8-2).

Essentially, the leader just has to resist this temptation and distribute the undesirable work fairly but there are a few things that can make this a little easier to do. Often the undesirable task has some kind of advantage that you can point out to reduce team members' resistance to doing it. For example, although unpleasant, the task may be vital to team function or vital to the client. (If you cannot say that it is necessary to do this work, then you need to reconsider why you are asking someone to do it.) Occasionally, it is also an opportunity to learn something new or to upgrade a skill to improve a future evaluation rating. However, pretending the job is desirable when it obviously is not will only promote resentment.

A mature group can probably handle the responsibility to decide how undesirable tasks will be distributed among team members. With an immature group the leader will probably find it necessary to either make the decision or to provide guidelines for making the decision in order to ensure that the criteria of appropriateness and fairness are met.

SUMMARY

The two major criteria to consider when delegating responsibility are the appropriateness and fairness of the assignment. Additional criteria include priority, efficiency, continuity, compatibility, learning, health, and staff preferences. Assignments should also be clear, concise, complete, written, and explained verbally.

Common problems encountered are difficulty delegating responsibility, achieving a satisfactory balance between specialist and managerial roles, inadequate staff, and delegating undesirable work.

Informal Evaluation: Seeking and Providing Evaluative Feedback*

Informal evaluation is the continuous process of giving and receiving feedback. It includes both positive and negative comments on people's effectiveness as caregivers and as coworkers, team members, and leaders. Although some of the feedback will be negative, it can still be constructive in the sense that it can promote growth and improve performance.

Everyone needs to know what impact they have had on a situation. They need to know how people respond to them, how well they have solved a problem, whether or not they have helped someone, and how effective their work is overall.

INFORMAL VERSUS FORMAL EVALUATION

The term *informal evaluation* is used here to distinguish it from the formal procedures such as performance appraisals and record audits that are mandated by organizations or by law. Formal evaluations usually have an explicit structure to them including specific forms to fill out or timetables for carrying out the procedures.

Formal evaluation procedures (which are discussed further in Chapter 10) may occur only once or twice a year, which is inadequate to provide the continuous guidance and recognition that people need at work. Providing frequent informal feedback can meet these needs and is an important function of the leader. You may recall that giving feedback was one of the actions listed in the components of effective leadership.

Informal evaluation occurs during the give and take of other work activities. It is a continuous process, an action that occurs often and whenever it is needed rather than according to a schedule. It is also an integral part of the activities of a well-functioning team. As an integral part of team function, seeking and providing feedback is the responsibility of every member of the team, not just the team leader, although the team leader has the extra responsibility of ensuring that it is done and done appropriately.

PURPOSES

People function better when they receive certain types of feedback. In particular, they need to know what is expected of them and they need to know that what they

---

*Written with P. George.

do is important.[11] Both formal and informal evaluation can meet these needs. Feedback verifies for people either that they did understand what is expected of them or that they need to clarify these expectations. People need adequate knowledge, skills, and practice to be proficient in their work. Feedback can confirm that they are performing well or that they need more training or practice. In this sense, feedback provides some indication of needs for continuing education. It can also communicate that what team members are doing is useful and important. Positive feedback meets those needs for esteem and recognition that all people have.

Informal evaluation also increases self-awareness and encourages growth and self-direction. Feedback can help people identify their strengths and weaknesses. Once these are clearly identified, the efforts of both the individual and the team as a whole can be directed toward reinforcing the strengths and developing more skill in the weak areas. Positive and negative feedback exchanged in a climate of open communication facilitates the functioning of the health care team.

Frequent feedback is one way to challenge caregivers to continually use the very best methods in providing health care. It also encourages people to use their best resources whenever they face a problem or difficult decision and to look for opportunities to upgrade their knowledge and skills. By serving these purposes, informal evaluation also improves the quality of the health care given.

PROVIDING FEEDBACK

Evaluation involves making judgments and communicating these judgments to others. People make judgments all the time about all types of things. Many times these judgments are based on opinions, preferences, and dislikes rather than on facts. Judgments are often made on the basis of inaccurate or partial information too.

Biased, hasty judgments offered as objective feedback have given evaluation a bad name for many people. Poorly communicated feedback has an equally negative effect. In fact, you will find that many of the people who fear or are threatened by evaluation have been the recipients of hasty, biased, poorly communicated evaluations in the past.

Evaluation can be a destructive process. When it is poorly done, evaluation can reinforce ineffective work habits, reduce self-esteem and destroy motivation. On the other hand, when it is well done, it can reinforce motivation, strengthen the team, and improve the quality of care given—it can fulfill all the constructive purposes mentioned earlier. The following sections discuss the need for both positive and negative feedback and offer some guidelines for ensuring that the feedback you give to your team members, clients, supervisors, and other caregivers is as constructive as possible.

Positive and Negative Feedback

Both positive and negative feedback are needed to fulfill all of the purposes mentioned. Neglect or avoidance of either will reduce your effectiveness as a leader.

Positive feedback may be easier to give, but leaders often neglect to do so. If questioned, people who do not give positive feedback will explain that, "If I don't say anything, that means everything is OK." Unfortunately, they don't realize that some people will assume that everything is *not OK* when they receive no feedback. Others assume that no one is aware of how much effort has gone into their work unless someone acknowledges it with positive feedback.

Providing positive feedback is one very useful way for the leader to promote job satisfaction. Most people want to do their work well. They also want to know that their efforts are recognized and appreciated and it is a real pleasure to be able to share the satisfaction of a job well done with someone else.

If you neglect to give positive feedback, you have failed to use a powerful and readily available motivator. Kron[12] calls positive feedback a "psychological paycheck" and points out that it is almost as important to people as their actual paycheck.

Negative feedback is just as necessary as positive feedback but more difficult to do well. Too often, negative feedback is critical rather than constructive. It is easier to just tell people that something has gone wrong or could have been done better than it is to make the feedback a learning experience for the receiver by suggesting ways to make the needed changes or working together to develop a strategy for improvement. It is also easier to make broad, critical comments such as, "You're too slow" than it is to very specifically describe the behavior that needs improvement such as saying, "Waiting in Mr. D.'s room while he finishes his breakfast takes up too much of your time," and then add a suggestion for change such as, "You could get your bath supplies together while he finishes eating."

Providing no negative feedback at all is the easiest but least effective solution to the problem of being too critical. Unsatisfactory work must be acknowledged and discussed with the people involved. The "gutless wonder" who silently tolerates poor work encourages it to continue and undermines the motivation of the whole team.[13] Avoiding negative feedback would seriously reduce your effectiveness as a leader.

Guidelines for Constructive Feedback

Evaluative feedback is most effective when it is given immediately, frequently, and privately. To be constructive, feedback must be objective, based on observed behavior, and skillfully communicated. The feedback message should include the reason why a behavior has been judged good or poor in order to promote growth and learning. If the message is negative it should be nonthreatening and include suggestions and support for change and improvement. Each of these criteria is listed and discussed further below:

Immediate. The most helpful feedback is given as soon as possible after the behavior has occurred. There are several reasons for this. Immediate feedback is more meaningful to the person receiving it. If it is delayed too long, the person may have assumed that your silence indicated approval or may have forgotten the incident altogether.

Also, like other confrontation situations, problems that are ignored often get worse and in the meantime, a lot of frustration and anger can build up inside. When feedback is given as soon as possible, there is no time for this build up and results can be seen immediately.

Frequent. Feedback should not only be immediate but also given frequently. Frequent constructive feedback keeps motivation and awareness levels high and avoids the possibility that problems will grow larger and more serious before they are confronted. Also, giving feedback becomes easier with practice. If it is a frequent and integral part of team functioning, giving and receiving feedback will be easier to do and less threatening to most people since it becomes an ordinary, everyday occurrence, one that happens spontaneously and is familiar to everyone to the team.

Private. Giving negative feedback privately rather than in front of others avoids embarrassment for all concerned. It also avoids the possibility that those who overhear the discussion may misunderstand it and draw erroneous conclusions from it.

Objective. It can be very difficult to be objective when giving feedback to others. The use of critical analysis techniques discussed in Chapter 5 can be helpful here. There are two other ways to increase objectivity. One is to always give a reason why you have judged a behavior as good or poor. The other is to use as broad and generally accepted a standard for judgments as possible and to avoid basing evaluation on personal likes or dislikes. Reasons should be given for both positive and negative messages. For example, if you tell a coworker, "That was a good interview" you have told that person nothing except that the interview pleased you. However, when you add to that message, "because you asked many open-ended questions that encouraged the client to explore personal feelings" you have identified the specific behavior that made your evaluation positive and reinforced this specific behavior.

Formal evaluations should be based on previously agreed upon, written standards of what is acceptable behavior. Informal evaluation is based on unwritten standards. If these standards are based on idiosyncratic personal preferences, the evaluation will be highly subjective. Objectivity can be increased by using standards that reflect the consensus of the team, the organization, the community, or the profession as a whole. Here are some examples of the differences between personal and general standards:

> A team leader who describes a female social worker as having a professional appearance because she wears skirts instead of pants to work is using a personal standard to evaluate that social worker.

A supervisor who asks an employee to stop wearing jewelry that could get caught in the equipment used at work is applying a more generally accepted standard of safety in making the evaluative statement.

The nursing home administrator who insists that staff include every resident in the weekly Bingo game is applying a narrower and probably personal standard than the administrator who insists that staff members offer every resident the opportunity to participate in weekly activities.

Based on Observable Behavior. An evaluative statement should describe directly observed behavior, not personality traits or attitudes that involve interpretation of behavior. The observation is much more likely to be factual and accurate than the interpretation is. It is also less likely to evoke a defensive response. Here is an example:

Saying, "You were impatient with Mrs. G. today" is an interpretive comment. Saying, "You interrupted Mrs. G. before she finished explaining her problem" is based on observable behavior. It is more specific and probably more accurate as the caregiver may have been trying to redirect the conversation to more immediate concerns rather than feeling impatient. The second statement is more likely to evoke an explanation than a defensive response.

Appropriately Communicated. An evaluative statement is a form of confrontation. Any message that contains a statement about the behavior of a staff member is confronting that staff member with information. All of the guidelines given in Chapter 4 about the appropriate way to confront another person or group apply to giving evaluative feedback. For example, it is particularly important to avoid sending put-down or blaming messages. The reader may want to review the confrontation section of Chapter 4 before providing evaluative feedback to other people.

As with other confrontations, the leader who gives evaluative feedback needs to be prepared to receive feedback in return and to engage in active listening. Active listening is especially important because the person receiving the evaluation may respond with disagreement and high emotion. Here is an example of what may happen:

Let's say that you point out to a coworker that the coworker's patients need to be monitored more frequently. The coworker responds emotionally about doing everything possible for the patients and not having a free moment all day for one extra thing. In fact, the coworker tells you about never even taking a lunch break and going home exhausted. Active listening and problem-solving with this coworker aimed at relieving the coworker's overloaded time schedule are a must in this situation.

When you give negative feedback, it is often necessary to allow time for ventilation of feelings and then for problem-solving with the individual to find ways to improve a situation. This is particularly true if the problem has been ignored long enough to become serious as in the example given.

Include Suggestions for Change. When you give feedback to someone that indicates some kind of change in behavior is needed, it is helpful to suggest alternative behaviors. This is easier to do when the change is a simple one.

When it is a complex change that is needed (as in the example given above of the exhausted coworker), you may find that the person is aware of the problem but does not know how to solve it. In such a case, simple solutions are inappropriate but an offer to engage in searching for the solution is appropriate. A demonstrated willingness to listen to the other person's side of the story and to assist in finding a solution also indicates that your purpose in providing the negative feedback was to help rather than criticize or attack the individual.

Nonthreatening. An appropriately communicated statement should not be threatening to the individual. Highly threatening messages reduce motivation and inhibit learning because they divert people's energies into activities aimed specifically at reducing the threat. While a small degree of anxiety may increase learning, too much fear immobilizes and reduces functional capacity to grow. The purpose of informal evaluation is to improve the function of the team and its individual members. When the feedback is negative, the focus of the message should be on the specific behavior, not on the person as a whole, which devalues the person and threatens self-esteem. Negative feedback often contains veiled threats or hints of dire consequences, probably in the mistaken belief that it will increase the person's motivation to change. The following are some common examples:

"You're not going to last long if you keep doing that."

"People who want to do well here make sure their assignments are done on time."

"Don't argue with the doctors, they'll report you to the nursing office.

When a person's behavior actually does threaten job security, a formal evaluation stating this fact and proposing needed changes is appropriate. The examples given above threaten job security but other evaluative statements can threaten other types of safety and security, self-esteem, or the need for love and belonging.

You may have assumed that people in the ranks above you (manager, head nurse, supervisor, director, and so forth) could not be threatened by feedback from you. This is not true. They are all human and as susceptible to feeling threatened as your coworkers are so that you need to follow these same guidelines in giving feedback to people above you in the organization as well as to your peers and coworkers.

SEEKING FEEDBACK

Just as important as knowing how to give feedback is knowing when to look for it and how to take it. The purposes for seeking feedback are the same as those for giving it to others. The criteria for evaluating the feedback you receive are also the same. It may be of some help, however, to point out the times when you need to seek feedback and offer some additional suggestions about how to respond to feedback.

When Feedback Is Needed

There are a number of different situations in which you need to seek feedback. For example, you could find yourself in a work situation where you receive very little feedback from any source except your own evaluation of your work. Or you may be getting only positive and no negative comments (or vice versa).

Another time when you need to look for feedback is when you feel uncertain about how well you are doing or whether you have correctly interpreted the expectations of the job. The following are some examples of these situations:

> You have been told that good patient care is the first consideration of your job but feel totally frustrated by never having enough staff to give good care.

> You thought you were expected to do case finding and health teaching in your community, but receive the most recognition for the number of home visits made and for the completeness of your records.

An additional instance in which you should request feeedback is when you feel that your needs for recognition and job satisfaction have not been met adequately.

Requests for feedback should be made in the form of "I" messages. If you have received only negative comments, ask, "'In what ways have I done well?" If you receive only positive comments, you can ask, "In what areas do I need to improve?" Or, if you are seeking feedback from a patient, you could ask, "How can I be of more help to you?"

RESPONDING TO FEEDBACK

When the feedback is positive but nonspecific, you may also want to ask for some clarification so that you can find out what that person's expectations are. Also, do not hesitate to seek that psychological paycheck. Tell other people about your successes—most are happy to share the satisfaction of a successful outcome or positive development in a patient's care.

There are times when it is appropriate to critically analyze the feedback you are getting. If the feedback seems totally negative or makes you feel threatened, ask for further explanation because you may have misunderstood what the person meant to say.

It is hard to avoid responding defensively to negative feedback that is subjective or laced with threats and blame. But if you are the recipient of such a poorly done evaluation, it may help both of you to try to guide the discussion into more constructive areas. You can ask for reasons why the evaluation was negative, what standard it is based upon or what the person's expectations were and what the person suggests as alternative behavior.

SUMMARY

Informal evaluation is a continuous process of seeking and providing feedback that should be an integral part of team function. The purposes of this type of evaluation are to provide recognition, increase self-awareness, clarify expectations, promote change and growth on the job, facilitate team function, and challenge staff members to improve their performances.

People need both positive and negative feedback. Constructive feedback is immediate, frequent, private, objective, based on observable behavior, appropriately communicated, nonthreatening, and includes suggestions for change. Seeking feedback is as important as providing feedback and follows the same guidelines. Responding to feedback is also important and may help to clarify both positive and negative feedback.

References

1. BRILL, N: *Teamwork: Working Together in the Human Services.* JB Lippincott, Philadelphia, 1976.

2. FRANCIS, D AND YOUNG, D: *Improving Work Groups: A Practical Manual for Team Building.* University Associates, La Jolla, California, 1979.

3. PARKER, AW: *The Team Approach to Primary Health Care.* University Extension, University of California, Berkeley, 1972.

4. WISE, H, BECKHARD, R, RUBIN, I, AND KYTE, AL: *Making Health Teams Work.* Ballinger Publishing, Cambridge, Massachusetts, 1974.

5. FRY, RE, LECH, BA, AND RUBIN, I: *Working with the primary care team: The first intervention.* In WISE, H, BECKHARD, R, RUBIN, I, AND KYTE, AL: *Making Health Teams Work.* Ballinger Publishing, Cambridge, Massachusetts, 1974.

6. SCHERER, JJ: *Can team building increase productivity or can something that feels so good not be worthwhile?* Group and Organizational Studies 4:3 (September 1979), p 335.

7. SCHEIN, E: *Process Consultation.* Addison-Wesley, Reading, Massachusetts, 1969.

8. BRAGG, JE AND ANDREWS, IR: *Participative decision making: An experimental study in a hospital.* Journal of Applied Behavioral Science 9(6):727 (November-December), 1973.

9. BROWN, BJ (ED): *Nurse Staffing: A Practical Guide.* Aspen Systems, Germantown, Maryland, 1980.

10. Douglass, LM and Bevis, EO: *Nursing Management and Leadership in Action.* CV Mosby, St Louis, 1979.

11. Mager, RF and Pipe, P: *Analyzing Performance Problems.* Lear Sigler/Fearon Publishers, Belmont, California, 1970.

12. Kron, T: *The Management of Patient Care: Putting Leadership Skills to Work.* WB Saunders, Philadelphia, 1981, p 22.

13. DelBueno, D: *Performance evaluation: When all is said and done, more is said than done.* Journal of Nursing Administration Vol 7, No 10 (December), 1977.

Chapter

Strategies for Planned Change

Planned Change

Planned change is deliberate. It is a conscious application of your knowledge and skills in order to guide and influence the direction of change.[1] The opposite of planning change would be to let it occur spontaneously, that is, to go along with whatever happens, which would not be an effective leadership approach.

MODELS FOR CHANGE

This chapter is organized around four major models or approaches to change. The first model is Watzlawick and colleague's[2] paradoxical model. This model divides change into first- and second-order types of changes and includes strategies that have a humorous turn to them. The other three models have a different perspective on change. They can be thought of as a continuum of change models from the low-key rational model to the midpoint normative model to the high-pressure power-coercive model (Fig. 9-1).

All four of these models for change can be used with open systems of various sizes, from individuals to entire communities, even to the profession as a whole. There are times when these models are appropriate for work with clients as well as with colleagues with the exception of the power-coercive model. Each model and the strategies that accompany it is based upon different, although not necessarily contradictory, assumptions about people and their behavior. It is interesting to see

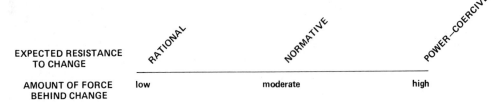

EXPECTED RESISTANCE TO CHANGE	RATIONAL	NORMATIVE	POWER-COERCIVE
AMOUNT OF FORCE BEHIND CHANGE	low	moderate	high

FIGURE 9-1. Three models of change placed on a continuum.

how the models help to explain the puzzling and sometimes contradictory ways that people react to change.

Attention will be given to the selection of the most appropriate model and strategies for a given situation. Each of the models is particularly appropriate for certain types of situations. As you read about the different models, you may find that some of your past attempts to bring about change did not work because you were not using the most appropriate model. The following is an example of how selecting the best model for the job can improve your effectiveness:

> After applying the normative model to a situation that had frustrated a community health nurse for a long time, the nurse said, "Now I understand why I couldn't get my team members to allow their clients more autonomy before. I had thoroughly assessed the need for this change and planned a smooth implementation of this new approach to case management. But I didn't analyze the sources of resistance because I had assumed that every health care giver would naturally support a change in procedure that improved their clients' ability to care for themselves."

READING THIS CHAPTER

In order to engage yourself actively in learning about the dynamics of change and application of the four models, it would be helpful for you to think of a particular change you would like to see happen and imagine using each model to bring about the change. This will also help you to appreciate the differences between the models. The following are some examples of different kinds of changes you could use:

Helping a client to stop smoking.

Starting a support group for families of cancer patients.

Implementing an employee wellness program.

Increasing communication between nurses and social workers.

Implementing an improved triage system in the emergency department.

Improving your team's efficiency in following up on referrals.

Getting legislation passed to provide more services for older adults.

Establishing a network of child care centers in your community.

Dynamics of Change

Change is essentially a repatterning of behavior. It is also a continuous process according to open systems theory. Growth and development, for example, is one kind of change that affects every human being over the entire life span. You may be aware of change occurring frequently and rapidly in your own life. But not every change in a system is obvious; change includes imperceptible shifts in the system's functioning or evolution as well as large-scale alterations in the pattern and organization of the system.

POTENTIAL FOR CHANGE

It is important to remember that the potential for change is inherent in every open system because people often make remarks, such as "Nothing ever changes around here," or "People here refuse to change," which seem to indicate that these systems have not or will not change. What they mean is that no rapid, large-scale changes have taken place or that there is a great deal of resistance to change. Whether it comes primarily from within the system or from the environment, some kind of change is inevitable in open systems.

Change in one part of a system will affect the whole system. In other words, when change occurs it affects the entire system as a whole and, therefore, will also affect its relationship with the environment. Even the person who attempts to guide and influence a change in a system will in some way be affected by the change process.

SYSTEM RESPONSE TO CHANGE

A system can respond in several different ways to an attempt to change it. If the system is neutral toward the change and does not see it as a threat, a small push can move the system in a new direction. A small force can also lead to great changes in a very unstable system. An example of this is how a little added force can make an angry mob turn violent and dangerous. On the other hand, if a system is very stable and considers the change a threat to its existence, it will take a strong force to change it because one of the basic needs of a system is to maintain its integrity as a system.[3] As you can see, there can be forces both for and against change both within the system and in the environment.

Myths About Change

There are common myths about change that people frequently mention and even apply to practice. The first myth is that people (and other systems) always actively resist change. The second is that change is always a positive occurrence, that it is always healthy for a system to change. Neither of these myths stands up under careful examination.

A system's need to maintain its integrity and identity as a unique entity does have a tendency to generate resistance to change. But systems do not always actively resist change. A mature, healthy individual, for example, seeks opportunities for further growth such as a new career challenge, learning a new sport, or meeting a person for the first time. One of the problems with bureaucracy is its built-in resistance to change and yet even the most bureaucratic organization can and does change voluntarily over time, although it may be a slow and imperceptible change.

Change per se is neither inherently good as implied by the second myth nor inherently bad. Some changes have a positive effect on a system, other changes have a negative effect. Change can be as welcome as a well-deserved holiday from work or school or as unwelcome as a speeding ticket.

Positive change is growth producing and as necessary as order and regularity are in the life of a human system. If you consider extreme sensory deprivation as an example of a system experiencing too little change, then you can understand why change can be a positive occurrence.

On the other hand, not every change in a system is a productive one for that system. In fact, resistance to change can sometimes be a healthy response. The following is an example of how a change can be unhealthy for a system:

> A midwestern community strongly resisted attempts to locate a new dump for chemical wastes on the edge of town. Residents picketed, protested, and wrote letters to their representatives in order to block the dumping of potentially hazardous wastes in their community. They saw this change as a threat to their own health and the health of their families and neighbors.

In this case, the change was seen as a threat to the integrity of the system. Resistance to the change was a positive response in terms of the health and safety of the community.

Multifactorial Influences

An open system's response to change is influenced by many factors. People react to change as whole persons in the same way that they react to other stimuli either from within themselves or from the environment. Their past experiences, present needs, culture, values, roles, and coping abilities may all have some influence on their responses. The same is true of groups, organizations, or communities as they respond to change. You will see that some of the models for change take this multifactorial influence into consideration more than others.

The apparent positive value of a proposed change is not the only factor that influences the amount of resistance that will be encountered. Health care givers frequently fail to recognize this fact when proposing a change in lifestyle for the purpose of improving an individual's or group's health. The following is a common example of resistance to a change that will improve health:

Consider for a moment how difficult it is for some people to quit smoking despite overwhelming evidence regarding the health benefits of quitting. Habit, psychological craving, pleasurable handling, stimulation, tension reduction, and the physical effects of nicotine are all factors that reinforce the smoking behavior and resistance to change. Cigarette advertising and the smoking habits of friends and colleagues also reinforce the habit. On the other hand, the health benefits and the fact that other friends have quit reinforce the motivation to change.

The outcome of the attempt to change smoking behavior depends on which set of forces is finally more influential, those for change or those resisting change.

Rate of Change

Not only the type but also the rate (or amount) of change that occurs within a given time will affect the system's response to the change. Holmes and Rahe's Stress Scale (Fig. 9-2)[4] is an example of the cumulative effect of too many changes occurring in a short period of time. As you can see, some of the changes such as "outstanding achievement" have positive value and yet too many of these changes occurring together can be a source of stress to the system.

Any kind of changes occurring at too rapid a rate may elicit resistance from a system. The changes are not limited to the ones listed by Holmes and Rahe. The following is an example of how a system may respond to a very rapid rate of change.

> A new Director of Rehabilitative Services was hired for the outpatient services of a large health care center. The Director thoroughly organized and modernized the entire department in six months. The Director purchased new equipment, moved the department into attractive new quarters, expanded the services offered, expanded the therapists' roles and increased their status within the complex, and hired several new employees.
>
> The result? Although the changes were needed and desired, the tension level in the department rose precipitously. Several people resigned and the rest of the employees in the department organized themselves into a bargaining unit and sought union representation for the first time. The Administrator of the complex summarized the reasons for the department employees' response this way: "We tried to make too many changes too fast. They couldn't take it."

The complexity of the forces within a system and in its environment makes it difficult to predict the results of the change with any real accuracy unless you have made a thorough analysis of that particular system and its relationship to the environment. The four models for change are useful in doing this analysis as well as in attempting to influence the direction that change takes within an open system. Though you cannot stop change or determine its exact outcome, there is enough order and pattern to change to allow you to influence and predict the outcome within a range of possibilities. The four models for change (paradoxical, rational, normative, and power-coercive) will be the subject of the remainder of this chapter.

EVENTS:	STRESS VALUE:
Death of a spouse	100
Divorce	73
Marital separation	65
Jail term	63
Death of a close family member	63
Personal injury, sickness	53
Marriage	50
Fired from job	47
Reconcile marriage	45
Retire	45
Illness in family	44
Pregnancy	40
Sex difficulties	39
Gain new family member	39
Change in business	39
Change in financial state	38
Death of close friend	37
Change line of work	36
Change in number of family fights	35
Mortgage over $10,000	31
Mortgage or loan foreclosed	30
Grown child leaves home	29
Change in job duties	29
In-law troubles	29
Outstanding achievement	28
Wife begins or stops work	26
Begin or end school	26
Change living conditions	25
Revise personal habits	24
Trouble with boss	23
Change work hours or conditions	20
Move to new home	20
Change schools	20
Change recreation	19
Change church activities	19
Change social activities	18
Mortgage or loan under $10,000	17
Sleeping habits change	16
Change in number of family get-togethers	15
Eating habits change	15
Vacation	13
Christmas	12
Minor violation of the law	11

Holmes and Rahe developed this scale to rate the amount of stress caused by many changes in life: major and minor, pleasant and unpleasant. To obtain your score, circle the ones that apply to you and then add up the total.

Follow-up studies show that people who accumulate more than 200 points in a year are high risks for physical or psychologic stress-related illnesses.

FIGURE 9-2. Holmes and Rahe's stress rating scale. (From Holmes, TH and Rahe, R: *The social readjustment rating scale*. Journal of Psychosomatic Research 2:213, April 1967, with permission.)

SUMMARY

Planned change is the deliberate application of knowledge and skills by the leader in order to bring about change. Change is inherent in open systems. It may be positive or negative, welcome or resisted by the system. Many factors influence a system's response to change including the perceived value of the change, the rate of change, and the needs, experiences, culture, values, and coping abilities of the system within a given environment.

Paradoxical Model

The originators of the paradoxical model for change have a background in psychotherapy that is apparent in their perspectives on change.[2] Their model is especially concerned with the way in which problems arise and why some persist while others are resolved. It grew out of their observation of a paradox: that logical, reasonable approaches to change often failed while illogical, backward-seeming approaches succeeded.

There are two different types or levels of change according to Watzlawick and associates. These two levels are called first-order and second-order changes. The first-order changes are those that seem logical; the second-order changes are those that seem illogical.

FIRST-ORDER CHANGE

In a first-order change, the patterns of behavior and the nature of relationships between the systems involved remains virtually the same. A first-order change has far less impact on the function of a system than a second-order change does. The following example illustrates a first-order type of change:

> The professionals on an interdisciplinary child care evaluation team have had difficulty relating to each other as peers. Instead of a pattern of communications between equals, the communications have been of a superior to subordinate nature.
>
> Whenever one member of the team approaches another team member as an equal, changing the pattern of communications, the other member retreats into a subordinate or superior position and so the overall pattern of interpersonal relationships remains the same. No permanent change in communication between equals occurs.

The Paradox

From the example, you can see that first-order changes do not significantly alter old behavior patterns and may actually reinforce them, making them even more entrenched than ever. This is the paradox operating: some attempts to solve a problem by bringing about change can actually make the problem worse. If the old behavior pattern is not the most effective one (as in the example given of the child care team) then first-order change is not adequate when you want to improve a system's ability to function. Let's return to the child care evaluation team example to see how first-order changes can reinforce old behavior patterns:

> The child care evaluation team has become divided into two groups: the lower-status professionals (teacher, nurse, social worker) and the higher-status professionals (physician, psychiatrist). This division is reinforced by a superior to subordinate communication pattern.
> The lower-status members try to improve their position on the team by thoroughly preparing their reports on each child evaluated by the team and by asserting themselves at team conferences. The more they assert themselves, the more the higher status professionals use a superior tone of voice and try to ignore their input in making decisions, even to the point of dictating the team's recommendations. The team is caught in this status struggle and the valuable input of several team members is lost under these circumstances, which impairs the function of the team.

The child care evaluation team example will be continued in the second-order change section to show the difference between these two types of change strategies.

Be Spontaneous

There is another kind of paradox that is especially common on the individual level of change. This is the "Be Spontaneous" paradox. It occurs in the form of a demand, from yourself or others, to engage in some kind of natural behavior that can only occur spontaneously. In fact, the harder you try to perform the desired behavior, the harder it becomes to do so. For example, urging depressed patients to "Cheer up!" is asking them to do the impossible. Paradoxically, it can make them feel even worse because they are unable to please you by being cheerful. Another interesting example of the "Be Spontaneous" paradox is insomnia. Falling asleep is a natural behavior but for insomniac patients, the harder they try to fall asleep, the wider awake they feel. The more conscious efforts they make to get to sleep on time, such as counting sheep or going to bed earlier, the less likely they are to succeed in falling asleep naturally.

Because of these paradoxes, first-order changes fail to break up old patterns of behavior and may actually result in reinforcing the unwanted pattern. A second-order change is needed in order to break up this pattern.

SECOND-ORDER CHANGE

Shifting from an unproductive first-order change to a second-order change requires taking a new perspective on the problem or situation you are trying to change. Watzlawick and associates[2] use a familiar puzzle to illustrate this shift from first-order change (Fig. 9-3). If you have not seen the puzzle before, try doing it as directed.

The solution to the puzzle requires going outside of the square. While the directions do not prohibit your doing this, most people can't figure out the puzzle

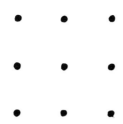

Puzzle: Connect the nine dots with four straight lines without lifting your pencil from the paper.

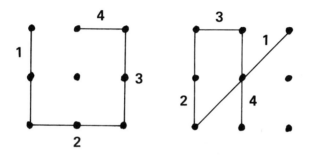

Wrong: First-order attempts to solve the puzzle.

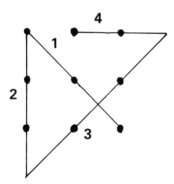

Solution: Second-order solution requires going outside the square.

FIGURE 9-3. An illustration of the difference between first- and second-order changes. (From Watzlawick, P, Weakland, J, and Fisch, R: *Change: Principles of Problem Formation and Problem Resolution.* WW Norton & Co, New York, 1974, with permission.)

because the edge of the square becomes an imaginary boundary that keeps them from looking outside the square for a solution. This is an example of a first-order attempt to change. A second-order change, requiring that you go outside the logical boundaries of the square, is needed to solve this puzzle. Once you see the second-order solution, it becomes clear why you couldn't solve it with a first-order change.

Reframing

As you can see in the puzzle solution, second-order change requires a rethinking of a problem from a new perspective. This is called reframing. Before considering more second-order solutions to problems, the steps suggested by Watzlawick for reframing the original problem will be considered. You may notice that these steps resemble the familiar problem-solving process somewhat. But these steps outlining the paradoxical model for change emphasize the need to reframe problems in order to eliminate the paradoxes that keep you from solving them. The steps are as follows:

1. Define the problem in concrete terms.
2. List the solutions attempted so far.
3. Clearly define a realistic change.
4. Select and implement a second-order change strategy.

The child care evaluation team problem will be used along with other examples to illustrate the application of this change model.

Step 1. Define the Problem in Concrete Terms

The purpose of this step is to help you to concentrate on the specific, solvable aspect of the problem or situation and to avoid trying to solve global or inevitable problems. Some problems are inevitable and cannot be changed although you can change the way in which you cope with them. You cannot, for example, remove the threat of a hurricane or tornado but you can either prepare for them or move out of their path. The storm itself is not amenable to change, but your response to the storm is amenable to change.

Example. In the same way, many social problems are amenable to change only over the long term and are not sufficiently concrete to tackle in order to gain relief from an immediate problem. To return to the child care evaluation team, here is a list of three possible ways to define the problem from the point of view of the nurse, teacher, and social worker:

> Our professional status is too low.
>
> Our value to the team is not recognized.
>
> Our input is ignored.

The first definition of the problem is too global to be amenable to immediate solution. It is a long-term problem that goes beyond the team and requires a change in social attitudes. The second definition of the problem is more specific and the third one is the most specific and concrete one. It also avoids analyzing the reasons behind the problem and defines the present dilemma of the lower status members of the team.

Step 2. List the Solutions Attempted So Far

Once you have defined the problem in concrete terms, you are ready to look for solutions to the problem. The solutions attempted so far are usually first-order changes that have failed to bring about any lasting changes in behavior and may even have made the problem worse than it was originally. The main purpose of this step is to help you avoid repeating previous unsuccessful attempts to change the situation.

Example. In the child care evaluation team example, the lower status professionals made several attempts to change their postition on the team. They repeatedly tried to do the following:

Relate to other team members as equals.

Prove their expertise by writing excellent evaluation reports.

Demonstrate their worth by working harder than the rest of the team and by being more thorough in their assessments than the rest of the team.

None of these solutions worked. In fact, they made the situation worse.*

Step 3. Clearly Define a Realistic Change

In this step you will define the goal of the planned change. Again, as in the first step, the emphasis is on the specific and concrete rather than on a goal that is too global, too vague, or attempts to solve a problem that is not amenable to change as stated (the inevitable storms, for example).

Example. The nurse, social worker, and teacher on the child care evaluation team wanted to achieve the following outcomes:

Raise our status.

Gain respect and recognition from the rest of the team.

Increase use of our input in making recommendations.

---

*These strategies frequently do succeed frequently in bringing about change. The emphasis in this chapter, however, is on situations in which these simpler attempts to change do not succeed and it is necessary to apply the strategies for planned change.

The first goal is global; it defines an attempt to change social phenomenon and is a long-term goal. The second is more specific but still vague in comparison with the third goal. The third goal, increased use of their input, is more specific and more amenable to immediate change than the first two. It would, therefore, be the most realistic of the three goals listed by the team members.

Step 4. Select and Implement a Second-Order Strategy

The most distinctive aspect of the paradoxical model for change is the type of strategies recommended to bring about change. When first-order change strategies have been tried without success, a second-order change is recommended. The previous steps were designed to help you to reframe the problem in need of solution so that you can shift into the second-order change perspective.

The key to designing a second-order change comes from the list of unsuccessful solutions rather than from the problem as is usually done. The second-order change is usually the *opposite* of the original attempts to solve the problem. In fact, it more closely resembles the problem than the original solutions. The second-order change is frequently an imaginative solution that brings a smile to the face of the person who is to carry out the strategy. Here is an example of this:

> Mr. D. had developed a fear that he would faint in hot, crowded stores. He could not shake this fear no matter how hard he tried to reason with himself that he was quite healthy and unlikely to faint (a first-order change strategy).
>
> Finally, a second-order change strategy was prescribed for Mr. D. He was told to go into a crowded department store at the busy noon hour and to lie down flat on the floor in the middle of the main aisle as if he had fainted. When he went to the store, he walked around looking for a place to pretend to faint, smiling to himself at the thought of deliberately stretching out on the floor, blocking traffic, and creating a hubbub.
>
> He did not acutally carry out the prescription; he had no need to do it because the unshakeable fear had been converted into a private joke he was tempted to play on the department store.[2]

You can see how closely the solution resembled the problem and was almost the opposite of the original first-order change in which Mr. D. tried so hard to avoid feeling faint. The same strategy can be applied to the fear of speaking in public. Instead of trying to cover up your fear (which often makes people more nervous because they are sure their fear is showing), try telling the audience how scared you are of speaking to them. By announcing your fear, you not only eliminate its worst consequence, but also win the support of the group to whom you are speaking.

The "Be Spontaneous" paradox can be dealt with in the same way. Insomnia was mentioned as one example of the paradox. The insomniac patients who can't force themselves to go to sleep are told to go to bed but to be sure to keep their eyes open. With their efforts turned away from trying to fall asleep, they are able to fall asleep naturally. Their original solutions (counting sheep, going to bed earlier, trying harder to get to sleep) had become part of the problem and were dealt with by reframing the problem: by trying to stay awake, the insomniac patients were able to fall asleep spontaneously.

Example. As you can see, every situation or problem calls for its own unique second-order strategy. Let's return once more to the child care evaluation team example to see what kind of second-order change strategy could be devised for this problem:

> The nurse, teacher, and social worker had defined the desired change to be "Increased use of our input in making recommendations." But they also had found that their attempts to prove their worth on the team only provoked more resistance and resulted in less recognition for their work rather than more.
>
> To implement a second-order change, the nurse, teacher, and social worker agreed with each other to change their strategy. Instead of working so hard to prove their ability, they started asking the physician and psychiatrist to do their work for them. They stopped trying to be recognized at the team conferences and began omitting important parts of their evaluations, asking the physician or psychiatrist to fill these parts in for them. Each one politely but insistently asked for time to meet with the physician and psychiatrist several times a week and telephoned them several times a day as well "just to check with you on this point."
>
> Within two weeks, the physician and psychiatrist were telling the nurse, teacher, and social worker that they were quite capable of doing their own work. They also began to encourage them to contribute to the team conferences, saying, "You can't expect the two of us to do all the work!"

COMMENTS ON THE PARADOXICAL MODEL

The paradoxical model seems particularly suitable for those situations in which every other solution has failed. In fact, the second-order change strategy was designed to deal with just this type of situation in which first-order change has not solved the problem. While this model can be applied to larger systems, it does not include strategies for communicating the paradoxical message to large numbers of people. In this sense, the model is not complete in itself but can be used in conjunction with other change strategies.

There are some drawbacks to this model. First of all, the person who carries out the second-order change strategy must be highly motivated in order to be willing to carry out a seemingly absurd strategy. While it is true that often people do feel a desperate need to change a situation and are willing to do almost anything to resolve their problems, the model does not provide a way to increase this motivation when it is lacking.

A second drawback to the model is that there is some risk that the strategy could backfire although people faced with a persistent problem may see the risk as negligible in comparison with the problem. Finally, reframing requires imagination and the kind of creativity needed to be humorous and a willingness to alter your perspective (that is, to step out of the nine dot box of the puzzle). In a sense, this is the same kind of creativity Greene[5] refers to when she talks about taking a stranger's point of view. In spite of these drawbacks, the creative leader will find the paradoxical model for change an effective approach for dealing with the persistent and seemingly unresolvable dilemmas that can arise in leadership situations.

SUMMARY

The paradoxical model for change divides change strategies into two types: first-order and second-order changes. The logical solutions to problems of the first-order type usually fail to break up old patterns of behavior and paradoxically may even make the problem worse. The second-order change strategy is usually the opposite of the logical first-order change. By reframing the problem, the second-order change resolves the paradox that prevented the solution to the problem.

Rational Model

Communication of a new idea is the main focus of the rational model for change.[6] This model is particularly concerned with an assessment of the characteristics of the proposed change and how these characteristics influence the rate of adoption or rejection by the target system. (The target system is the group, organization, community, or other system in which the leader proposes to bring about change.) The original research that led to the development of this model came from such diverse sources as the study of the introduction of a new hybrid corn to farmers; research on the adoption of educational innovations (adding the kindergarten year or adopting modern math, for example); and research on the pattern and rate of adoptions of a new drug by physicians.

ASSUMPTIONS

The rational model is the least power-oriented of the three models on the continuum (see Fig. 9-1).[1] It assumes a relatively passive or neutral attitude on the part of the system you want to change and, therefore, does not emphasize the use of strategies designed specifically to overcome resistance to change.

A logical response is also assumed. The rational model assumes that people behave rationally, that is, that their behavior is guided by reason and logic. This means that their behavior would be guided by rational self-interest once it is revealed to them. In other words, once you have informed people about a better or easier way to do something, they are expected to adopt this new way.

According to the rational model, ignorance and superstition are the main stumbling blocks in the way of change. Therefore, once people become better informed, they will adopt the new change willingly. The process of passing on new information is typically done through the media or other educational channels. This approach (informing the people) appeals to the American belief in the ability of science and technology to solve a wide range of problems, from curing disease to improving the quality of life.

Rogers' *diffusion of innovation,*[6] one of the best known of the rational models for change, will be used to describe this approach to change and the accompanying strategies. There are three steps in the diffusion of innovation;

1. Invention of the change.

2. Diffusion (communication) of the information regarding the change.

3. Consequences (adoption or rejection) of the change.

Each will be described in the following discussion of the steps and strategies of the rational approach to change.

STEP 1. INVENTION

The change you want to implement must first be developed or invented. One way would be to develop a new method of doing something. Or you could find a new solution to a problem through research. Another way would be to collect all the information people would need to implement a particular change. As you can see, the focus here is on the change itself rather than on the target system. The leader's attention is directed toward thorough preparation of the proposed change.

Example. The rational model for change is frequently used in health education. An example from a community health program will be used to illustrate the application of the rational model for change:

> A community health center nurse noticed that many clients with hypertension were not following their prescribed sodium-restricted diets. Most did avoid using the salt shaker but ate liberal quantities of cold cuts, cheeses, and other more hidden sources of sodium.
> The nurse consulted references for the latest information about sodium-restricted diets and spoke with the dietitian, who offered to assist the nurse in gathering educational materials. Together they developed an outline of the basic information needed to follow the diet correctly. They also collected and evaluated booklets from a number of sources (such as the American Heart Association) to find the best materials to give to clients with hypertension.

STEP 2. DIFFUSION

The next step is to diffuse or communicate the idea or information developed in the first step. Step 2 includes the selection of a way to communicate the change and an analysis of the characteristics of the change and their effect on the ease of diffusion. The goal is to ensure adequate dissemination of the information to all the people in the target system. Not only does the information have to reach all the people in the target system, but it must also be presented in such a way that the people can understand it and will accept it.

Using Mass Media

The mass media are effective channels of communication for increasing people's knowledge and awareness. You are probably familiar with many of the following examples of the use of mass media in health education:

Immunization campaigns.

Food and Drug Administration warnings.

Health messages during Heart Month.

Anti-smoking posters, pamphlets, buttons, and bumper stickers.

Radio and television talk show discussions of various health concerns from infertility to relaxation exercises.

Newspaper articles and health columns.

While these methods are quite effective in terms of reaching large numbers of people, some experts, including Rogers, believe that a more personal communication is needed to change attitudes toward the innovation. More personal communications would include individual and small group methods.

Example.   The next step was to consider the different ways in which information about sodium-restricted diets could be communicated to the people who need it (that is, the target system):

The health center nurse and dietitian considered several options for disseminating the information they had put together. They could make copies of their outline and distribute it to their clients or they could have the information printed in a colorful pamphlet to give to their clients. To be sure that each person understood the information, the nurse and the dietitian could review the material with each one individually or they could organize a class in which to do this. They decided to try the classroom approach.

If the nurse and dietitian had decided to enlarge their target system to include the whole community, they could consider using mass media methods of communication. They could, for example, organize a campaign to inform the community they served by using radio spot announcements, newspaper columns and interviews, distributing posters and pamphlets, and so on.

Estimating Diffusibility

The degree of difficulty in diffusing a new idea or information varies considerably. Every idea has certain characteristics that make it easier or harder to diffuse successfully. These characteristics include the relative advantage of the new idea over old methods or ideas; its compatibility; its complexity; the possibility of trying it out on a trial basis first; and the observability of the results. Each of these five characteristics will be described below and the sodium-restricted diet example will be used to illustrate how the characteristics can be used to evaluate the diffusibility of a particular innovation.

RELATIVE ADVANTAGE. Is the proposed idea or method in some way better than what it replaces? It is important that the change be perceived as having some advantage over the present method or information being used. There are many possible ways in which the innovation may be better. It may be more efficient, more satisfying, easier, more visually attractive, faster, cheaper, or safer to name just a few ways in which it could have a relative advantage over the old idea or method of doing things.

Example. What is the relative advantage of the sodium-restricted diet?

> The diet itself has the advantage that it can improve health and reduce serious risks (of stroke and heart attack, for example) if followed as part of a long-term treatment plan. This advantage can be pointed out in the printed material and in other communications.
>
> The information put together by the nurse and dietitian also has some advantages. It is more complete, more accurate, and easier to understand than the old diet instructions that the health center had been handing out with little or no explanation in the past.

COMPATIBILITY. To what extent is the innovation consistent with existing values and behavior patterns? Target systems that are generally open to communications from outside and have positive attitudes toward learning and change are usually more receptive to innovations. Some knowledge of the target system's norms, values, and needs is necessary in order to evaluate the degree to which the innovation will be compatible. The system's past experiences with other changes may also affect its response to another change. Compatibility, then, is a measure of the "fit" or congruence between the proposed change and the target system.

EXAMPLE. Is the proposed class on sodium-restricted diets compatible with the health center client's values and behavior patterns?

> This characteristic is a little more difficult to evaluate than the first one was. If the center's clients have been making some attempts to restrict their sodium intake, then the proposed change will be compatible with current behavior. If the clients have not been trying to follow the diet, then the proposed change lacks compatibility in this regard and this may be a problem area.
>
> Compatibility will also be increased if the center's clients are accustomed to seeking information on their health problems, to using health information as a guide to behavior, and if they feel comfortable in a classroom setting.

COMPLEXITY. Is this innovation difficult to use? If the target system perceives the proposed method or new idea as being hard to understand or difficult to use, there will be less acceptance of the change. A simple change is easier to communicate and is also easier to implement.

Example.   How complex is a sodium-restricted diet?

> One factor that increases the complexity of the sodium-restricted diet is that salt is not the only dietary source of sodium. Another related factor that increases the complexity is that foods may contain a lot of sodium and yet not taste salty at all. A sodium-restricted diet is also hard to follow when eating out in restaurants or cafeterias.
>
> If the diet could be reduced to a single, simple phrase such as, "Don't eat salt," it would be more easily communicated but this oversimplifies the information too much. Despite this, if the information is communicated in a clear, concise manner, it should not be too difficult for most people to learn.

TRIALABILITY.   Can the innovation be tried out on a limited basis? People are often more willing to try something new if they can do it on a trial basis first. They are more likely to be reluctant to implement a change if it requires a full-time commitment right from the start.

Example.   Does a sodium-restricted diet have trialability?

> This diet could be implemented gradually although it is not going to be effective until it is followed on a full-time basis. The trialability seems to be adequate.

OBSERVABILITY.   To what extent are the results of the change visible? Observable results encourage people to continue their efforts to implement the change. Seeing positive results reinforces the innovative behavior. The old saying, "Nothing succeeds like success" is another way of saying that the observability of results encourages the change activity.

Example.   How observable are the results of implementing a sodium-restricted diet?

> Most people are not aware of any symptoms when they have elevated blood pressure so they will also not be able to notice that the diet has helped lower the blood pressure.
>
> However, a lower blood pressure reading at the next visit to the health center could be one way to provide observable results. Another good substitute for observable results would be praise and encouragement from the center's staff when a client follows the diet.

STEP 3. CONSEQUENCES

The result of the effort to diffuse an innovation throughout a target system may be adoption of the change or it may be the ultimate rejection of the change. A particular change is more likely to be adopted if it has the five characteristics described in Step 2. Also, the system that is more open and has a positive attitude about learning and change is more likely to adopt an innovation than a relatively closed system that has had negative experiences with change in the past.

When a change is adopted by the target system this adoption process usually has three phases. These phases are called trial, installation, and institutionalization. Each successive phase indicates an increasing degree of acceptance of the change as follows:

TRIAL.   The change is first tried out on an experimental basis on the part of the target system. The attitude of the target system is generally one of "OK, we'll try it once and see how it works."

INSTALLATION.   If the trial is successful, the change becomes accepted enough to make it part of the regular routine and the attitude becomes one of "From now on, we'll do it this way."

INSTITUTIONALIZATION.   This phase begins when the once new idea has become so deeply enmeshed a part of the system's behavior pattern that the attitude toward it can be described as "We always do it this way."

Example.   The health center's clients may also go through the three phases of adoption in the following manner:

> When the clients first attend the class and try to follow the diet correctly, the change is in the trial phase.
>
> If the clients accept the diet sufficiently to make it a part of their everyday routine, the change has become installed.
>
> If they follow the diet so well that they don't even need to think much about it anymore, it has become institutionalized and the change has been successfully implemented.

DISCUSSION

When is the rational model a good choice? The rational model works well when there is almost universal readiness for change within the target system. For example, when the polio vaccine was developed years ago, most people were eager to obtain it because they had been very worried about outbreaks of the disease and had great faith in the ability of medical research to develop an effective vaccine. Many technologies—all kinds of mechanical inventions and new ideas—have been quickly adopted using this model.

However, the rational model's assumption that people act logically ignores the fact that as holistic beings they also react emotionally to attempts to change them. Any change that violates a norm, threatens a cherished tradition, or even disturbs a comfortable routine is not going to be accepted as readily as one that does not. Entire groups can react on the basis of a shared group feeling or norm that has developed. Let's return to the sodium-restricted diet example once more to analyze under what circumstances the rational model will be effective:

If the class consists of a highly motivated group of clients who are concerned about following their diets correctly, then the rational model will probably be effective. But food has emotional and social significance and is a part of many religious and cultural traditions. A restricted diet frequently conflicts with these other meanings.

As was mentioned before, people often experience no symptoms when they have high blood pressure and, therefore, may not be motivated to even try following a restricted diet. It is also difficult to see or feel immediate benefits from following a restricted diet and some people are easily discouraged. The described change project using the rational model ignores all these and other potential sources of resistance.

The rational model works best when the planned change is easy to understand, easy to implement, and provokes very little resistance from the target system. It assumes readiness to change and a tendency to respond rationally; it ignores social, cultural, and emotional responses to proposed changes. In other words, the rational model is most useful when the entire situation is conducive to change. However, when there is more resistance to change, you will find that the next change model, which pays more attention to the twin problems of developing readiness to change and reducing resistance, will be the more appropriate choice.

SUMMARY

The rational model is based on the assumption that people will respond in a logical fashion to change. It works best when there is little resistance to change. This model has three steps: invention, diffusion, and consequences. A change is more easily communicated or diffused if it has an advantage over the old way, is compatible, is not too complex, can be tried out on a limited basis, and if the results are observable. In the last phase, the change may be either accepted or rejected. If it is accepted, it will usually pass through three phases: trial, installation, and institutionalization.

Normative Model

The normative models of change are more holistic in their approach than the rational models are. One reason is that they focus on the target system and the actions of the leader as change agent as well as the characteristics of the change itself when planning the change strategy. Normative models also recognize and deal with the influence of people's needs, feelings, attitudes, and values on their response to change.

ASSUMPTIONS

Normative change models are located around the midpoint of the power continuum between the rational and power-coercive models (see Fig. 9-1). Some resistance is anticipated but it is expected that this resistance can be overcome. Both the leader and the target system are expected to be active, not passive, participants in the change process.

Normative models recognize the ability of the target system to resist, modify, or accept the proposed change and therefore emphasize the need to include the target system and the need to use stronger tactics in addition to the educational ones of the rational model when implementing the change. These tactics are not as strong as those used in the power-coercive models, however.

Normative models also emphasize that needs, values, attitudes, and norms affect the target system's response to change. They do not deny rationality as a basis for behavior but correctly point out that it is only one of many factors influencing behavior.

TYPES OF NORMATIVE MODELS

There are a number of different normative models, each having some variations in their approach to change. The two that will be discussed here have had a major influence on the development of change theory and its use in leadership. The first model originated with Lewin's[7] work and was further developed by Schein and Bennis,[8] and others. This first model divides the change process into phases (unfreezing, changing, and refreezing) and emphasizes the need to first analyze the forces for and against the change, a concept of a particular value to leaders.

The second model combines Havelock's[9-10] and Lippitt's[11] steps and offers a logical sequence for implementing the change process using a democratic leadership style. This model is also the source of the widely used term "change agent."

LEWIN'S PHASES OF CHANGE

Driving and Restraining Forces

Lewin recommends that you begin the change process by analyzing the entire system involved in order to identify the forces for and against change. These are called the driving and restraining forces. You can see that this is quite different from the rational model that began with the development of a new or better idea.

The forces operating within the system that push the system toward change are the driving forces. Those forces that pull the system away from change are called the restraining forces (Fig. 9-4). When the existing restraining forces are the same or stronger than the driving forces, the leader will need to use normative or power-coercive change strategies to reduce the restraining forces and increase the driving forces in order to implement the change.

In order to accurately assess these opposing forces, a thorough knowledge of the target system, the environment, the characteristics of the change, and the potential responses to change is needed. The leader may have to spend some time becoming better acquainted with one or all of these elements before an accurate appraisal of the situation can be made. When this analysis is done, the forces are mapped out as shown in Figures 9-4 and 9-5.

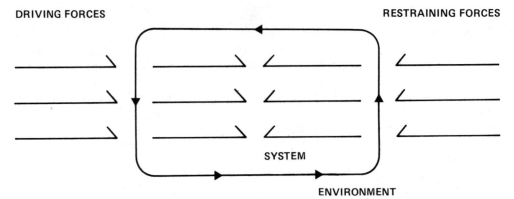

DRIVING FORCES

RESTRAINING FORCES

SYSTEM

ENVIRONMENT

FIGURE 9-4. Opposing change forces in a system. (Adapted from Lewin, K: *Field Theory in Social Science: Selected Theoretical Papers.* Harper & Row, New York, 1951.)

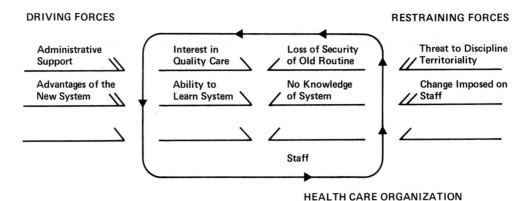

DRIVING FORCES

RESTRAINING FORCES

| Administrative Support | Interest in Quality Care | Loss of Security of Old Routine | Threat to Discipline Territoriality |
| Advantages of the New System | Ability to Learn System | No Knowledge of System | Change Imposed on Staff |

Staff

HEALTH CARE ORGANIZATION

FIGURE 9-5. Diagram of opposing change forces in computerized patient information example.

Example. An example of a very common type of change within health care organizations will be used to illustrate the analysis of driving and restraining forces in a system and its environment. The following is a description of the situation:

> The nurse educator of a small health care organization was asked to carry out the implementation of a new computerized patient information system. The new system has several advantages over the old one: it requires less writing, eliminates repetition, and allows quicker access to stored information; it combines notations from all caregivers into one format that provides a total picture of the client's progress; and it can be modified for use with different kinds of health care programs. The system is also strongly supported by the administrators and executive board of the organization.

However, none of the staff who will be using the new system have ever used it before and do they know how to use the new equipment. They also have not expressed any need to change the old system and seem satisfied with it. Aside from this, most staff members seem concerned about providing high quality care and believe that they are doing so.

The nurse educator identified the following driving forces:

Advantages of the new system.
Administrative support for the change.
Staff concern about quality care.
Staff ability to learn the new system.

On the other hand, the nurse educator also found the following restraining forces:

Lack of staff participation in the selection of the system.
Little or no staff knowledge of the new system.
Potential threats to staff feelings of security when giving up their old routine.
Potential threat to territoriality of various disciplines because of equal access to information in the new system.

These opposing forces are diagrammed in Figure 9-5. The diagram shows you what factors will help and hinder your efforts to bring about change. In some situations you might also want to note which of the forces are especially strong by adding extra lines as was done in Figure 9-5 for illustrative purposes only.

Unfreezing

Target systems usually need a push to get them moving toward change. Technically, an open system cannot actually be frozen but they can be very resistant to change and so appear to be frozen to the leader trying to introduce a change. Particular patterns of behavior can be so entrenched that it takes a great deal of energy to change them. The leader must then deliberately stir things up to unfreeze the situation.

There are three main tactics used to unfreeze the target system. These are creating disconfirmation, inducing guilt and anxiety, and providing psychologic safety; each one is explained below. These tactics are used together to get the system ready to change.

DISCONFIRMATION. Introducing disconfirmation is a confrontation with conflicting evidence. This confrontation makes the target system feel uncomfortable or dissatisfied with its present condition so that it will want to change. The disconfirming evidence may be information, examples, or experiences that challenge the status quo.

People often resist disconfirmation. They may try to ignore the evidence or to rationalize that the evidence is ambiguous or atypical. Or they may blame the problem on someone else. These responses may be defensive behaviors aimed at protecting security, esteem, or some other need.

GUILT AND ANXIETY. Inducing guilt and anxiety will overcome resistance to disconfirmation. This is done by demonstrating that a goal or value that is important to the target system is not being met or upheld. Doing this upsets the balance between the driving and restraining forces and raises the tension level within the target system.

PSYCHOLOGIC SAFETY. Providing psychologic safety is the third tactic. Making a change requires some risk on the part of the target system so the leader needs to provide sufficient security to minimize the risk. This would seem to be in conflict with the second tactic of inducing guilt and anxiety but it is not really because the guilt or anxiety induced is specific to the planned change while the feeling of security is developed as a general climate of trust and acceptance.

Many changes are resisted mainly because they present some kind of threat to the target system. If this threat is reduced or removed, people will feel comfortable enough to reduce their defensive behavior and attempt the change.

Much time and energy may be needed to unfreeze the target system enough to get it moving toward change. As a general rule, most energy is needed to reduce or eliminate the strongest restraining forces and to strengthen the weaker driving forces. For a large-scale change it may take weeks or even months to achieve unfreezing. Even the ordinary change situation described in the computerized information system example may require several weeks for unfreezing.

Example. The example of the change to a new computerized record keeping system will be continued here to show how each of the three tactics for unfreezing can be applied to a specific situation. In order to unfreeze the staff, the nurse educator took the following actions:

Disconfirmation	Meet with every staff member in small groups to discuss the inadequacies of the current system.
	Present examples of problems found in the old system.
Inducing Guilt and Anxiety	Demonstrate ways in which the old system interferes with quality care.
	Indicate that the staff is not doing the best job possible in using the old system.
	Tell staff members how strongly administrators and board members support the new system. (This implies that they would be unhappy with the staff if the new system were not accepted.)
Providing Psychologic Safety	Assure staff members that they will have ample time and opportunity to learn the new system.

Indicate that staff will be involved in planning the implementation phase.

Point out similarities between the old and new systems and that the new system will not change the routine too much.

Express approval of staff's concern for the quality of the care given and confidence in their ability to learn the system.

Assure the continued identity of each discipline; use examples for each one; show how others will be better able to see and appreciate each discipline's contribution with the new system.

You can see that each of the driving and restraining forces are dealt with in at least one of the three tactics. Many situations have more or stronger restraining forces than this example does and may require more emphasis on the disconfirmation and guilt inducing tactics than is shown above.

Changing

This is the implementation phase of the change process. Once the target system is unfrozen and moving toward change, the leader can begin putting the planned change into effect. The leader still plays a very active role in this phase.

The following is a list of the activities in which the leader will be engaged during the changing phase:

1. Introduce any new information that is needed to implement the change.
2. Encourage the new behavior so that it becomes part of the system's regular patterns of behavior. Allow practice and experimentation with the change behavior if possible.
3. Continue to provide a supportive climate to avoid an increase in defensive behavior and resistance to the change.
4. Provide opportunities to ventilate the guilt and anxiety deliberately aroused as well as other feelings, such as anger or hostility, that are aroused by the change process.
5. Provide feedback on progress and clarification of goals to reinforce the change process and to keep people from getting sidetracked.
6. Present yourself as a trustworthy person in order to keep communications open.
7. Act as an energizer to keep interest high and to keep the change process moving forward.
8. Overcome resistance that may still arise by using the tactics of the unfreezing phase.

You probably noted that most of the leader actions listed above were just basic leadership skills that come from the components of effective leadership.

Example. The following list shows how these change activities were translated into specific actions taken by the nurse educator to implement the new record keeping system already described:

Introduce New Information	Teach the staff how to use the new system.
Encourage the New Behavior	Begin with practice using examples from real situations. Then have the staff begin using the new system according to the plan they devised for implementation.
Continue the Supportive Climate	Allow adequate time for learning and practice before implementation.
	Point out how the staff is raising its standards of care.
Provide Opportunities for Ventilation	Ask staff how they feel about the new system and listen and respond to what they say about it.
Provide Feedback and Clarification of Goals	Check computerized records to evaluate progress.
	Ask staff how well the new system is working.
	Remind staff personally and through memos as needed about the use of the system and why it is being implemented.
Present Yourself as Trustworthy	Make sure that all staff were included in the implementation planning as promised.
	Follow through on other promises as well.
	Keep communications open and direct.
Overcome Resistance	Repeat, increase, and if necessary, expand the tactics described in the unfreezing phase. If, for example, staff continue to use the old system, confront them with this evidence and with its consequences.
Act as an Energizer	Take every opportunity to promote the new system at meetings, mention it in newsletters, and so forth.
	Demonstrate interest in staff progress.

Refreezing

The purpose of the refreezing phase is to stabilize and integrate the change so that it becomes a part of the regular functioning of the target system. It is similar to the institutionalization stage of the rational model.

At the beginning of this phase the situation is still fluid. Because the target system is still in the process of changing and could still take a different course than planned change, the guidance of the leader is needed to ensure that the new pattern of behavior persists. However, the leader role does become a less active one in this phase than it was in the preceding phases.

In order to facilitate the integration of the planned change, the leader continues to act as an energizer and to guide the new behavior but also increasingly delegates responsibility for the change behavior to other people in the target system. Each of these actions is discussed below.

CONTINUE ACTING AS AN ENERGIZER. Although high interest and even excitement about the change was more important in the previous phases, continued interest and support is still needed to keep the target system moving toward integration or refreezing. It is important to maintain the visibility and credibility of the change during this phase so that the integration process continues to proceed to completion.

DELEGATE INCREASED RESPONSIBILITY. By the time this phase is reached, there should be other interested and capable people ready to accept responsibility for continuing the new behavior. The leader can gradually reduce participation as other people become increasingly involved.

CONTINUE GUIDING NEW BEHAVIOR. The leader does this only as long as necessary to ensure correct implementation. Because change continues to take place in an open system, some kind of continued supervision of the new behavior may also be needed. In some cases, the leader relinquishes all responsibility for continued supervision at the end of this phase but in others this supervision becomes a part of the leader's regular functions.

Let's return to the patient information system example one more time to see how the refreezing phase is accomplished in a specific situation.

Example. Once the nurse educator succeeded in implementing the new patient information system, the nurse educator wanted to ensure its continued use. To do this, the nurse educator took the following actions:

Continue Acting as Energizer	Keep the new system visible through memos, newsletters, frequent mention at meetings, and so forth.
	Continue to show interest in staff progress and feelings about the new system.
	Praise staff for genuine progress.
Continue Guiding New Behavior	Continue to check computerized records to see how well the new system is working and to intervene if problems arise.
	Help staff correct mistakes and provide needed information.
	(Delegate both of these responsibilities as much and as soon as possible.)
Delegate Increased Responsibility to Others	Designate certain staff members as resources for staff to turn to for help.
	Turn over responsibility for checking implemetation to supervisors.

The nurse educator continued to orient new staff members to the new patient information system and to act as a resource person when other staff people did not have the information needed to answer questions. The nurse educator also continued to show some interest in the outcome of the new system but otherwise turned over all other responsibility for the system to staff members and their supervisors by the end of this last phase of Lewin's change model.

HAVELOCK AND LIPPITT'S STEPS IN THE CHANGE PROCESS

This second normative change model is derived from Havelock[9-10] and Lippitt's[11] work. It is oriented more directly toward the action of the leader rather than toward the evolution of the change as Lewin's phases were. This model is also more specific in its description of steps to follow when planning a change within a target system. You will see that these steps emphasize the use of the democratic, participative leadership style in the planning and implementation of change.

Assumptions

These steps focus on the use of communication skills and the development of a good working relationship between the leader and the person or people of the target system. In this model, the target system is more involved in the initial planning of the change process than in any of the other models described in this chapter. This emphasis on involvement is based on assumptions similar to those humanistic assumptions of the motivational theories and the democratic styles of leadership: that people will be more cooperative if they are included in decisions about things that will affect them and that most people will make appropriate decisions given sufficient time, information, and motivation.

This particular normative change model begins with the development of a relationship with the target system and then proceeds by engaging the target system in the problem-solving process. The last step deals with integration of the change into the regular behavior patterns of the target system and its environment.

Step 1. Build a Relationship

In order to work effectively with the target system, the leader must first earn that system's trust and respect. This is done by taking several actions. The first way to earn trust and respect is by using good communication techniques, especially active listening. Offering some kind of help or assistance is another way to develop positive ties with the system. Openness and honesty are also needed to gain people's trust.

There are two commonly used ways to gain the target system's respect. The first is to provide people with information about your skills, credentials, and relevant past experiences. The second is to demonstrate your ability to the group in some way. .

Building an effective working relationship is fairly simple when the target system is a group of people who already know, trust, and respect you. Both clients and coworkers are frequently in this category. However, some of your colleagues in other professions may not recognize the full range of skills and knowledge possessed by a nurse and so your credibility and respectability would have to be further developed with them. Some clients' respect for the nurse may also have to be reinforced but building trust is more frequently needed. Clients may lack trust because of negative experiences with health caregivers or because they see the leader as someone who does not have the same background or experience they have had. This lack of trust may also be found in some coworkers for the same reasons.

Example. A situation in which a new relationship had to be developed with a client system is described below.

> A nurse from a community service organization obtained permission to offer health services to the people held in a county jail. The nurse had never been inside the jail before except to meet with prison officials to get permission to work with the prisoners.
> Prison officials asked the nurse, Miss W., to begin by working with the women held in the jail, so she arranged to meet with the women and their guards (correction officers). In general, prisoners do not trust people easily. Miss W. knew that she could not pretend to understand how it feels to be arrested and imprisoned. She told the women honestly that she did not know what it was like to be in prison and that she needed to learn this from them before she could help them effectively. The nurse told the women about her past nursing experience and credentials in order to gain credibility and their respect but mostly she encouraged them to talk about their experiences and their health needs in order to begin developing a positive relationship with them.

In this situation, both trust and respect had to be developed in order to begin the change in the target system.

Step 2. Diagnose the Problem

The purpose of this step is to identify a felt need, that is, something that the target system itself considers important and in need of change. The people in the target system are actively involved in this process.

There are many ways to get the input of the people in the target system into the diagnosis of the problem. Individual and group meetings, conferences, informal discussion, surveys, questionnaires, telephone interviews, and casual conversation may all be used. Whatever method is used, the leader must ensure that people feel free to express their personal feelings and opinions and that each person's input is in some way reflected in the final diagnosis of the problem.

Some face-to-face interaction should be included in order to allow for exchange and clarification of ideas leading to some consensus from the group (including the leader) regarding the problem in need of change.

This consensus among the people in the target system and with the leader is an essential element of this change model. When the entire group has been involved in identification of the problem and has agreed that it needs to be changed, resistance to change is decreased and motivation to change is increased. The planned change is perceived as coming from within the group rather than being imposed from the outside. It is a change that the group believes is needed. Through this approach, the group becomes committed to the change process because the change meets the needs of the group and belongs to the group.

The leader's role in this process has several dimensions. The leader usually initiates the change process. Although this initiative could come from the group, the leader is more often the initiator of the process because many people who've been working within a system for any extended period of time just move along with the currents of the daily routine and fail to recognize the need for change. They become so accustomed to the system's patterns that they do not think about ways to change or improve these patterns until stimulated to do so. Others simply fail to take the initiative to begin the change process or have given up trying to change the system.

The leader also acts as an energizer in stimulating and continuing the exchange and guides the choice of methods for obtaining input from members of the target system and maintaining the exchange of opinions and ideas. The leader provides input to the discussion and facilitates the exchange by engaging in open, honest communication and by promoting a climate of trust.

Finally, the leader encourages and guides movement toward the development of consensus on the problem. Generally speaking, the group should choose the problem of most concern or the one on which there is the greatest agreement in order to increase the motivation to change. However, when the group is immature and not highly functional, it is wise to start with a problem that has a good chance of being resolved. The success of the first attempt at planned change improves the group's function and increases the group's confidence in its ability to solve a harder problem next time.

Example.   The group of women prisoners described above was not a highly functional group due to its high turnover rate and the fact that the women were very concerned about their own problems and therefore unable to concentrate on group concerns. These characteristics of the group had to be taken into consideration in the process of diagnosing the problem.

> The nurse encouraged the women to talk about their health needs. Many problems arose in the discussion: needed diagnostic tests were not done; blankets were not cleaned between prisoners; no showers were allowed on Sundays; starchy high-calorie meals thwarted dieters; the women had fewer exercise times and TV privileges than the men; they had difficulty contacting lawyers and families; there were interpersonal and racial conflicts among the women; and many women were concerned about young children left with friends or placed in foster care.
>
> When so many problems face a group, a decision must be made about where to begin. The problems could not all be dealt with at once, especially by an immature group, but several of them could be dealt with at one time because they had a common source. The nurse encouraged them to choose one of the problems to work on first. The women decided that they would work on the inequity between the men and the

women in the prison. They focused their attention on a particularly irritating but simple problem—they were not allowed to shower on Sunday and Sunday was visiting day.

Step 3. Assess Resources

Once a consensus has been reached on the diagnosis of the problem, the resources available to the group are assessed. The resources can belong to the leader or to the target system or they can come from the environment in which the change is to take place.

The particular resources needed to bring about change varies depending upon the type of change the target system selects. In general, however, there are certain categories of resources to consider in making this assessment. These categories are the following:

Motivation and commitment to change.
Knowledge and skills needed to implement the actual change behavior.
Sources of power and influence that support the change.
Economic resources available.
Time and energy available.
Social norms, roles, and values that support the change.

This assessment of resources is somewhat like Lewin's analysis of the driving and restraining forces except that it emphasizes the forces for change while neglecting the forces resisting change. In spite of this drawback, this assessment does indicate when a group's resources are inadequate to bring about the change. More often, the assessment shows a group that they had more resources than they realized and so it encourages them to continue their movement toward change. Also, once you are familiar with these change models, you can combine their different strategies to suit a particular situation. You could, for example, use Lewin's analysis of the driving and restraining forces within the Havelock/Lippitt model.

Example. It may seem that a realistic assessment of the resources available to a group of prisoners would be discouraging. But even this group had some resources they could draw on to bring about change. These resources included the following:

Knowledge of the informal system of the prison, especially what rules could be broken without punishment and what type of complaint prison officials were likely to respond to.
Ability to gain the sympathy of their guards.
Motivation of the women and the nurse to work for change.
Potential support from the community; conditions in the jail were publicized.
Prison officials' recognition of the nurse's professional status and ability.

After assessing their resources, the group decided that their resources were adequate for the selected change.

Step 4. Set Goals and Select Strategies

After diagnosing the problem and assessing the resources, the group is ready to set specific goals and to decide how they will implement the actual change behavior. The people in the target system are as actively involved as they were in diagnosing the problem (Step 2). The leader continues to act as guide, resource person, supporter, and energizer in this step.

The goal set by the group should be specific in order to provide direction and attainable in order to avoid discouragement. When the goal has been specifically stated and agreed upon, the group can then decide how to implement their goal. Again, the group is actively involved in this decision-making process. The strategies selected need to be realistic in terms of the resources available to the group and appropriate for the change desired and the setting in which it takes place.

Beginning with a *leverage point* is often a good idea. A leverage point is a point at which it is most easy to get movement toward change. A person or group that is very likely to be receptive to the proposed change is one such leverage point.

Example. The women prisoners began with one strategy for change and shifted to another more power-oriented strategy when the first one failed to bring quick results. The goal they set and the two strategies they used were as follows:

GOAL   The immediate specific goal set by the group was to get permission to shower on Sunday. In addition, they wanted TV and exercise privileges equal to those of the male prisoners.

1st STRATEGY   The women asked the nurse to speak to jail officials on their behalf. The nurse first spoke to the guard on duty with the women present. The guard said that showers were not allowed on Sundays because it was a visiting day and that the guard could not change the rule. The nurse then met with Warden L. who said he would think about the women's request.

At this point, the reader may note that the target system has actually been enlarged to include the guards and jail officials. However, these people were not included in the planning of the change and so were likely to resist the change.

2nd STRATEGY   The next day, Saturday, was very hot. The women asked the guard if they could take showers on Sunday. The guard responded, "No, the rule hasn't been changed." The women became more and more frustrated and angry. When they were put back in their cells after TV privileges ended at 8 o'clock, they set fire to their mattresses.

The fires were quickly extinguished but the incident frightened the guard and led to a meeting with the warden later that night during which the women presented their requests directly.

On Sunday, the women were allowed showers before visiting hours, given equal TV privileges, and promised equal outdoor exercise time.

The women had used a power tactic to take advantage of the warden's concern about public criticism of the way the jail was run.

Step 5. Stabilize, Consolidate, and Reinforce the Change

This important last step is similar to Lewin's Refreezing and Rogers' Institutionalization. The leader's role in this step is to continue action to maintain the change, provide feedback on progress, and to support the change.

Example. Once the women succeeded in implementing the change they had been involved in planning, their motivation remained high enough to complete the change process and accomplish integration of the change:

> The women continued to remind their guards about their new privileges and took full advantage of the privileges. The nurse followed through on the change with prison officials until equal privileges became a written regulation of the prison.

You can see from this example that when you involve the target system in the whole process, both the process and the change can turn out quite differently from what the leader originally had in mind. In this case, a normative change strategy evolved into a power-coercive strategy.

DISCUSSION

The normative models for change are holistic, responsive, democratic, flexible, and adaptable. They are responsive and democratic in approach, particularly the Havelock/Lippitt steps in which the target system is actively involved in the planning of the change. Both encourage responsiveness to the characteristics and needs of the target system. They are also far more holistic in their approach than the rational model is and applicable to a wider range of situations than the paradoxical model is. In fact, the normative models are so flexible that they can be applied to almost any change situation. In Research Example 9-1, you will see that the researcher attempted to determine what factors in a situation increase the likelihood of success for a planned change and came up with recommendations that parallel the strategies of the normative approach.

Although they are effective in a wide range of situations, the normative approaches do not always work. Normative change models work well when there is a low to moderate amount of resistance to change. They are basically persuasive, problem-solving methods. But there are individuals and even whole groups of people who are not easily persuaded, if at all.

There are also times when strong resistance to change is due to conflicting beliefs, norms, or values that cannot be made compatible with each other. The controversy over abortion is an example of conflicting values in which each side uses moral or ethical beliefs to support their arguments. Normative models will not work when people cannot eventually reach some kind of consensus.

There are other situations in which the resistance to change is very strong because the target system feels that the change will be detrimental to its position

Research Example 9-1. Successful Planned Changes

What factors facilitate planned change? What factors increase resistance? Schermerhorn[12] asked middle managers from hospitals of different types in New England to rate the effect of a number of different factors on a typical planned change. Most of these changes were common events such as altering admission procedures, asking lab employees to begin wearing lab coats, or trying to change the attitudes of uncooperative employees. A total of 70 actual successful and unsuccessful attempts to implement change were analyzed.

The factors rated by the managers as having increased success included the presence of a felt need, providing information about the change, using coercion and personal attraction to induce change, frequent communications, direct assistance, and top management support. Success in implementing change decreased when alternative actions were available. The perception that coercion was effective but that the use of special incentives (rewards) was not seemed to surprise the researcher.

The managers surveyed also thought that conflict increased when coercion or data gathering was done but decreased when a problem existed that created a felt need to change. The data gathering may be threatening to some people. Resistance was perceived to increase when information was provided or when alternatives to the change were available but decreased when there was a felt need, personal attraction to the person implementing the change, and top management support.

On the basis of these results, the researcher suggested the following guidelines for implementing change:

Build the change around a felt need.

Conduct data-gathering in a nonthreatening manner.

Use effective communication skills when presenting information and any alternatives.

Maintain good interpersonal relations with staff in order to use the influence of personal attraction.

The pressure of coercion may help to unfreeze a situation.

Encourage free exchange of ideas to develop a sense of participation.

Provide assistance and avoid overloading the group to facilitate the change process.

---

or well being. There are, for example, many individuals and groups who value their positions of prestige, power, influence, or economic strength. A change that threatens any one of these will be strongly resisted.

When the restraining forces such as those mentioned above are too strong, the normative approach will not be effective. In these situations, a more powerful model is needed to bring about planned change—the power-coercive model.

SUMMARY

Normative change models deal with people's needs, feelings, values, and potential resistance to change. The first model, derived primarily from Lewin, began with an analysis of the forces for (driving) and against (restraining) change. The leader then proceeds to work through the unfreezing, changing, and refreezing phases of change.

In the second normative model, derived from the work of Havelock and Lippitt, the leader begins by developing a positive relationship with the target system. The target system itself is then actively involved in the rest of the change process: diagnosing the problem, assessing resources, choosing a goal and selecting strategies, and finally, reinforcement and integration of the change into the function of the target system.

The normative approach works best when the resistance to change is low to moderate and when some consensus on the planned change can eventually be reached.

Power-Coercive Model

The power-coercive model for change focuses on resistance to change and how to overcome that resistance. This model is also concerned with the target system and the actions of the change agent. While it recognizes the influence of people's needs, feelings, attitudes, and values on change, the power-coercive model does not necessarily respect them.

ASSUMPTIONS

The power-coercive model is located on the far end of the power continuum, at the opposite end from the rational model (see Fig. 9-1). A great deal of resistance is anticipated in this approach, so much resistance that only an exercise of power is expected to be able to overcome this resistance. It is assumed that a consensus cannot be reached through the use of the softer, more persuasive approaches of the rational or normative models.

The power-coercive model is neither democratic nor participative in its approach. The target system is truly a target in this model. The members of the target system are very resistant, sometimes actively resistant to the change and are not included in the decisions made during the change process. This approach is not responsive to the needs of the people of the target system except when this responsiveness would bring about the desired change.

Power-coercive strategies emphasize the use of some type of force that pushes the target system toward change. Its use is appropriate when the less powerful approaches fail. The leader who decides to use this approach is entering a win-lose situation and assumes the risk of losing the contest. However, when you consider that the alternative is to not fight at all, the benefits often outweigh the risks of using the power-coercive model.

In the next part of this section, the term power as used in this model for change is defined. Then the many sources of power will be listed and finally the steps for carrying out a power-coercive strategy will be given. These steps are not as orderly as those of the previous models, but they do serve as an outline to guide you in the use of this powerful leadership strategy.

POWER

Power is the ability to change people's behavior whether they want it changed or not. It has also been defined as the ability to impose your will on others, even when they resist you.[13] Power involves the use of some type of force although it is not necessarily physical force that is used. The force may be gentle or it may be harsh but it is used to overcome whatever resistance there is to the change.

Power tactics involve the use of coercion to bring about change.[14] This means that the target system is not willing to change but is forced to by the use of power. Many power tactics also involve the use of threats to bring about change. For example, in collective bargaining, an employee group can threaten to strike if the employer does not agree to the group's demands.

SOURCES OF POWER

Although power is not evenly distributed among the individuals or groups, everyone has some power and, therefore, some resources for using power tactics. The sources include physical strength, ability to threaten harm, positional power, money, legal power, public recognition and support, expert power, the power of an idea, strength in numbers, and control of access to resources.

Each of these sources is interrelated so this listing of sources has many overlaps. It is not meant to provide clear cut categories. Its purpose is to provide a guide for assessing your actual and potential power and your opponent's actual and potential power.

Physical Strength

Physical force can be used to change behavior. For example, a parent will bodily remove a toddler from an immediate danger rather than try to persuade the child to move away from the danger. Police use physical force when necessary but usually try to use their other powers (legal and positional) first. Nurses occasionally use force to restrain patients in danger of doing harm to themselves or others. A leader may step bodily between two arguing staff members to break up a fight.

With these few exceptions, physical force is rarely considered appropriate for use in leadership situations. A serious drawback to the use of physical force is that it can provoke return physical force and an escalation of hostility into violence. Its use also violates many social norms and values in most situations.

Ability to Harm

The ability to inflict some kind of harm to others is another source of power. For example, an employer can fire an employee but employees can also quit, leaving the employer without anyone to do the work. There are many other more subtle kinds of harm that can be threatened such as public embarrassment, loss of prestige, or loss of popularity.

The threat of harm does not have to be made directly to influence another's behavior. For example, an employer negotiating with a union knows that the union can call a strike and does not have to be told this directly. In fact, the veiled, ambiguous threat of harm is often more frightening and therefore more effective than the direct threat in which the threatened person or group knows exactly what is risked by continuing to resist.

Positional Power

Some positions or offices, both public and private, have inherent power. The office of the President of the United States is an example of a very powerful position. On a less lofty level, the person who is the Director of Nursing has some power over the entire nursing department. The Director makes decisions that affect everyone working in the nursing department and the Director's requests or orders are usually obeyed by everyone in the department because of the power of the Director's position as head of the department.

Postitional power comes from the position itself rather than from the individual who holds that position. Part of this power is delegated. For example, an elected official is given power by the voters. A supervisor or head nurse has power delegated by the administration of the agency or institution. Another part of this power comes from those who work under the direction of the person with positional power. They grant the person this power by respecting the position and being willing to carry out the requests made by the holder of this position. Another source of positional power comes from having a social position with high status. Two examples of this are being known as a community leader or being the spokesperson for a particular group such as the women's movement.

Since positional power is delegated and granted by others, it is not too effective against very strong resistance, especially from those who have granted this power. But it is often effective when used in combination with other sources of power.

Money

Money is thought by some to be the greatest source of power and is certainly a very effective power source in many situations. The opportunity to gain monetarily or the fear of losing money affects much behavior. For example, money in the form of a salary influences the behavior of many workers. Since money is needed to purchase the basic necessities of food, clothing, and shelter, the loss of salary threatens these basic needs. As a result, people tend to behave in a way that they believe will keep that salary secure.

Economic motivation works at other levels too. For example, the organizations in which most people work need money to survive and those organizations that lose too much money will cease to exist. It is not surprising then that much behavior in organizations is aimed at bringing money into the organization or preventing the loss of money already earned.

People or groups who are able to control access to money have a tremendous source of power. There are indirect ways in which this source of power can be tapped. For example, information that leads the public to believe that an institution's services are inferior will indirectly lead to economic losses for that institution by reducing the number of people seeking and paying for its services. A poor evaluation that means a staff member will not receive a raise this year is another example of an indirect way to control economic resources. You can see that even if you do not have direct control over economic resources, you may be able to influence access to these resources and therefore gain power.

Legal Power

The legal system is a more specific source of power than some of the sources already mentioned. When the behavior you want to change is contrary to an existing law, you can use the law to force the target system to change. For example, nurse practice acts define the legal scope of the profession and may be used to support efforts to expand nursing functions. There are also laws regarding fair employment practices, health and safety standards for employees, legal precedents in malpractice cases, and regulations defining adequate health care for reimbursement purposes. These are just a few examples of ways in which laws can be used to support your efforts to bring about change. You can also challenge existing laws in the courts or work to get them changed at the local, state, or federal level of government.

Using legal power is not a simple thing to do. It requires knowledge of the law, of the way courts and legislatures operate, and money to support your effort. However, many important changes have been brought about through the legal system. The laws against discrimination in employment are just one example of these changes.

Public Recognition and Support

Although public recognition and support may seem to be a nebulous entity, it can be a very useful source of power. Most people want to avoid embarrassment or disapproval and will often change their behavior to do so.

Pressure from peers can be an effective way to change behavior. For example, aides who have gotten into the habit of coming in to work late will change their behavior if their coworkers begin to criticize their lateness.

People also seek recognition and approval. For example, letters of thanks from former patients or a favorable article in the newspaper about the high quality care given on a particular unit strongly reinforces the caregivers' desire to function at a high level. This public recognition not only raises morale but also keeps the administration from trying to make any unwanted changes on this popular unit.

Hospitals and other health care organizations find it very difficult to operate in a climate of unfavorable public opinion. Public recognition and support is so important that large health care organizations actually have public relations departments whose major purpose is to win this approval and recognition. Favorable public opinion about an organization brings increased numbers of clients and it also brings increased financial contributions to the organization.

Public sympathy can also be aroused and used to bring about change. For example, you can use public sympathy for abused children to support the expansion of family counseling and child protective services.

Expert Power

Expert power is based upon the education, skills, and experience of the individual or group. Patients often follow the nurse's directions simply because they believe the nurse is the expert on health matters. A well-known example of the use of expert power by a group is the American Dental Association's endorsement of fluoride toothpaste.

Expert power is gained by first preparing yourself as an expert, identifying yourself as an expert, and then seeking recognition as an expert. It is especially useful in influencing public opinion to support your side. By itself, expert power is not usually sufficient to overcome strong resistance but is useful in establishing the legitimacy of your claims to power and in combination with other sources of power.

Power of an Idea

Ideas by themselves have a certain amount of power. For example, a nursing home staff can be depressed and discouraged by the idea that they are only providing a place to store old people to wait until it is time to die. The idea that a nursing home is a rehabilitation center that aims to send some people home can completely change the feelings of the staff and the climate of the nursing home.

In order for an idea to have power, it must be heard. The idea (in the example above) that a nursing home means rehabilitation not warehousing could not have had any effect if it had not been effectively communicated to the staff. The power of an idea is also enhanced when the idea can be simply stated, easily remembered, and when it is accepted by large numbers of people.

Strength in Numbers

The sheer number of people who support a change are an important source of power (Fig. 9-6). It is so important that organizing a following is one of the basic steps in carrying out a power-coercive change strategy.

FIGURE 9-6. Strength in numbers. The number of people who support a change is an important source of power. The side with the most supporters appears strong while the side with fewer supporters appears weak.

The larger the number of people who support a change, the harder it becomes for others to oppose the change. When other factors are equal, the side with the most supporters appears strong and the side with fewer supporters appears weak. Gaining many supporters for your side increases the strength of the entire strategy for change.

Control of Access to Resources

This last source of power overlaps several of the others already mentioned. The person or group who controls access to money, communications, or to information has a potentially enormous source of power available because very little can be accomplished without money, communications, or information.

BASIC STEPS OF THE POWER-COERCIVE MODEL

The steps given here are derived primarily from the work of Alinsky[15] and Haley.[16] Both Alinsky and Haley have concentrated on the use of power by people who are "have nots" in contrast to the "haves" (to use Alinsky's terms). In other words, these are the tactics used by people who do not have the advantage of holding high positions, great wealth, or other vast resources to support their desire to bring about change. The "haves" tend to be especially afraid of losing their power and react defensively to any challenges to their power.

The following tactics are designed to take advantage of the sources of power most available to the have-nots.

Step 1. Define the Issue and Identify the Opponent

As with most strategies for change, you need to be clear about exactly what change is desired. In a power-coercive strategy you also need to reduce the change to a single issue around which you can polarize (divide into groups for and against) people and rally support.

The issue must be specific enough that people can take sides for or against it. It also needs to be expressed in a few simple words that can be easily communicated to a large number of people and can serve as a slogan or battle cry. Finally, the issue should express a goal that is realistic and has the possibility of being achieved.

In a power strategy, the target system becomes the opponent. The opponent is the person or group that has the ability to bring about the desired change. The target is not necessarily the person or group who will actually implement the change but whoever controls the behavior targeted to be changed. You need to identify the opponent as sharply as the issue in order to focus all the pressure on this point later on.

Example. This example will illustrate how health caregivers can use the power-coercive model to fight restrictions on their professional roles:

Several incidents had come to the attention of the Chief of the Medical Staff in regard to patient teaching. Two very traditional obstetricians complained about the post-partum exercises their patients were taught. Then, an oncologist found a patient weeping and the physician complained that the nurses had spoken to this patient about dying. Finally, one patient called the attending physician because the patient had discovered during routine preoperative teaching that the scheduled surgery would be much more extensive than the patient had expected.

The Chief of the Medical Staff brought these complaints to the hospital Administrator and asked the Administrator to do something about them. The Administrator then asked the Director of Nursing to tell all nurses that they could do no patient teaching without a physician order. The Director protested strongly and listed all the reasons why nurses are expected to teach patients as needed and pointed out that other staff also did some patient teaching. The Administrator was adamant and told the Director "If you do not take care of it, then I will." The Director replied "You are making a mistake."

The next day, a memo from the Administrator was distributed to every nursing unit. The memo stated that nurses in that hospital would do no patient teaching without a physician's order.

A head nurse, Miss B., who had been planning an extensive new patient teaching program with her staff was infuriated by the memo. She decided to fight this new rule. The issue as she saw it was nurses' rights to teach their patients and her opponent was the Administrator who signed the memo.

Step 2. Organize a Following

You may be completely alone when you begin to implement this strategy but you cannot remain alone and succeed. You can remain the leader of the strategy but you need to form a group to support you.

Actually, two kinds of groups are needed. The first is a small cadre of people who are just as strongly in favor of the change as you are and who are willing and able to help you plan and carry out the tactics needed. This cadre will be the core group, the key people on whom you can depend throughout the rest of the steps.

The second group is a larger following of people, as many as possible, who will support you and take part in some of the tactics. These people do not have to be as dedicated or skillful as the key people, but it will be important to keep up their interest and motivation. This larger number of people is needed to provide the strength of numbers. The size of the group will be one demonstration of your side's power.

Some organizing tactics may be needed to develop a following. The issue and the identity of the opponent need to to be clearly and simply communicated to anyone you want to recruit. The opponent is defined as the enemy of your following, an enemy who threatens harm to your group. Identification of a common enemy increases the cohesiveness of your following and appeals to the needs or interests of the people on your side. It is important to define your side as having the ability to bring about the desired change and as being right in demanding this change while the other side is defined as wrong and as a threat to your group that can and must be overcome.

It may be difficult to attract a large following immediately. If this happens, Alinsky has a formula for dealing with this problem:

> If you have a vast number of people, "you can parade it visibly" and "openly show your power . . ."
>
> If you have a small number of people, conceal them in the dark but make a lot of noise so it sounds like a lot of people . . .
>
> If you have a tiny number, "too tiny even for noise, stink up the place."[17]

Example. In the example so far, the head nurse had decided to fight the new rule limiting nurses' rights to teach their patients:

> Miss B. talked with two of her friends after the head nurse meeting about the memo. Both were angry about it but not sure what to do. Miss B. suggested that they meet after work to talk about it some more.
>
> After work, the three head nurses met. One had brought the evening supervisor, who was known to be in agreement about nurses' rights, to join them. They discussed the problem for a while. They all thought that most of the nurses in the hospital were unhappy about the memo so they decided to collect as many signatures as possible to send with a reasonable letter stating their position to the Administrator.
>
> The first head nurse mentioned including the Director of Nursing but the supervisor suggested that they wait until the signatures were collected. Each of the four nurses took a section of the hospital and they planned to collect the signatures immediately so that the letter could be sent within 48 hours.

Step 3. Build a Power Base

This step lays the groundwork for the implementation of specific tactics in the next step. The development of a following was the beginning of the power base that now needs to be expanded. The leader and key people need to carefully assess what types of power they have or can develop. As many as possible of the power sources listed earlier in this section should be used to build the power base from which pressure can be put on the opponent.

The power available to your opponent should also be assessed. Even more important is an assessment of the opponent's weak points, which will be the targets of the power tactics in the next step. For example, if your opponent is violating a law or regulation, this violation is an obvious weak point. Or your opponent may be particularly sensitive to public opinion, which would then be a logical target. No opponent has an unshakeable power base—there is always an Achilles heel to attack if you search hard enough for it.

Example. The four nurses found that most of their colleagues supported their fight for nurses' rights.

Several nurses offered to collect signatures and within the 48 hours, they had signatures from more than half of the nurses working in the hospital. The first head nurse also prepared a letter to the Administrator that gave a rationale for patient teaching and pointed out that it was an independent function mentioned specifically in their state's nurse practice act.

The Administrator, Mr. C., was impressed with the number of signatures and began to wonder if he'd acted too hastily. However, he was concerned that if he gave in to this petition, the hospital staff would think they could always get him to change his mind by presenting a petition. So he decided to ignore the petition and did not respond to it at all. When the head nurse called his office, his secretary told her that no action would be taken.

The head nurse called the key people together again to plan their next move. They reassessed their position. What could they do next? They had several sources of power available: many nurses on their side (numbers), the law supported but did not demand they be allowed to do patient teaching (some legal power), the patients wanted the information the nurses gave and most physicians and other staff appreciated their teaching (potential public support), and they were good at it (expert power). Also, they could refuse to work (threat of harm) and paralyze the hospital although they did not want to do this. The Administrator had the power of his position, economic power, and the support of some physicians, but seemed susceptible to a change in public opinion or to pressure from others with position power.

Step 4. Begin Action Phase

In the action phase of the power-coercive model for change, tactics that will push the opponent into accepting the desired change are selected and implemented. These tactics are designed to create fear, confusion, and anger in the opponent. Conflict and controversy are encouraged in this approach to change in contrast to other models for change.

There are several factors to consider in the selection of the tactics to use. First, the tactic must suit your following. For example, health care professionals are likely to be more comfortable with petitions and even picket signs than with any tactic that is illegal or dangerous. The tactic should also be one that your group can enjoy carrying out. One that has drama or humor in it is more fun and usually more effective. Paradoxical tactics have this element of humor in them.

Alinsky was a master at creating tactics that people enjoyed and were very effective. For example, he figured out a harmless way to completely tie up a busy airport: have your people go into the restrooms and keep them occupied—for hours. A bank can be paralyzed the same way by large numbers of people opening up new accounts with small amounts of money.

Alinsky also used ridicule effectively. He found that it not only infuriates the opponent but it is very hard to counterattack. When obeyed to the letter, most rules become absurd and this can be an effective way to ridicule an opponent's rule.

Threats have already been mentioned as effective tactics. However, if you decide to a use a threat, be sure that you can fulfill it because your opponent may challenge you to carry it out. In other words, do not bluff.

Haley recommends that you set yourself up as an authority or expert on the issue and speak to the opponent as an equal or better, never as a subordinate. It is also important to respond to any attack on your side with either a question or another attack, not with a defensive reply because it will be perceived as a sign of weakness.

At the same time, you can paradoxically define yourself as not seeking power— this makes your opponent appear to be the power hungry one. You can also say that you are not calling for a change and then call for a change—this confuses your opponent and makes it harder to attack your side. This is a pretended meekness that makes your opponent appear to be the bad guy and builds public sympathy for your side.

You cannot actually be meek when implementing a power-coercive strategy. An effective strategy demands strength. Each of these tactics demonstrates your group's power and challenges the power of your opponent.

Example. Based on their assessment of the power available to them and to their opponent, the four nurses planned a tactic that they believed their following would be willing and able to carry out:

> The four nurses decided to launch a compaign to publicize their fight and build more support. They distributed buttons to all nurses who would wear them saying "Nurses' Rights." Many patients, visitors, and staff members asked what the buttons meant and expressed support for the nurses' group.
>
> The Administrator began to wish he had just let the nurses keep on teaching but he was still concerned about the physicians who had originally complained and about appearing weak (losing power) by giving in to the nurses. So he decided to live with both the buttons and with his memo.

Step 5. Keep the Pressure On

It may be necessary to continue the pressure on your opponent by carrying out several different tactics until your opponent agrees to the desired change. This pressure is continued by changing tactics. The changes serve two purposes. First, they keep your opponent off balance and unable to predict your next move. Second, they keep your following interested and excited. A single tactic used for a long time becomes predictable and boring. New tactics help to keep your group's motivation high.

Example. Although the administrator was definitely feeling the pressure, he had not agreed to change after both the petitions and buttons with the "Nurses' Rights" slogan on them had won some public support for the nurses:

> The four nurses decided that it was time to increase the pressure on the Administrator by getting increased public support and by using ridicule. They asked the people in their group to encourage anyone who expressed support to call the Administrator. The

nurses also asked every physician who supported them to stop by the Administrator's office to tell him what they thought as the Administrator seemed to be susceptible to physician's influence.

In the meantime, the key people in the group began telling hospital staff members that the only reason the memo had been sent was because the Administrator was afraid of one of the outspoken physicians. They started referring to the Administrator as "Chicken Charlie." They also decided to meet with the Director of Nursing.

Because the Administrator originally issued the memo in response to physician complaints, the Administrator assumed he had their support until they began to visit his office. The number of calls to his office increased that day to the point that his secretary threatened to resign. The Administrator went home a little earlier than usual that day.

Step 6. The Final Struggle

Neither side can continue to give or take such pressure indefinitely. If the opponent has not yet agreed to the desired change despite several different tactics, it is time to increase the pressure enough to force a decision. Several new and stronger tactics are needed to do this.

Example. The four nurses felt that they were close to winning and wanted to force a decision:

> The four nurses met with the Director of Nursing who had closely followed their activities and quietly supported their efforts. They asked the Director for more direct support. With the Director, they planned the final attack.
>
> The attack focused on two points: making the Administrator look foolish by over-obeying his rules and bringing on pressure from outside the hospital for the first time. The four nurses went back to their group and asked each nurse to point out to the physicians every time there was an indication that a patient needed any information at all. At the same time, the Director of Nursing cancelled all prenatal classes held at the hospital, declaring that they were in violation of the Administrator's rule. In order to inform the people who attended the classes, the Director asked the local newspaper and radio stations to announce the cancellations.
>
> After it was all over the Administrator could not remember whether it was the Chief of the Medical Staff or the President of the Board of Trustees who called him first. The President of the Board demanded to know why they were going to be the only hospital in the city without those very popular prenatal classes and ordered the Administrator to stop the public announcements. The Chief of Staff told the Administrator to stop being ridiculous and let the nurses get on with their work so that the physicians could get on with their work.
>
> The four nurses celebrated their victory with their following. Along with several members of their group, they were asked to serve on a Nursing Advisory Committee that made recommendations about any new policies affecting nurses. The Director of Nursing took advantage of the situation to strengthen the power of the Director's position in relation to the Administrator so that any future policies affecting nursing would come only from the office of the Director of Nursing.

Not every power-coercive strategy will end in victory. Effective implementation of a power-coercive strategy demands a great deal of time and energy from the leader and from supporters. However, since it is used when other change strategies are ineffective, deciding not to use the strategy is actually an acceptance of defeat on that issue.

Power tactics are used frequently in work situations so an effective leader needs to be able to recognize them and respond to them with equally strong tactics as well as to initiate the use of a power-coercive strategy for change.

SUMMARY

Power is the ability to change people's behavior in spite of their often strong resistance. Everybody has some sources of power available to them that can be used to carry out a power-coercive strategy for change. These sources include physical strength, ability to threaten harm, positional power, money, legal power, public recognition and support, expert power, the power of an idea, strength in numbers, and control of access to resources. After defining the issue and identifying the opponent, the leader organizes a following, builds a power base, and then carries out the power tactics needed to pressure the opponent into the desired change in behavior.

References

1. BENNIS, WG ET AL: *The Planning of Change,* ed 3. Holt, Rinehart & Winston, New York, 1976, p 2.

2. WATZLAWICK, P, WEAKLAND, J, AND FISCH, R: *Change: Principles of Problem Formation and Problem Resolution.* WW Norton & Co, New York, 1974.

3. MATHWIG, G: *The Nurse as a Change Agent.* (mimeographed) New York University, New York, nd.

4. HOLMES, TH AND RAHE, R: *The social readjustmant rating scale.* Journal of Psychosomatic Research 2:213, April 1967.

5. GREENE, M: *Teacher as Stranger.* Wadsworth, Belmont, California, 1973.

6. ROGERS, EM AND SHOEMAKER, FF: *Communication of Innovations,* ed 2. The Free Press, New York, 1971.

7. LEWIN, K: *Field Theory in Social Science: Selected Theoretical Papers.* Harper & Row, New York, 1951.

8. SCHEIN, EH AND BENNIS, W: *Personal and Organizational Change Through Group Methods.* John Wiley & Sons, New York, 1975.

9. HAVELOCK, RG: *The Change Agent's Guide to Innovation in Education.* Educational Technology Publications, Englewood Cliffs, New Jersey, 1973.

10. HAVELOCK, RG AND HAVELOCK, MC: *Training for Change Agents: A Guide to the Design of Training Programs in Education and Other fields.* University of Michigan, Ann Arbor, 1973.

11. LIPPITT, GL: *Visualizing Change: Model Building and the Change Process.* University Associates, La Jolla, California, 1973.

12. SCHERMERHORN, JR: *Guidelines for change in health care organizations.* Health Care Management Review 6(3):9, Summer 1981.

13. HOOK, S: *The conceptual structure of power—An overview.* In Harward, DW (ED): *Power: Its Nature, Its Use, and Its Limits.* Schenkman Publishing, Boston, 1979.

14. ZALTMAN, G AND DUNCAN, R: *Strategies for Planned Change.* Vintage Books, New York, 1972.

15. ALINSKY, SD: *Rules for Radicals: A Practical Primer for Realistic Radicals.* Vintage Books, New York, 1972.

16. HALEY, J: *The Power Tactics of Jesus Christ and Other Essays.* Avon Books, New York, 1969.

17. ALINSKY, SD: op cit, p 126.

Chapter *10*

Organizations

Organizations as Complex Systems

Up to this point, most of our attention has been on leadership in relation to individuals and groups. We move now from these relatively small numbers of people to consideration of much larger numbers of people in more complex systems—the organizations and communities in which health care professionals work. Even those caregivers who are in independent practice find it necessary to work with organizations and communities.

These larger systems are much more complex than the small groups and teams that have been discussed so far. They are actually suprasystems made up of many smaller, interrelated systems and subsystems. These larger systems are important because the way in which they are structured, their overall climate, and their patterns of interaction have a great deal of influence on the way people function within them.

A different, broader perspective is needed when studying organizations and communities. It is not possible to directly observe or record everything that is happening in these systems. It is possible, however, to identify and evaluate the system's structure, climate, and patterns of interaction once you know what to look for. You can also learn how to function more effectively within these larger systems.

This chapter describes the basic characteristics of organizations: types of organizations, the organization as an open system, the formal and informal levels of operation, official and operative goals, distribution of power and authority, some common patterns of interaction in organizations, and two related types of conflict, reality shock and burn-out, experienced by health care professionals who work in organizations. Research Example 11-2 indicates some additional sources of satisfaction and dissatisfaction experienced by health caregivers in the hospital setting. Chapter 11 goes into more detail on the subject of working in organizations and then Chapter 12 discusses communities as complex systems.

TYPES OF ORGANIZATIONS

Nurses practice in many different types of organizations. Most of these are health care organizations such as hospitals, clinics, health maintenance organizations, community health agencies, nursing homes, health-oriented centers, community mental health centers, neighborhood health centers, and so forth. But others are organizations in which health care is just one of many functions, a service offered to their clients or to the people employed by the organization. Schools, camps, businesses, day care centers, and prisons are examples of this type of organization.

Health care organizations vary widely in the type of services they offer, the people they serve, and the way they are financed. Some are highly specialized, offering only preventive services, or counseling, or treatment of a specific disease. Others, such as general hospitals, offer a wide range of services from prenatal classes to ambulatory surgery and intensive care units. Despite even this wide range of services, however, the organization that offers truly holistic health care is rare.

Many health care services are designed to serve a specific, limited population. They may be available only to employees of a particular company or to children in a specific school district. Some services are designed only for the aged, for women, or for people with a particular problem such as alcoholism or drug abuse. Some are available only to the poor, or to those who can pay or are enrolled in a health plan. These limitations frequently result in people being excluded and unable to obtain a needed service.

Health care organizations can also be classified by the way in which they are financed. Those that are operated for profit are called *proprietary* organizations. Their funds come from the same sources as any other business, including operating income and the sale of bonds or shares in the company. Payment for services comes from private insurance, government reimbursement, or out of the pocket of the person receiving the service. Because they are operated for profit, proprietary organizations usually cannot survive for long if they are losing money.

Voluntary organizations are not operated for a profit. They have no owners or stockholders for whom they are expected to make money but their administrators must answer to the board of trustees, to government agencies providing reimbursement, and to their contributors if costs become excessive. They also need to consider retaining a surplus in order to meet future, usually escalating, operating costs in order to remain solvent.[2] Voluntary organizations receive funds from private gifts, bequests, donations, and grants as well as from insurance, government reimbursement, and direct payments from their clients. Many of these voluntary organizations were established by religious or other charitable organizations and by community groups.

Another not-for-profit health care organization is the *public* agency or institution. These organizations are directly supported by funds from the local, state, or federal government. Their services are often free or offered at a reduced rate to those who cannot pay the full cost. Although they are not operated for profit, their administrators are answerable to the sponsoring government agency and boards directly, and indirectly to elected officials and the taxpayers who provide the money for their support. The amount of support is strongly influenced by public opinion and the prevailing political climate.

You may have noticed that increased government support of health care costs (for example through Medicare and Medicaid) has blurred the lines of distinction between the public, proprietary, and voluntary types of health care organizations. However, the motives for establishing and continuing the services still differ substantially and influence the organization's structure and goals.

ORGANIZATIONS AS OPEN SYSTEMS

Wholeness and Individuality

An organization is more difficult to comprehend in its entirety than a group or individual is. But organizations also have characteristics as a whole that are different from and greater than the sum of its parts. This means, for example, that even when many people join or leave an organization, the organization as a whole can continue to function and retain its identity. It also means that a change in one part of the organization has an effect on the whole. For example, a change in the operating hours of the hospital laboratory could affect the work on inpatient units, in the operating room, in the ambulatory clinics, and so forth.

Organizations also exhibit individuality—they are not all alike by any means.[3] Like groups, organizations can be characterized by a certain climate or emotional atmosphere. It is both interesting and informative to ask people who work in an organization to describe its atmosphere or personality. People may describe their organization as "open and informal," "schizophrenic," "suffering growing pains," or "hungry" (that is, looking for more clients or funds). You may find some differences if you ask several people from different parts of the organization to describe its personality but a very definite pattern usually emerges from the answers to this question.

You can also identify these characteristics by observing people's behavior and paying attention to your own responses to the organization. Some organizations have a climate that is warm and friendly and seems open to new people and new ideas. Others present themselves as cold, hostile, and suspicious of new people or new ideas. The following is an example of how you might get an initial impression of these differences:

First Organization: Imagine what your first impression of a mental health center would be if a guard blocked your way when you approached the door until you explained that you were a community health nurse and had come to consult with the psychologist treating one of your clients. When the guard finally says, "Go ahead," you enter a bare lobby and go over to the glass window. The switchboard operator slides back the glass and says, "Yes?" You repeat your explanation and the operator slides the glass shut without another word. A minute later, the operator opens it again and says, "Room 203 on your left."

Second Organization: Now, if the guard had said, "Good morning, may I ask who you are going to see?" and if there were some comfortable chairs in the lobby and the receptionist had smiled at you while dialing the psychologist's office, wouldn't you have gotten a very different impression of the center?

Can you imagine how differently clients would feel about walking into these two places?

The work climate of health care organizations can differ in other ways as well. For example, research studies have shown that the level of anxiety among staff members varies from department to department and from one organization to another. The degree of alienation in the staff has been found to differ substantially from one organization to another. It was also found that effective leadership interventions could influence the prevailing climate. In particular, it was found that respect for the dignity and worth of the individual employee, open communications, administrative support, and taking action on problems as needed affected the climate of the organization in a positive way.[4-5]

You can expect, then, that the emotional climate of one organization may be very uncomfortable while the climate of another may be just the opposite. This difference has implications not only for leadership action but also for selecting an organization in which you want to work. The powerful effect of the organizational climate on the perceptions and behavior of people within that organization is described in Research Example 10-1.

Hierarchy

The simplest organization is divided into a number of different groups and the very complex ones are made up of many levels of systems and subsystems that are given names such as divisions, areas, units, departments, groups, and teams. These different levels form a hierarchy within the organization.

Most organizations have clearly identifiable hierarchies in which people are ranked according to their function and the amount of authority they have. This hierarchy can be thought of as a pyramid having the smallest number of people with the greatest amount of authority at the top and the largest number of people with little or no authority at the bottom (Fig. 10-1). People are also ranked according to the amount of status and salary paid from the lowest status and pay at the bottom of the pyramid to the highest at the top. While it illustrates the existence of the hierarchy, the pyramid actually oversimplifies the structure and especially the patterns of interaction in organizations. Although it would not be as clear, a hierarchy of interacting circles would be a more accurate model of an organization.

Research Example 10-1. Being Sane in Insane Places

In this provacative and frequently quoted study, Rosenhan[1] asked whether the characteristics that lead to a diagnosis of mental illness are really found in the patients themselves or in the organizational context, that is, the environment. Eight "sane" people (three psychologists, a graduate student, a pediatrician, a psychiatrist, a painter, and a housewife), five men and three women, presented themselves at the admissions offices of hospitals in five different states. Each person complained of hearing strange voices that were often unclear or sounded "empty" or "hollow". All eight were admitted immediately and placed in a psychiatric ward. Seven were diagnosed as schizophrenics.

Once on the psychiatric wards, these pseudopatients, as the researcher calls them, no longer claimed to hear voices and behaved as they usually did. Except for giving false symptoms and false names, they related their own ordinary life events when asked for their life history. But once they had been labeled as sick, the label stuck—all were discharged with the diagnosis of schizophrenia in remission after an average stay of 19 days (the range was 7 to 52 days).

Many of the real patients detected the pseudopatients and accused them of being journalists or evaluators checking up on the hospital. But there was no evidence that any staff member (for example psychiatrist, nurse, or attendant) ever questioned the assumption that they were genuinely ill despite patient records describing them as friendly, cooperative, and showing no abnormal behavior.

The researcher found that the staff's perceptions of the pseudopatient's behavior, no matter how normal it was, was so strongly shaped by the diagnosis that it was considered disturbed. An example of this effect is the staff's response, or more accurately nonresponse, to the fact that the pseudopatients took notes. The staff never questioned this behavior although the real patients did. One physician told a pseudopatient that he did not have to write down the name of his medicine but could ask if he forgot it. Another pseudopatient had the comment "Patient engages in writing behavior" written in his chart. Apparently, the writing was presumed to be part of the disturbance.

The researcher also found that the source of any disturbance was always assumed to be the patient and not the staff's behavior or the effect of the environment. For example, when a pseudopatient was found walking the halls a nurse asked him if he were nervous. Actually, he was bored. The researcher concludes that the staff's perceptions of behavior were controlled by the situation. The organizations themselves had a climate in which the behavior of their inmates was easily misperceived.

Complexity

Organizations are complex, intricate systems. The number of interacting levels of groups just described is one indication of their complexity. Also, as the number of people in a system increases, the number of different relationships possible between people increases geometrically. (For example, there are only four different relationships possible in a group of three people; nine in a group of four people, and 9801 in a group of 100 people.)

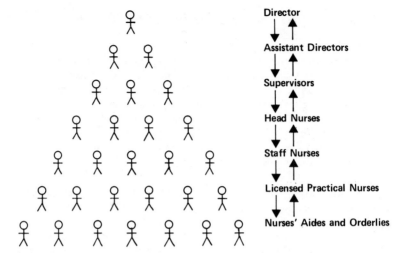

A TYPICAL NURSING HIERARCHY IN HOSPITALS AND LARGER NURSING HOMES

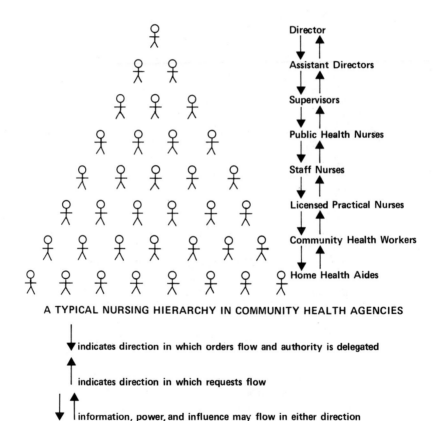

A TYPICAL NURSING HIERARCHY IN COMMUNITY HEALTH AGENCIES

↓ indicates direction in which orders flow and authority is delegated

↑ indicates direction in which requests flow

↓↑ information, power, and influence may flow in either direction

FIGURE 10-1. Common nursing hierarchies in organizations.

Because of their great size and complexity, most organizations have multiple rather than single purposes, goals, and functions and these are often in conflict with each other.[6] For example, cost cutting done to increase the profits of a proprietary organization may conflict with the goal of delivering quality care. This complexity is the existence of different levels of goals in most organizations.

Openness

Every open system, including organizations, affects its environment and is affected by its environment. For example, health care organizations located in resort areas experience much higher demands for their services during the tourist season than off season. This fluctuation in demand also affects the organization's need for staff. The health care organization in turn affects the people who seek its services. The organization may welcome them, heal them and send them away feeling better, or it may reject or harm them and send them away feeling worse.

An organization exchanges information and energy with its environment. Health care organizations can provide the specialized skills and information needed to promote or restore health. These skills are exchanged for money and recognition. This basic exchange between the organization and its clients is influenced by many factors in the environment such as the number of other organizations offering the same services, the actual and perceived need for the service and government regulation. Also, some health care organizations cannot find sufficient staff to offer needed services or find that their service is not valued and that people are not willing to pay for it. In other cases there is insufficient knowledge available about a problem to be able to offer satisfactory care. All of these factors and many more interact to produce a very complex health care system.

Pattern

Like other living systems, organizations have identifiable rhythms and cycles. For example, although most business organizations function during the day and close down at night, many of those that offer health care operate 24 hours a day, every day of the year. Within those 24 hours, the day shift is usually the busiest and the night shift usually has the least number of people working (even if it is busy).

The most typical growth pattern for organizations is early, rapid growth followed by a slower rate of growth or even no growth in the late stages of the life cycle. Some organizations experience spurts of new growth later in the life cycle but eventually all of them experience a decline in growth and eventually cease to exist.[7]

Like groups, organizations can also develop and increase their effectiveness but they do not all succeed in this during the time they exist. Organizations can have a structure and climate that encourages the free movement of information up and down the hierarchy or they can have limited communication networks in which very few people know what is happening or feel as if they had anything to say about what is happening. Some organizations promote the growth and development of the many groups and individuals who are a part of the organization while other organizations stifle creativity and inhibit growth.

The patterns of relationships between people in organizations also become complex. Two patterns of relationships that develop in some organizations and create problems for health care professionals are the paternalistic and the victim-persecutor-rescuer patterns that will be discussed later.

There is another important pattern that emerges as organizations become increasingly complex. Ideally, an organization functions according to agreed upon procedures and carries out its stated goals but organizations do not actually operate in this simple and straightforward manner. Instead, there are many informal, unstated goals and ways in which the work actually gets done in organizations. Being able to recognize the difference between these two levels and the ways in which they affect the functioning of the organization is an important part of learning how to work effectively within an organization. These two levels of operation will be discussed in the next section of this chapter.

SUMMARY

Health care organizations vary in the type and comprehensiveness of services offered and populations served. They may also be categorized as either voluntary (not-for-profit), proprietary, or publicly financed organizations.

Organizations are complex suprasystems made up of large numbers of people grouped hierarchically into smaller systems and subsystems. Because of their size and complexity they frequently have multiple purposes, goals, and functions. They also have identifiable characteristics, including their climate and structure, and exhibit patterns of behavior such as growth activity cycles and patterns of interaction.

Levels of Operation

In order to understand what is happening in an organization and to be able to influence that organization, you need to know about and use both the formal and informal levels of operation. The classic approach to organizations was to study only the formal organization but it eventually became apparent that too many important factors were being ignored.[8] Knowing about just one or the other of these levels would give you only half of the entire picture, so it is important to look at both levels in order to understand the organization as a whole.

FORMAL LEVEL

The formal level of operation is the official, stated structure and function of the organization. If you asked an administrator of an organization to describe the organization to you, the administrator would probably describe only this formal level of operation to you. The description would probably include the way in which employees are divided into groups, the kind of work each group does, and who supervises the work of each group. The following is an example of the way in which the director of an ambulatory care center might describe their formal level of operation:

> This is the main clinic in which we have our administrative offices as well as our comprehensive ambulatory care clinic. Clients can see the physicians, nurses, social worker, dietitian, or community worker as needed here. We have three satellite clinics staffed by nurses practitioners and a social worker. We also have an outreach team that is based here at the main clinic but travels to different locations each day of the week and also responds to emergency calls. Clients who need to see a physician or dietitian must come to the main clinic. Also, the bookkeeping and billing are done from the main office but people can call the satellite clinics to make appointments.

The description would go on to say who is in charge of each clinic, who manages the entire organization, the specific services offered, the fees charged, the hours each clinic is open, and so forth.

If you expressed interest in further information, the administrator might give you a *table of organization*. The table of organization is a diagram showing the formal relationships between employees of the organization, the way in which they are grouped together, and who reports to whom. (Fig. 10-2). The table of organization clearly shows the pyramid shaped hierarchy (turned on its side) of the organization that is wide at the bottom and narrow at the top.

The table of organization represents the formal level of operation. On the formal level, communication flows along the established lines shown in the diagram, for example from the administrator to the assistant administrator to the director of the main clinic to the supervisors, the rest of the staff, and back again. These established lines of communication are often referred to as the ''proper channels of communication.''

The board of trustees delegates authority to the administrator who in turn delegates some authority to the assistant administrators and so on down the line. Staff members who are at the bottom of the pyramid have authority over no one except perhaps the clients served by the organization who do not even appear on most tables of organization. Work assignments and directions are also passed down the line in the same way. It is often said of these organizational hierarchies that orders come down and requests go up.

Bureaucracy

Some degree of bureaucracy is characteristic of the formal operations of virtually every organization. In fact, even deliberately informal work groups take on some of these characteristics when they become larger and more complex in spite of attempts to avoid becoming bureaucratic. This happens because these arrangements

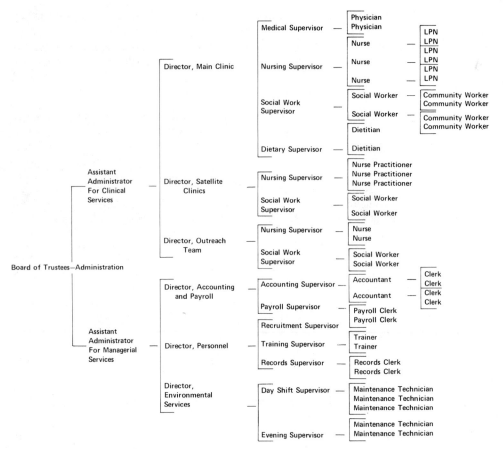

FIGURE 10-2. Sample Table of Organization.

known as the bureaucracy are designed to promote smooth operations within a large and complex group of people.

Weber[9] said that bureaucracies have the following four characteristics:

1. *Division of Labor:* specific parts of the job to be done are assigned to different individuals or groups. For example, nurses, aides, physicians, dietitians, and social workers all provide parts of the health care needed by one patient.
2. *Hierarchy:* employees are organized and ranked according to their degree of authority within the organization. For example, administrators and directors are at the top of most hospital hierarchies while aides and maintenance workers are at the bottom.
3. *Rules and Regulations:* acceptable and unacceptable behavior and the proper way to carry out predictable tasks are specifically stated, often in writing. For example, procedure books, policy manuals, by-laws, statements, and memos prescribe many

types of behavior from acceptable aseptic techniques to vacation policies in health care organizations.

4. *Emphasis on Technical Competence:* People with certain skills and knowledge are hired to carry out specific parts of the total work of the organization. For example, a community mental health center will have psychiatrists, psychologists, social workers, and nurses to do different kinds of therapies and clerical staff to do the typing and filing.

There are varying degrees to which an organization can be bureaucratized. A highly controlled and bureaucratized approach is based on the belief that employees must be told what to do, must be closely supervised in order to ensure that they will do it, and also that some employees are more skilled and responsible than others and should, therefore, have authority over the others. An organization that is managed according to these beliefs would have many detailed rules and regulations, close supervision of employees, and little autonomy allowed individual employees, even those who are professionals capable of functioning independently.

People generally respond negatively to the word bureaucracy. One reason for this is that in most bureaucratic organizations with their long lines of delegated authority and decision-making, you often cannot identify exactly who is responsible for having made a certain decision or created a certain unpopular rule. Arendt calls this "rule by nobody"[10] because the source of these decisions and rules is faceless, no one person takes full responsibility for their outcome and nobody seems to know where they originated.

One of the greatest frustrations people experience in trying to relate to a bureaucratic organization either as employees or as clients is the diffusion of responsibility and subsequent refusal to make a decision. For example, to get something done in some organizations, you need the approval of six different people on six different forms, all in triplicate, and each of the six people refuses to give you an OK until the other five have given theirs. This is not true of every organization that has a hierarchy, division of labor, set of rules, and emphasis on technical competence, but it is one very common negative outcome of bureaucratic organization. This difficulty in obtaining a final decision is often called "bureaucratic red tape."

In extremely bureaucratic organizations, employees feel that they are being controlled by impersonal rules and regulations. Having no influence on decisions within the organization leads to a feeling of powerlessness and alienation.

An extreme division of labor extends the "rule by nobody" to responsibility for the end product of the organization. For example, when 6, 8, or even 20 people in one health care organization have given care to a patient, how can you say who is responsible for the outcome? Another problem arises from an extreme division of labor: how can people derive any satisfaction or pride in their work when it is difficult to identify their contribution? When patients or clients are transferred from one unit to another as their needs change, the health caregivers are involved in only one segment of their care and most never even know what the eventual outcome is. The following is one example of this fragmentation:

In a child health clinic, a nurse observed that one younster was flushed, restless, and had some abdominal pain. The child was immediately referred to a physician who diagnosed the problem as appendicitis.

The child was admitted to the hospital and prepared for surgery. The operating room nurse and recovery room nurse both offered support and reassurance when the child seemed frightened by this new experience and strange environment.

Several nurses cared for the child on the pediatric unit until the child was sent home. The child recovered quickly at home and returned to school in two weeks.

However, the child health clinic nurse's original assessment was not confirmed to the nurse until the child returned to the clinic a year later. The operating room and recovery room nurses never found out whether or not their intervention had left the child less fearful and the nurses on the pediatric unit never found out whether or not the child did well at home and in returning to school.

Each of these caregivers had an important but limited part in the child's care. The lack of involvement in the whole process and of feedback about the child's progress to recovery meant that none of them received confirmation of the ultimate effectiveness of their intervention, resulting in a failure to meet their needs for recognition and self-actualization, both important sources of motivation.

Alternatives to Bureaucracy

There is no single, widely accepted alternative model for organizations that eliminates the problems of bureaucracy and yet promotes the smooth and efficient operation of a large organization. But there are several approaches that have been suggested to alleviate these problems and increase the effectiveness of the organization.[11-13]

It has been increasingly recognized that organizations need to be not only efficient but also adaptable. Organizations need to be prepared for uncertainty and for rapid changes in their environment. In addition, they need to provide an internal climate that not only allows but also motivates employees to work to the best of their ability.

These newer approaches emphasize increased flexibility of the organizational structure, increased participation in decision-making, and more autonomy for working groups or teams. For example, rigid department or unit structures can be reorganized into semi-autonomous teams that are each given a specific task or function to carry out. These teams or work groups are given much more authority than is ordinarily done in a bureaucratic organization. The teams themselves are responsible for their own self-correction and self-control. Together team members make decisions about work assignments and how to deal with any problems that arise. In other words, the teams supervise or manage themselves to a much greater extent. (See Research example 8-1)

As you can imagine, working on such a team would require much more consensus among team members than is required in more traditional departments where the head of the department makes most of these decisions. The increased participation in decision-making by each employee reduces the feelings of powerlessness and alienation that can arise in bureaucracies.

Some of these teams are temporary task forces that are put together in order to accomplish a specific task within a given amount of time. People with different skills needed to complete the task may be drawn from many different parts of the organization to form the team. The advantage of using these temporary task forces is the greatly increased flexibility to respond to changing needs of the organization but a disadvantage is the potential disruption of the departments or areas from which people were taken to form the team. The creation of temporary task forces may also threaten some people's feelings of security if these needs are not met in another manner.

Supervisors and administrators can also be given different functions. Instead of spending their time closely watching and controlling other people's work, they can become planners and resource persons. Providing the conditions required for the optimum functioning of the teams becomes their most important responsibility. They need to ensure that the support, information, materials, and budgeted funds needed to do the job well are available to the team. They also need to provide more coordination between the teams so that the teams are working toward congruent goals, cooperating rather than blocking each other and not duplicating effort.

Very large organizations can also be divided into functional areas that operate as if they were smaller organizations. This reduces the complexity of each of the divisions and allows each division to be better integrated when integration of the entire organization as a whole becomes almost impossible because of its great size, complexity, and diversity although it may make communication between divisions more difficult.

INFORMAL LEVEL

The informal level of operations includes all those unwritten, unofficial relationships that develop in an organization (Fig. 10-3). It includes norms and traditions about the way people work together and has a strong influence on what actually happens in an organization. The informal level of operations exists alongside the formal level but it is not necessarily congruent with the formal level.

The informal level operates even in the most highly controlled bureaucratic organization. For example, you may find that some rules and regulations are circumvented, that the hierarchy is ignored or that lines between specific jobs are blurred. Also, alternative paths are created by which requests are made and filled without multiple approvals; tasks are completed quickly and messages are communicated across and around the so-called proper channels of communication. These alternate methods for getting things done are the informal level of operations. The following is an example illustrating the informal level of operations in a highly controlling organization:

FIGURE 10-3. Informal organization. The informal level of operations in an organization includes all those unofficial relationships that develop in the organization. It provides a lively and often efficient informal communication network and can be a source of esteem, support, and friendship not provided by the formal organization.

> A prison is a highly controlling organization in which its clients (the prisoners) are not even allowed to leave without permission. There are many restrictions placed on both the guards and the prisoners about who can visit, what possessions the prisoners are allowed, and so forth. At the same time, some prisoners are able to buy and sell drugs, liquor, and sex, all absolutely forbidden by the formal organization. They are able to do this through the informal level of operation that exists even in prisons.

Interrelationship With Formal Level

Because they occur within the same organization and affect the same people, the formal and informal levels of operation are always at least somewhat interrelated. The two levels can be complementary or they can be in conflict. When they are complementary, the informal level can provide a way of dealing with absurd regulations as in the following example:

> If you visited a small town and were told that there was a local law requiring horses to wear bonnets on Sunday, you would probably laugh about the archaic law and leave your horse bareheaded. You would not expect anyone to even say anything to you about your horse, not even the police whose formal duty is to enforce the law. Informally, you know that you are not expected to obey that particular law.

At the same time, you would also know that there are other laws that you are expected to obey and that you would definitely hear about it if you did not obey them.

In this example, the informal level complements the formal level by providing a socially acceptable way of dealing with an absurd regulation, that is, ignore it. This often happens in organizations too: the informal level facilitates operations by ignoring or revising formal relationships, rules, and regulations. When complementary in this way, the informal level can humanize the impersonality and facelessness of a large bureaucratic organization.

The informal level of operations also provides a lively and often efficient informal communication network commonly known as the grapevine. Although the grapevine is best known for spreading rumors that are often false or misleading, it is not always a negative force in an organization. The grapevine often provides employees with needed information that the formal system is slow or neglectful about sharing with them. It is also useful as a way to test a new idea or change without having to go through the frequently cumbersome formal level of operations.

Informal role expectations can be blended with formal ones so that people are not overly restricted by formal job descriptions. This blurring can provide needed flexibility but it can also cause some confusion, especially for the new employee who does not understand the informal system yet. Blurring of roles can also lead to increased territorial conflicts between individuals or groups within the organization.

The informal level often provides needed supports for people in an organization that fails to provide support on the formal level. However, when this support is extended to protecting or covering up for inept employees, it can reduce the organization's effectiveness. Another way in which the informal level can reduce effectiveness is when employees informally agree to limit the amount of work they do and put pressure on their coworkers to do the same.

Like the formal level, the informal level of operation can either facilitate the functions of the organization or impede them. The informal system can supply rewards such as esteem or friendships that the formal system cannot do but it can also hurt people by circulating false rumors or by encouraging them to do poor quality work. The informal level can promote effectiveness by meeting basic human needs ignored by the formal organization but it can also be the arena for conflicts and power struggles that the formal level would suppress.

Although the informal level can be facilitative, it can also lead to serious problems when there are unresolved conflicts with the formal level. The following is an example of how a problem can arise when the levels conflict:

Officially, nurse aides are not allowed to give medications to patients but, occasionally, a busy nurse will informally ask an aide to take an oral medication to a waiting patient or to stay with the patient who takes a long time to swallow several tablets.

One day, an aide gave a medication to the wrong patient who experienced some serious side effects from the drug. As required, the incident was reported and both the nurse and the aide were fired for failing to obey the official rules.

Incongruency between the informal and formal levels can also lead to some less serious but common difficulties for those who do not understand the differences between the two levels. The following is an example of a failure to understand the difference:

> A community health agency officially prohibited payment for overtime but staff members often had to stay late to finish their work. Informally, their supervisors allowed them to leave early when things were quiet or when they had an appointment in order to compensate for the extra time they had worked.
>
> The Director of the agency was aware of this informal procedure and tacitly allowed it to continue because it resulted in staff members feeling that they were being treated fairly. However, when a naive staff member demanded to be given earned compensation time in the middle of a very busy week, the staff member was told that there was no such thing as compensation time and that staff members were not allowed to work overtime and so could not possibly have earned any compensation time.

This staff member had made the mistake of trying to deal with an informal procedure as if it were a formal regulation. As a result, no staff member was granted any compensation time until the formal and informal levels had been clearly separated again. Then the informal procedure was reinstated.

Using the Informal Level

The informal level can work for or against you. On the plus side, it can provide you with the opportunity to expand your role or to expedite matters when the formal level is too restrictive. It can be a source of much needed support and can be an alternate channel for acquiring information. On the negative side, the informal level can reinforce poor work habits or be a source of false information for you or your coworkers. It can also be a source of conflict with the formal level or frustrate your attempts to bring about change if you are not aware of its influence.

It is important to recognize and understand the operation and interrelationship of the formal and informal levels of any organization in which you work. It is especially important to avoid being misled into ignoring what is happening on the informal level. Many efforts to bring about improvements or changes have failed because the person planning them thought it could be done by just setting up a formal procedure. The following example illustrates the difference between using only the formal level and using both:

> Two different nurses working in a large city hospital had what they thought were good ideas for improving patient care in that hospital. The first nurse had some ideas for improving the patient assessment form and asked the head nurse how a suggestion is supposed to be sent to the Director of Nursing. The head nurse told the nurse to put the idea in writing, including the reasons why the nurse thought it would improve nursing care, and to give two copies to the supervisor, one for the supervisor to keep.
>
> The nurse typed a three-page report explaining the idea and how it would increase efficiency and promote better patient care. The nurse gave the report to the supervisor as directed.

Three months later the nurse received a note from the Director expressing appreciation for the suggestion and saying that it would be shared with the head nurses and supervisors to find out if they thought it would work. By the time the nurse received the note, the nurse had almost forgotten about the idea and it was apparently received without enthusiasm by the head nurses and supervisors as it was never implemented.

The second nurse followed the procedure that other people used successfully in that hospital. The second nurse talked with the head nurse and one of the supervisors at lunch one day about an idea for improving admission procedures and why the nurse thought it would work. Both seemed interested so the nurse asked them, ''How can we try out this idea?'' They suggested that the nurse ask to be included on the agenda for their next meeting and come to explain the idea to the group.

The nurse asked the head nurse and supervisor to help plan the presentation. They worked out the details of the plan with the assistance of one of the hospital's inservice educators. At the meeting, the idea received sufficient support to try it out on several units to see if it would work.

The first nurse using only the formal channels of communication and the idea moved along them without gathering any support or having any impact. Although the first nurse did exactly what was advised, the nurse failed to observe how the informal level operated in the implementation of an idea. The first nurse also neglected to find out who was interested in the idea and likely to give it support.

In contrast, the second nurse had observed that many ideas come from the head nurses and supervisors and that the people the nurse talked to were often interested in new ideas. This is only the first phase in bringing about a change but it is an important one. Without the use of the informal level of operation it is very likely that the second nurse's idea would also have been ignored.

SUMMARY

The formal level of operation is the official, stated structure and function of the organization, which can be represented by a diagram called the table of organization. The formal level often has the bureaucratic characteristics of a hierarchy, division of labor, rules and regulations, and emphasis on technical competence but there are alternative models for the formal level that are more flexible and participative. The informal level includes the unwritten, unofficial relationships, norms, and traditions that develop in an organization. The informal level may complement the formal level or be in conflict with it. In order to work effectively within an organization, it is important to know and use both levels of operation.

Goals

In much the same way as there are two levels of operation in an organization, there are also two kinds of goals, the official stated goals and the unstated operative goals.[14] Many decisions made by people in organizations seem to be irrational until you know what the operative goals are in that organization. Knowing both the official and operative goals—and the difference between them—can also save you from some surprises and disappointments when you try to bring about change in the systems or when you are seeking some reward from the system.

OFFICIAL GOALS

The official goals of an organization are the goals that appear in public statements about the organization. They are the goals you would be told about if you asked a representative of the organization what its purpose was or the goals you would find if you read in an official statement of its purposes.

Official goals tend to be general, public-spirited, and idealistic. They are designed to sound benevolent and impressive. The following are examples of typical official goals in health care organizations:

Promote the health and well-being of the clients we serve.

Protect the people of this country.

Foster a spirit of cooperative concern for those in need of our services.

It is usually easy to determine the official goals of an organization because they are publicly announced goals. In fact, most organizations want the public to hear about their official goals and make an effort to publicize them because they promote the desired image of a public-spirited organization that really cares about the people it serves. However, official goals do not explain the entire purpose or behavior of an organization. Much of the behavior of the organization is directed toward achieving another set of goals known as the operative goals.

OPERATIVE GOALS

The operative goals of an organization are those goals that the organization is actually pursuing in its day to day operation. They are usually not verbalized and tend to be far less rational or public-spirited than the official goals.

Operative goals are not only different than the official goals but often are in conflict with them. Operative goals focus on the survival and growth of the organization rather than public benefit.

Health care organizations depend on their environments for a continuous supply of clients, money, and personnel. Without these resources, they cannot continue to exist and these needs are reflected in their operative goals. As a result of these needs, operative goals are commonly aimed at achieving financial gain, efficiency rather than effectiveness, quantity versus quality and maintenance of a positive public image. They are also aimed at avoiding public criticism and legal problems, especially expensive lawsuits. Operative goals are also influenced by the personal needs and ambitions of people who have power and authority in the organization. Each of these is discussed in this section.

Identifying Operative Goals

Operative goals are more difficult to determine than official goals because they are unstated and unannounced. In fact, stating them directly can provoke denial of the existence of an operative goal and an insistence on the official goals from some members of the organization.

Careful observation of behavior in the organization is needed to identify the operative goals. In particular, you need to look at the decisions that are made, what kind of behavior is rewarded, and the actual (not stated) priorities that are implied by these actions. The examples given in this section should provide you with an idea of the types of operative goals that exist in health care organizations and the kind of evidence to make note of when looking for them.

Financial Gain

The overall goal of continued existence or growth of the organization leads to financial gain taking priority over more idealistic goals. Even non-profit health care organizations pursue financial gain at the public's expense. The following are some examples:

> Some hospitals have told people who can obviously afford the extra cost that there are no semi-private rooms available so that their higher priced rooms are not left empty and unproductive.[15] Other hospitals have refused care to people who could not pay, insisted on payment in advance, or refused to release patients who cannot pay their bills, keeping them extra days while the bill becomes even higher.

As you can see, the pursuit of profits can subvert caregiving goals. The recurring nursing home scandals have demonstrated that the goal of increasing profits for the organizations' owners can result in serious neglect of its clients' needs.

There are many other sources of profit in the health care industry. Most people are aware of the substantial incomes earned by physicians but do not think about the profits of companies who manufacture and sell the drugs, equipment, and supplies used by health care organizations (and paid for by the health care consumer). There are many others who also profit indirectly from health care and will exert their influence on the operative goals of the organization in order to increase their profits. For example, just the expansion of an existing hospital can bring profits to lawyers, bankers, architects, planners, and various consultants.[16]

Efficiency

Efficient operation means greater output per dollar spent but it is a goal that is not always congruent with increased effectiveness of the care given. For example, the assembly line approach to health care is used in many organizations to increase efficiency. The individual client is divided into separate parts (for example, heart, lungs, psyche) each to be treated skillfully and efficiently by someone who is a specialist in taking care of that part. Unfortunately, this approach to health care is often ineffective because it fails to consider the interrelationships of these parts and the person as a whole.

Staffing in many health care organizations also reflects the operative goal of improving efficiency. The functional mode of organizing nursing care (in which one person gives all the medications, another does all the treatments, and so forth) is one example of the priority of efficiency over effectiveness. Another example is the hiring of the person with the least amount of skill (such as the nursing assistant) rather than the person who can do the job best but may command a higher salary.

Staff nurses frequently find themselves praised and rewarded for completing assignments and charting on time rather than for their perceptive observations or professional judgments, another example of the priority of the operative goal of efficiency over the official goal of providing effective care.

Quantity versus Quality

The priority of quantity over quality as an operative goal leads to what is often called the "numbers game" in organizations. Departments are asked to report the numbers of things done rather than how well they are done, and are rewarded for producing quantity rather than quality.

In health care, the priority of quantity translates into counting and reporting how many people a nurse practitioner can see in one day rather than the thoroughness of the assessments done and the effectiveness of the resulting interventions. Inservice educators find themselves rewarded for holding many classes rather than for the amount of learning and change that took place. Public health nurses find their agencies reporting the number of home visits made rather than the results of those visits.

Other departments have the same experience: getting food trays to patients quickly is more likely to be praised than the ability to make a restrictive diet palatable; seeing many patients in physical therapy is more likely to be rewarded than the ability to motivate patients to continue their exercises after discharge.

Public Image

A positive public image is important to health care organizations because it affects the number of both clients and contributors the organization can attract. This operative goal can conflict with official service goals. For example, what happens to an individual patient is much less apparent to a hospital's potential clients and benefactors than an attractive, modern building so money needed for additional staff may be spent on renovation and landscaping instead of staff.

On the other hand, you can also take advantage of the operative goal of promoting a positive public image. For example, to gain support for a birthing room, you can point out that it would be the first birthing room in the community, that many people have asked for one, and that it would receive much favorable publicity when the organization announced its introduction.

Avoiding Criticism

Many health care organizations will go to great lengths to avoid criticism that would tarnish their public image or otherwise threaten their existence. The following is an example of the effect of this operative goal:

> A county health department hired a pediatric nurse clinician to conduct child health clinics. The clinics were well attended and the parents were very satisfied with the family-centered care they received. In fact, they were so satisfied that many reduced their pediatrician visits, which provoked a strong protest from area peditricians. In response to the protest, the pediatric nurse clinician's clinics were limited to families who could not pay for a private physician.

Avoiding Lawsuits

Many health care organizations are also very concerned about avoiding expensive lawsuits. Excessive concern can result in unnecessary restrictions on both staff and patients. For example, ambulatory patients who have every functional capacity needed to take their own medications are not permitted to do so because of concern about legal responsibilities. Many efforts to expand nursing roles have been blocked by the same concern. Community health nurses may not be permitted to make a second home visit because a client does not have a physician. Concern about legal repercussions is sometimes used as a convenient excuse to constrain health caregivers.

The operative goal of avoiding lawsuits can also be turned into an advantage. For example, if discharge planning is inadequate, you can point out that the organization could be held legally responsible if patients are given inadequate information about self-care before discharge and injure themselves as a result.

Individual Needs

Personal needs, desires, and ambitions influence the decisions of people with power and authority in organizations but may have nothing to do with the organization's official goals. For example, caregivers may meet their own needs by encouraging clients to be dependent on them long after they could be independent. Surgeons may perform unnecessary surgery to keep their skills sharp or their practices busy. An administrator may propose purchasing expensive new equipment because the administrator wants to be part of a technologically advanced organization. These individual needs can set in motion operative goals that are often in conflict with the official goals of the organization.

SUMMARY

Official goals are the stated or written goals of the organization. Operative goals are the unstated goals that the organization is actually pursuing in its day-to-day operation. The operative goals of health care organizations are usually harder to identify and much less idealistic and public-spirited than the official goals. Financial gain, efficiency, quantity versus quality, maintenance of a good public image, avoidance of criticism, and avoidance of lawsuits are common operative goals in health care organizations. These goals are also influenced by the personal needs and ambitions of the people working in the organization.

Patterns of Relationships in Organizations

POWER AND AUTHORITY RELATIONSHIPS

Authority is a specific type of power that originates in the official position that a person holds within the organization. Authority exists only because other people are willing to accept and obey the decisions made by the person in authority.[17] It is an important source of power and influence in organizations but it is by no means the only source of power and influence in organizations.

Every individual within an organization has some resources for power and influence, but not everyone has authority in an organization. The amount of authority a person has in a particular organization is related to that person's position in the hierarchy. There is a purpose for this unequal distribution of authority: it is delegated to a relatively small number of people who are expected to exert some control over the way the rest of the organization functions.

Authority and the Hierarchy

Health care organizations typically have a board of some kind, known as the board of directors, trustees, or governors, at the top of the hierarchy. The trustees, who are often influential business people, professionals, or representatives of the community, are legally and morally responsible for the operation of the organization.

The board members usually delegate most of this responsibility and accompanying authority to the administrator (who may also be called a president or director). But this does not always happen: sometimes board members get involved in everyday operations. This may occur in a crisis or when some members have difficulty delegating their authority. An example of this difficulty in delegating authority was a board whose members questioned the brand of grape juice being served and complained about the color of the paint being used.[14]

Generally speaking, however, the function of board members is to set general policies and not to get involved in the day-to-day operation of the organization. Health care is a highly complex and technologically advanced field and most board members find that they do not have either the time or the expertise needed to make many of the important decisions involved in running a health care organization, such as trying to control spiralling costs without reducing the quality of care. The professional administrator usually has the time and training needed to thoroughly assess the situation and make these decisions after getting sufficient input from the staff.

A third element of the top administration of hospitals is the medical staff. The medical staff has been called the "shadow organization" because it has its own admission requirements, hierarchy, rewards, and sanctions and because most physicians are not employed by the organization. Many abuses of power by physicians have been documented including frequent power plays to control the functions of the organization, exploitation and domination of nurses and other health caregivers, and discrimination within medical staffs.

In those health care organizations in which physicians are involved, the board, administrator, and medical staff form a triad of power and authority at the top of the organizational hierarchy.[18] Several trends are changing and challenging this triad. More physicians are being employed directly by organizations. If this trend continues, it will bring them further into the organization's structure and out of the "shadows." Governmental regulation has become an increasingly powerful influence on health care organizations as it has moved toward more evaluation, restriction, and control of the health care delivery system. Consumer representation on planning and advisory boards also has the potential for increasing organizational responsiveness to people's needs but so far has not had a substantial impact on health care organizations.

Nurses have also challenged the traditional organizational triad. Nursing service administrators are more aware of their potential power as leaders of the largest group of health care professionals in most health care organizations. At the present time, most directors of nursing are immediately below the triad at the top of the hierarchy, but many are no longer satisfied with the limited amount of power and influence they have had in the past.

Nursing in the Hierarchy

Nursing service administrators often find themselves in the middle, between the conflicting expectations of two different levels in the hierarchy. They are expected to support the interests of nursing in their relationships with other departments of the organization, with physicians, with the organization's board and administrator, and with the community. From the nursing point of view, the Director of Nursing should be an advocate rather than a "policeman" of the nursing staff. At the same time, they are expected to represent the board and administrator (often the medical staff as well) in their dealings with the nursing staff. The expectation of the organizational triad is that they will direct and control the nursing staff but the Director of Nursing needs the cooperation of the nursing staff to do this effectively. Remembering that it is the board and administrator who hire, evaluate, and give salary increases to the Director of Nursing, you can see that the Director of Nursing walks a "rather delicate tight-rope" in trying to work effectively with both groups.[19]

After considering the conflict faced by nursing service administrators, it may not surprise you that they are often described by nurses lower in the hierarchy as the source of most of their problems. Staff nurses rate lack of support from nursing service administration, inadequate staffing, and restrictions on giving the best patient care as some of their major problems, all of which can be influenced although not necessarily controlled by the Director of Nursing.[20] Staff nurses who lack open communications, fair treatment, and the support of nursing administration tend to feel powerless and isolated within the hierarchy of the organization.

Before concluding this section on authority relationships in the organizational hierarchy, it is important to point out that nurses are neither powerless nor at the bottom of the hierarchy. Depending on the particular organization, nurses have positional authority over other nurses, practical nurses, aides, orderlies, and people from other professions and departments. It is also worth noting at this point that many other health care professionals (such as physical therapists, dietitians, social workers, and so forth) are located in similar positions in the organizational hierarchy and face much the same kinds of conflicts as nurses do in dealing with the expectations of people above and below them in the hierarchy and at the same time promoting the practice of their professions.

Other Power Relationships

No one's power or authority in an organization is absolute. Each person, no matter how high up in hierarchy, is susceptible to the power of others either within or outside of the organization.

Nor is anyone, no matter how low on the hierarchy, completely without power. While people at lower levels of the hierarchy have little or no authority, they have other sources of power that can counterbalance the authority of people above them in the hierarchy. For example, people in high-level positions depend on their staffs to carry out their decisions. A head nurse could not carry out all the work that must be done if the staff left.

Research on organizations has shown that people at all levels in organizations tend to attribute more power to others than to themselves.[21] In a college, for example, the faculty felt that the students and administrators had most of the power, the administrators felt that the faculty and students had most of the power, and the students felt that the faculty and administrators had all the power. It may help you to remember this when you are dealing with persons in authority in an organization: these people probably feel much less powerful than they seem to you.

RELATIONSHIP GAMES

You may recall from the section on confrontation in Chapter 4 that games are a repetitive and unproductive pattern of relating to others. Organizations play similar games. There are two that health care organizations are especially likely to play. One is paternalism in which the organization acts as parent and relates to its employees as if they were children. The second is the Karpman Triangle, which can occur in any organization but is especially a problem in health care organizations where it is played with clients as well as employees.[22]

Other games that you are likely to observe or perhaps experience while working in an organization are I told you so and the bear trap.[23] Both of these games affect the way in which employees are hired and promoted and can create a great deal of unhappiness for the unwary individual who accepts employment in an organization that plays these games.

Paternalism

Many organizations treat their employees as if they were children instead of mature adults. One of the problems with this approach is that it is likely to provoke childish behavior such as rebelliousness or dependency in return. It also has a tendency to inhibit the growth and development of employees and subsequently affects their ability to contribute to the best of their ability. An authoritarian or directive type of management in which employees are allowed little or no voice in decision-making because their supervisors think that they know what is best for them and do not expect them to be able to make wise decisions is just one of many ways in which paternalism occurs in organizations.

Paternalism can appear to be benevolent. For example, many organizations show interest and concern for what happens to their employees outside of working hours. However, when this commendable concern is extended paternalistically into telling or even requiring employees to conduct their lives in a certain way, it is no longer benevolent.

Paternalistic organizations are also likely to give thier employees turkeys on Thanksgiving or to hold expensive celebrations on such occasions as the anniversary of the organization. The paternalistic aspect of this becomes more apparent when you realize that many employees would prefer to make their own decisions about how to spend the money used to hold these celebrations rather than being given a piece of birthday cake and balloons to take home from work.

The examples given so far are of the milder forms of paternalism. Organizational paternalism can become much more restrictive and suffocating. Ashley's[24] history of hospitals' paternalistic treatment of nurses provides a good example of this more serious kind of paternalism:

> Until the 1950s, many hospitals employed only a limited number of graduate nurses and used student nurses for most of the hospital nursing staff positions. Nurses were poorly paid and poorly educated women who accepted society's definition of them as servants and physicians' helpers. For example, it was considered more important for nurses to get meals served while the gravy was still hot than for nurses to know anything about their patients' needs. Physicians continually exerted control over nurses and nursing education, denying their value at the same time that they depended on nurses to care for their patients 24 hours a day. Many of the nurses who held positions of authority in hospitals supported this definition of nursing instead of fighting it, which reinforced the pattern of poor self-image and passivity that others have capitalized on since the 1900s.

Although much has changed since then, there is still some passivity and low self-esteem evident in the behavior of nurses and the approach of many health care organizations (and physicians) toward nurses is still paternalistic.

Because of its seemingly benevolent intention, it can take some time to identify the pattern of paternalism is an organization. Many of the restrictions and frustrations experienced by health care professionals in organizations stem from a paternalistic stance.

Calling the other's game by refusing to respond in a childish manner is one way to confront paternalism. However, a planned change strategy may be necessary to change the way an organization treats its employees.

Karpman Triangle

This is another counterproductive game that service organizations play with both clients and employees. There are three different roles to choose from in the Karpman Triangle: victim, persecutor, or rescuer (See Fig. 4-1). Participants switch from one role to another around the triangle to play this game.

This counterproductive game (explained in Chapter 4) of moving from one role to another around the triangle can be played by the organization as well as by individuals. The following example shows how an organization can play the different roles in relation to its clients:

> A health department decided to offer free immunizations to people who were going to travel in foreign countries, most of whom could afford to pay for this service (rescuer). When they were overwhelmed by the crowd of people appearing at their door for the first travelers' clinic, the health department announced that further clinics would be cancelled, claiming that people who could really afford to pay for the service were taking advantage of the health department (persecutor).

Organizations also play these games with their employees as in the following examples:

> An agency had very harsh personnel policies including the immediate dismissal of any employee caught taking even a pencil home (persecutor). When questioned about these extreme policies, a spokesman for the agency said it was necessary because so many of its employees were not interested in the welfare of the organization (victim).

> Due to inadequate planning for summer vacations, a hospital suffered a serious shortage of maintenance workers and asked its maintenance workers to work two double shifts a week all summer to cover the shortage (victim). These employees had a union contract so they were paid time and a half for the extra shifts. When this group was due for a salary increase in the fall, the hospital said it would not grant an increase because the maintenance workers had taken so much overtime all summer (persecutor).

As with the paternalism, refusing to play any of these roles is one way to counteract this game. It is often necessary, however, to use planned change strategies to change an organization's pattern of relationships with its employees.

I Told You So

This is another potentially destructive game that some organizations have developed (consciously or unconsciously) in response to pressures to promote more women and people from minority groups into positions with some authority within the hierarchy. Instead of selecting the individual from these groups who has the best qualifications for the job, an individual who lacks the ability, education, or experience needed is chosen and placed into a position that that person is not prepared to fill. The almost inevitable result is that many of these individuals fail to carry out the responsibilities of their new positions as well as others within the organization, occasionally with disastrous results. Their failure provides the organization with an excuse for continuing its inequitable promotion practices. It also gives the people who oppose the equitable promotion of women and members of minority groups a chance to say "I Told You So."

It can be very difficult for individuals who are offered a promotion to a position beyond their present capabilities to reject that attractive, even flattering, offer unless they are aware that they are being set up for failure. Once such a person is in the position, it is often possible for coworkers to offer sufficient help and support for that person to succeed despite the trap that has been set.

Bear Trap

This is another trap into which the unsuspecting prospective employee may fall. The bear trap is set by organizations that enter agreements with people seeking employment and later do not honor those agreements. Although it is natural for representatives of an organization to make known only its more positive aspects to someone they wish to hire, some organizations go beyond this to what can only be called a serious misrepresentation of the conditions of employment in that organization. An organization's success in doing this is greatly enhanced by the naiveté and eagerness of the job applicant.

Typically included in this trap are promises of an exciting, challenging job, fast promotions, job security, and impressive flexibility regarding working conditions and transfers between departments. The following are examples of some common traps set by organizations:

> Miss K., a new graduate chose a particular agency because they promised her two weeks vacation in December for her wedding. She began working at the agency in July and was generally satisfied with the position until she was told that no one is ever allowed to take time off in December or January and that her request for time off was denied.

> Another prospective employee, Mr. S., who requested a staff position in the Emergency Room was promised a transfer to the Emergency Room after completing a required three months on a general medical or surgical unit of the hospital. After completing the three months he was told there were no openings in the Emergency Room. He finally left the hospital after two years during which no opening in the Emergency

Room ever came up at a time when he could be transferred, although he knew of at least two new nurses who had been added to the Emergency Room staff while he worked for that hospital.

An experienced nurse administrator, Mrs. T., was hired by a large agency after a six-month search for someone with her expertise. She accepted the position primarily because she was promised a great deal of freedom and autonomy to hire her own staff and to develop the services to be offered on the basis of an assessment of client needs. After beginning work, she found that the agency actually had a rough plan for the project which she was expected to implement immediately without conducting a needs assessment. She was also given a list of six current employees from which to choose her four staff members because the agency could not afford to hire additional staff, hardly the freedom and autonomy she had expected.

Astute questioning and observation of both managers and staff members during employment interviews can substantially reduce the possibility of falling into such traps after accepting a position, perhaps rejecting what might have been a better offer, and committing your time and energy to that position. Any agreements made should be obtained in writing. Once in the trap, you have to decide whether you are going to fight for change and for the fulfillment of promises made, accept the organization's failure to fulfill its agreements with you, or resign.

SUMMARY

Authority, which is derived from holding certain positions within the organizational hierarchy, is greatest at the top of the hierarchy but other sources of power are available to people with little or no authority. *Paternalism,* the *Karpman Triangle, I told you so,* and the *bear trap* are unproductive relationship patterns often found in health care organizations. In paternalism, the organization acts as parent to its employee children; in the Karpman Triangle, the organization plays the roles of victim, rescuer, or persecutor; in I told you so, the organization promotes unqualified people; and in the bear trap the organization enters agreements that are not honored. Confrontation and change strategies can be used to repattern this organizational behavior.

Professional-Organizational Conflict: Reality Shock and Burn-out

Reality shock and burn-out are two related conflicts that are experienced by a number of people in the helping professions. Both of these terms refer to the conflict between a person's professional goals and ideals and the realities of the work situation. Reality shock refers specifically to the occurrence of this conflict when nurses leave school and begin their first job.[25-28] Burn-out is a broader term describing the way this conflict is experienced by people in any of the human service professions, such as teachers, social workers, nurses, counselors, and so forth.[29-30]

Both reality shock and burn-out are discussed along with some suggestions for dealing with these very common conflicts.

REALITY SHOCK

Reality shock occurs when the new graduate suddenly becomes aware of the discrepancy between the real world and the ideals of the nursing profession. The shock stems from the sudden realization that the way the graduate was taught to do things in school and believes is the right way to do things is not necessarily the way things are actually done on the job.

The Honeymoon

The first few weeks on a new job are often called the honeymoon phase. During the honeymoon phase, the new employee is excited and enthusiastic about the new position and everything seems rosy. Coworkers usually go out of their way to make the new person feel welcome and overlook or brush aside any problems that arise.

Honeymoons do not last forever. The new graduate is soon expected to behave just like everyone else and discovers that expectations for a professional employed in an organization are quite different than expectations for a student in school. Those behaviors that brought rewards in school are not necessarily valued by the organization. In fact, some of them are critized by coworkers and supervisors. The new graduate who is not prepared for this change feels hurt, angry, disillusioned, and shocked. The tension and stress of the situation can become almost unbearable if it is not resolved.

The Conflicts

What are these differences in expectations? Kramer,[1-4] who has studied reality shock for many years, found some substantial differences between professional goals and ideals and organizational goals and expectations. These discrepancies include a mechanistic versus holistic orientation, the priority of efficiency over effectiveness, the way expectations are communicated, and the way feedback is given.

Ideally, health care should be comprehensive. Not only should it meet all the patient's or client's needs but it should be delivered in a way that considers the person as a whole, as a member of a particular family that has certain unique characteristics and needs, and as a member of a particular community as well. But most health care professionals are not employed to provide comprehensive, holistic care. Instead, they are asked to give medications or to provide counseling or to make home visits or to prepare someone for surgery, but rarely to do all these things. These tasks are divided among different people, each a specialist, for the sake of efficiency rather than continuity or effectiveness.

When efficiency is the goal, the speed and amount of work done is rewarded rather than the quality of the work. This also creates a conflict for the new graduate who was allowed to take as much time as needed to provide good care in school.

Another conflict arises from differences in the way in which expectations are communicated. In school, an effort is made to provide explicit directions so that students know what they are expected to accomplish. In many work settings however, instructions are brief and many expectations are left unspoken. New graduates who are not aware of these unspoken expectations (which are part of the informal level of operations) may find that they have unknowingly left tasks undone or are considered inept by coworkers who believe they know the "right" way to do things. The following example describes a common occurrence of these unspoken expectations:

> A new graduate was assigned to give medications to all the patients cared for by the team. Because this was a fairly light assignment, the graduate spent some time looking up the medications and explaining their actions to the patients receiving them. The graduate also straightened up the medicine room and filled out the order forms, which the graduate thought would please the task-oriented team leader.
>
> At the end of the day, the graduate reported these activities with some satisfaction to the team leader. The graduate expected the team leader to be pleased with the way the time had been used. Instead, the team leader looked annoyed and told the graduate that whoever passes meds always does the blood pressures too and that the other nurse on the team who had a heavier assignment had to do them. Also, since supplies were always ordered on Fridays for the weekend, it would have to be done again tomorrow so the graduate had, in fact, wasted time.

If this new graduate had been more aware of the existence of the informal level of operations with its unspoken expectations, the graduate would have discussed the plans with the team leader earlier in the day. Of course, an effective leader would also have communicated the leader's expectations more clearly, but many people in leadership positions are not very effective leaders.

The example of the new graduate also illustrates some differences in the way feedback is given by the ineffective leaders who are often found in organizations. The feedback given was all negative and it was given too late. Other common problems with feedback are messages that are too vague or global such as "You're doing fine," very indirect messages such as grumbling under the breath or redoing something that has just been done, or a complete lack of feedback until something goes wrong.

Additional Pressures on the New Graduate

The first job a person takes after finishing school is often thought of as a proving-ground for testing new knowledge and skills. People often set up mental tests for themselves that they feel must be passed before they can be confident of their ability to function in this new professional capacity. Passing these mental tests also confirms achievement of identity as a practitioner rather than a student.

It is important to take a positive, assertive approach to your abilities at this time and to avoid minimizing them. For example, when you need to ask for assistance or information, you can make a point of first telling your coworker what you do know and then indicate where you need help rather than presenting yourself as a helpless person or saying you have never done something before, which is damaging to your confidence.

A feeling of uncertainty about your competency can also come from the ambiguities of a situation. For example, there are many clinical situations that demand professional judgment because there is no single right way to handle them. It has also been suggested that nurses are socialized into being very concerned about not making a mistake or harming the patient rather than into feeling confident of their abilities.

At the same time that new graduates are testing themselves, they are undergoing testing by their coworkers. The coworkers are also interested in finding out whether or not the new graduates can handle the job. This testing is somewhat like the teasing and hazing of freshmen entering high school or college. The new graduate is entering a new group and the group will decide whether or not to accept this new member. This testing is usually reasonable but sometimes new graduates will be given a task they are not ready to handle. If this happens, Kramer[1-4] recommends that you refuse to take the test rather than fail it. Another opportunity for proving yourself will soon come along.

The discrepancies in role expectations and the need for a feeling of competency are the top two concerns of new graduates, according to most surveys. Next in order of concern are the system that must be dealt with, self-concept, and the type of feedback that is given (or not given). Some other problems, such as dealing with resistant staff members, cultural differences, and age differences, have already been discussed in the chapter on team leading. Before considering ways to resolve these problems, we will look at some less successful ways to cope with these problems.

Unsuccessful Coping Efforts

When faced with reality shock, some new graduates give up their professional goals and ideals and adopt the organization's operative goals as their own. By doing this, they eliminate their conflict but they also become less effective caregivers. This coping strategy results in putting the needs of the organization before the needs of either the professional or the client. It also reinforces operative goals that might better be challenged and changed.

Other people give up their professional ideals but do not adopt the organization's goals nor any others to replace them. This has a deadening effect on people: they become automatons believing in nothing relating to their work except in doing what is necessary to earn a day's pay. Their profession had become just another job.

Of those who do not give up their professional goals and ideals, many try to find an organization that will support them. Some will succeed but others will find themselves switching from one job to another until they find what they seek. A significant percentage of those who do not want to give up their professional ideals escape these conflicts by leaving their jobs and not returning to their profession.

Resolving the Conflicts

Some of the shock experienced by the new graduate can be prevented. The new graduate who understands the difference between the formal and informal levels of operation in an organization and knows how to identify its operative goals and the types of games that organizations play will not be as shocked as the naive individual who thinks that every employee's efforts are directed toward meeting the official goals and that this behavior will be rewarded.

Experience also helps. Opportunities to challenge your competence and develop your identity as a professional can begin in school. Success in meeting these challenges can immunize you against the loss of confidence that accompanies reality shock.

When you begin a new job, it is important to learn as much as you can about the organization's formal and informal levels and operative goals. This not only saves you from some nasty surprises but also gives you some ideas about how to work within the system and how to make the system work for you. The following is an example of how one team leader figured out how to use the system:

> A new team leader realized that patient care conferences were never held in the home health agency but were needed to improve the care given. When the team leader approached team members (who were all long-term employees of the agency) about this, they expressed no interest in having conferences. The supervisor's response was also negative.
>
> The agency was an extremely rigid and bureaucratic one that allowed team leaders very little authority so the team leader could not begin the conferences without the supervisor's approval. (The team members would not attend them unless they were approved anyway.) However, the agency did have a strong bias in favor of education, held many classes for its employees, and rewarded employees for accumulating large numbers of education credits or contact hours.
>
> The new team leader took advantage of the value placed on education. The team leader adopted the patient care conference format to focus on the teaching and learning aspects of it and presented the idea to the supervisor as twice weekly seminars for staff. The supervisor recognized the seminars' similarity to patient care conferences but felt a need to approve the plan because of the strong emphasis on education in the agency. The staff agreed to attend because it was a good way to accumulate educational credits on work time. The patient care conference/seminars became an accepted part of the team's operation and the team leader was later praised for interest in meeting the educational needs of the team.

The team leader in the example did not abandon or even compromise the goal to improve care, adapting it instead to the realities of the situation in which the leader was employed. When your goal cannot be adapted without seriously compromising it, then one of the change strategies in Chapter 9 is needed.

It is helpful to keep in mind that a great deal of energy goes into learning a new job. At the same time, implementing a change takes time and energy on your part. Make a choice from a number of different changes and improvements that you see are needed. It is also a good idea to make a list of these things not only to make your choice but also so that you do not forget them later when you have become socialized into a part of that system.

There are three other actions that can help to reduce the shock effects of these conflicts. The first is to *seek feedback often and persistently*. This not only provides you with needed information, but also pushes the people you work with to be more specific about their expectations of you. A second and related action is to *use confronting communication to deal with the problems that can arise with coworkers*. The third action is at least as important and helpful: *develop a support network for yourself*. Identifying colleagues who have also held onto their professional goals and sharing with them not only your problems but the work of improving the organization is a very helpful cushion against reality shock. The mutual support of colleagues reinforces your self-confidence if it wavers in the face of many conflicts and challenges. Their praise of your work can keep you going while rewards from the organization are meager. A support network is a source of strength when resisting pressure to give up professional ideals and a source of power when attempting to bring about change. You can see that work on developing your potential in each of the components of effective leadership can help to prevent the problems of reality shock.

Reality shock may occur whenever you begin a new position, even if you are not a new graduate (See Research Example 1-1). Because reality shock and burn-out are related conflicts, you may also find some of the suggestions for counteracting burn-out helpful in coping with reality shock.

BURN-OUT

The term burn-out refers to a state of exhaustion, a depletion of energies that seems to be a particular problem for people in helping professions. It begins with frustration, disillusionment, or doubts about your work and leads to the loss of ideals, purpose, and energy.

The burned out individual may feel apathetic, alienated, or exhausted. Stress-related physical symptoms such as headaches, backaches, indigestion, and lowered resistance to infection may be experienced. Family difficulties and social problems may also occur. Like reality shock, the cost of burn-out to individuals, their families, friends, colleagues, and clients is enormous.

People who enter helping professions usually do so with a lot of enthusiasm and idealism. They want to help people and expect that their interventions will have a great deal of impact. The system needs changing and they frequently intend to do something about that too. Support and success nourish all their high hopes. But when they meet continuous resistance, disinterest, and failure to meet their goals, many of them begin to burn-out.

The factors that contribute to burn-out are discussed next and then some suggestions for avoiding or reducing the effects of burn-out are offered.

Factors Contributing to Burn-Out

Burn-out can occur at any time in your career. In some ways, it is an extension of reality shock when the initial conflicts have not been satisfactorily resolved.

Burn-out is the result of the negative interaction between the expectations and behavior of the health care professional and the systems with which the professional is working. The following is a list of the factors most commonly involved in this negative interaction:

Low Pay. When compared with the salaries of professionals in other fields, many health care professionals are poorly paid for the amount of education they have and the degree of responsibility they are given. For example, nurses are still paid less than sanitation workers or grocery store cashiers in some communities.

Long Hours. Not only is the work demanding but many health care professionals find themselves working well beyond the typical 40-hour week. For example, nurses are frequently asked to work rotating shifts or 16-hour days, both of which are a considerable stress on the individual's health.

Too Much Paper Work. People who enter helping professions derive their satisfaction from interacting with people, not with paper. When much of their time is spent on filling out forms, charts, and reports, they become frustrated by the loss of time that could be spent with their clients.

Lack of Success with Clients. When you commit yourself to helping people, their failure to recover can be felt as a personal disappointment. Health care professionals find that the people they counsel often return to destructive behavior and that many they care for do not recover but die. This happens to intensive care nurses, oncology unit staff, counselors, rehabilitation workers, and many others. The continual loss of patients alone can result in burn-out.

Lack of Appreciation and Understanding. Getting intangible rewards or a psychological paycheck meets an important need for esteem and recognition. Patients or clients do express their appreciation many times but supervisors frequently fail to comment favorably on a job well done. Also, the public does not understand what many health care professionals do and does not appreciate how demanding some of these jobs are. For example, there are still many people who think of nurses as bedpan carriers and doctors' helpers until they require the services of a nurse and find out what nurses really do.

Lack of Support. Many health care professionals find themselves working in organizations that do not support their efforts to improve the quality of the services offered. Continually fighting for the right to practice in a professional manner has left many burned out.

Unresponsiveness to Client Needs. The health care system's lack of responsiveness to client needs (for example, impersonal, fragmented care, restrictive eligibility requirements, lack of respect for the dignity of the individual, and so forth) conflicts with the professional ideals of a helping person. Finding out that the operative goals of a health care organization emphasize efficiency and monetary gain over the needs of the people served leads to much frustration and disillusionment.

Powerlessness. A feeling of powerlessness can contribute to burn-out. This feeling stems from a failure to recognize and use the potential power available to any large group that performs a vital function. Many people in the helping professions feel it is wrong, or at least not nice, to use their power. This same attitude leads to a reaction of dismay and discouragement when they find themselves the target of a power play. Both of these attitudes contribute to burn-out.

Discrimination. Although progress has been made in reducing discrimination, you will still find more women and minorities in the lower status, lower paid positions in health care. The majority of physicians are still men; the majority of nurses are still women and they still find themselves resisting physician dominance and the myths that women are weaker, less dependable, or less intelligent than men. This problem is quite evident in the health care field but not unique to it.

Inadequate Advancement Opportunities. People at the lower levels in the helping professions are often frustrated and discouraged by the educational prerequisites for moving up the career ladder. Those who are higher up on the ladder find that further advancement means moving into management or teaching and further away from the people they want to help. This frustration is not unique to the helping professions.

Counteracting Burn-Out

It is difficult to devote much energy to counteracting burn-out when your energies are depleted and you feel exhausted. For this reason, it is a good idea to intervene for yourself and others before burn-out becomes too severe.

Some of the suggestions given previously for dealing with reality shock (especially those related to developing leadership effectiveness) are also helpful for counteracting burn-out. The suggestions offered here focus on long-term interventions.

You may have noticed when reading the list of factors contributing to burn-out that several of them were based on the helping person's unrealistic expectations. People who define success in terms of having all their patients recover or all their clients rehabilitated have set themselves up for failure. In contrast, if you are able to define success as having made some contribution to the health and welfare of *some* of the people you care for, then you have set yourself up for success.

You can also divide overall goals into partial goals that you are more likely to succeed in meeting. For example, if your goal is to completely rehabilitate a stroke patient, you may fail, especially if the patient has another stroke. But if you set several partial goals or separate steps leading to the patient's full recovery, such as finding a new means of transportation or being able to prepare meals, you have a much greater probability of meeting at least some of these goals. In general, a focus on your successes rather than on your failures helps to reduce feelings of discouragement and disappointment.

Along with focusing on success and defining it realistically, you can also redefine the extent of your responsibility to your clients. If you recall the victim-rescuer-persecutor roles of the Karpman Triangle, you'll see that helping persons who take on full responsibility for what happens to a client are acting in the role of rescuer. In contrast, helping persons who recognize that their clients have some responsibility too and who allow clients to exercise that responsibility have taken a burden off their shoulders and at the same time become more effective helping persons. This strategy has more utility in some settings than in others but even in intensive care units, caregivers can learn to recognize their own limits and can focus their thoughts on the people who would not have survived without their care rather than seeing the deaths of some patients as a sign of failure.

The use of effective leadership actions was mentioned as a way to cope with reality shock. They are equally helpful in dealing with burn-out. It is especially important to learn how to use change strategies to fight back when work situations are unsatisfactory. In particular, it is important to overcome the idea that the use of power tactics is unprofessional. Power tactics can and will be used on you by other people (including other professionals) so you will need to know how to use them in return. Many people in the helping professions are reluctant to let go of the myth that rewards somehow come automatically to those who do their work well. While this happens occasionally, more often the rewards go to those who know how to ask for and even demand them.

Stress reduction, relaxation techniques, exercise, and good nutrition are all helpful in keeping your energy levels high. However, while they can prepare you to cope with the stresses of a job, they are not solutions to the conflicts that lead to reality shock and burn-out and are supplements rather than substitutes for the other strategies discussed here.

When your work takes up too much of your time and energy, there is little left for other important activities and relationships. Your job can become the center of your world and your world can become very small. When your interests and satisfactions are limited to your work, you are more susceptible to burn-out; trouble at work becomes trouble with your whole life. There are two ways out of this: set limits on your commitment to work and expand the number of satisfying activities and relationships you have outside of work.

Many people in the helping professions have difficulty setting such limits on their commitment (especially if they often play the rescuer role). If you enjoy working extra hours and taking calls at night and on weekends, that's fine; but if it exhausts you, then you need to stop doing it or risk serious burn-out. When you are asked to work another double shift or the third weekend in a row, you can say no. At the same time that you are setting limits at work, you can expand your outside activities so that you live in a large world in which a blow to one part can be cushioned by support from other parts.

SUMMARY

Reality shock and burn-out are related conflicts between a person's professional goals and ideals and the realities of the work situation. Reality shock occurs when nurses leave school and discover the discrepancies between professional and organizational goals: a holistic versus mechanistic orientation, the priority of efficiency over effectiveness, the way expectations are communicated, and the way feedback is given. Burn-out stems from the frustration and disillusionment of unsatisfactory working conditions and unrealistic expectations. Strategies for counteracting these problems include obtaining adequate knowledge, confidence, and skills to do the job; seeking feedback; using confrontation; developing a support network; improving and using leadership skills; redefining success; setting realistic goals; setting limits on your work responsibilities; and expanding your world outside of work.

References

1. ROSENHAN, DL: *On being sane in insane places.* Science 179(4070): 250, January 1973.

2. YOUNG, DW: *"Nonprofits" Need Surplus Too.* Harvard Business Review 60(1):124, January-February 1982.

3. MINTZBERG, H: *Organizational Design: Fashion or Fit?* Harvard Business Review 59 (1):103, January-February 1981.

4. McCLURE, M: *The Reasons for Hospital Staff Nurse Resignations.* Unpublished doctoral dissertation. Teachers College Columbia University, New York, 1972.

5. REVANS, RW: *Psychosocial factors in hospitals and nurse staffing.* In LEVINE, E (ED): *Research on Nurse Staffing in Hospitals.* US Department of Health, Education, and Welfare, Washington, DC, 1972.

6. HUSE, EF AND BOWDITCH, JL: *Behavior In Organizations: A Systems Approach to Managing.* Addison-Wesley, Reading, Massachusetts, 1973.

7. MEYER, MW: *Theory of Organizational Structure.* Bobbs-Merrill, Indianapolis, Indiana, 1977.

8. DALTON, M: *Formal and informal organizations.* In ETZIONI, A (ED): *Readings on Modern Organizations.* Prentice Hall, Englewood Cliffs, New Jersey, 1969.

9. WEBER, M: *Bureaucratic organizations.* In ETZIONI, A (ED): *Readings on Modern Organizations.* Prentice Hall, Englewood Cliffs, New Jersey, 1969.

10. Quoted by GREENE, M: *Self-consciousness in a technological world.* In FITZPATRICK, ML (ED): *Present Realities/Future Imperatives in Nursing Education.* Teachers College Press, New York, 1977, p 4.

11. LAWRENCE, WG: *Exploring Individual and Organizational Boundaries.* John Wiley & Sons, New York, 1979.

12. McKELVEY, B AND KILMANN, RH: Organization design: A participative multivariate approach. Administrative Science Quarterly 20(1):24, March 1975.

13. DRUCKER, PL: *People and Performance: The Best of Peter Drucker on Management.* Harper & Row, New York, 1977.

14. PERROW, C: *The analysis of goals in complex organizations.* In ETZIONI, A (ED): *Readings on Modern Organizations.* Prentice-Hall, Englewood Cliffs, New Jersey, 1969, p 71.

15. Citizens Board of Inquiry into Health Services for Americans. *Heal Yourself.* American Public Health Association, Washington, DC, 1972.

16. NICHOLS, B: *Oklahoma crude: Everything's gushing up hospitals.* In KOTELCHUCK, D (ED): *Prognosis Negative.* Vintage Books, New York, 1976.

17. MERTON, R: *The social nature of leadership.* American Journal of Nursing 69:12, December 1969.

18. LONGEST, BB: *Management Practices for the Health Professional.* Reston, Virginia, 1976.

19. McCLURE, M: op cit, p 146.

20. FUNKHOUSER, GR: *Quality of care: Part II.* Nursing '77 7(1):27, January 1977.

21. LINDQUIST, JD AND BLACKBURN, RT: *Middlegrove: The Locus of Campus Power.* American Association of University Professors Bulletin 60:367, 1974.

22. JONGEWARD, D: *Everybody Wins: Transactional Analysis Applied to Organizations.* Addison-Wesley, Reading, Massachusetts, 1973.

23. JONGEWARD, D AND SEYER, PC: *Choosing Success: Transactional Analysis On The Job.* John Wiley & Sons, New York, 1978.

24. ASHLEY, J: *Hospitals, Paternalism and the Role of the Nurse.* Teachers College Press, New York, 1976.

25. KRAMER, M: *Reality Shock: Why Nurses Leave Nursing.* CV Mosby, St Louis, 1974.

26. KRAMER, M: *Coping with Reality Shock.* Workshop presented at Jackson Memorial Hospital, Miami, Florida, January 27 and 28, 1981.

27. KRAMER, M AND SCHMALENBERG, C: *Path to Biculturalism.* Contemporary Publishing, Wakefield, Massachusetts, 1977.

28. SCHMALENBERG, C AND KRAMER, M: *Coping with Reality Shock: Voices of Experience.* Nursing Resources, Wakefield, Massachusetts, 1979.

29. EDELWICH, J AND BRODSKY, A: *Burn-Out: Stages of Disillusionment in the Helping Professions.* Human Sciences Press, New York, 1980.

30. FREUDENBERGER, HJ: *Staff burn-out.* Journal of Social Issues 30(1):159, 1974.

Chapter *11*

Working In Organizations

This chapter continues the study of organizations begun in Chapter 10 but moves further from the broad focus on the entire organization as a complex system to a narrower one concentrating on the experience of people working in an organization. Several topics of particular interest and concern to those who are working in health care organizations are discussed, including the different ways to organize the delivery of nursing care; using objectives as a guide to planning and evaluating your work, the process of budgeting, formal evaluation procedures, and labor relations activities.

The Organization and Delivery of Nursing Care

The four most common ways to organize and deliver nursing care are discussed here. These are the case method, functional method, team nursing, and primary nursing.[1, 2] Each of these approaches has certain advantages and disadvantages in terms of their effect on staff members and on the quality of the care given.

Most health care organizations make some adaptations in whichever approach they choose. These adaptations vary a great deal. Some successfully modify the approach to meet the needs of that particular organization but other adaptations defeat the original reason for selecting that approach.

CASE METHOD

The case method is the assignment of one nurse to the total care of one or more patients or clients. The assigned nurse is responsible for providing all the nursing care that is needed.

The work of the private duty nurse is one example of the case method. Community health agencies often use this method to assign cases to individual nurses, and intensive care units often use a modified version of this method for delivering nursing care. It is also used extensively for student assignments.

Advantages

Although it is the oldest of the four modes, the case method is still considered by many to be the ideal way to deliver nursing care. The case method is simple and direct in comparison with the others. It does not require the complex assignment planning that some of the others do and the lines of responsibility are clear: the nurse assigned to the patient is responsible for the outcomes of that patient's care.

The primary advantage, though, is that the care given using the case method is comprehensive, continuous, and promotes the holistic approach. The likelihood of the care being fragmented, discontinuous, or full of serious gaps is greatly reduced when the case method is used.

Disadvantages

With so many advantages, you might wonder why the case method is not used universally. The major difficulties with the case method are related to the number and complexity of health care problems and the settings in which care is given. One of the arguments against the case method is that it is less efficient than some of the other methods since it uses highly skilled, higher paid professionals to do work that can be done by less skilled, lower paid people such as nursing assistants. The case method cannot be used to assign patients or clients to these ancillary staff members. In addition, with the number of specialties that have developed in the health care field, it is very difficult for an individual professional to be knowledgeable in all areas and to provide the most expert care for patients or clients with a wide variety of needs.

There are also some disadvantages that relate specifically to inpatient care. Care that must be given around the clock, seven days a week cannot be done by one person. Also, inpatient units are organized in such a way that interaction with many different departments is necessary for obtaining such services and supplies as drugs, linens, meals, laboratory tests, different therapies, and so forth. Having a number of different nurses independently interacting with each of these departments could create a lot of confusion. In such complexly organized settings, more coordination than the case method offers seems to be needed.

FUNCTIONAL METHOD

The functional method of delivering nursing care is based on a division of labor similar to that used on an assembly line. Individual caregivers are assigned to do specific tasks rather than being assigned to a certain number of patients or clients.

Assignments are based on the criterion of efficiency: tasks are given to the lowest skilled, lowest paid worker who is available and can do them. The usual result in a hospital or nursing home is that one nurse is assigned to be in charge of the unit, another nurse administers all medications, a practical nurse is asked to take blood pressures, and an aide takes all the temperatures, passes out meal trays, and so forth. In a home health care agency, implementation of the functional method would mean that a nurse would visit a client to counsel, teach, or carry out complex care techniques while a home health aide would visit to assist with bathing and personal care. Nursing care in the home is rarely divided into as many discrete pieces for different level workers because of the inefficiency of making multiple visits, but it can and is done frequently in ambulatory care settings.

Advantages

The major advantage of the functional method is its efficiency. This method makes it possible to use more unskilled or lesser skilled people to get the work done. When caregivers are given the same assignments on a regular basis, each person becomes quite adept at them and can finish the tasks quickly.

Using the functional method makes it easy to give clearly defined assignments and to check later to ensure that the assignments were completed. Once the tasks are defined and the assignments are made, there is usually very little overlap or confusion about who is expected to do a particular job and so the time required for coordination of staff members is minimized. It is interesting to note that even when team or primary nursing is the usual mode for delivering care, organizations frequently fall back on the functional method to deliver care if a serious shortage of staff occurs.

Disadvantages

The functional method may not be as efficient as it is generally thought to be. From the point of view of getting the work done the need for coordination may be kept to a minimum but the need for it is increased from the point of view of the recipient of this care. Consider, for example, how inefficient it is to have three different staff members enter a room, one to give a medication, the second to take a blood pressure reading, and a third to check a dressing. An even more serious drawback to this method of care is the extreme fragmentation of care that results. Because it uses an assembly line type of division of labor, the functional approach is mechanistic, impersonal, and emphasizes the more technical aspects of nursing care. Both staff and patients are likely to be dissatisfied with the way care is given.

For the staff, the work becomes repetitious and boring. Doing the same disconnected tasks prevents them from experiencing the satisfaction of seeing anything done completely from beginning to end. For example, if a patient has a quick and uneventful recovery from surgery, no one staff member can take pride in having assured the patient's comfort and prevented postsurgical complications. The patient, too, is confused and sometimes irritated by the large number of people going in and out of the patient's room or home, each one doing only one or two things and refusing to do others because it is someone else's job. Potentially more serious for the patient is the fact that communication between staff members may be minimal and rushed so that no one is aware of everything that is happening to an individual patient. While the nurse in charge is theoretically responsible for all care given, responsibility is so diffused among various caregivers that a serious gap in care can occur without anyone realizing it. As you can see, holistic nursing is virtually impossible under the functional mode.

TEAM NURSING

Team nursing is the delivery of nursing care by a designated team of staff members including both professional nurses and nonprofessional (ancillary) staff. There are several elements considered necessary in team nursing. These are as follows:

1. The leader of the team should be a registered professional nurse, not a practical nurse or other staff member. The team leader also has delegated authority to make assignments for team members.
2. The leader is expected to use a democratic or participative style of leadership in interactions with team members.
3. The team is responsible for the total care given to a certain number of patients or clients that have been assigned to the team.
4. Communication among team members is built into this mode and is essential to its success. This includes written patient care assignments, nursing care plans, reports to and from the team leader, team conferences in which patient care problems and other concerns of the team are discussed, and frequent informal feedback among team members.[3-5]

Team nursing was designed at the end of World War II to make the best use of the nursing staff available and to alleviate the problems created by the functional method. As more workers with minimal on the job training were hired in the health care field, it became necessary to reorganize the delivery of care so that appropriate assignments could be made for these less skilled workers. At the same time, it was also hoped that the use of team nursing would increase both staff and patient satisfaction and improve the quality of care.

The team leader has a pivotal role in team nursing. The leader is expected to closely supervise ancillary staff and to provide informal training for them as it is needed. The leader is also expected to be thoroughly acquainted with the needs of every patient or client assigned to the team, even if not directly involved in their care. In hospitals or nursing homes, the head nurse selects the team leaders, designates the scope of the team's responsibility, and is responsible for overall management of the nursing unit, meeting the more formal education needs of staff, and formal evaluation. In community settings, the supervisor usually fulfills these roles.

Advantages

Although team nursing was not designed to make up for inadequate staffing, it does make it possible to deliver quality care using a relatively large proportion of ancillary personnel. In comparison with the functional method of delivering care, team nursing is far more satisfying to both patients and staff when it is done well. The abilities of each staff member are more likely to be recognized and fully utilized. The increased amount of cooperation and communication among team members raises staff morale and generally improves the functioning of the staff as a whole. Team members also have a greater sense of having contributed to the outcomes of the care given. Especially in hospital settings, most nurses working on teams find that they know both their patients and fellow staff members better than when using the functional method.

Even though patient care is still divided among several people in team nursing, it is far less fragmented that it is in the functional method because of the increased communication between team members and because of the extensive coordination efforts of the team leader who is expected to be familiar with all aspects of the patient care given by the team. The team nursing approach allows comprehensive, holistic nursing care when the team functions at a high level of maturity.

Disadvantages

One of the greatest disadvantages of team nursing is that it is so often poorly done. Team nursing is far more than simply dividing staff into equal parts and then assigning an equal number of patients to each group of staff. Yet this is often called team nursing even though it usually is much more like the functional method in everything but name.

Team nursing requires a great deal of cooperation and communication from all staff members. It demands even more of the team leader who spends a lot of time coordinating and supervising team members and needs to be highly skilled both as a leader and as a practitioner. Not every nurse practicing today is prepared to assume these roles.

Some efficiency is lost due to these demands for increased interaction among staff members. Also, the large number of people attending the same patient in the functional method is not substantially reduced in team nursing.

Although the leader of the team is a professional nurse, a large proportion of the staff is not and much of the care is given by persons other than nurses. In contrast, both the case method and primary nursing emphasize care given by professional nurses.

PRIMARY NURSING

Primary nursing incorporates the concept of assigning total care and responsibility for one patient or client from the case method into a modality particularily designed for inpatient care, though adaptable to ambulatory care as well. Every patient or client has a designated primary nurse who is responsible for planning their care and for ensuring that the plan is implemented around the clock, seven days a week. When the primary nurse is not at work, the implementation of the care plan is delegated directly to an associate nurse but the primary nurse is still responsible as well and may be called upon if a serious problem arises.[6]

When primary nursing is implemented, the inpatient unit is usually divided into districts or small modular units with a primary nurse assigned to each district. In some settings, primary nurses select their patients. The primary nurse provides all the nursing care needed by each assigned patient including the baths and vital signs that are usually delegated to ancillary personnel under the functional or team methods. The head nurse functions as the coordinator of the entire unit and consultant to the primary nurses. Conferences to discuss patient care problems are planned to include members of the entire health care team.

Advantages

Primary nursing has many of the advantages of the case method. Nurses have more autonomy in this mode than in the functional or team approaches and are challenged to work to their full capacity. They spend less time in coodinating and supervising activities and more time in direct care activities. Along with the increased autonomy and involvement in direct care, the primary nurse is also more accountable because responsibility is focused rather than diffused.

Once they have become accustomed to this mode, primary nurses generally feel that they are more effective working under this system. In fact, many studies have shown that both cost and turnover are reduced though evidence of its impact on the quality of care is still inconclusive.[7] They also gain more satisfaction from being involved in the entire care of a patient and from being able to give more holistic care.

Patients also seem to appreciate the more personalized and holistic care that can be given in primary nursing. They are especially pleased to be able to say "This is my nurse." People from other disciplines also appreciate the fact that they can consult with one particular, identifiable nurse who knows all about the patient.

Disadvantages

As with team nursing, most of the disadvantages of primary nursing come from problems with implementation. While proponents of primary care argue that it is no more costly than other ways to deliver care, its detractors point out that it requires a much higher proportion of professional nurses to ancillary personnel. It has also been noted that even with primary nursing the hospitalized person is cared for by at least six nurses (three nurses to cover the three eight-hour shifts in a day and another three associates to substitute for them on their days off).

Primary nursing demands increased independence, accountability, and the ability to make thorough assessments and plan nursing care accordingly. Unfortunately, not every nurse feels prepared for this, especially those who are accustomed to the routinized work done under the functional method. Some are threatened by these additional demands, others find that they need additional education before assuming the primary nurse role. Ancillary workers often feel a sense of loss when their direct care activities are reduced under primary nursing.

One of the major differences between primary nursing and team nursing is the conceptualization of the way care is given, especially by whom. Team nursing was developed in order to include ancillary personnel in caregiving roles appropriately and emphasizes the supervising, teaching, and coordinating functions of the nurse. On the other hand, primary nursing focuses on the nurse as the caregiver and does not clearly define the roles of ancillary personnel. In fact, there is much disagreement over the issue of practical nurses assuming the primary nurse role and many variations of primary nursing have arisen from attempts to make appropriate use of ancillary personnel in the primary nursing approach to delivering nursing care.

SUMMARY

Case, functional, team, and primary nursing are common ways to organize and deliver nursing care. The case method is the total care for one or more patients by one nurse, but it does not allow for 24-hour coverage or roles for ancillary personnel. The functional method is an assembly line type of division of tasks often selected for its apparent efficiency but resulting in fragmented care. Team nursing focuses on the coordination and supervision of care given by the team including ancillary staff. Primary nursing returns to the focus on the nurse as caregiver with associate nurses covering the other hours of the day. Both team and primary nursing are more difficult to implement than the functional or case method.

Management by Objectives

Management by objectives, often called MBO, is a well-known approach to planning and evaluating the work done in organizations.[8] Although MBO is usually described as a tool for managers, it can be used by leaders who do not necessarily hold the official title of manager. In fact, in the way it is described in this section, MBO can be used by any individual or group at any level in the organization or for the organization as a whole.

The essential elements of this approach are quite simple: set meaningful goals written in the form of objectives, work on carrying out the objectives, then evaluate how well the objectives have been met. This procedure follows the order of the familiar problem-solving process except that it assumes that a thorough collection of data and definition of the needs or problems in the work situation have already been done. The purpose of using objectives in this way is to set out clearly what direction the work should take and what specific accomplishments (outcomes) are expected within a given period of time. In other words, the objectives serve first as a guide to the planning of your work and later as a guide to evaluating your work.

A few examples of this use of objectives for both individuals and groups will be given and then the advantages and disadvantages of MBO will be discussed.

SET OBJECTIVES

Assuming you have adequate data, the first step is to write a set of objectives describing your goals for a given period of time. These objectives should begin with an action verb and describe an activity that can be measured or at least observed. When possible, the objectives should also state a quantifiable end result to increase the objectivity of the evaluation done at the end point.

In addition to being observed or measurable, the objectives should also be meaningful and either congruent with the goals of the system in which you are working or deliberately aimed at changing its goals. Meaningful goals are those which describe some kind of change or progress in the work being done or an entirely new direction. Meaningless objectives tend to describe the routine activities that accompany any job or specify no action at all such as "have a positive attitude toward work."

Most of your objectives will probably be congruent with official and operative goals of the systems in which you are working. But when changes are needed, your objectives may be deliberately in conflict with some of your team's or organization's goals. If you find that all or most of your individual objectives are in conflict with those of the team or organization then you need to consider moving to another team or organization.

The time set for completing the objectives depends on the nature of the work being planned, the proportion of the work day set aside to work on the objectives and any other factors that will affect the speed with which the work can be done. Common time frames used in organizations are one month, three months, six months, and one year.

Individual Objectives

When objectives are used as the basis upon which a formal evaluation is made, you may be either given a set of objectives, asked to write your own objectives or asked to write them with your immediate supervisor. Of course, there is a great difference between being encouraged to set your own objectives and being handed a predetermined set of objectives. The first approach increases motivation and encourages self-management; the second approach discourages self-management, reduces motivation, and becomes primarily a means for controlling employees.[9]

Whether or not you have an employer who uses MBO, you can develop your own set of objectives to guide your career planning and professional growth. Because examples of objectives used in formal evaluations are given in the next section of this chapter, the following example describes objectives used to guide professional growth:

Imagine that you have begun working in a new position in a respiratory care unit. For the first few weeks in this new position, your primary objectives would be to learn the new job and to become acquainted with both the people you're working with and the organization in which you are now working.

At the end of three months, you feel more comfortable with the work you are doing and have also become familiar with the informal level of operation of the organization, its operative goals, and so forth. At this point you can either let yourself go along with the routines of the job and accept whatever changes in assignment are made for you or you can decide on the direction you would like to see your career take and set objectives for yourself that will take you in that direction.

If you decide to set your own course, there are several questions to ask yourself:

How can I improve my practice?
What do I want to gain from this position?
What do I want to accomplish?
Where do I go from here?

The specific objectives you write will depend on your answers to these questions, your overall goal, and your current position. Both short- and long-term objectives are helpful. For example, you may want to learn how to assemble, use, and adjust the new respirator that is going to be used on your unit within the next month. This would be one of your short-term objectives. You may also want to write a protocol for use of the new respirator by the end of the month, implement full use of the respirator in three months, and complete an evaluation of its effectiveness in a year.

Long-term goals may need to be broken down into steps. For example, a year from now you may want to have taken a course to become a clinical specialist in respiratory care. You can develop a time line to follow in working toward this long-term objective as follows:

1 month: Obtain information about courses and programs available.
3 months: Complete application to selected program.
6 months: Begin course in respiratory care nursing
1 year: Complete first course.

You can see that it would take longer than one year to fulfill the objective to complete an entire clinical specialist program.

The individual objectives given here as examples are only a sampling, not an entire set of objectives.

Work Group Objectives

As the leader of different types of working groups, you will also find objectives useful guides for planning and evaluating their work. The criteria for writing objectives for work groups are the same but their scope and content will differ from the individual objectives. The following objectives would be appropriate for a task force or committee:

1 month: Invite a speaker on home care services to the next meeting.
3 months: Select a method for surveying the availability of home care services in the community.
6 months: Survey the availability of home care services in the community.
1 year: Prepare a report on the availability of home care services in the community.

It is less common and yet probably more important for health care teams to develop a set of objectives because they can very easily become immersed in their daily routines and lose sight of future goals or directions for improvement and change. The following list is a sampling of objectives for health care teams:

Increase the number of completed discharge plans.
Invite people from other agencies to client-oriented conferences.
Plan, organize, and initiate a support group for families of developmentally disabled children.
Design a new crash cart system to decrease current response time.
Revise outpatient chemotherapy procedures to decrease waiting time and increase patient comfort.

IMPLEMENT OBJECTIVES

Once the objectives have been set and a time for accomplishing them has been determined, the next step in MBO is to carry out the work indicated by the objective. The objective itself defines the action needed to fulfill it but it does not tell you how to go about carrying out this action. For example, the health care team objectives about including people from other agencies in client-centered conferences tells you that these people should be invited but it does not tell you exactly which people, how many people, or how to extend the invitation. In other words, the objective serves as a guide telling you what to do but not how to do it.

It was mentioned before that a time line may be a helpful guide in working out a long-term objective. When the objective is a complex one, it may also be necessary to break it down even further into separate steps or components in order to have an adequate guide for your work.

The objectives and time estimates are meant to be flexible guides, not rigid expectations, because circumstances change and external factors can interfere with fulfilling an objective. For example, if you need one more course to complete a clinical specialist program but that course is cancelled at the last minute, you may not be able to fulfill the objective in the previously reasonable estimated time unless you are able to find an alternative way to complete the program requirements.

EVALUATE OUTCOMES

If the objectives were well written, they included a brief description of the expected outcome in measurable or at least observable terms. Evaluation of accomplishments is based on the degree to which this outcome was met. For example, one of the health care team objectives was to increase the number of completed discharge plans. If 25 percent of the discharge plans were completed before setting this goal, then an outcome of 50 percent now completed would indicate that the objective had been met. If the objective had stated that all discharge plans would be complete, then a 50 percent completion rate would not have fulfilled the objective.

The degree to which the individual or work group has control over all the factors that affect the fulfillment of the objective is a source of concern in the evaluation phase of MBO, especially when the objectives are used as the basis for formal evaluation of employees and decisions about raises, promotions, and so forth. This concern about other factors that influence the outcome of work toward an objective has led to a more complicated MBO system in which major obstacles in the way of fulfilling an objective are listed as well as the types of support and resources that are needed from others in order to fulfill the objective.

ADVANTAGES AND DISADVANTAGES

Depending on the way in which it is used, MBO can either be a helpful guide for planning and evaluating the work done in organizations or it can be just another means of control or empty work imposed on employees. Probably the biggest advantage to using MBO is that it directs attention and energy to where it is most needed and in this way helps people to be more productive. Using the objectives as a planning guide helps to organize work and to set priorities. The objectives encourage goal-directed behavior rather than random or unplanned behavior, and help people at every level to avoid getting so caught up in the daily routine that they lose sight of their long-term goals.

When individuals and work groups set their own objectives the result is usually a high level of motivation to complete the objectives. It also encourages self-direction and professional growth. However, when MBO is used in an authoritarian manner, the objectives become another set of orders given to employees and evaluation of the degree to which the objectives were met becomes a source of control over employees. This use of MBO would eliminate one of the primary advantages of the approach.

Another advantage to setting objectives and sharing them with others is that it provides an opportunity for everyone involved in a particular job to know what expectations each one has of oneself and of others. Using these same objectives to evaluate performance helps to eliminate the subjectivity that is so often a problem in evaluation.

MBO is only as good as the objectives that are written and the manner in which they are used. For example, unless the need to allow for changes in circumstances that affect the accomplishment of the objectives is recognized, MBO can be rigid and confining and can result in unfair evaluations. It can also become an empty routine if the objectives are not meaningful or if people do not take them seriously.

SUMMARY

Management by objectives (MBO) is the process of planning and evaluating work on the basis of a set of predetermined objectives. These objectives may be written for an individual, work group, or an entire organization. The purpose of using MBO is to guide and direct the work being done and to provide a clearly specified set of expectations regarding the outcomes of that work. The use of MBO increases motivation and self-direction when employees are involved in setting their own objectives but it can have the opposite effect when they are not.

Budgeting in Organizations

For the majority of people who work in organizations, the process of developing and implementing a budget seems remote from their everyday activities. But the budgeting process actually affects many aspects of everyone's work in the organization including the salaries offered, the number of people available to do the work, and the quality and quantity of needed equipment and supplies available. The following are some examples of important organizational decisions based primarily on budgetary factors:

> A hospital with limited revenues (income) may decide to close its obstetrical unit because it is not usually filled to capacity and is operating at a loss to the hospital.

> A home health agency may choose to serve only private pay and Medicare clients because Medicaid does not pay as much per visit as it costs to make the visit. The agency may also limit the time allowed per visit in order to increase efficiency.

> A nursing home may keep staffing levels to the minimum required by law in order to reduce costs and increase profits.

Each of these decisions affects both the people working in the organization and those who are served by the organization. You can also see that such budgetary decisions reflect the goals and values of the organization.

In some organizations, budgeting is a highly participative process in which input is sought from virtually every individual staff member. However, in the more authoritarian type of organization, even people in lower level management positions are either not included on the process or their input is ignored and the budget is almost literally "delivered from on high" having been written by high-level fiscal administrators based on guidelines from the Board of Trustees and top administrators.[10] Managers and employees who are lower in the hierarchy are expected to accept and abide by the budget as written. This authoritarian style of budgeting predominates in most health care organizations.

If you work in an organization that uses a participative budgeting process, the information in this section about the basic components of a budget, purposes of the process, and the two common approaches to budgeting will help you to participate intelligently in the process. However, if your organization uses the authoritarian style, you will still find the find the information useful in helping you to avoid becoming caught up in the blaming-the-budget games and in recognizing the budget as a reflection of the flow of economic power within the organization. Those who can understand and influence the budget have access to an effective force for or against change in organization.

BUDGETS

Components of a Budget

A budget is a document that describes the amount of money coming into the organization (income) and the amount going out (expenditures). These dollar amounts are very specifically divided among the various subsystems of the organization and also into different categories according to the type of income or expenditure. For example, a hospital budget is broken down into the various services such as nursing, pharmacy, dietary, laboratory, radiology, housekeeping, and so forth. Some of these departments, such as radiology and laboratory, charge separately for their services and can show specific revenues that come into the organization as a result of their work. Unfortunately, in larger health care organizations (except community health agencies) nursing services are usually lumped together with other general charges such as clerical, maintenance, and dietary so that it is more difficult to identify revenue generated by nursing services.[11]

Income and expenditures are broken down into a number of different categories. Income may be divided into categories by its source such as philanthropic contributions, private payment, Medicare, Medicaid, and other third party payers.[12] Within each department, expenditures are usually divided into such categories as employee salaries and benefits, equipment (everything from furniture to monitors and respirators), supplies (from paper to dressings and syringes), staff travel and education, overhead (the cost of operating and maintaining the building), and so on (Fig. 11-1). The categories differ somewhat according to the type of services provided by the organization and the way in which the budgeting process is carried

BUDGET SUMMARY
EXPENSES

Department _____

Month Ending _____

	MONTH			YEAR TO DATE			BUDGETED YEAR
	Actual Expense	Budgeted	(Variance) + or –	Actual Expense	Budgeted	(Variance) + or –	
LABOR							
Salaries	$125,347	$135,000	$ (-9653)	$	$	( )	$
Benefits	$ 11,281	$ 13,250	$ (-1969)	$	$	( )	$
MATERIAL							
Supplies	$ 1,473	$ 1,340	$ (+1133)	$	$	( )	$
Equipment	$ 7,897	$ 11,810	$ (-3913)	$	$	( )	$
OTHER							
Education	$ 330	$ 330	$ (0)	$	$	( )	$
Travel	$ 1,255	$ 650	$ (+ 605)	$	$	( )	$
CAPITAL EXPENDITURES							
OVERHEAD (Fixed Expenses)	$ 29,050	$ 29,050	$ (0)				
TOTALS	$176,633	$191,430	$ (-13,797)	$	$	( )	$

FIGURE 11-1. Example of a monthly budget report of departmental expenses. (Some figures are included for illustrative purposes.)

out in that particular organization. Two common approaches to budgeting are the incremental budget and the zero base budget, which are discussed later in this section.

Purposes

The primary purpose for preparing and using a budget for an organization is to ensure that the organization and its members do not spend more money than can be brought into the organization within a given time period, usually within a specific year. Budgeting has two other important functions—planning and control.[13] The planning function is achieved primarily during the preparation of the budget while control is achieved primarily during implementation.

Budget preparation requires planning in the form of predictions about how much money the organization will bring in in the next year and how much it will need to spend in order to continue operating and to grow. Most health care organizations depend upon an adequate money supply for their continued survival and growth. Those that use their money efficiently and effectively thrive while those that do not may cease to operate entirely.

The people who contribute to the writing of the organization's budget must be able to look ahead and to consider such trends as economic inflation or recession, community needs and demands, availability of qualified staff, changes in health care methodology and technology, and competition from other organizations. Failure to consider any of these factors can result in an inadequate budget and eventual depletion of resources. However, a careful study of previous patterns of income and expenditure combined with an accurate assessment of future trends prepares an organization and its members to meet future demands adequately.

After the budget has been prepared and approved it becomes a means for control. For example, the amount of money budgeted for salaries determines whether or not raises can be given and new staff members hired. Substantial budget cutbacks in salaries could mean that some staff members will lose their jobs due to insufficient funds to pay their salaries. The budget may also specify what type of new staff members may be hired and for what positions. There may, for instance, be money available to hire a much needed clerical person but not to hire an equally needed clinical specialist for a stroke unit. The result of this budgetary decision would be that the paperwork of the unit is done more thoroughly but the rehabilitation of the unit's stroke patients is not, unless the unit's head nurse can obtain permission from the supervisor and administrator to reallocate (move from one category to another) the funds for the head nurse's unit or obtain additional funds by changing the budget. In these and innumerable other ways, the budget controls employee actions.

Another way in which the budget is used to control employees is its use as a measure of performance. For example, a department that manages to stay within its budget may be evaluated as more efficient than the one that did not on the basis of this measure alone. While the ability to stay within a given budget is an appropriate measure of a department's function, some problems arise if this measure is used exclusively or is overemphasized. A number of factors other than effective management can affect a department's expenditures or costs. For example, an increase in the severity and complexity of disabilities of the patients comprising the caseload of a home health agency will affect the services, equipment, and supplies needed by each patient as well as the time required to complete each home visit. Under these circumstances, an increase in cost per visit cannot be blamed on the inefficiency of the community health nurses or their supervisor.

Another problem arising from overemphasis on this measure of performance is the response of the people being evaluated. Supervisors and administrators whose effectiveness is being measured by their ability to stay within their budgets will try to pad their budgets in order to allow for unexpected expenses and also may make decisions that sacrifice quality of care for apparent efficiency of operation.

Blaming the Budget

The budget itself is just a document, a piece of paper listing numerous figures distributed according to a series of decisions made by designated people within the organization. But once it is completed, the budget frequently has a great deal of power ascribed to it.[10] This is the game of *blaming the budget*, in which power and authority are ascribed to the budget itself rather than to the people in positions of power and authority in the organization who have created the budget and subsequently enforce adherence to it.

The budget is frequently blamed or used as an excuse for unpopular decisions. For example, you might be told that "the budget won't allow us to hire more nurses" or that "the budget says we cannot modernize the nursery this year." While it is certainly true that some figures in the budget such as reimbursement levels and the cost of new equipment are not within the control of administration, much of the allocation of funds to one department or the other within the organization certainly is, although you would not think so when you hear administrators blaming the budget.

INCREMENTAL BUDGETING

Incremental budgeting is the traditional process in which budgets, divided into components similar to the ones previously described, are prepared every year on the basis of what was spent the year before. The budgeting process begins with an analysis of the income and expenses of the previous year with special attention given to departments and categories that were substantially overbudgeted or underbudgeted and the reasons for these deviations from the previous budget. These reasons are taken into consideration in projecting the next year's income and expenses. Budgeting projections are also based upon plans to expand or limit services, add new staff, renovate or add new space, begin new projects, and raise salaries and benefits for employees. Any of these actions requires a change in the budget, usually an increase, which is the reason why this type of budget is called an incremental budget.

After this analysis of the organization's future goals and activities is done, dollar figures are assigned to all departments and categories on both the income and expenditure sides of the budget. Individual departments may be given some flexibility in allocating funds to various categories or may be restricted to using funds only as designated in the budget. The complete budget for the entire organization is a compilation of all sources of income and expenses for every subsystem and may be a very complex document. The formulas used to estimate such items as overhead costs may not be readily comprehensible unless you obtain an explanation from the organization's fiscal officers or budget committee. For the organization as a whole, the income or credit side of the budget is expected to equal the expense or debit side of the budget; although this same balancing of the budget is generally not required of each separate department within the health care organization.

Once the budget is completed and approved, anyone in a supervisory or administrative position who has authority to spend money is expected to work within the guidelines set by the budget. The degree to which this is done is usually monitored on a monthly or quarterly basis and explanations are required when any substantial deviations occur. Adjustments in the budget can be made during the year but requests for these changes generally meet resistance.

ZERO BASE BUDGETING

Zero base budgeting is a more complex and usually more participative process than incremental budgeting. It is based upon the idea that no expense should be assumed to be absolutely necessary. The result is that every expenditure must be justified as essential to the function of the organization, at least in theory. The zero base budget begins each year with a blank slate rather than building upon the previous year's budget.

The use of the decision package[14] is the core of the zero base budgeting process and the feature that distinguishes it from the traditional incremental process. Decision packages consist of several basic elements including a listing of all current and proposed objectives or activities of a given team, department, or unit; alternative ways of carrying out these activities and the different cost for each alternative; the advantages of continuing the activity; and the consequences of discontinuing the activity. The following is a simplified example of a decision package (without cost figures) for an occupational health setting:

Objective:	Provide CPR (cardiopulmonary resuscitation) instruction for all employees.
Advantages:	Every employee will be prepared to respond immediately to an emergency situation.
	May save an employee's life and prevent lawsuits.
	Additional benefit to employees.
	Good public relations—a community service.
Disadvantages:	Time away from work required for CPR classes.
	Cost of part-time CPR instructor.

Alternative Approach # 1:	Require each employee to acquire CPR instruction from community organization.
Major Advantage:	No cost to this organization.
Major Disadvantage:	Employee resistance and resentment over use of off-work time.
Alternative Approach # 2:	Do not require CPR instruction.
Major Advantage:	No cost, no resistance, or resentment.
Major Disadvantage:	Potential avoidable loss of employee life and lawsuit vulnerability.

The listed activities are then ranked from the most essential ones required to maintain minimal operation of the team, unit, or department to those that are nonessential but desirable if sufficient money is available to support them.

The zero base budgeting process begins with the identification of individuals who will be assigned to the task of developing these decision packages. General information about projected trends and resources for the coming year and some direction for completing the decision packages is usually provided. Head nurses, coordinators, and supervisors are frequently asked to participate in this process and may seek the assistance of their staff in the gathering of information and prioritization of needs. The packages are then compiled for the entire organization and further prioritizing is done on the basis of organizational goals and resources. The zero base budget is then implemented in much the same way as the incremental budget.

In comparison with incremental budgeting, zero base budgeting demands more thought and precision in planning future activities. It also encourages a more participative approach because information from people at all levels is needed to adequately analyze and prioritize the activities of each team, unit, or department within the organization. The requirement of reducing the budget to the most essential elements helps to eliminate padding of the budget and facilitates decisions on which projects or activities to add and which to delete. However, zero base budgeting is also far more work and requires more time to complete than the incremental process. Its major purpose is to improve planning but it may also help to reduce costs, rationalize expenditures, and increase employee understanding and support of budgetary goals.

SUMMARY

A budget is the detailed documentation of an organization's income and expenditures. Its purposes are monitoring the flow of money in and out of the organization, planning and control, including the measurement of performance. The budgetary process may be participative or authoritarian. It begins with an analysis of the organization's goals and resources, followed by preparation, approval, and implementation of the budget. An incremental budget is developed from prior budgets while a zero base budget is based on a set of prioritized decision packages.

Formal Evaluation Procedures*

Formal evaluation is the planned process of giving and receiving feedback that occurs within most organizations. Formal evaluations are much less frequent than the informal kind but they are usually more structured and employee participation in these procedures is usually required by the organization.

Formal evaluation begins with the setting of standards against which the individual or group will be judged. These standards should be objective, in written form, and communicated in advance to those who will be evaluated.

PARTICIPATION IN FORMAL EVALUATION

As a leader, you are likely to be involved in formal evaluation procedures in several different ways. Nurses should be involved in the setting of standards for the evaluation of nursing care and they should also be well represented on any committee or task force involved in designing an overall quality assurance program in any health care organization. Nurses are often involved in the gathering of data and should have input into the analysis of the data. For these roles, you need to know what aspects of care to measure, how to determine standards, and how to use them.

You may also be involved in evaluating staff members. To do this effectively, you need to know the purposes of the evaluation, how to develop and use standards, and how to write objectives. Even more important is the ability to be objective in your evaluation and to use communication skills effectively in sharing the evaluation with the person or group that was evaluated. You can see that you need to have learned leadership well to be an effective evaluator. This is so important that many organizations hold workshops on evaluation and schedule skill-training sessions for people who do performance appraisals (employee evaluations).

As an employee, you will also be the subject of evaluation procedures. When this is the case, you still need to know what constitutes an objective evaluation and how to communicate effectively. You also need to know what you can reasonably expect from your employer.

Although formal evaluation has some of the same purposes as informal evaluation, it also has some additional purposes, which will be mentioned here. The three aspects of health care—structure, process, and outcome—that need to be included in a comprehensive evaluation will be explained and then the most common types of formal evaluations found in health care organizations will be discussed including audits, utilization review, performance appraisal, peer review, and quality assurance programs.

PURPOSES

Most of the purposes of informal evaluation described in Chapter 8 (providing recognition, increasing self-awareness, clarifying expectations, and promoting

---

*Written with P. George.

change and growth) also apply to formal evaluation. Formal evaluation also has some additional purposes that are related to the function of the organization, to the regulatory agencies that mandate the procedures, and to the professions that are involved in the procedures. These purposes include accountability, administrative intervention, developing reward systems, identification of educational needs, and development of a data base. Each of these purposes is briefly discussed below.

Accountability

Evaluation is an important demonstration of both the individual's and the health care organization's sense of responsibility for the services provided. It is a demonstration to the public that efforts are being made to provide quality care.

Individual health care professionals are accountable for the care they give. Participation in evaluation procedures in which the caregiver is judged against an accepted standard is one way to achieve accountability.

Entire health care organizations should also be accountable for the health care that they offer to consumers. The development and implementation of comprehensive quality assurance programs is one way for organizations to achieve accountability. Not every organization has been willing to do this but pressure from the state and national levels has helped promote the development of organizational accountability.

Administrative Intervention

Evaluation that is taken seriously by the administrators of an organization can be a stimulus for change in that organization by documenting success or failure in meeting objectives and identifying specific obstacles in the way of achieving these objectives.

Regular evaluation of the individual practitioner, entire teams or departments, programs, and the institution as a whole can help to identify weaknesses and problems before they become major obstacles to achieving the desired objectives. If these evaluations are based on the goals and standards of the organization, they can answer such questions as the following:

Are expected objectives being achieved?
Are patients' needs being met?
Are nurses teaching effectively?
Is the program/institution serving the community's needs?
Are services accessible to the community?

Since the leadership and administration of a program can be crucial to its effectiveness, they should also be evaluated. Evaluations should consider such factors as leadership styles, management policies, operating procedures, and staffing patterns. Factors that are external to the organization such as funding sources, department regulations, and reimbursement requirements may also need to be considered in evaluating the effectiveness of an organization.[15]

Rewards

Formal evaluations can serve as the basis upon which employees are given raises and promotions as rewards for satisfactory or better performance. They are also a way to provide reinforcement for a job well done.

An objective, comprehensive evaluation of an employee's work (often called a performance appraisal) can identify the person's potential growth. It can also help in the identification of experiences that would contribute to that person's professional growth and development.

Formal evaluation procedures point out deficiencies in a person's work and help in the identification of ways to improve that person's performance. Formal evaluation may also be the basis for termination of employment when consistently poor appraisals follow substantial efforts to remedy the problem.

Identify Educational Needs

This purpose is related to several of the others already discussed. The data resulting from formal evaluation procedures can be used to analyze the continuing educational needs of the people who work in that organization. For example, the analysis could point out a specific need such as inconsistency in diabetic teaching or more general educational needs of the staff such as exploring new approaches to practice or improving leadership skills.

Data Base

Although it is not usually the main purpose for doing formal evaluations, the information collected and recorded during evaluation procedures can serve as a valuable data base for the analysis of health care procedures.

There are many problems in health care for which complete solutions have not been found. For example, many diabetic patients do not follow their diets, many alcoholic patients are not sufficiently motivated to stop drinking, and too many hemiplegic patients are not restored to maximum function. The chances of finding a way to achieve better results are improved if we look for solutions in a number of places including the data from evaluation procedures. Evaluation seeks to answer at the specific, individual level the same questions that research addresses in a broad, general way; in this instance, "What are effective helping behaviors?"

STRUCTURE, PROCESS, AND OUTCOME

There are three different aspects of health care that can be evaluated: the structure in which the care is given, the process of giving that care, and the outcome of that care. To be comprehensive, an evaluation program must include all three aspects of health care.[16-18]

Structure

Structure refers to the *setting* in which the care is given and the *resources* that are available. It is the easiest of the three aspects to measure and yet is still overlooked in some evaluation procedures. The following is a list of some of the structural aspects of a health care organization that can be included in a formal evaluation:

1. *Facilities:* comfort, convenience of layout, accessibility of support services, and safety.
2. *Equipment:* adequate supply, state of repair, up to date, and staff ability to use it.
3. *Staff:* credentials, absenteeism, turnover rate, and staff-patient ratios.
4. *Finances:* salaries, adequacy, and sources.

None of these structural factors alone can guarantee that good care will be given but they are factors that make good care more likely to occur. High nurse-patient ratios and low staff absenteeism rates, for example, are structural factors that are associated with quality nursing care.[19]

The most common pitfall in evaluating structural factors is to neglect the other two aspects (process and outcome). The following is an example that illustrates the problems that occur when evaluating only structure:

> One hospital measured the quality of nursing care given in its eight bed critical care unit by comparing its staffing ratio with the standard ratio of one nurse to two patients. The inadequacy of this structural measure became apparent during a period when the unit had six (out of a total of eight) patients who each required the care of one nurse. Under the standard that was set, there were four nurses on duty, which created a severe staff shortage because seven nurses were actually needed to provide adequate care.

Process

Process refers to the *actual activities* carried out by the health caregivers. It can include leadership skills and writing care plans as well as actual patient/client interventions. It also includes psychosocial interventions such as teaching and counseling as well as physical care measures.

There are several ways to collect process data. The most direct way is by observation of caregiving activities. Another is self-report of the caregiver. A third source of data is the chart or record that is kept (the use of this source is called an audit).

Whichever source of data is used, some set of objectives is needed as a standard with which to compare the activities. This set of objectives can be very specific such as listing all the steps in a catheterization procedure or it can be a very general list of objectives such as ''offer information on breastfeeding to all expectant parents'' or ''conduct weekly staff meetings.''

Outcome

Outcome refers to the *results* of the activities (or process) in which the health caregivers have been involved. Outcome measures evaluate the effectiveness of these activities by answering such questions as: Did the patient recover? Is the family more independent now? Has team functioning improved?

These questions are very general and reflect overall goals of health caregivers and the organizations in which they work. The outcome questions asked during an actual evaluation should be far more specific and should measure observable behavior such as the following:

Patient:	Good appetite.
	No elevated temperature.
	Absence of infections.
Family:	Increased time between visits to the emergency room.
	Applied for food stamps.
Team:	Decisions reached by consensus.
	Participation in discussion by all team members.

You can see that some of these outcomes, such as temperature or time between visits, are easier to measure than other equally important outcomes, such as increased satisfaction or changes in attitude. While these less tangible outcomes can't be measured as precisely, it is still important to include them because omitting them may imply that they are not important outcomes.[20]

A major problem in using outcome measures in evaluation is that outcomes are influenced by many factors, not by just one factor or by just one person. Here is an example that illustrates how many factors affect the outcome:

The outcome of patient teaching done by a nurse on a home visit is affected by the patient's interest and ability to learn, the quality of the teaching materials, the presence or absence of family support, the information given by other caregivers (which may conflict), and by the environment in which the teaching is done. If the teaching is successful, can the nurse be given full credit for the success? If it is not successful, who has failed?

You can see that it would be necessary to evaluate at least the process as well as the outcome in order to determine why an intervention such as patient teaching succeeds or fails. A comprehensive evaluation would include all three aspects: structure, process, and outcome.

STANDARDS

Although standards have been mentioned already, they are such an important influence on the quality of an evaluation procedure that the information is restated here.

An evaluation standard is a criterion for judging the work of an individual, team, or organization. It supplies a basis for comparison. The following are examples of standards that have been mentioned before in this chapter:

Structural Standard   A ratio of one nurse to two patients in the critical care unit is maintained at all times.
Process Standard: Every expectant parent is offered information on breastfeeding.
Outcome Standard: All families who qualify will have applied for food stamps before discharge.

The major reason for setting standards is to increase objectivity by defining as clearly as possible what is acceptable and what is not acceptable. Without these standards, the judgments that take place in the evaluation process can be very subjective and susceptible to the whims of the evaluator.

A second function of these standards is to communicate clearly to everyone involved with the organization (including staff, administrators, consumers, accreditors, and regulators), what quality of service is expected in that organization. This function can only be carried out if the standards are available to all these people.

The standards and measurements used for evaluating performance may vary with the institution, the purpose of the evaluation, and the evaluator. They can become outdated and should be reviewed regularly. Outdated standards can perpetuate the use of ineffective practices.

TYPES OF EVALUATION PROCEDURES

Some of the most common formal evaluation programs in health care organizations are utilization review, audit, performance appraisal, peer review, and quality assurance. Quality assurance is the broadest of these programs and will be discussed last.

Utilization Review

Utilization review was originally mandated by the Federal Government as a quality care control measure tied to Medicare reimbursement. Basically, a utilization review asks the question "Does this patient have to be here?" and then, if the physician has shown in the record why the patient does have to be here, the utilization review answers "OK, but only for this many days." Utilization review is done in any health care agency where care is reimbursed by Medicare including hospitals, health departments, and any other community or private agency that has an agreement to accept Medicare payment in place of private payment.

The utilization review process has been increasingly formalized over the years to ensure that reimbursements are not being made for trivial or unjustified expenses. For example, patients must have acceptable diagnoses and the length of their hospital stays must conform to the guidelines set for that particular diagnosis. The following is an example of these guidelines:

A 65-year-old man who is admitted to the hospital with a diagnosis of appendicitis and has an appendectomy would be expected to be discharged by the sixth postoperative day.

Complications that require further treatment and a longer stay must be justified. For example, if the 65-year-old man could not be discharged by the sixth day, the physician would have to record the development and treatment of the new problem such as atelectasis, wound infection, thrombophlebitis, or urinary tract infection. It would not be acceptable to simply say that the patient cannot go home yet because he is too weak or there is nobody at home to take care of him.

The utilization review process has generated a new department within the hospital for documenting patients' legitimate needs for hospital care and treatment. The person who performs the mechanics of the utilization review is paid by Federal money if the hospital is in compliance with the regulations. If not, that money goes to pay the regional surveyor, who not only does surveillance but also assists organizations in setting up their own procedures according to guidelines. The findings are reviewed on a regular basis by a committee of physicians, nurses, and other caregivers called the Professional Standards Review Organization (known as PSROs). This review provides an opportunity for health care professionals to evaluate care not only for conformity to utilization review standards but also to acceptable practice standards.

Health care organizations that do not do utilization review or do it poorly, risk losing reimbursement (insurance payments) for the care they give to Medicare patients. By requiring hospitals to set standards in order to receive reimbursement, utilization review is a potential force for the improvement of care.

Audits

Audits are surveys of records done to evaluate both the care given and the outcomes of that care. Audit may be done *concurrently,* which is while the patient is receiving care, or *retrospectively,* which is some time after the patient has been discharged.[21]

In hospitals, audits are often done by people in the Medical Records Department who have ready access to patient records. They may also develop a coding and filing system that makes it easier to pull out records for the patients who are on a particular service unit, have a particular diagnosis, or were discharged within a certain time period.

The standards of care and expected outcomes for a nursing audit are prepared by the nursing staff. The data recorded by the auditors is then examined by a nursing audit committee or by the staff of a particular service area so that the evaluation can be done and the results can be communicated to the entire staff involved. Sometimes nurses themselves conduct the entire audit.

No matter who retrieves the information from the chart, the audit of the record is based on previously developed standards of care for particular health care problems. For example, the standards of care (evaluating process) for a diabetic patient at home might include the following:

1. Teach and observe patient drawing up insulin accurately and self-administering correctly.
2. Teach patient importance of skin and foot care and what constitutes such care.
3. Teach patient to recognize and respond appropriately to episodes of hypoglycemia and hyperglycemia.

A concurrent or retrospective audit would look for documentation of these nursing behaviors in the chart.

Documented outcomes can also be compared to the expected (standard) outcomes of care. The following list gives some examples of the outcomes of teaching a diabetic patient, which could be found in a chart audit:

1. Patient was observed drawing up insulin accurately and injecting correctly, rotating sites.
2. Patient states importance of good foot and skin care, but refused to inspect feet daily, answered the door barefoot, and stated it was too much trouble to put shoes on all the time.
3. Patient states signs of hypoglycemia and hyperglycemia and appropriate intervention. Keeps orange juice on hand.

The outcomes listed above are typical in the sense that while two standards were met, one was not completely met.

One of the problems with audit, especially in the early stages of its use in quality assurance, is that it only gives information about what is actually documented in the record. For example, if the auditor is looking for evidence of patient teaching, the failure to find evidence of that care and its outcome *could* mean that what actually happened was not documented. If so, audit may point up a need for staff inservice about documentation. Audits can serve several different purposes. Feedback to the staff about the results of audit is a crucial part of the audit process because it reinforces individual accountability for the care given, the outcomes achieved, and proper documentation of both, as well as giving each practitioner information that may be useful in self-evaluation.

Concurrent audits provide immediate feedback to caregivers about adequacy of care while there is an opportunity to make immediate corrections and improvements that will benefit the patient. Information from audits can be used in appraising an employee's performance.

The effectiveness of inservice education programs can also be evaluated through a chart audit. For example, an audit of improvements in the self-care abilities of diabetic patients would look for an increase in the number who are able to give their own insulin at the time of discharge after an inservice program on diabetic teaching was given.

Performance Appraisal

Performance appraisal is the term generally used to describe the evaluation of an employee. The employee's behavior is compared with a standard describing how the employee is expected to perform. The standards are often written in the form of objectives. Actual performance is evaluated, not good intentions.

In the ideal situation, a performance appraisal begins when the employee is hired. Based on the job description, the employee and employer or supervisor agree on the standard of performance and write a set of objectives that they feel the employee can reasonably accomplish within a given period of time. The objectives should be written at a level of performance that demonstrates that some learning, attainment or refinement of a skill, or advancement toward some long-range objective has taken place. The following are examples of objectives that could be set for a patient educator to accomplish in six months:

> Conduct a survey of patient use and response to the closed circuit television patient education programs.
> Include staff in development of a proposal for a cardiac rehabilitation program.
> Continue to conduct diet and exercise classes for the community.
> Implement proposed series of Stop Smoking classes.

Six months later, at the previously agreed time, the employee and supervisor sit down again and evaluate the employee's performance in comparison with the previously set goals (Fig. 11-2). The evaluation should be based on both the employee's own assessment and the supervisor's observation of specific behaviors, but this is not always done. New objectives and plans for achieving them may be agreed on at the time of the appraisal or at a separate meeting.[22] The new objectives will be used to evaluate the employee's performance at the next evaluation. A copy of the performance appraisal and the projected goals must be available to the employee for periodic checks on the employee's progress.

It is important for the employee and the person doing the evaluating to set aside adequate time for the feedback and goal-setting processes. Each should come to this session with data already collected for use at this session. The variety of data brought to an evaluation session should include a self-evaluation by the employee and observations by the evaluator of the employee's activities and outcomes. Data may also be obtained from peers and patients or clients. Some organizations use surveys for getting this information from patients.

The guidelines for providing informal evaluative feedback discussed in Chapter 8 apply to the conduct of performance appraisals. Performance appraisals are not as frequent or immediate as informal feedback but should be just as objective, private, nonthreatening, and skillfully communicated.

Many organizations, unfortunately, have employee evaluation procedures that are far from the ideal. Their procedures may be inconsistent, subjective, and even unknown to the employee in some cases. The following is a list of standards for a fair and objective employee evaluation procedure you may want to use to judge your employer's procedures:

1. Standards are clear, objective, and known in advance.
2. Criteria for pay raises and promotions are clearly spelled out and uniformly applied.

3. Conditions under which employment may be terminated are known.
4. Appraisals are part of the employee's permanent record and have space for employee comments.
5. Employees may inspect their own personnel file.
6. Employees may request and be given a reasonable explanation of any rating and may appeal the rating if they do not agree with it.
7. Employees are given a reasonable amount of time to correct any serious deficiencies before other action is taken.

FIGURE 11-2. Formal evaluation. During a formal evaluation, the employee and the supervisor sit down together and evaluate the employee's performance in comparison with previously set goals. Performance appraisals should be objective, private, constructive, and skillfully communicated.

Peer Review

Peer review is the evaluation of an individual's practice by colleagues (known as peers) who have similar education, experience, and occupational status. Its purpose is to provide the individual with feedback from those who are best acquainted with the requirements and demands of that particular position. Peer review is usually concerned with both the process and outcomes of practice.[23-24]

Whenever peers meet to audit records or otherwise evaluate the quality of care they have given, they are actually engaging in a kind of peer review. However, formal peer review programs are often one of the last formal evaluation procedures to be implemented in a health care organization.

On an informal basis, professionals frequently observe and judge their colleagues' performance. But many people feel uncomfortable about telling others what they think of their performance and so the evaluations made are not shared with the individual practitioner as often as they could be.

Formal peer review begins with precisely defining the scope of professional practice and setting standards for quality care. Observations of performance are made by one or more peers, compared with previously set standards and then shared with the person being reviewed. The reviewer is expected to look for those behaviors indicated by the standards and to avoid making judgments based on personal standards or subjective feelings.

There are a number of possible variations in the peer review process. For example, the observations may be shared only with the person being reviewed or with the person's supervisor or with a review committee. The evaluation report may be written by the reviewer or it may come from the review committee. However, the use of a committee defeats the purpose of peer review if the committee members are not truly peers of the individual being reviewed.

Peer review reinforces good performance and stimulates health care professionals to scrutinize their own practice and continue their learning in order to maintain or improve their level of practice. Although peer review is often perceived as threatening when it is introduced, it can be a rewarding experience for those involved when it is conducted according to the guidelines for providing objective, nonthreatening, evaluative feedback.

Quality Assurance

Quality assurance is a broad term that encompasses all the evaluation procedures mentioned here and some others as well. A comprehensive quality assurance program would consider all aspects of the entire organization's structure, processes, and outcomes. Such a program can include not only utilization review and performance appraisals but also evaluation of the policies and regulations of the organization, management styles, comprehensiveness of special services offered, and their ability to meet the needs of the community serviced, audits of all records to evaluate the quality of care, and a survey of such structural factors as the number of people served and the accessibility of services.

The quality and comprehensiveness of an organization's quality assurance program is an indication of that organization's commitment to providing the highest quality services possible.

SUMMARY

Formal evaluation procedures in organizations serve as a source of data, a demonstration of accountability, an identification of educational needs, and as the basis for the reward system and for administrative intervention. A comprehensive evaluation program considers structure, process, and outcome data and should be based on objective standards. Quality assurance programs include utilization review, audits, peer review, performance appraisals, and other procedures designed to evaluate the whole organization in terms of its effectiveness in the delivery of health care services.

Labor Relations

This section is concerned with labor relations, another important aspect of working in organizations. More specifically, the issues involved in joining a labor organization are discussed and the process of organizing a bargaining unit, negotiating a contract, and administering the contract are described. The section begins with an introduction to collective bargaining including an explanation of commonly used terms, consideration of its purposes, and some of the arguments for and against it that have been raised by people in the health care professions.[25-27]

COLLECTIVE BARGAINING

Explanation

Collective bargaining is the joining together of employees for the purpose of increasing their ability to influence their employer and improve working conditions. In labor relations parlance, the employer is often referred to as managment and the employees are referred to as labor, even if they are professionals.

Anyone involved in the hiring, firing, disciplining, and evaluating of employees or in scheduling the work of employees is considered part of management and cannot be included in a collective bargaining unit. People in management can form their own groups but are not protected by the collective bargaining laws discussed here and are often too small a number in one orgainzation to benefit from the same kind of collective bargaining. This definition of management includes directors of nursing service, assistant directors, and supervisors but usually not head nurses.

The National Labor Relations Act and its amendments are the primary laws that protect an employee's right to engage in collective bargaining. This act also established the National Labor Relations Board (NLRB), which has two major functions. The first is to ensure that employees are able to freely choose whether or not they want to be represented by a particular bargaining agent. For nurses, this bargaining agent is usually the professional association or an affiliate of a national labor union. The second function of the NLRB is to prevent or remedy any violations of labor law. These violations are usually called unfair labor practices.

Nonprofit health care organizations, including hospitals, nursing homes, larger visiting nurse associations, clinics, and other health care centers, have only been subject to these laws since 1974, making them relative newcomers to collective bargaining. Special rules designed to safeguard the welfare of patients apply to health care organizations. Proprietary organizations are also covered by these laws but government operated health care facilities are subject to an entirely different set of rules that generally afford less protection of the employees' collective bargaining rights.

Purposes

The fundamental purpose of bargaining collectively is to equalize the power distribution between labor and managment. Collective bargaining is a power strategy based on the principle that there is increased strength in numbers. An individual employee who attempts to bargain with an employer is far more vulnerable to potential threats or reprisals from the employer that is an entire group of employees. As with other power strategies, collective bargaining is usually employed when other efforts to get fair treatment or to bring about change have failed.

Basic economic issues such as salaries are usually the first concern of people joining a collective bargaining unit. Despite the demand for nurses and even some serious shortages of nurses, hospitals have kept their wages artificially low, often by setting up agreements with other area institutions to keep wages down. In fact, some nurses have found that other employees of the same organization who have less responsibility are making equal or better salaries. Other economic concerns covered by collective bargaining include shift differentials, overtime pay, holidays, personal days, the length of the work day, sick leave, maternity and paternity leaves, payment for uniforms, lunch and rest periods (breaks), health insurance, pension plans, and severance pay. Also of concern are staffing and scheduling matters such as days off, rotating shifts, working on call, and adequate staff levels. Promotion policies, transfers, layoffs, seniority rights, and the posting of job openings are also bargainable.

Collective bargaining also deals with areas in which management has been or is likely to be arbitrary or unfair. Arbitrary treatment can be anything from being the only one who has to work three weekends in a row to being passed over for a promotion without explanation to being fired because a physician thought your assertive protection of a patient's rights was "insubordinate." Perhaps the most important protection against this arbitrary treatment is the inclusion of a grievance procedure in the collective bargaining agreement that enables an employee to bring a complaint to management without having to fear later reprisals for assertiveness. The way in which grievance procedures are used will be discussed later in this section.

Research Example 11-1. Nurses' Purposes and Management's Perceptions in Collective Bargaining

Are nurses primarily concerned with economic issues or with professional issues when they bargain collectively? Do managers know what issues are actually important to their staff members?

Bloom, Parlette, and O'Reilly[28] interviewed 78 public health and registered nurses and 11 supervisory nurses from three large community health care agencies in California for this study (two of the agencies had recently settled work stoppages). These nurses had worked an average of 7.5 years for the county and all county employees were represented by an international labor union. The nurses were asked to rate the importance of 17 different issues on a four point scale from not a factor at all to a major factor in the decision to strike. Ten top management people, including the Director of Nursing, three Assistant Directors of Nursing, the Director of Public Health, and the County Manager were also asked to rate the same 17 issues.

Very little relationship was found between the ratings of the nurses and people in management over what issues were important (the correlation was 17). The nurses considered support for nurses in their unit, difficulty communicating with management, management's authoritatian behavior, a belief in collective bargaining as a way to balance the power between management and employees, and the need for more nursing positions (the only economic issue) to be most important. In contrast, the people in top management positions thought that the most important factors in the strike decision were a pay increase, allowing two nurses to share a fulltime position, a union attempt to gain power, and pressure from other nurses to go on strike. None of the four issues rated important by management were actually important to the nurses.

The researchers ask why people in management fail to use principles of effective communication and the basic concepts of the well-known motivational theories when dealing with collective bargaining. They concluded that management thought that the industrial type of bargaining issues such as wages and job security were the critical issues, but that the nurses were actually more concerned about professional issues, especially with improving communication with management and increased participation in organizational decision-making.

Proponents of collective bargaining also believe that it is one means by which nurses can increase and maintain control over their practice. For example, some nurses' bargaining units have succeeded in putting the entire American Nurses Association Code of Ethics into the contractual aggreement with their employers. Adequate staffing, acceptable standards of care, and other quality of care issues and standards can also be negotiated with employers. Research Example 11-1 describes some sources of dissatisfaction experienced by hospital employees.

Professional and Ethical Issues

Most objections to collective bargaining center around convictions that it is an unprofessional activity, that it is damaging to the profession, and that some activities involved are unethical.

Many people associate unions with truck drivers and factory workers and feel that it is unprofessional for health care professionals to engage in the same type of activity. They feel that collective bargaining activities do not fit the image of the nurse as a professional and that other means should be found for achieving the goals of collective bargaining. Yet, many professionals such as pharmacists, engineers, college professors, and even some employed physicians are members of unions. The NLRB defines nurses as professionals because their work requires advanced specialized training and making critical judgments and the NLRB allows both nurses and physicians to have separate bargaining units because of their unique character-istics. A favorite response of union organizers to the argument that collective bargaining is unprofessional is that accepting low salaries and poor working condi-tions is also unprofessional. Another response, from nurses who support collective bargaining is that control over practice is the essence of professionalism.[30]

Most health care professionals have a strong set of values emphasizing the priority of the patient's or client's health and welfare. The safety of their patients takes precedence over their own personal gain and needs. These values conflict with some of the strategies used in collective bargaining, especially with any type of work slowdown or stoppage. Many health care professionals feel that they could not abandon their patients during a strike under any circumstances.

The opposing argument is that the poor and sometimes intolerable conditions under which many nurses work are also a threat to patients' safety and that the threat of a strike is needed to improve these conditions. It can also be pointed out that the law requires giving 10 days notice before striking and has other provisions that reduce the possibility of a strike in a health care organization. The 10-day strike notice allows time for management to make preparations for the patients' safety such as reducing elective surgeries and admissions or transferring patients to other facilities.

When the American Nurses Association had a no strike policy (prior to 1968), nurses who tried to bargain collectively with their employers found that they had little or no success. Their employers ignored them, refused to bargain, or gave them platitudes about how important they were and then raised other people's salaries faster than the nurses' salaries were raised. Without the clout of a potential strike, nurses could not get their employers to listen to them or to respond to their requests.

A third serious objection to collective bargaining is its potentially divisive effect on the profession. State nurses associations have acted as bargaining agents for many groups of nurses, yet many supervisors and directors of nursing are members of these associations and many hold offices at both the state and national levels. For these management nurses, there is a potential conflict of interest in being a member of an association that supports strikes, perhaps even a strike against their own institutions. On the other hand, there is also a potential legal conflict of having management people attempting to influence the association in its function as a labor organization.

These conflicts have evoked strong emotions and led to many debates about the role of the association, even threatening to split it into management and nonmanagement factions. Some nurse administrators feel torn between representing management and supporting their own professional association. Others feel angry and bitter about the collective bargaining efforts of their fellow nurses. Collective bargaining does draw a clear line between management and labor and tends to make their relationship an adversarial one. But it also has enabled staff nurses to bring about some of the same changes that nursing administrators have been trying unsuccessfully to implement through persuasive means.

Finally, some people (especially administrators) say that collective bargaining is unnecessary, that management and labor can work together better without the interference of a third party. In some instances this is true. An organization with a proactive management that recognizes employee concerns and acts quickly to resolve them, creates an open, participative, growth promoting work environment, and one that treats employees fairly and pays substantial wages will probably not have to deal with a union. But the majority of organizations are far from this ideal. In fact, some union representatives will admit that management's failure to do these things is the union's best weapon when organizing. Research Example 11-2 describes some of the reasons that nurses engage in collective bargaining.

ORGANIZING

In this first phase of the collective bargaining process, a labor organization is formed and that organization seeks recognition as the employees' bargaining agent. It is possible to form an independent group for the purposes of bargaining with your employer and be protected by the same laws but the professional association and unions have already established themselves as bargaining agents and have developed expertise on the applicable laws and in the multiple strategies needed to bargain effectively with management. Health care organizations frequently hire consultants to help them fight unionization and sometimes pool their resources with other area institutions in order to improve their own expertise and bargaining position. Their access to this expertise would put an independent group at a disadvantage.

Organizing Council

The movement toward unionization begins when a group of interested employees forms an informal organizing council. This council becomes the core group that gets other nurses interested and involved in joining a union by pointing out the need for one. The need is usually based on a combination of some or all of the items listed under the purposes of collective bargaining (economic, scheduling, staffing, equitable treatment, and quality of care issues) in which management failed to meet the needs of the employees. The council can ask for assistance from the professional association or a union or it can attempt to form an independent bargaining unit. Sometimes, the initiative to organize comes from a union or competing unions but the core group of committed employees is essential to the success of an organizing effort.

Research Example 11-2. Hospital Employees' Opinions About Their Work

What do hospital employees like and dislike about their jobs? Holloway [29] reported the results of a survey of the attitudes of 21,748 employees of 29 voluntary (nonprofit) community hospitals. These hospitals were located in New England, California, and the Midwest and Holloway points out that, although the sample was large, it was not a random sample and therefore may not be representative of all hospital employees in the U.S. The size of the hospital had no relation to employee satisfaction with the work environment in this sample.

Employees were asked to rate their satisfaction with many different aspects of the work environment. Their responses were reported in terms of percents of the sample that were satisfied with each factor. Some examples from the different categories:

Work Productivity: 55 percent rated the amount of job pressure as unsatisfactory.

Coordination of Work: 55 percent rated teamwork satisfactory, 42 percent rated interdepartmental cooperation as satisfactory.

Administrative Procedures: 75 percent rated the procedures fair but only 55 percent rated the handling of complaints as satisfactory.

Salary and Benefits: these were found generally satisfactory but only 40 percent thought the promotion incentives were satisfactory.

Communications: most employees rated their hospitals highly on communication of hospital policies and fire and disaster procedures. However, only 30 percent rated communication between departments and grievance procedures as satisfactory.

Organizational Orientation: again grievance procedures were the lowest rated factor (20 percent found them satisfactory). First impressions of the institution, cleanliness, and job security were rated high by 80 percent of the sample.

Staff Relationships: acceptance of new staff was highly rated (80 percent) but only 20 percent were satisfied with physician-staff relationships.

Job Enrichment: education and training were rated satisfactory by 60 percent, 65 percent thought that good use was made of their talents.

Staff Appraisal and Development: career planning and the availability of career ladders for advancement within the organization were not highly rated (35 percent and 40 percent respectively), nor was the amount of praise given (40 percent). The fairness of the appraisals and resultant corrective actions taken were rated higher—65 percent found them satisfactory.

Even the survey itself was rated: 75 percent of those responding trusted that the results would be kept anonymous.

On the basis of these findings, grievance procedures, lack of administrative response to complaints, and lack of mutual respect among managers, professionals, and other staff seemed to be of major concern to employees, according to Holloway. Job pressures and staffing patterns were also serious problems as were a lack of recognition for performance, lack of career ladder, and lack of communication between departments and with administration. Holloway suggests that many of these concerns are due to management problems and the lack of effective leadership, for example, using the old trait approach in evaluation procedures: inconsistency in enforcing personnel policies; inadequate career planning and mobility for employees, supervisors, and department heads who perform tasks instead of managing; rapid change and turnover so that supervisors cannot explain policies to employees; and the failure to develop an open, participative, organizational climate.

The organizing council usually meets outside of working hours in a nonwork setting to plan its organizing strategies. As they persuade other nurses that a union is needed, core group members ask them to sign authorization cards. These cards indicate their desire to be represented by a particular labor organization. (The cards are checked by a neutral third party; management does not see the signatures at any time.) When a majority of the nurses employed in the organization have signed these cards, the employer is asked to voluntarily recognize the union. Employees usually do not do this and so an election supervised by the NLRB is held.

Elections

The pre-election campaigning on both sides can become intense. Management often plays on nurses' feelings of guilt, implying that they are planning to abandon the patients who depend on them or that they are betraying the director who has worked so hard on their behalf. Other tactics may be aimed at stirring fear of reprisals (such as being fired) but actual threats or coercion or even promises of benefits for those who vote against the union are illegal.

An entirely different strategy sometimes used by management is to take a positive approach. Suddenly, the pay scale for nurses is raised and supervisors become very attentive to the needs of individual employees. This attentiveness fades quickly if the organizing effort ends.

The union side has its own strategies. Unions often mount an educational campaign explaining what a union is and what it can do for employees. These campaigns often include responses to criticisms that collective bargaining is unprofessional or unethical. Unions also use fear by pointing out how vulnerable an employee is without the protection of a union. The unsatisfactory conditions that led to the interest in collective bargaining are emphasized and individual incidents may be exaggerated to stir anger against management. Any threats or coercion from the union are also illegal.

All fulltime and most part-time nurses who are employed by the health care organization but are not in management positions are eligible to vote for or against the proposed bargaining agent. The bargaining agent that wins the election is certified by the NLRB and the employer must bargain with this designated representative of its employees.

NEGOTIATING A CONTRACT

Once a bargaining agent has been certified by the NLRB, collective bargaining enters the second phase in which an agreement on a contract is reached. This contract is a legal document, which both management and labor must abide by after it is signed. All of the items listed earlier under the purposes of collective bargaining can be included in this agreement. Items about union membership and payment of dues (called union security items) are also included in the contract.

Negotiations

Both management and labor groups form negotiating teams and designate one member of the team as their spokesperson. Before negotiations begin, each team meets separately to decide what their priorities are and what items they are willing to compromise on at the bargaining table. As with other types of negotiations, each team begins by asking for a list of everything they might possibly want, but usually avoids making any completely unreasonable demands. When an expiring contract is being renegotiated either side may ask for something they lost at the last contract negotiation.

During the initial negotiating sessions, both sides present their proposals or demands. As a rule, management is very reluctant to give up any of its power or to spend more money; the union attempts to equalize the power-balance between labor and management and to gain benefits for its members. These recitations of who-wants-what can go back and forth for many meetings but they do have some purpose. During this time, the negotiating teams find out what the key issues are and where compromise is possible.

Much of what happens in these early rounds of negotiating are demonstrations by each team aimed at gaining public support for their side. There is often a great deal of posturing and showmanship during these early rounds of talks. Often, the serious bargaining is done later behind closed doors, during which the really difficult issues are dealt with and necessary compromises are made in order to reach an agreement.

An important difference in this particular type of negotiation is that each side is *obliged by law* to bargain in good faith. Good faith means that both parties must agree to meet at reasonable times, to send representatives with the authority to negotiate to the bargaining table, and to bargain with the other side. Presenting a take-it-or-leave-it package of demands and refusing to negotiate any changes in that package is not bargaining in good faith.

Stalemates

Despite good faith bargaining, negotiations may reach a stalemate in which the two teams are unable to reach an agreement on one or more items, usually key issues in the agreement. If this happens, both sides must notify the Federal Mediation and

Conciliation Service (a government agency). There are several actions that may then be taken to break a stalemate: mediation, fact-finding, binding arbitration, and work stoppages. Each of these is discussed below:

Mediation.   A neutral party provided by the Federal Mediation and Conciliation Service may meet with each of the negotiating teams to explore the nature of the stalemate and then bring the two sides together to try to work out a settlement of the dispute. Both sides must cooperate with this Federal mediator but they do not have to accept the mediator's recommendations.

Fact-Finding.   The Federal Mediation and Conciliation Service may also appoint a fact-finding board of inquiry to investigate the situation and make recommendations. This board's report and recommendations are made public and can be used to pressure one or both sides to move toward an agreement.

Binding Arbitration.   Arbitration is a third alternative. Like the mediator and fact-finding board, the arbitrator is a neutral party who thoroughly investigates the situation, meets with each side, and makes a decision regarding a settlement between the two. However, both sides must accept the arbitrator's decision so both management and labor are reluctant to voluntarily limit their bargaining power by submitting the dispute to binding arbitration unless there are no better alternatives.

One of the risks of binding arbitration is that either side may lose something gained during previous negotiations. For example, the arbitrator could reverse a hard won agreement to reduce the probation time of new employees from six months to two months. Reinstating the six-month probation would be a victory for management because it means that benefits do not have to be paid for these first six months and it slows down pay raises for new employees.

Work Stoppages.   When talks reach an impasse, employees have a fourth alternative. They can slow down or stop working. Employers can also lock employees out but they are usually reluctant to do this. The union must give 10 days notice before striking unless management has committed an unfair labor practice.

At this point, the tension builds rapidly. In fact, the prospect of a strike usually leads to more intense negotiating and often to a last minute settlement. Generally speaking, no one really wants a strike and the decision is preceded by a great deal of discussion with the membership of the bargaining unit. Unions do not want to strike unless their members are solidly in support of the action.

While management is preparing for the loss of the nurses' services, the union has to organize the strike, set up strike headquarters, and build up support from the members, the public, and other unions for its strike. Strikes usually continue until some kind of settlement is reached.

Ratification

When an agreement is finally reached the union negotiators take it back to the membership for their approval. A vote is taken and, if approved, the agreement becomes a legally binding contract under which management and labor now have to work together.

CONTRACT ADMINISTRATION

Collective bargaining does not end with the signing of the agreement. The often hard-won agreement now has to be enforced.

Grievances

Almost every collective bargaining agreement includes provisions for a grievance procedure to deal with any dispute or complaint from the employer or any employee in the bargaining unit regarding implementation of the contract. The contract usually specifies certain steps to be taken and the time limits for each of these steps. For example, employees may be given a limit of five days after the incident occurs to file a grievance with their immediate supervisors and the supervisors must respond within another five days.

If the problem is not resolved at this first step, it proceeds through further steps. The grievance may be brought next to the director of personnel and then to the administrator of the organization. If the grievance is still not resolved at the end of these steps, it can then be taken to arbitration.[31-32]

A typical grievance begins when an employee feels mistreated and contacts the union delegate (a fellow employee who represents a particular work group at union meetings) to find out if this perceived mistreatment is a violation of the contract. The delegate then discusses the situation with the employee and decides how to handle the complaint. The following is an example of the kind of complaint handled by a delegate:

> An employee informed the delegate about not receiving a raise that was due. The delegate spoke to the employee's supervisor who said it was just an oversight, and the problem was quickly resolved.

If the problem affects other employees too, the delegate will also speak to them before deciding how to handle it. Here is an example:

> The supervisor of the intensive care units told the day-shift nurses that they would have to work an extra weekend for the next three months. One of the nurses informed their delegate. The delegate spoke with several other nurses who confirmed that they had been told the same thing. The delegate then went to the supervisor and told the supervisor that this was a violation of the contract and showed the supervisor the relevant clause in the contract. The extra weekend work was removed from the schedule before it was posted and was not mentioned again.

Often the delegate needs to use personal understanding of human behavior and some effective communication techniques in dealing with grievances because supervisors may take a grievance personally and become defensive about having made a mistake or feel threatened by the power the delegate represents. The following is an example of a solution that the delegate handled tactfully to avoid making the supervisor defensive:

After an unusually busy week when the staff could not get all their work done on time and everyone was becoming tired and short tempered, an irritable supervisor decided that staff members were spending too much time in the lavatories and tried to limit them to one trip a day. Most of the staff ignored the order but a few became angry and one threatened to use the supply room sink. The delegate approached the supervisor privately and told the supervisor that staff members could not obey the rule and that it could not be enforced. The supervisor realized that the head of the department would not approve of the absurd rule and dropped the whole matter after thinking about the conversation with the delegate.

As you can see, many grievances are minor and can be resolved in an informal manner by the employee, immediate supervisor, and delegate at the first step of the grievance procedure.

Any disputes more serious or complex than the examples given above are usually brought to a union employee, often called an organizer, to handle. The organizer has more experience in resolving grievances and is in a less vulnerable position than the delegate, who is an employee of the organization. The organizer is not emotionally involved in the situation, cannot be harassed by management, and can be more objective than the other people involved. This is an instance in which it is an advantage to be represented by a large union that has locally based organizers available to represent employees throughout the steps of the grievance procedure.

The organizer is likely to confront supervisors more directly than a delegate would. The following are two examples in which the organizer confronted the immediate supervisor and resolved the problem at the first step of the grievance procedure:

A nursing assistant, Miss M., felt that she was being treated unfairly by her head nurse who often criticized her, never praised her, and never granted her requests for a particular assignment or day off. The aide brought her problem to the delegate who referred it to the organizer. The organizer was direct with the head nurse. The organizer told the head nurse, "You don't have any respect for this nursing assistant as a person. She's a human being." The head nurse responded somewhat defensively but did begin to treat the nursing assistant more like a human being after the confrontation.

A nurse, Mr. P., requested a particular day off in order to take care of some important personal business which had to be done during work hours, but his supervisor denied the request. The organizer accompanied the nurse to meet with the supervisor and repeat the request. The supervisor said the nurse could have the day off only if he found someone to work his shift. The organizer said "Are you asking the nurse to do your job for you?" The supervisor backed down, rearranged the schedule and allowed the nurse to take the day off.

The organizer plays the same roles as mediator and defender of the employee's rights if the grievance is not resolved at the first step but has to be taken through the next steps, which involve management higher up in the hierarchy of the organization. If the grievance is a very serious matter, such as the firing of an employee, it may be taken directly to the administrator of the organization.

Binding Arbitration

When the previously mentioned steps of the grievance procedure fail to resolve the dispute, the problem can be taken to binding arbitration. This kind of arbitration is much the same as the arbitration used during contract negotiations except that it is done in this case to resolve a disagreement over implementation of the contract.

The contract usually specifies the way in which an arbitrator is selected. Most often an arbitrator is selected from a list supplied by the American Arbitration Association, which acts like a clearing house for arbitrators. Both sides must agree with the choice.

Again, there is some reluctance to go to arbitration because the decision is binding on both parties and the arbitrator's fees, which are paid by both sides, can be substantial. If the employee has been offered a reasonable compromise at an earlier stage and does not have a strong case, the organizer will encourage the person to accept the compromise. If the employee is completely in the wrong in the dispute, the organizer may refuse to proceed with the arbitration. This refusal can be appealed to the union board.

The arbitrator acts very much like a judge in hearing the case except that the rules of evidence are not as strict as they are in a courtroom. The arbitrator's duty is to decide whether or not the contract was violated and what action is to be taken. The following are two examples in which the firing of a hospital employee was taken to arbitration:

A shipment of perishable materials was due some time during the day and a pharmacy aide was assigned to unpack and store the materials. The shipment arrived just before quitting time and the pharmacist said that the aide had to stay. The aide refused saying, "I would have stayed if I had been asked earlier in the day." Because the aide had received disciplinary warnings in the past, the aide was fired for insubordination.

Because this was a serious case, the union organizer began the grievance procedure at the second step with the personnel department. Eventually, the case was brought to arbitration. The contract stipulated that management could ask employees to work overtime and this employee had been warned about insubordination in the past so the employee lost the arbitration and remained fired.

In another case, a new technician who was in a training program suffered a convulsion, fell down a flight of stairs, and broke several bones. The technician was fired by the hospital for excessive absenteeism while out of work on disability. The hospital claimed that the technician was incapable of completing the training program or doing the job for which the technician was hired. The technician said, "I just forgot to take my Dilantin that day," but the hospital would not reinstate the employee.

The union brought this case to arbitration and the arbitrator ruled in favor of the employee noting that it was an accident, that anyone could make that kind of mistake. This employee got the job back.

The grievance procedure provides employees with two safeguards not always available to employees who have not organized. The first is a guarantee of a fair hearing and a response within a given time. The second is that employees have someone to represent and defend them and do not have to face an authority figure alone.

SUMMARY

Collective bargaining is the joint action of a designated group of employees in order to gain economic benefits, improved staffing and scheduling, equitable treatment, and improved care standards from their employer. Opponents of collective bargaining by health care professionals say that it is unprofessional, unethical, divisive, and not necessary.

Collective bargaining begins with the formation of an organizing council and recognition of a bargaining agent, usually the professional association or a national union, by the employer, either voluntarily or after an election. Then contract negotiations begin between representatives of management and the bargaining unit. If stalemated, mediation, fact-finding, binding arbitration, or work stoppages may be used to bring about an agreement. Once a contract is signed, it must be enforced, usually through grievance and arbitration procedures specified in the contract.

References

1.   BROWN, BJ (ED): *Nurse Staffing: A Practical Guide.* Aspen Systems, Germantown, Maryland, 1980.

2.   ROWLAND, HS AND ROWLAND, BL: *Nursing Administration Handbook.* Aspen Systems, Germantown, Maryland, 1980.

3.   KRAMER, M: *Team nursing—A means or an end?* Nursing Outlook 19(10):648-652, October 1971.

4.   KRON, T: *The Management of Patient Care.* WB Saunders, Philadelphia, 1981.

5.   LAMBERTSEN, EC: *Nursing Team: Organization and Functioning.* Teachers College Press, New York, 1953.

6.   MARRAM, GD, BARRETT, MW, AND BEVIS, EO: *Primary Nursing: A Model for Individualized Care,* ed 2. CV Mosby, St Louis, 1979.

7.   FAIRBANKS, JE: *Primary Nursing: More Data.* Nursing Administration Quarterly 5(3):51, Spring 1981.

8.   DRUCKER, P: *People and Performance: The Best of Peter Drucker on Management.* Harper & Row, New York, 1977.

9. LEVINSON, H AND LaMONICA, EL: *Management by whose objectives?* Journal of Nursing Administration X(9):22, September 1980.

10. DILLON, RD: *Zero-Base Budgeting For Health Care Institutions.* Aspen Systems, Germantown, Maryland, 1979.

11. HIGGERSON, NJ AND VAN SLYCK, A: *Variable billing for services: New fiscal direction for nursing.* Journal of Nursing Administration XII (6):20, June 1982.

12. BERMAN, HJ AND WEEKS, LE: *The Financial Management of Hospitals,* ed 4. Health Administration Press, Ann Arbor, Michigan, 1979.

13. SWEENY, A AND WISNER, JN: *Budgeting Fundamentals for Nonfinancial Executives.* AMACOM, New York, 1975.

14. PYHRR, PA: *Zero-Base Budgeting: A Practical Management Tool for Evaluating Expenses.* John Wiley & Sons, New York, 1973.

15. DAUBERT, EA: *Patient classification system and outcome criteria.* Nursing Outlook 27(7):450, July 1979.

16. DONABEDIAN, A: *A Guide to Medical Care Administration. Vol II Medical Care Appraisal—Quality and Utilization.* American Public Health Association, New York, 1969.

17. DONABEDIAN, A: *Evaluating the quality of medical care.* Milbank Memorial Fund Quarterly 44(Part 2), p 166, July 1977.

18. BROOK, RH, DAVIS, AR, AND KAMBERG, C: *Selected reflections on quality of medical care evaluations in the 1980s.* Nursing Research 29(2):127, (March-April 1980).

19. CHANCE, KS: *The quest for quality: An exploration of attempts to define and measure quality nursing care.* Image 12(2):41, June 1980.

20. LYNCH, EA: *Evaluation: Principles and processes.* NLN Publication No 23-1721, 1978 (32 pp).

21. PHANEUF, M: *The Nursing Audit: Self-Regulation in Nursing Practice,* ed 2. Appleton-Century-Crofts, New York, 1976.

22. BEER, M: *Performance appraisal: Dilemmas and possibilities.* Organizational Dynamics Winter 1981, p 24.

23. STETZER, SL: *Implementing peer review in the hospital.* Journal of the New York State Nurses Association 9(4):44, December 1978.

24. VENGROSKI, SM, AND SAARMANN, L: *Peer review in quality assurance.* American Journal of Nursing 78(12):2094, December 1978.

25. FOSSUM, JA: *Labor Relations: Development, Structure and Process.* Business Publications, Dallas, Texas, 1979.

26. LOCKHART, CA AND WERTHER, WB (EDS): *Labor Relations In Nursing.* Nursing Resources, Wakefield, Massachusetts, 1980.

27. O'ROURKE, K AND BARTON, SR: *Nurse Power: Unions and the Law.* Robert J Brady, Bowie, Maryland, 1981.

28. BLOOM, JR, PARLETTE, GN, AND O'REILLY, C: *Collective bargaining by nurses: A comparative analysis of management and employee perceptions.* Health Care Management Review 5(1):25, Winter 1980.

29. HOLLOWAY, RG: *Management can reverse declining employee work attitudes.* Hospitals, Journal of the American Hospital Association 50(20):71, October 1976.

30. LUTTMAN, PA: *Collective bargaining and professionalism: Incompitable ideologies?* Nursing Administration Quarterly 6(2):21, Winter 1982.

31. THOMSON, AWJ AND MURRAY, VV: *Grievance Procedures.* Saxon House, DC, Westmead, England, 1976.

32. Collective Bargaining Agreement Between League of Voluntary Hospitals and Homes of New York and District 1199 National Union of Hospital and Health Care Employees RWDSU/AFL-CIO, 1980-1982.

Chapter *12*

Working in the Community

Communities are even larger and more complex open systems than those considered so far. They contain many people and may have many different kinds of organizations as subsystems within them. A community can be the setting in which the health professional works or it can be the "client" of one health professional, or both. The tremendous size and complexity of some communities can make it even more difficult to see them as systems that have characteristics as a whole, but they do, in much the same way that organizations have these characteristics.

In this chapter, the concept of a community and its characteristics as an open system are considered in the first section. Then, leadership in the community is discussed including the power and authority structures of a community, the process of community action, and strategies for influencing the flow of power and decision-making in the community.

The Concept of Community

DEFINITIONS OF COMMUNITY

There are many definitions and uses of the term community. Most of these uses fall into one of two main categories—those that emphasize geography or place and those that do not. Both types of definitions emphasize the common bonds and interrelationships between people that are the basis of a community.[1-4]

With either type of definition the basic elements of the concept of community are the people and whatever they share that makes them a community.

Geographic Community

Those definitions that emphasize place define a community as an open system comprised of a number of people who share a common place and common resources, interests, or needs. This type of community may be a neighborhood, parish, ghetto, village, town, city, metropolitan area, county, or other locale. Its boundaries may be defined by rivers, mountains, streets, fields, or politically by boundary lines such as those drawn between a city and its suburbs. A geographic community usually contains a number of different organizations within its boundaries and usually has a political and legal structure as well as the informal relationships that develop among people who have common bonds.

Community of Interest

Those definitions that do not emphasize place define a community as an open system comprised of a number of people who have common resources, interests, or needs, and have a potential sense of belonging or identification with each other. This community of interest may be a religious community, a migrant population, people in the same occupation such as coal miners or asbestos workers, people with a physical disability such as blindness, people with a psychosocial problem such as alcoholism, or people with a common ethnic background. People who belong to any of these groups have a common need or interest and could identify with each other on the basis of that common need or interest.

Community of Solution

The concept of a community of solution helps to bridge the gap between these two different definitions of community by overlapping both of them. It is also a helpful way to look at a community for health care givers and planners. A community of solution is comprised of a number of people who have an identifiable need or problem and is the system within which the solution to this problem can be implemented. To be a viable community of solution, a system must have a sufficient number of people with the same problem or need, sufficient resources to meet this need or solve the problem, and the capability and authority to carry out the solution. The following is an example of a community of solution:

> A large number of migrant workers comes through a small farming community every year to pick fruit. The migrant workers have some serious health needs but this small farming community has neither the money nor the trained people to meet these needs. Several other farm communities in the area also have migrant workers coming through but no resources to provide for their health care needs. However, the county health department has access to the funds and health care professionals needed to meet these needs, so all the migrant workers who came through the county became the community of solution for this particular problem.

The community of solution was defined by both the need and the capability to meet the need.

FUNCTIONS OF A COMMUNITY

Communities are formed and maintained because they fulfill several important functions for the people who belong to them. The functions of a community are generally broader than those of an organization, which are usually quite specific (such as providing a certain type of health care or producing a certain kind of equipment). As you read the following list of community functions, you will see that people band together in communities in order to meet some basic needs. It is the ability of a community to meet these needs that makes most people willing to contribute in some way to the continuation of their communities.

The basic functions of a community are to provide the following to its members:

1. **Safety and Security.** Communities provide their members with protections against fire, crime, natural disasters, and other threats to their physical safety by organizing and supporting such services as fire departments, rescue squads, and police protection, and by mobilizing members of the community during an emergency. People usually feel more secure when they know that they can call on others for help.
2. **Mutual Support.** The community also offers sources of mutual support in ways similar to the provision of safety and security measures. This mutual support can include psychologic support and help during a crisis, such as assistance with household tasks, care for the sick, food, clothing, and money for people who do not have enough.
3. **Network for the Distribution of Resources.** Communities provide networks through which people exchange information, materials, and services. In modern communities, this network for distribution has become extremely complex and specialized so that there are specific networks for distributing information, for providing health care, for the sale and purchase of goods, and so forth.
4. **Socialization.** Communities are also networks of shared meanings and values. They are sources of beliefs, values, attitudes, norms, and role definitions that pattern people's behavior.
5. **Significance.** A person's membership in a community meets a basic need for belonging. The community in which a person lives can also become a part of the person's identity. For example, people may identify themselves as New Yorkers or Southerners, or as members of the black community or members of the medical community.

From your own experience with communities, including the ones in which you have lived, you may already be aware of the fact that they differ widely in the degree to which they fulfill the functions listed above. Nongeographic communities of interest are more likely to emphasize the provision of mutual support, socialization, and significance than the provision of safety measures or distribution of resources.

THE COMMUNITY AS AN OPEN SYSTEM

Wholeness

The community as a whole is greater than and different from the sum of its parts. The community has attributes that characterize it as a whole which cannot be identified by observing only a part of it.

There are many dimensions to a community as a whole. Among its many attributes that can be measured or at least observed are its age, size, and location. A community may be a new one recently formed or it could be a long-established one in existence for hundreds of years. Its size would include both the number of people in it and the area encompassed by the community. The richness or paucity of its resources is also important. For geographic communities, location is another important attribute and would include its climate, elevation, topography, physical shape and boundaries, and its position in relation to other communities.

The quantity and quality of the relationships among people are also important. Some communities are highly integrated wholes in which there are active ties between most of the people and organizations within them. Others are poorly integrated with few ties between their various subsystems. There may be conflicts among these subsystems, for example, among different age groups, ethnic groups, or political organizations. In fact, conflict may characterize the interactions in some communities while others may be characterized by friendly and cooperative interactions among subsystems.

A community as a whole can also be described as healthy or unhealthy. The health of a community has traditionally been measured in terms of its morbidity (illness) and mortality (death) rates but other measures, such as its emotional climate and prevelant lifestyles, are also indications of a community's health.

Uniqueness

No two communities are alike. Each has variations in its attributes and an identifiable personality or character to it as a whole. When you observe a community, its colors, sights, sounds, smells, and the feelings you pick up about relationships within the community give you an indication of its overall personality or character. Another excellent source of information about a community's personality are local informants, people who know a community well but who are also able to look at it objectively and describe it to others.[5]

When you consider a community in this way, you may find that it is a warm, vibrant, lively place that welcomes newcomers and visitors. Or you may find that the community is wary and suspicious of strangers and that it is difficult to become acquainted with it. Others are as bleak and colorless as their surroundings and tend to respond with indifference.

Some communities are highly integrated wholes in which there is a great deal of communication and other exchanges among its subsystems but others are highly differentiated with limited interaction among their subsystems. These and the many other characteristics mentioned throughout this section contribute to a community's uniqueness. Whatever similarities you may find in a particular community, it will be different in some way from any other community.

Hierarchy

There are many systems within systems in a community, creating a hierarchy with as many or more levels than an organization, but without the same flow of authority from top to bottom as is found in a bureaucratic organization. The flow of power, authority, and decision-making in a community is more diffuse than in an organization and will be discussed later is this chapter.

Beginning with the basic unit of a leadership situation, the individual, we can see how the hierarchy of systems in a community develops. The individual may be a member of a family, the next level in the hierarchy. The individual also lives in a particular neighborhood, which would be the third level and is a subsystem of the community as a whole (Fig. 12-1).

However, this hierarchy of individual, family, neighborhood, and community oversimplifies the community because it overlooks a large number of other subsystems of which this hypothetical individual may be a member. At the same level as the family, this hypothetical individual also has friends, acquaintances, coworkers, and neighbors with whom the individual interacts. At the neighborhood level, the

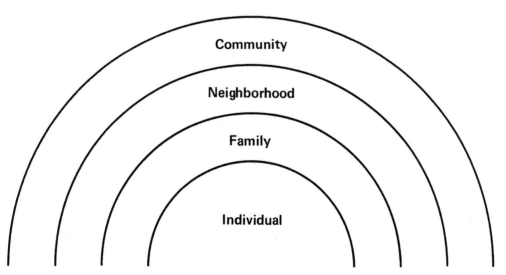

FIGURE 12-1. Hierarchy of subsystems of a community.

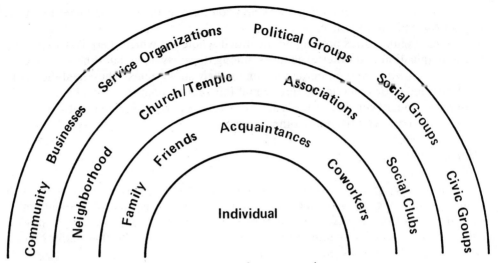

FIGURE 12-2. Additional subsystems of a community.

individual may be a member of a church or temple, a neighborhood association, and a social club. At the community level, the individual may be a member of social, civic, and political groups and may also interact with many different businesses, merchants, and service organizations (Fig. 12-2).

This second model is still oversimplified because it does not include any of the organizations with which a person may interact during the course of the individual's work, or the interrelationships with people and groups in other communities, or in the even larger systems at the county, state, and national levels. However, it does give you an idea of the number of systems within systems that can be found in even the smallest community. A thorough knowledge of the interrelationships of these systems can help one leader devise ways to communicate in some way with the large number of people that makes up a community.

Openness

Communities are open systems that influence and are influenced by their environment, including other systems in their environment. The political structure can be used as an example of this influence moving in both directions. The people in the community elect representatives for the state legislature and for Congress. Both the legislature and Congress will pass laws that the community and its members must obey. However, if the people are dissatisfied with the laws supported by their representatives, they will not re-elect them and could even have them removed from office. So the influence flows both ways: the community decides who will represent them in the legislatures and the legislatures decide what laws the community must obey.

This mutual influence operates laterally as well as vertically within the hierarchy of systems so that communities are not isolated from other communities within their environment. For example, a rising unemployment rate in neighboring communities will mean that these nearby communities will not be good sources of employment and they will not be able to purchase as many goods or services from the community's business if their people have reduced incomes. The health of other communities is another example of mutual influences. Infectious diseases do not recognize community boundaries and a flu outbreak in one community can quickly spread to others. (This is also an example of the difference between a geographic community and a community of solution.)

Growth and Development

Like other living systems, communities show evidence of growth, development, and an eventual termination of existence. However, their growth and development patterns are quite variable and it is not possible to describe a single-pattern characteristic of all or even most communities.

New and developing communities usually lack a complete network of relationships between subsystems and often do not have as many services available as the well-established communities do. Those communities that experience rapid growth are often unable to develop supports and services fast enough to keep up with demands, often a source of frustration for professionals and consumers alike. Communities experiencing a loss of resources, including people, may also be unable to continue to offer as many services as they once did despite continuing demand, a phenomenon that is occurring in many of our older cities where declining populations and shrinking tax revenues affect the community's ability to provide services.

Community growth is usually accompanied by increased differentiation among the subsystems of the community. The following is an example of how this differentiation occurs within health care services as a community grows:

> A small rural community had one physician and one nurse who provided some home care services on a part-time basis. Any health care needs that could not be met by these people were either neglected or necessitated a long drive to one of the three urban centers that served the region.
>
> The community experienced rapid growth and a great increase in demand for services that the two practitioners could not meet alone. The physician and nurse formed a partnership and opened a small clinic, which expanded and diversified rapidly. At the same time, the community began its own health department, which absorbed the home care functions of the original nurse. Several years later, a small hospital was built and offered additional services.

The increased differentiation in the example brought with it the need for more integration, that is, for developing more relationships among the new and expanded subsystems offering health care services. The communication network becomes far more complex when all these new connections are added. For example, individuals in that rural community now have to know which service they need, and each service agency needs to know what services the others provide and how to link up with them. You can see that a procedure for making referrals among the three services will be needed and will probably begin as an informal procedure that becomes more formalized as the community and numbers of services continue to grow. It also becomes apparent that the need for coordination and cooperation grows as the community becomes more complex, often a challenging task for the leader.

Pattern

Communities also have distinctive rhythms and patterns that are evident in the ebb and flow of activities within them. For example, some communities are busy and brightly lit at night while others are dark and quiet and its people will jokingly say "we roll up our sidewalks at 9:00 PM here."

Like organizations, many communities have differences in activities between weekdays and weekends. Many health care services, for example, are available only on weekdays, often only during working hours. In communities where people commute long distances to work, a predictable flow of traffic in and out of the community can be observed.

Longer rhythms are also evident. Political campaigns and elections may occur annually with an accompanying build up of interest and energy expenditure up to the election and then a slackening off until the next campaign begins. Many charitable organizations also have annual fund drives and those services that depend on grant funds will move through cycles based on the need to apply for additional funds to continue each year.

The health needs of a community may also show evidence of patterning. For example, hospital emergency rooms are usually busiest on weekend nights and health departments usually begin their immunization drives in the fall of the year.

The patterns of communication and decision-making in the community are of particular interest to the leader. Upon careful observation, you will note in some communities that people interact most with those who live nearby and those with whom they share a common interest, and that communications between different interest groups within the community are minimal. This type of communication pattern has important implications for the leader attempting to communicate a message to everyone in the community.

There are also identifiable patterns to the way decisions are made. You may note, for example, that certain people and groups are influential in a large number of decisions, while others are occasionally involved, and still others seem to never be involved in decision-making. This information is valuable when you are attempting to influence a decision within the community. Another behavior pattern of interest to the leader who wants to bring about change is the way in which a community responds to change and the kinds of changes that seem to provoke resistance.

Energy

The major energy resource of a community is its people. Energy in the form of information, materials, money, and services is constantly being exchanged in a community. An adequate flow of energy within the community is vital to its ability to grow and prosper. For example, people who live in a community need many different kinds of information in order to function effectively. They need to know where to obtain food, fuel, and other essentials, how to obtain health care and other services, how and where to complain if they have a problem, and so forth.

An adequate amount of energy in the form of materials and services is also vital to the community. Materials such as food, clothing, building supplies, and fuel are required to meet people's basic needs. Some services are also considered vital— the disruption that occurs when police officers, transportation workers, or nurses go on strike is evidence of the community's need for such services.

A balance in the flow of energy in and out of the community is also important. For example, if the community is spending more money on such services as police, fire, rescue, schools, welfare, and health care than the community is taking in as taxes, it will eventually run into financial trouble and be unable to offer any services. The economic resources of a community are finite and there are usually more requests for money than there is money available. This means that decisions have to be made about how to allocate this scarce resource, which often leads to competition for funding among various agencies.

Because of the community's dependence on an adequate flow of energy, the ability to influence or control this flow is an important source of power in a community.[3] People who are in a position to affect the flow of money (such as bankers and people in government), or the flow of goods (such as merchants and other businessmen), or the flow of information (such as professionals and people in the media) may be sources of considerable influence in the community.

Goals

Like organizations, communities have both official and operative goals. However, the difference between these spoken and unspoken types of goals is probably a less significant consideration in community leadership because more people seem to be aware of the fact that the official goals of communities have their unspoken, covert counterparts that are equally or even more influential.

One of the best ways to identify the community's operative goals is to observe what happens and where the community's energies are spent, especially its scarce resources. For example, does the community use its limited funds to improve its schools and health services or is the money spent on a new municipal building? If the community's operative goal is to educate its children and keep its people healthy, the money will be spent on the schools and health services. But if the community's operative goal is to have a more attractive town hall than its neighbor does, the money will be spent on that municipal building.

There are also different levels of goals within a community, both laterally and vertically up through the hierarchy of systems. For example, an individual has personal goals, the individual's family has its goals, the organization in which the individual works has another set of goals, and so on through the hierarchy of systems. Laterally, the individual's neighbors, friends, acquaintances, and coworkers all have sets of goals. These goals may or may not be congruent. When they are not, conflict and stress are predictable consequences.

Different socioeconomic or cultural groups within a community often have different and conflicting goals. The following is an example of such a conflict:

> A group representing several churches from a low to moderate income neighborhood requested permission from the town council to use an empty town-owned building for a youth drop-in center. The group was concerned about the delinquency rate in their neighborhood and wanted to find a positive solution that would help troubled adolescents and be of benefit to the community as well.
>
> A second private group, from a more affluent part of the community, offered to purchase the building from the town. They intended to renovate the building and convert it into meeting rooms that could be rented to a number of different social groups, primarily groups of adults with moderate to high incomes. They argued that the town would gain financially from the sale of an unused building, which would go back on the tax rolls when sold to this private group.

Both groups felt that they could make good use of the building and that their plans for the building would be of benefit to the community. However, their plans were not congruent and led to a long and bitter conflict between the two groups and dissension among town council members until the problem was finally resolved.

Incongruence among the goals of different socioeconomic or cultural groups within a community can have serious consequences for the community. A community's ability to resolve this type of conflict among goals in such a way that all the people involved feel that their needs and interests were fairly considered is very important. In an organization, every person can be consulted (as was described in the discussion of Theory Z), although it is rarely done. But this is far more difficult to do in a community except through special elections or old-fashioned town meetings (which are virtually impossible to conduct in heavily populated communities). Instead, community leaders frequently rely on their ability to identify and consult with groups and individuals who represent a cross section of community opinion and their own intuitive sense of community feeling developed from their knowledge and interactions with the community in order to resolve such conflicts in accord with community feelings on the issue.

SUMMARY

A community may be defined as a geographic place, a group of people with shared interests and needs, or as a group within which a problem can be solved. The functions of a community are to provide safety and security, mutual support, socialization, significance, and a network for the distribtuion of goods and services. A community is an open, living system that has unique characteristics as a whole that are different from those of its many subsystems. Its subsystems can be ordered hierarchically in terms of increasing size and complexity. These subsystems are connected in varying degrees by a network of communication and other interactions and have their own sets of goals, which may or may not be congruent. Like other living systems, communities have identifiable rhythms and patterns of activity, including growth patterns. They also exchange energy in the form of information, materials, money, and services with their environment.

Power and Political Structures

This section considers the distribution of power and political authority within the community. Although the two concepts are interrelated, they are somewhat arbitrarily divided here. The distribution of power is considered first and then the political authority and influence of governmental systems in relation to health care services will be reviewed.

POWER DISTRIBUTION

The question of who has power and the ability to influence decisions within a community has been a difficult one to answer or even to study. A community is far too large and complex to recreate in a laboratory for careful study, which has been done with groups. It is less difficult to observe the community in its natural setting but the power, authority, and influence relationships are multiple, interconnected, and at the same time can be quite subtle and difficult to observe by an outsider.

One of the early solutions to the problem of identifying the power distribution in communities was to ask people to list the most influential leaders in their community. It was found that a small number of people were consistently named. These people, primarily from the top ranks of commerce, finance, and industry in the community, were considered the ruling elite, the group that made the decisions in the community.[6]

However, when additional methods (such as studying actual participation in decision-making; memberships in community organizations; and positions within business, government, educational, labor, and religious organizations) were used, it was found that different people were influential in regard to different issues. Power and influence were found to vary according to the particular issue and the particular resources controlled by the individual or group. The power structure of a community is not a single hierarchy of the elite but a complex network of many actors, each with varying amounts of power and influence and diverse, often conflicting, interests.[7-10]

One useful, although simplified, way of visualizing the distribution of power in the community is to divide those who are powerful into three major groups, the influentials, the effectors, and the activists. The institutional leaders or *influentials* are the people who head the largest business, government, political, educational, and other types of organizations. They are the people mentioned earlier who have a reputation for being influential that is based on their positions within these organizations. It is interesting to note that most of the influentials are not particularly active in community affairs. Their influence is felt primarily by their prestige and support of one side or other on an issue but also through the next group, the effectors.

Effectors are very active in the community's decision-making processes. Although they are not heads of organizations as the influentials are, they are professionals, government officials, and employees of corporations. They often become involved in the community's decision-making processes through specific work assignments and are most influential in decisions that require technical or specialized knowledge.

The *activists* are different. They come primarily from clubs or voluntary, civic, or service organizations. While they do not have the effectors' power bases of a government agency or large corporation behind them, they influence decisions by committing their time and energy to involvement in community affairs. The activists are less likely to be involved in economic decisions than are the influentials and effectors.

The people who participate regularly in decisions that affect the community are a diverse but powerful group. Their power comes primarily from the positions they hold, from their individual characteristics and from connections with power sources outside the community. Power derived from their positions is based on their authority relationships; ability to control the flow of money, credit, and jobs; and expert technical knowledge unavailable to most people in the community. Power derived from individuals' characteristics is based on their reputations as people who can mediate negotiations, respect for their ability to get things done in the community, connections with other influential people, and influence in community organizations such as political parties or voluntary organizations. Outside political and economic ties are also power sources. People who are influentials, effectors, or activists usually have a cluster of these characteristics rather than just one or two of them.

For most purposes, the leader will find that the categories of influential, effector, and activist are sufficient for analysis and action. However, the power distribution in a community is actually more complex than these categories indicate. In fact, it is a large network of people and groups with different types and amounts of resources and links with the decision-making processes of the community. To further complicate matters, different issues are settled in different arenas within the community so that certain people and groups will be close to one decision-making process but completely removed and not even interested in other decisions.

It is evident from the description of the three major categories of people who regularly influence community decisions that power is unevenly distributed in the community. But those people in the community who do not regularly participate in community decisions do have some potential sources of power and influence on decisions and may become participants in the process. When they do participate, there are two general patterns that participation may take, the high-initiative, direct-action type of pattern or the low-initiative, more passive pattern of participation.[11]

The high-initiative pattern includes collective actions such as consumer boycotts, picketing, agitation, and protest marches. It also includes such direct actions as hiring professional advocates (for example, lawyers) and using ombudsman organizations, consumer protection agencies, outside auditors, and investigative agencies to bring about desired changes. The low-initiative pattern includes collective actions such as holding formal meetings and presenting formal requests for change. Individual actions include letter-writing, telephoning, and meeting with those who will make the decision and presenting individual requests for change. Although these are low-pressure tactics, they can influence the outcome of community decision-making processes by providing feedback to the decision-makers about community values and positions on particular issues that decision-makers, especially politicians and public office holders, know they cannot completely ignore without risking community protest.

GOVERNMENT STRUCTURE

Although a number of other sources of authority, from parental authority to organizational authority, can be found in the community, one of the most influential is the hierarchy of government officials and organizations, which begins at the local level and continues through the county, state, and national levels. The influence of government in the community is of particular concern to the leader in the health care fields because the government has become increasingly involved in the planning, financing, delivery, and regulation of health care. The fact that we are reaching a point where nearly half the money spent on health care comes through government channels is just one indicator of the public sector's increasing influence on health care.[12-14]

Federal Level

Although its influence is often indirect and therefore not always apparent to the individual, the federal level of government is considered by many to be the ultimate source of power and influence within the government hierarchy and has a wide range of economic and legal sanctions (such as fines and imprisonment) through which it can wield its power. While the federal government is technically concerned only with matters that cross state or federal boundaries, its influence reaches beyond these areas through an intricate net of laws, policies, and operational procedures.

The ways in which the federal government exerts its power and authority in the health care field can be divided into five categories: direct health care delivery, subsidies, entry restriction, rate-setting, and quality control. The federal government is not a health care provider for the majority of the population but it is directly involved in providing health care for specifically defined populations such as people in the military, veterans, and some American Indians.

The federal government also provides funds for numerous programs that are carried out at the state or local level by various state and local government agencies, educational institutions, and nonprofit organizations. These federal monies have "strings" attached to them that increase the government's power and influence. Federal subsidies in the form of direct funds, loans, and tax exemptions are granted for a wide variety of health services, construction, research, educational projects, and training in the health care field. The strings through which the government maintains control include such things as criteria for eligibility, specifications about the way in which funds are used, and the extraction of certain promises in return for the money (for example, the Hill-Burton Act required hospitals to provide a certain amount of free care, and some training grants stipulate service after graduation). Grants are often made to support efforts in areas that have previously been neglected or in which it is difficult to attract people unless additional money is offered.

Entry restrictions, rate-setting, and quality control are more direct means of control. They can also be tied to the availability of federal money—those who do not follow these regulations and guidelines do not receive federal money. One of the most effective entry restrictions is a federal requirement that states adapt certificate of need laws. Under these laws, a health care organization must obtain approval from the local and state planning agencies before making any major changes in its services or beginning any major construction project. Although the purpose of requiring these certificates of need is to keep costs within reasonable limits, most health care organizations see them as a restriction of their freedom to expand as they wish.

The fee schedules and reimbursement rates for Medicare and Medicaid are the best known examples of rate-setting done at the federal and state levels. The PSROs (Professional Standards Review Organizations, mentioned in Chapter 11) are one example of quality controls of individual practitioners. The certification of organizations as eligible for Medicare and Medicaid reimbursement is an example of quality control on the organizational level and also of the way federal money is used to regulate the health care industry.

State Level

Most of the mechanisms through which the federal government wields its power over health care are also available to the states. For example, the states regulate entry into the health care professions through their licensing laws. But the states have less money to use and a smaller jurisdiction, which limits their scope of influence in comparison with the federal government. In fact, one of the reasons often given for developing or funding programs at the federal level is that the poorer states will not be able to provide the service to their citizens without assistance.

Individual states may also add their own regulations, which are usually more restrictive and sometimes in conflict with federal regulations. The same can happen at the local level. A story told by administrators of nursing homes, which are subject to a number of inspections, is that an administrator in one locality kept two sets of garbage cans, one plastic and one made of metal. The administrator brought out one set to meet the requirements of the state inspector and the other set to meet the local inspector's requirements—a case of conflicting requirements.

An additional power available to the states is known as police power and is defined as the power to protect the safety and health of the people in the state. This means that the state or the agency to which its power has been delegated (such as a local board of health) can inspect, remove, use, or destroy private property if necessary to protect the health and safety of the community. For example, persons with a highly contagious and dangerous disease could have their freedom restricted by a health officer exercising police power in order to protect the rest of the community.

The existence of these police powers is not well known, probably because most health officers exercise this police power with sufficient restraint and reasonableness that it does not disturb the people in the community. The following example illustrates a community's ignorance of and response to police power at the local level:

The health board of a rural midwestern county prepared a new set of environmental sanitation regulations and announced the date for a public hearing. Ordinarily these hearings were attended by 10 or 20 people at most. However, several farmers in the county heard about a particularly irritating new regulation that certain organic materials could be left standing in the fields only for strictly limited periods of time to prevent rodent infestation. The farmers could be fined for violating this regulation.

The farmers' protest led to a much closer than usual scrutiny of the board's proposed regulations. Among the many regulations was a series of rules concerning food inspection. Several people noticed that the inspection policy could include food prepared by people in their own kitchens and served at social affairs such as church suppers. The women in the community who were proud of their cooking skills and of their church suppers were offended and some of them were furious. People began writing letters to the local newspaper complaining about these violations of their freedom and right to privacy. Ministers denounced the board of health from their pulpits and the health board was inundated with telephone calls from county residents.

The stunned health board tried to explain that they had always had these police powers but no one listened. Instead of one hearing, the board held a series of well-attended, lively hearings in every part of the county. They finally rescinded the new farm regulation and promised to leave church suppers alone unless an outbreak of food poisoning occurred—which, they quickly added, was unlikely. The rest of the regulations went into effect without further protest but the community remained watchful of the health board's activities.

This example not only shows that most people are not fully aware of the extent of governmental powers but that the people of a community have powers of their own with which to counteract these governmental powers.

Like the federal government, states also are involved in the delivery of health care to some specific populations. Probably the best known examples are the statewide systems of mental health institutions and other mental health services.

However, another major state responsibility is to set and enforce state policies and to assist agencies at the local level both technically and financially.

Local Level

Much of the power and authority of the local level has already been mentioned in the discussion of the federal and state levels. Local governments provide direct care through a number of different agencies, which include city and county health departments, community mental health centers, and a wide range of other health, safety, and social service programs. The local level usually has police powers delegated by the state (as illustrated in the health board example) and can use economic and legal sanctions such as withholding funds, controlling entry, and setting regulations. The degree of local autonomy varies from state to state.

Probably the most important consideration in regard to the local level is the fact that it is at this level that the majority of people in the community interact with government officials and agencies. Although much of what is done at the local level has been determined at the state or federal level, the local level is the main point of contact and communication for many people in the community, although any of the these levels can become the target of their criticism.

SUMMARY

Power is unevenly distributed in the community. People who regularly influence decision-making can be categorized as influentials, effectors, or activists. Others in the community participate at irregular intervals and can be categorized as having high- or low-initiative patterns. The three levels of the government hierarchy wield much power and influence on health care through their involvement in direct delivery of care, subsidies, entry restrictions, rate-setting, and quality control. The states also have police powers that can be delegated to the local level.

Community Action

Working with members of the community to help them initiate action to meet their own needs is the intent of community action. It is a process based on the principles of democratic leadership and closely resembles Havelock and Lippitt's model for change (Chapter 9). Because it is a normative (moderate in strength) approach to change, it is most effective with minimal to moderate resistance. When there is organized, extensive resistance to change, Bachrach and Baratz's model (discussed later in this chapter), which analyzes and utilizes the sources of power in the community, is more appropriate.

Leaders working in the community quickly learn that they must gain the support of the community in order to succeed with any project intended to improve the health of the community. If the members of the community do not want a particular service, they can ignore it, not use it, or refuse to support it (Fig. 12-3).

416

FIGURE 12-3. Empty clinic. Leaders working in the community quickly learn that they must gain the support of the community in order to succeed with any project intended to improve the health of the community. If the members of the community do not want a particular service, they can ignore it, not use it, or refuse to support it.

For example, if you offer them health information for which they see no need, they may listen politely but they will not use it. If the offered service offends them, they may even ask you to remove it, although this is less likely to happen. The ability of a community to reject your offer of help is part of both the frustration and the challenge of working with communities. This is particularly true when working in a community whose culture is somewhat or very different from your own.

Community action is a mutual problem-solving process. Its purpose is to help the community learn how to meet its own needs as much as to find ways to meet an immediate need. It also serves to develop more connections among people and increase their sense of belonging as they learn how to help themselves and others.

Ross developed a series of steps for community action. These steps begin with the mutual identification of a community's needs, followed by prioritizing those needs, developing the community's motivation, taking stock of the resources available and building up the community's confidénce, developing a plan of action, implementing that plan, and then evaluating the results.[16-17] Each of these steps is discussed briefly below.

MUTUAL IDENTIFICATION OF NEED

Once you have identified the community with which you are going to work and established some kind of contact with that community, you are ready to find out from the people themselves what they consider their needs to be.

As a knowledgeable professional, you could generate a list of the community's health needs and select several that are of top priority by yourself. But however accurate your list might be, doing it without the input of the community fails to generate any interest or commitment from the community. You may also find that the people in the community have a very different idea of what their needs are and if you do not find out what their ideas are, you may waste your time developing and offering unwanted and unused services.

Although they may not all respond, it is important to try to reach everyone in the community with which you are working. If you plan to hold a community meeting, personal contacts before the meeting will help to make individual people feel that their attendance is needed and desired. A door-to-door survey is another way to meet with members of the community; it can be quite informative but can also be very time consuming.

When it is not possible to involve every member of the community, it is important to try to get a representational cross section of the population in order to accurately assess the needs and priorities of the community as a whole.

People in the community may have trouble identifying their needs at first, partly because they have become accustomed to whatever standard of health care is available. The leader may have to offer some ideas to get the discussion started. Questions aimed at discovering areas of discontent and dissatisfaction usually lead to an identification of needs.

Example. A student was assigned to a clinic that served the three apartment buildings of a small, senior retirement community in an urban area. The student tried to find out what health care needs of the community were not being met:

> In order to find out what kind of project would be of most use to the people who lived in the retirement community, the student distributed flyers asking everyone living in the three buildings to meet with the student the next week. The student expected that these older people would have many physical problems and that they would want information about their problems.
>
> Only 10 people came to the meeting. The student was disappointed but went ahead with the plan and began by explaining the purpose of the meeting. The student

asked the people who came to suggest ways in which they thought their health care could be improved. Most of the people told the student that they had private physicians and were quite satisfied with the services provided by the clinic nurses. At that point, the student expressed disappointment at the small number who came, and the people told the student that this happened whenever they had a tenants' meeting or community function. They began talking about the problem of apathy in their community and by the end of the meeting they had decided to meet again to discuss ways to reduce the apathy of their community.

PRIORITIZE NEEDS

The community's priorities may also be quite different from those of the leader. For example, you might expect that a group of parents would agree that having their children immunized would be a top priority and be surprised to find that their priority is to get an extra police officer stationed at a dangerous school crossing. Both, of course, are important, but you will find that the community is much more cooperative and actively involved when you begin with their priorities.

Example. In the retirement community, the people had identified apathy as their primary concern so a listing of priorities was not needed at that time.

DEVELOP MOTIVATION

The next step is to generate sufficient interest and motivation in the community to sustain action and involvement. To motivate people to take action, the project and its outcomes have to have some personal meaning to each individual community member. This is part of the reason why it is important to begin with the need identified by the community as a top priority. It is important to get people excited about what they are doing and to believe in its importance. The effective leader will also encourage the development of good working relationships among the people involved in the project.

Example. Probably the most effective way to engage people in the process of improving their own community is to help them see the connection between the proposed action and a strongly felt personal need, as the student does in this example:

> The same 10 people came to the second meeting and began to talk about the lack of interest of other members of their community. The student noticed that many were saying "What's the use? They'll never come out of their apartments" and wanted to revive their sinking enthusiasm. So the student led them into talking about the effects of the prevailing apathy on each one of them personally—how it depressed them, how it discouraged them from suggesting any activities, and how it kept them from enjoying life in that community as much as they could. By the end of the discussion, the people were all angry about the way the apathy was cheating them and preventing them from deriving some pleasure from their residence.

TAKE STOCK OF RESOURCES AND BUILD CONFIDENCE

Community groups frequently feel unable to do anything about their identified needs. The leader can help them take a more realistic view of their own resources and the resources available to them. The leader can also encourage and support their efforts and offer assistance where necessary. Once people begin to evaluate their own resources and look outside the group for other help that is available, they usually begin to feel capable of carrying out the action needed to solve their own problems.

Example. The group from the retirement community felt at first that they could not handle the apathy problems alone:

> The group asked the student to offer some suggestions but the student turned the question back to them and asked them what it is that gets them out of their apartments to attend meetings. After they gave several answers, the student pointed out that they might have some ideas about getting other people to meetings. They agreed, and began to discuss who else might be able to help them fight the apathy. They decided that they might want to call on the City Recreation Department and the Agency on Aging for some help in carrying out their plan.

DEVELOP A PLAN OF ACTION

Although it may take longer, it is important to involve the community in the development of a plan of action. Learning how to approach a problem and solve it may actually be more valuable for the future than the resolution of the present problem. The leader's willingness to let the community develop the plan communicates the leader's confidence in their ability to handle this responsible task.

Involving the community does not mean that the leader allows the group to formulate a completely inappropriate or unrealistic plan. The leader's role in planning is to offer information when no one else in the group has that information and to guide the group in developing an effective plan. Asking questions about the feasibility of suggested actions is one way to guide the group toward a realistic plan. Encouraging consideration of alternative actions also helps people to develop an effective plan.

Example. By this time, the group had begun to take some initiative:

> Most people in the group knew others in the apartment who did not attend any meetings. They talked about some of the reasons why these friends and neighbors did not become involved. They came up with several common reasons: physical disabilities that made it difficult to go out; a life-long pattern of noninvolvement; a lack of any sense of belonging to the community, which was self-perpetuating; and lack of interest in the few activities available.
> They developed a three-stage plan: Stage 1: Personally contact all residents in the three buildings to find out what activities they would enjoy and to invite them to

the next meeting. Stage 2: Begin a support group to help people with physical disabilities get out more often. Try to involve the new people who come to the next meeting in this project. Stage 3: Ask the City Recreation Department to help them establish a better activity program based on the results of their survey.

The student was impressed with the plan, especially with their intent to get other community members involved. The student also realized that not even Stage 1 of the plan could have been carried out by the student alone before the assignment to the clinic was over.

IMPLEMENT THE PLAN

The next step is to carry out the plan. Again, the members of the community should be involved as much as possible. For example, they can contact other agencies, seek new funds, get involved in writing proposals, and assist in the delivery of health care services. The degree to which the community is involved has a great effect on the maintenance of the project after the leader withdraws or has to turn attention to another problem.

Example.   The group immediately implemented Stage 1 of their plan:

> The 10 residents and the student were excited about beginning the visits. They planned to keep in touch with each other to see how the visits were going and in case they ran into any problems.
> The next community project meeting attracted 50 people. Most of the new people were interested in the original group's plans for reducing the apathy of their community and offered to help complete the visiting of each resident.
> The next meeting attracted even more people who formed committees to analyze the data collected about desired activities and to plan the operation of a support group.

EVALUATE RESULTS

It is always helpful to pause at frequent intervals during a project to evaluate the progress made so far and to decide whether or not new strategies are needed to complete the project successfully. The dynamics of the group and the degree to which the members of the community are involved in the activities of the project and in the decisions being made should also be evaluated.

Example.   After the meeting in which the committees were formed, the student met informally with the original 10 group members:

> These residents felt that they had successfully launched their project and had already reduced the apathy somewhat by getting more people to attend their project meetings. They decided that it would be important to continue to involve as many people in the project as possible and that they would have to take responsibility for keeping up the community's interest and enthusiasm after the student left.

The original 10 members were preparing themselves to assume the leadership of the project after the student left. Their leadership would be a very important factor in maintaining the success of the project.

SUMMARY

The goal of the community action process is to involve members of the community in helping themselves and others. The leader's primary roles are to act as a catalyst, energizer, supporter, and source of information. The process begins with the mutual identification of needs and a prioritizing of those needs by the community. The next steps are to develop motivation, take stock of the resources available and build community members' confidence in their ability to help themselves, develop a plan of action, implement the plan, and evaluate the results.

Political Action: Influencing the Flow of Power and Decision-Making

The community action process just described cannot be used for the implementation of all projects and changes in a community. When there is strong resistance to a proposed change, an approach is needed that recognizes and deals within the opposing sources of power and influence.

Bachrach and Baratz[15] developed a model that outlines the process of decision-making in the community, the directions in which power and influence flow, and the major bariers encountered en route to implementing a change. While this model (Fig. 12-4) is applicable to a wide range of decisions at either the local, state, or national level of decision-making, it is only an outline of the process. The details must be filled in by the leader based on the leader's knowledge of the particular situation.

This model is particularly useful as a guideline for analyzing a decision-making situation in which a large number of variables are involved. It is especially helpful in sorting out the complexities of the situation. Once the situation has been analyzed using this model, the leader can see where it is possible to have an impact on the decision-making process.

According to this model, once the proposal or issue is clearly understood the analysis begins with the identification of the individuals and groups who will support the change and those who will oppose it. Then it follows the proposed change through the decision-making channel past four major barriers (community values, blocking procedures, the decision-making arena itself, and administrative interpretation and enforcement) until it is finally implemented effectively. At any barrier, the proposed change can be defeated or delayed indefinitely by the opposing group. This model uses elements of Lewin's analysis of driving and restraining forces and some tactics of the power-coercive approach to change (see Chapter 9).

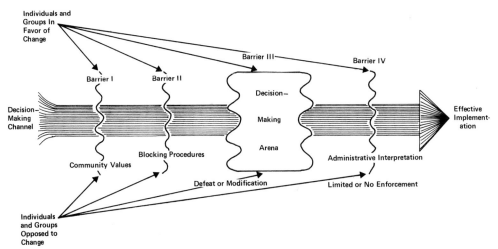

FIGURE 12-4. Flow of decision-making in the community. (Adapted from Bach-rach, P and Baratz, MS: *Power and Poverty: Theory and Practice.* Oxford University Press, London, 1970.)

ENTERING THE DECISION-MAKING CHANNEL

When entering the decision-making channel, it is important to clearly identify the basic elements involved in the process: the proposal or desired change and the way in which different individuals and groups in the community feel about the change.

The Proposal or Desired Change

There are so many different types of decisions made in a community that it is difficult to categorize all of them except in terms of the broad functions of a community listed earlier in this chapter (the provision of safety and security, mutual support, distribution of resources, socialization, and significance). In the health care field alone, myriad decisions are made about the kind of services to offer, who will be eligible for them, how to support them, and how they will operate and by whom and so forth.

The proposal for change may come from any individual or group, including health care organizations; government officials; civic, social, and religious groups; interest groups; professionals; concerned citizens; and individuals who are in need of the service. They may also come from individuals and groups outside the community.

Example. The proposal that will be followed through the decision-making channels to illustrate the use of this model is one that came from concerned professionals who lived in the community:

Two community mental health nurses who were employed outside the community became concerned about reports of inadequate health care in a correctional facility located in their community. News items about problems with the county jail included stories about serious incidents arising from the neglect of the prisoners' health needs. Two prisoners had committed suicide within the past month and one died from a neglected perforated ulcer, although the prisoner had pleaded for medical attention.

After confirming these reports and trying unsuccessfully to work with prison officials to improve the situation, the two nurses decided to become involved in a campaign to improve the health services at the jail.

Identify the People For and Against the Change

Every proposal or desired change involves some kind of issue around which people can align themselves as being for or against the proposal. At this early stage of the process, many will be potential rather than actual supporters or opponents. There will also be individuals and groups who remain indifferent or uninformed about the issue.

The individuals and groups who are in favor of the proposed change will try to push it through the decision-making channel while the opposing forces will try to keep it out of the channel or, once it gets into the channel, to slow or stop its progress. These individuals and groups must be identified in order to estimate their strength and the sources of their power (which could be physical strength, the ability to threaten harm, positional power, economic power, legal power, public recognition and support, the strength of members, control of access to resources, or the power of an idea).

Example. In the example being used, the correctional facility was becoming a controversial issue in the community because of the many news stories, so there were a number of individuals and groups on each side of the issue:

The two nurses found several groups in favor of improving conditions at the jail. A key citizens' organization in the community, the Civic Union, was considering doing a study of the situation and invited one of the nurses, who was a member of the organization, to head the study group. The Interfaith Council, which included representatives from every church and temple in the community, had been trying to begin some social services at the jail and so was very much in support of the proposed change. The major political parties were divided on the issue but a few in the majority party of the county legislature (which provided the funds to run the jail) supported the idea of making improvements but had not yet worked out the details of any improvement plan. A number of individuals also spoke out against the present conditions in the facility and called for reforms. Among them were several inmates and the parents of the young man who died in the jail.

Opposing any changes were many individuals who believed that being in prison was supposed to be a punishment. Among them were several people who had been victims of crimes committed by people in the prison. The county Sheriff, who was responsible for operating the jail, opposed any changes at the jail except improvements of the building. The Sheriff was supported by most members of the Sheriff's political party, which was currently the minority party in the county legislature but had only two seats less than the majority party. Two active taxpayers' groups from different parts of the county opposed spending any more money on the jail at all if it would mean raising taxes.

At the time the nurses joined the movement to improve the jail, most members of the community were beginning to be concerned about what had happened at the jail but were not sure what should be done about it.

BARRIER I. COMMUNITY VALUES

Those individuals and groups who are opposed to the change will try to keep it from being considered in any decision-making arena. In order to do this, they will reinforce existing community values that support the status quo (present situation). These values are the first barrier to any proposed change in the community and are already in place when the change is proposed. You can almost always find some community values that can be called on in support of the change but there will usually be more or stronger prevailing values that support the status quo, which the proponents of change will have to overcome.

Example. Strong community values supported spending as little as possible on the jail but the recent reports of problems at the jail threatened to upset the status quo:

> The county prison was constructed as a place to detain people accused of crimes and to punish those found guilty of relatively minor offenses. Those who were given long sentences for serious crimes were not held at the county prison but sent to the state prison.
>
> Most people in the community preferred to ignore the jail and leave it to the Sheriff and the Sheriff's administrators to operate in such a way that it didn't cost the taxpayer too much but did keep the inmates securely inside. The prevailing value, then, was to provide the minimum necessary for the jail and its inmates. There was also an undercurrent of feeling that the victim of a crime was more neglected than the person who committed the crime.
>
> Values in support of improving the correctional facility were primarily based on a belief in humane treatment of any individual regardless of past behavior, and a belief that most people found in county jails would be more accurately described as troubled than as evil and dangerous.
>
> When people in the community heard news reports of a series of escapes from the jail, they began to wonder if even the minimal necessities were presently taken care of at the jail and they began to think about their own safety and feelings of security in a community that had frequent prison escapes.
>
> The incidents at the facility (especially the deaths) sparked a grand jury investigation that uncovered numerous instances of inhumane treatment, including neglect of the most basic health needs, even emergency treatment. Dissemination of the grand

jury findings through news stories and discussions at gathering places throughout the community upset the status quo—the community could no longer ignore the jail and too many of its values were in conflict with conditions at the jail.

The proposed change passed Barrier I when it became apparent to the community that the jail was not well managed and that its inmates were treated far worse than they had imagined.

BARRIER II. BLOCKING PROCEDURES

Once the first barrier has been passed, the opponents of the change will try various maneuvers to block its movement into the decision-making arena. This is a stage at which a working knowledge of the community and its organizations and of the different levels and branches of government is vital information when you want to set up blocks or maneuver around them.

Those who oppose the change will try both avoidance tactics and direct blocking tactics. The specific tactics used vary somewhat according to the situation but there are some common ones used in many situations. The following is an example:

> If you were trying to get a change made in a particular social service but the administrator, Mr. D., and his staff are opposed to your idea, the administrator will first try avoidance tactics, such as not returning your calls and not answering your letters. When you finally succeed in speaking with him (perhaps catching him at a public meeting) he will be politely evasive. If you persist, he may claim that you do not understand the situation and therefore cannot understand why your proposal cannot be implemented. If pressed further, he will probably say he cannot make the decision alone but will not tell you who can make the decision. When you try to approach others in the agency you may find that they have been instructed to direct all inquiries back to the administrator. If you try to go around him to his supervisors, you will find that he has been there first and that they have issued a new policy that all requests for changes in the agency's services must come through the administrator.

When these so-called normal channels of communication are effectively blocked, it becomes necessary to circumvent them or to open them up.

The type of avoidance and blocking described above is very common. It succeeds in discouraging all but the most persistent agent for change. However, no person or group is completely immune to public pressure to change, so if the channels are blocked, you can break down the barrier through the use of power tactics.

Example. In the prison situation, it became necessary to use some power tactics to finally move the issue into the decision-making arena, which was the county legislature:

At first the Sheriff simply refused to comment on the news stories about the jail. When the grand jury report was released the Sheriff told reporters that it was full of erroneous statements. These avoidance tactics succeeded for several months. Finally, the legislators felt that they had to do something about the rapidly deteriorating situation and placed the prison on the agenda of their next meeting. The Sheriff came to the meeting and told the legislators that since a Sheriff is a duly elected official of the county they could not tell a Sheriff how to run the county jail. This direct block succeeded and the issue was dropped for the time being.

The groups supporting the proposal searched for a way around this block. The Civic Union study group, led by one of the nurses, met with several county legislators who were known to oppose the Sheriff and support the proposed change. The legislators decided to bring the study group's data and the grand jury reports to the attention of the state investigation commission. At the same time, a group of former inmates decided to sue the Sheriff for inadequate medical care. These two actions kept the jail on the front page of the county's newspaper and kept up the pressure on the county legislature.

State investigators visited the jail and issued yet another critical report on prison conditions. Based on this new report, unidentified sources in the Governor's office were quoted as saying that they were looking into ways to remove the Sheriff from office. When this news story broke, county legislators were spurred back into action. They found a different way to deal with the prison situation—through control of the funds needed to operate the jail.

Supporters of the proposals to improve the jail finally had succeeded in moving the issue into the decision-making arena.

BARRIER III. THE DECISION-MAKING ARENA

Once an issue reaches the decision-making arena, both the supporters and opponents are likely to become more open about their viewpoints and the lines between the groups become clearer. The decision-making arena often provides an opportunity for the groups or their representatives to face each other directly for the first time to debate the proposal. Evasion is more difficult at this point but stalling and blocking tactics can still be used by opponents of the proposal.

The arena itself varies according to the particular issue. The legislatures at any of the three levels of government are frequent arenas but the courts and administrative arms of government are also common arenas. In the prison issue discussed here, for example, the former inmates' lawsuit could have become the decision-making channel if the county legislators had failed to respond, and the courts could have ordered improvements at the prison if the inmates won their suit. The executive branch of government can also conduct investigations and hearings that become arenas for decision-making. The election process is another arena for community decision-making.

There are also arenas outside of government. Schools, colleges, and a wide range of community organizations can hold meetings and forums that have the potential to be decision-making arenas. Neighborhood gatherings and formal meetings of representatives from various organizations can also become arenas. The media—especially newspapers, radio, and television stations—disseminate information, encourage debates on issues, and sometimes support one side but are not usually decision-making arenas.

Example.   The prison issue has finally been brought before the county legislature:

> At the preliminary hearing of the legislature, a number of proposals were presented. A coalition between the Civic Union group led by the two nurses and the Interfaith Council presented a well-developed, comprehensive plan for changing the administrative structure of the jail, providing a wide range of health, social, and vocational services for the inmates and petitioning the state legislature to remove the county prison from the Sheriff's control. One of the supporting legislators presented a similar but less expensive plan.
>
> Another legislator who supported the Sheriff presented a proposal that simply allocated more funds for the jail, which would be used at the Sheriff's discretion. The Sheriff had previously requested more money to renovate the prison building and this request was read to the group. A representative of one of the taxpayers' groups cautioned the legislators against getting caught up in the emotionalism of the issue and against throwing money at problems instead of trying to solve them inexpensively.
>
> The lines were clearly drawn. Both sides supported an increase in funds for the jail but one side wanted the money to be spent on services and to remove control of the prison from the Sheriff. The other side wanted the Sheriff to retain control of the prison and any additional funds.
>
> As often happens, the positions and proposals of the two sides were reduced to two-word descriptions and they became known as the anti-Sheriff and pro-Sheriff groups. The division also followed political lines with most members of the Sheriff's political party supporting the Sheriff and many from the other party opposing the Sheriff.
>
> The Sheriff was a well-known, popular figure in the community. At the legislative hearing, the Sheriff spoke persuasively of a long fight to retain law and order in the community and implied that the other side wanted to coddle the prisoners and let them run loose in the community. One of the guards (correction officers) at the jail described the unruly behavior and abusive language guards had to deal with daily. The county engineer described the deteriorating condition of the prison building.
>
> The anti-Sheriff group, including the two nurses, described the inhumane treatment of the inmates in dramatic tones, implied that the Sheriff was not capable of operating the prison properly and that the Sheriff's methods would turn relatively harmless people into dangerous criminals by the time they were released back into the community. The parents of the young man who died described their pleas for help and the way their son was treated in the hours before he died. The hearing lasted six hours and received extensive news coverage.
>
> The legislature adjourned at 2:00 AM and reconvened the next afternoon to vote on the proposals. The coalition's proposal to expand services was approved after cuts were made in the budget section. However, the proposal to remove control of the jail from the Sheriff was defeated by a small margin. Both groups claimed victory but neither side actually felt satisfied. The Sheriff retained control of the prison but was now supposed to provide more services for the inmates.

BARRIER IV. ADMINISTRATIVE INTERPRETATION AND ENFORCEMENTS

It would seem that once a decision is made, especially if it is in the form of a law, that battle would be over, but it is not that simple. As is done with the official goals of an organization, official laws can be ignored or partially enforced if the community does not support the law and pressure a reluctant administrator to firmly and fully enforce the law. In addition, some laws are so vaguely worded that they can be interpreted in several ways, depending on the wishes and desires of the administrator.

The same is true of any decision. Any ruling, procedure, or decision can be ignored or evaded by its opponents if its enforcement is not closely followed by its supporters.

Example. The results of the county legislature's decisions left a situation in which limited enforcement was almost a predictable outcome:

> The Sheriff continued to control the prison. After the funds were appropriated, the Sheriff quickly initiated renovation plans and publicized the physical improvements being made. However, the introduction of new services did not conform with the approved plan. A part-time social work student and licensed practical nurse were hired but given little direction or support. One community group was given permission to visit inmates once a week, but group members were treated so rudely by some of the guards that they did not want to return.
>
> Although news items about the jail decreased considerably, both the coalition and supporting legislators continued to pay close attention to what was happening at the jail. When it became apparent that only token attempts to improve health, social, and vocational services were being made, they brought their data and complaints back to the state investigating commission, which renewed its investigation. The Governor's office quietly renewed its pressure on the Sheriff (the threat to remove the Sheriff from office was a real possibility although it was a rare occurrence) and the Sheriff finally hired an experienced and capable administrator for the jail. The new administrator appointed several community advisory boards to develop plans for improving conditions in the prison, and within a year most of the services described in the coalition's original proposal were implemented.

The tremendous amount of time and energy required to implement the proposal described in the example was due not only to the strength of the opposing side but also to the community's basic lack of interest in what happened at the prison so long as members of the community did not feel that it affected them personally. The combination of strong opposition, initial community disinterest, and conflicting beliefs and values made it very difficult to move the issue through the channels of decision-making to effective implementation.

You may have noticed that the nurses in the example were only a small part of the group that finally succeeded in improving prison conditions. A number of different individuals and groups within the community and outside the community were eventually involved and brought their collective power and influence to bear on the situation. Without this convergence of power and influence from many sources, the change would not have taken place. As an individual leader, you can act as a catalyst in bringing these forces together and, as an energizer in helping to keep up interest and momentum, you can greatly extend your influence in the community.

EFFECTIVE COMMUNITY LEADERSHIP

Before concluding this section, a review of the way in which the components of effective leadership were used to influence the outcome of the community decision-making process in the prison example may help to summarize the many different concepts that can be applied in community leadership.

GOALS. Although the goals of the various individuals and groups who supported the change were far from identical, they were sufficiently congruent for the people to work together. The two groups that formed the coalition identified and agreed upon mutuals goals through the development of the written proposal for improving the county prison.

SKILLS AND KNOWLEDGE. A great deal of knowledge and skill was needed to implement this change. Knowledge of the conditions at the jail and what was needed to improve conditions was frequently used as data to support the desired change. Familiarity with the community's beliefs and values helped the group to overcome the first barrier by indicating how the community's values were in conflict with the status quo at the jail. Use of the legislators' knowledge of the way in which the state government could apply pressure was a turning point in bringing the issue to the legislature and in forcing full enforcement of the decision.

SELF-AWARENESS. The need for self-awareness was not as evident in this particular situation as it is in some others. However, it entered into the development of effective working relationships within the groups forming the coalition and among all of the individuals and groups forming the supporting side. The people who led the movement for change also had to be aware of their own motives because if their desires for individual recognition or power had overridden their desire to bring about change, it could have destroyed the coalition.

COMMUNICATION. Communication between the individuals and groups forming the coalition was essential, first, in bringing the people together and, later, in coordinating their actions. Even more essential to the success of the entire project was the steady flow of communication with other people in the community through the media, meetings, and personal interaction. Without this communication, the supporting side could not have gained the support from the community, and the pressure from the media needed to press the county legislature to act. It also involved as many people in the community as possible in the movement to bring about change.

ENERGY. As mentioned earlier, a great deal of energy was required to initiate and maintain interest in the issue, particularly at the barrier points, where the opposition nearly succeeded in blocking the proposed change completely. Energy was also needed to keep the supporting group interested and excited about their work and to follow-up on enforcement, a time when energies are likely to flag because the battle appears to be over.

ACTIONS. The initiative of the two nurses helped to bring the two community groups together into a coalition. This is a good example of the linking function of leaders. Other vital actions included the frequent use of the media and other forms of communication, the number of times they called meetings (for example of the study group, with the legislators and with the state investigation commission), and their continuing presence and participation in the many meetings and hearings about the jail.

SUMMARY

The model for analyzing the flow of power and decision-making in the community begins with the identification of the proposed change, its supporters, and its opponents. The four barriers in the way of effective implementation are prevailing community values, blocking procedures, the decision-making arena, and administrative interpretation and enforcement of the change. Using the components of effective leadership, the leader can act as a catalyst and energizer in bringing together the sources of power and influence in the community needed to move a proposal past the barriers and into effective implementation.

References

1. BRADEN, CJ AND HERBAN, NL: *Community Health: A Systems Approach.* Appleton-Century-Crofts, New York, 1976.

2. GOTTSCHALK, SS: *Communities and Alternatives: An Exploration of the Limits of Planning.* Schenkman, New York, 1975.

3. HANCHETT, E: *Community Health Assessment: A Conceptual Tool Kit.* John Wiley & Sons, New York, 1979.

4. WARREN R: *The Community in America.* Rand McNally, Chicago, 1963.

5. KLEIN, DC: *Community Dynamics and Mental Health.* John Wiley & Sons, New York, 1968.

6. HUNTER, F: *Methods of study: Community power structure.* In AIKEN, M AND MOTT, PE (EDS): *The Structure of Community Power.* Random House, New York, 1970.

7. COLEMAN, JS: *Notes on the study of power*. In LIEBERT, RJ AND IMERSHEIN, AW (EDS): *Power, Paradigms, and Community Research*. Sage Publications, Beverly Hills, 1977.

8. FREEMAN, LC ET AL: *Locating leaders in local communities: A comparison of some alternative approaches*. In AIKEN, M AND MOTT, PE (EDS): *The Structure of Community Power*. Random House, New York, 1970.

9. MARSDEN, PV AND LAUMANN, EO: *Collective action in a community elite: Exchange, influence resources and issue resolution*. In LIEBERT, RJ AND IMERSHEIN, AW (EDS): *Power, Paradigms, and Community Research*. Sage Publications, Beverly Hills, 1977.

10. POLSBY, NW: *How to study community power: The pluralist alternative*. In AIKEN, M AND MOTT, PE (EDS): *The Structure of Community Power*. Random House, New York, 1970.

11. LITWACK, E, MEYER, HJ, AND HOLLISTER, CD: *The role of linkage mechanisms between bureaucracies and families: Education and health as empirical cases in point*. In LIERBERT, RJ AND IMERSHEIN, AW (EDS): *Power, Paradigms, and Community Research*. Sage Publications, Beverly Hills, 1977.

12. HANLON, JJ AND PICKETT, GE: *Public Health: Administration and Practice,* ed 7. CV Mosby, St Louis, 1979.

13. MacINTOSH, DR: *Systems of Health Care*. Westview Press, Boulder, 1978.

14. WILLIAMS, SJ AND TORRENS, PR: *Introduction to Health Services*. John Wiley & Sons, New York, 1980.

15. BACHRACH, P AND BARATZ, MS: *Power and Poverty: Theory and Practice*. Oxford University Press, London, 1970.

16. McDOWELL, D: *The New Older Citizen's Guide: Advocacy and Action*. Office for the Aging, Pennsylvania Department of Public Welfare, Harrisburg, 1977.

17. ROSS, MG WITH LAPPIN, BW: *Community Organization: Theory, Principles and Practice,* ed 2. Harper & Row, New York, 1967.

Index

An italic number indicates a figure.
An asterisk after a number indicates a Research Example.

Initiator, 171
Insecurity
  leader, 155
  group, 154-155
Interaction
  environment, open system groups and,
    151-152
  group
    group development and, 162
    leader, 62
  patterns of
    agendas and, public and hidden, 179-
      181
      communication patterns, 175-181,
        175-176
    groups and
      group roles, 171-175, *173-174*
      problem-solving conferences and, 217
Interactional theories
  complex man and open systems, 60-61
  discussion of, 62
  explanation of, 60
  leader-group interaction, 62
  leader situation elements, 61
Interest, community of, 402
Interpretation
  administrative, 429-430
  communication and, 102
Intervention, administrative
  evaluation and, 375
Invention, planned change and, 285
Inventory, energy, 87
Issue(s)
  central, critical thinking and, 142
  correctly identified, critical thinking and,
    146
  delegating responsibility and, 257-261,
    260
  emotional, negotiation and, 126
  ethical, labor relations and, 387-389
  identification of, planned change and,
    311-312
  key, negotiation and, 126
  professional, labor relations and, 387-389
  proliferation, 123
  substantive, negotiation and, 126

JUDGMENTS, complex
  critical thinking and, 139

KARPMAN Triangle, 117-119, *118*, 344
Knowledge
  information conferences and, 226, 230
  leadership
    community, 430
    critical thinking and, 74
    getting ahead of the group and, 74
    leadership elements and, 72
    need for, 72-73
    value of, 75*
  need for, 71-72
  nursing
    authority and, acceptance of, 74-75
    building, 73-74
    routine and
      acceptance of, 74-75
      effects of, 76
  prerequisite, information conferences
    and, 226

LABOR, division of, 328
Labor relations
  collective bargaining, 385-389, 387,* 390-
    391*
  contract administration, 394-397
  negotiating a contract, 392-394
  organizing, 389-391
Laissez-faire leader, 43, *43*, 44,* 47
Language, cultural differences and, 25
Lawsuits, goals and, 339
Leader
  action
    dominant synchronizers and, 184
    group development and
      ajourning stage of, 169-170
      forming stage of, 155-157
      norming stage of, 163-164
      performing stage of, 167-168
      storming stage of, 159-161
    public and hidden agendas and, 181
  authoritarian, *43*, 43-45, 44*
    one-way communication and, 177
    stilted communication and, 177
  behavior
    categories of, 48
    descriptions of, 47-48
  change and, 300
  competence, effect of, 75*

Model—*continued*
  types of, 291
  paradoxical
    comments on, 283
    drawbacks to, 283-284
    first-order change and, 277-278
    second-order change and, 278-283, *279*
    success of, 283
  power-coercive
    assumptions in, *272,* 305-306
    basic steps of
      begin action phase, 314-315
      build a power base, 313-314
      define the issue and identify the opponent, 311-312
      final struggle, 316-317
      keep the pressure on, 315-316
      organize a following, 312-313
    power of, 306
    sources of power in
      ability to harm, 307
      control of access to resources, 311
      expert power, 309
      legal power, 308
      money, 307-308
      physical strength, 306
      positional power, 307
      power of an idea, 309
      public recognition and support, 308-309
      strength in numbers, 309-311, *310*
  rational
    assumptions in, 272, 284-285
    consequences and, 288-289
    difussion and
      estimating, 286-288
      mass media, 286
      purpose of, 285
    discussion of, 289
    invention and, 285
Money. *See also* Budget; Salary.
  planned change and, 307-308
Monopolizer, 173
Motivation
  development of, community action and, 419
  factors, motivational theories and, 52-53
  human needs and, 14-22, *14, 19*
  information conferences and, 221

  theory of, 14, *14*
    factors in. *See* Needs, human.
Motivational theories
  behavioral management, 55, 55-56*
  explanation of, 50
  hygiene and motivation factors in, 52-53
  Theory X, 51
  Theory Y, 51-52
  Theory Z, 53-54

NATIONAL Labor Relations Board
  collective bargaining and, 385-386, 388
  negotiating a contract and, 392
  organizing council and, 390, 391
Nature
  human
    open systems and, 60-61
    Theory X and, 51
    Theory Y and, 51-52
  relationship of people with, 23
Needs
  burn-out and, 353
  dependency, 18
  educational, evaluation and, 376
  human
    esteem, *14,* 20-21
    hierarchy of, 14, *14*
    love and belonging, *14,* 18-20, *19*
    motivation and, *14,* 14-22, *19*
    physiologic, *14,* 15-16
    safety and security, *14,* 16-18
    self-actualization, *14,* 21-22
  identification of, community action and, 418-149
  individual, goals and, 339
  physiologic, *14,* 15-16
  prioritization of, community action and, 419
  safety, *14,* 16-17
  security, *14,* 17
  stability, 17-18
Negotiation
  change strategies and, 129-130
  continuing, 127-129
  identify key issues in, 126
  labor relations and, 392
  leader, group development and, 159-160
  need for, 125
  opening move, 126-127, 128*

questions during, 125
rewards in, 130
setting the stage for, 125-126
strategic influences in, 129-131
threats in, 130-131
win-win not win-lose in, 125-126
NLRB. *See* National Labor Relations Board.
Nonconformity, role stress reduction and, 31
Normative model. *See* Model, normative.
Norming stage, group development in
explanation of, 161
group climate and behavior in, 162-163
group tasks in, 162
individual tasks in, 161
leader actions in, 163-164
Numbers, strength in
planned change and, 309-311, *310*
Nurse, private duty, 358
Nursing
care. *See* Care, nursing.
knowledge. *See* Knowledge, nursing.
primary
advantages of, 362
disadvantages of, 362-363
explanation of, 361-362
team
advantages of, 361
disadvantages of, 361
explanation of, 360

OBJECTIVES. *See also* Goal(s); Purpose.
affective, 223-224
cognitive, 223-224
content areas for
explanation of, 224
need for, 224-225
sequencing of, 225
implementation of, 366
individual, management and, 364-365
information conferences and, 224-225
management by
advantages and disadvantages of, 367
evaluate outcomes, 366-367
explanation of, 363-364
implement objectives, 366
set objectives, 364-366

pyschomotor, 223-224
setting, 364-366
specific behavioral
categories of, 223-224
common mistakes, 222-223
information conferences and, 222-224
sharing, 224
work group, management and, 365-366
Open system. *See* System, open.
Openness
environment and, 8-10, *9*
open system community and, 406-407
open versus closed, 8
organizations and, 325
Operation
level of
formal, 326-331, *328*
informal, 331-335, *332*
Opinion giver, 172
Opinion seeker, 172
Opponent, identification of
planned change and, 311-312
Opportunities
burn-out and, 353
learning, staffing decisions and, 256
Organization(s)
budget in
blame and, 371
components of, *369,* 369-370
explanation of, 368
incremental, 371-372
purpose of, 370-371
zero base, 372-373
burn-out in, 351-355
characteristics of, 319-320
complex systems, 319-326, *324*
goals of, 335-339
group forming and, 155
information conferences and, 221-222
level of operation in
formal, 326-331, *328*
informal, 331-335, *332*
nonprofit, 320
open systems
complexity in, 323-325
hierarchy in, 322, 323*
openness in, 325
pattern in, 325-326
wholeness and individuality in, 321-322

Processing—*continued*
  pros and cons of, 121
Professional Standards Review Organiza-
    tion, 380
Projection, human behavior and, 34
Proliferation, issue, 123
Promotion(s), Theory Z and, 54
Proximity, physical
  groups and, 150
PSRO. *See* Professional Standards Review
    Organization.
Publicity, problem discussion meetings and,
    191
Purpose. *See also* Goal(s); Objectives.
  shared, groups and, 150

QUALITY
  assurance, evaluation and, 384-385
  quantity and, 338
Quantity, quality and, 338
Question, open-ended
  communication and, 107

RATIFICATION, negotiation and, 393-394
Rational model. *See* Model, rational.
Rationalization, human behavior and, 35
Reality shock
  actions to reduce effects of, 351
  additional pressures on new graduate
      and, 348-349
  conflicts and, 347-348
  explanation of, 346-347
  honeymoon and, 347
  resolving conflicts and, 350-351
  unsuccessful coping efforts and, 349-350
Reassurance
  human behavior and, 35
  support and, 111
Recognition
  leaders and, 91
  public, planned change and, 308-309
Recognition seeker, 173
Recorder, 172
Recordings, tape, 119-120
Refreezing, planned change and, 296-298
Refreshments
  problem discussion meetings and, 192,
      192

problem-solving conferences and, 214
Regulations, bureaucracy and, 328-329
Reinforcement, group development and,
    160
Relations
  labor
    collective bargaining
      explanation of, 385-386
      professional and ethical issues in,
          387-389, 390-391*
      purposes of, 386-387, 387*
    contract administration
      binding arbitration in, 396-397
      grievances in, 394-396
    negotiating a contract
      explanation of, 392
      negotiations in, 392
      ratification in, 393-394
      stalemate in, 392-393
    organizing council
      elections in, 391
      explanation of, 389
Relationships
  games in
    bear trap, 345-346
    explanation of, 342-343
    I told you so, 345
    Karpman Triangle, 117-119, *118,* 344
    paternalism, 343-344
  nature and, 23
  orientations, task versus, *49,* 49-50
  others and, 24
  people in authority and, 25
  power and authority
    authority and the hierarchy in, 340-341
    explanation of, 340
    nursing in the hierarchy in, 341-342
    other power relationships in, 342
  spatial, 25
  systems and, 11-12
Relaxation techniques, human behavior
    and, 36
Repression, human behavior and, 34
Reserves, energy, 86-87
Resources
  access to, planned change and, 311
  budgeting and, 377
  community, 403

taking stock of, 420
Responding
  pitfalls in, 106
  reason for, 103-104
Responsibility
  delegation of
    communicating assignments in, 257
    criteria for making assignments in, 253-256
    difficulty in, 257-258
    issues and problems in
      assigning undesirable work, *260, *261
      inadequate staff, 259-261
      manager or specialist or both, 258-259
    planned change and, 297
    teamwork and, 253-261, *260*
  teamwork and, 240
Responsiveness, 78-79
Results
  analyze, 232
  evaluation of
    community, 421-422
    problem-solving and, 138
  use of, 233
Review
  peer, 384
  utilization, 379-380
Rewards
  evaluation and, 376
  negotiation and, 130
Rhythm. *See* Patterns.
Role(s)
  bargaining, role stress reduction and, 29-31
  conflict
    reality shock and, 28, 30*
    staffing decisions and, 258-259
  existence of, 27-28
  group
    analyzing, 174-175
    explanation of, 171
    functional group building roles in, 172-173
    functional task roles in, 171-172
    nonfunctional individual roles in, 171-174, 173-174
    problem-solving conferences and, 217

individual, problem discussion meetings and, 207-209
  stress
    reduction of
      nonconformity, 31
      problem-solving, 29
      role bargaining, 29-31
      withdrawal, 31
    sources of
      ambiguity, 28
      incompetence, 29
      overload, 29
      overqualification, 29
      role conflict, 28
    team-building and, 242-243
Routine
  acceptance of, 74-75
  effects of, 76
Rules, bureaurcracy and, 328-329

SAFETY
  community, 403
  individuals and need for, *14,* 16-17
  psychologic, planned change and, 294-295
Salary. *See also* Pay.
  burn-out and, 352
  collective bargaining and, 386
Script, problem discussion meeting, 195-205
  analysis of, 205-211
Scrutiny, teamwork and, 240
Security. *See* Safety.
Self, openness to, 77
Self-acceptance, 77-78
Self-actualization, need for, 21-22
Self-awareness
  community leadership and, 430
  effective leadership and, 76-77, 94*
  importance of
    responsiveness to others and, 78-79
    self-acceptance and, 77-78
  increasing, 79
  information conferences and, 230
  openness to self and, 77
  stages of, 79-80
Self-esteem, 20
Self-insight. *See* Self-awareness.
Sentience, 13

Summarizing
  problem discussion meetings and, 193
  problem-solving conferences and, 216
Supervision, indirect
  Theory Z and, 54
Support
  burn-out and, 352-353
  community, 403
  group forming and, 154, 155
  group development and, 160
  public, planned change and, 308-309
  reassurance and, communication skills
      and, 111
  teamwork and, 239
Suppression, human behavior and, 34
Suprasystems, 5-7, 6
Synchronizers, dominant
  definition of, 182-183
  groups and, 182-185
  leader action in, 184
  problem discussion meetings and, 210
  problem-solving conferences and, 217
  types of, 183-184
Synergy, teamwork and, 238
Systems
  attributes of, 5, 7, 11-12
  characteristics of, 5, 7, 10
  closed, definition of, 8
  components of. See Systems, objects of.
  complex, organizations as, 319-320
  energy fields in, 10
  growth in larger, 11
  growth of, 10-11
  hierarchy of, 5-7, 6
  individuality in, 12-13
  interaction with environment, 8-10, 9
  levels of, 5-7, 6
  objects of, 5
  open. See also Community, open system.
    closed versus, 8
    communities as
      energy in, 409
      goals of, 409-410
      growth and development of, 407-408
      hierarchy in, 405-406, 405-406
      openness in, 406-407
      pattern of, 408
      uniqueness in, 404-405

    wholeness and, 404
    complex man and, 60-61
    definition of, 8
    groups as
      growth and, 151
      interaction with environment and,
          151-152
      patterns and, 152
      wholeness and, 151
    organizations as
      complexity in, 323-325
      hierarchy in, 322, 323,* 324
      openness in, 325
      pattern in, 325-326
      wholeness and individuality in, 321-
          322
    openness in, 8-10, 9
    patterns of, 11-12
    relationships in, 5, 11-12
    support, mobilization of, 91
    wholeness and, 7-8

TAPE recordings
  confrontation and, 119-120
  self-awareness and, 79
Tasks
  group, group development and
    ajourning stage of, 169
    forming stage of, 154
    norming stage of, 162
    performing stage of, 165, 166
    storming stage of, 158
  individual, group development and
    ajourning stage of, 168-169
    forming stage of, 153-154
    norming stage of, 161
    performing stage of, 164
    storming stage of, 158
  relationship orientations versus, 49, 49-
      50
Teaching, autotutorial, 227-228
Team(s). See also Teamwork.
  cohesiveness, 243-244
  composition of, 235-236
  function of, 237-238
  identity, 243-244
  leadership in, 236-237